Ochoa, George.

The timeline book of
the arts.

Tl

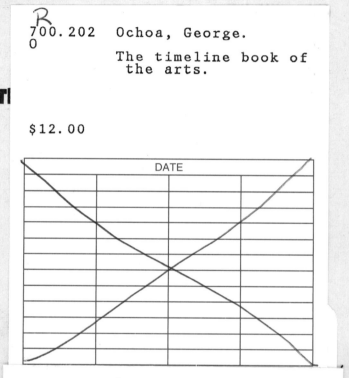

DATE			

Books in the same series:

The Timeline Book of Science
The Timeline Book of Great Ideas *
The Timeline Book of History *

* Forthcoming

The Timeline Book of the Arts

George Ochoa and Melinda Corey

A Stonesong Press Book

Ballantine Books • New York

Copyright © 1995 by The Stonesong Press, Inc.

All rights reserved under International and Pan-American Copyright Conventions. Published in the United States by Ballantine Books, a division of Random House, Inc., New York, and simultaneously in Canada by Random House of Canada Limited, Toronto.

Library of Congress Catalog Card Number: 94-96512

ISBN: 0-345-38264-1

Cover design by Kathleen Lynch

Typography by Noble Desktop Publishers

A Stonesong Press Book

Cover photo of Great Pyramid at Giza © Telegraph Colour Library/FPG, Int'l. Photo of Guttenberg Bible © Gunther-Keystone Pics/FPG, Int'l. Etching of Mozart © FPG, Int'l. Photo of Van Gogh's *Starry Night*, MOMA © Sondak/FPG, Int'l. Photo of "I Love Lucy" © FPG Int'l.

Manufactured in the United States of America

First Edition: March 1995

10 9 8 7 6 5 4 3 2 1

To Martha

TABLE OF CONTENTS

ACKNOWLEDGMENTS

We are indebted to John Cameli, Andrea Orrill, and Timothy Wright, diligent researchers and contributors. We also thank Tom Brown for keyboarding parts of the manuscript. Finally, we thank Paul Fargis and Sheree Bykofsky of The Stonesong Press and Phebe Kirkham, our editor at Ballantine.

INTRODUCTION

Beginning with prehistoric rock engravings in Australia and ending with art installations in SoHo, the more than 3,800 entries in *The Timeline Book of the Arts* answer a basic question: What do artists do? By tracing hundreds of artists' accomplishments over hundreds of centuries, it becomes clear that what an artist does is work, and in great variety. Often, as with Michelangelo or Joan Miró, it is in many different forms; with haiku poet Bashō or TV comedian David Letterman, it is almost exclusively in one artistic arena. Sometimes, as with poet Emily Dickinson or photographer Eugène Atget, it is with little or no outside acknowledgment; other artists, like filmmaker Akira Kurosawa or composer Richard Wagner, are recognized in their day. The amount of work can also vary: Shakespeare wrote dozens of plays and sonnets, Thoreau one book of lasting fame.

By placing artists' work in a timeline format, the book also offers a broad view of the artistic world of a given age. We include both popular and elite forms: Art objects in the eighteenth century include statuary as well as tableware; music in the 1970s spans both disco and Philip Glass's *Einstein On the Beach*. Readers will also see what art forms were gaining favor at a particular time. For example, from the number of significant plays produced, the English Renaissance shows the rise of dramatic art. Similarly, the number of poetry collections published during the nineteenth century (writers as varied as Tennyson, Whitman, and Baudelaire, to name a few) points to the strength of poetry as an art form. The breadth and quality of films made in one single year, 1939, suggests the strength of that art: *Gone With the Wind, The Wizard of Oz, The Rules of the Game*, and *Stagecoach*, among many others.

The sidebars and quotations sprinkled throughout *The Timeline Book of the Arts* further showcase or comment on the artistic process. A sidebar on photographer Walker Evans's technique for portraiture suggests the inherent voyeurism of the photographic art. Another on the painter Goya and the composer Beethoven spotlights how the two artists responded to their shared deafness. Still another uncovers the link between the Beatles and the Singing Nun. Quotes by Pablo Picasso, Queen Victoria, and James Stewart comment respectively on the redeeming powers of art, historical attitudes toward Shakespeare, and the enduring popularity of the movie western.

INTRODUCTION

The vastness and variety of the arts throughout the ages is comforting, but it forced us to make choices. In *The Timeline Book of the Arts* we have concentrated on the artistry of the western world because that is the tradition in which most of us were raised, but we have also included representative examples from nonwestern cultures. We have focused on such well-established art forms as painting, sculpture, architecture, literature, and film. However, we have included emerging art forms, such as performance art and installations, as well as the oral traditions and decorative art forms of nonliterate societies.

Rivers of facts, be they grocery lists or names of artworks, cannot be memorized without end. That is one reason books exist: to free people of the need to memorize. But through the facts in this book, we also think that larger truths about art emerge. Art is work, it is created by people of all kinds, it is intended to reach others, and it changes in form and in public perception over time.

A NOTE TO THE READER

The Timeline Book of the Arts is arranged by year, and within a year by category. The categories are as follows:

ARCH	Architecture
DANCE	Dance
DECO	Decorative arts
DRAMA	Theatrical works, including drama, comedy, musicals, and performance art
FILM	Film
GRAPH	Graphic arts, including printmaking and illustration
LIT	Literature, including prose and poetry
MISC	Miscellaneous
MUSIC	Music
PAINT	Painting and drawing
PHOTO	Photography
SCULP	Sculpture
TV&R	Television and Radio

In the timeline, B.C. dates are indicated by negative numbers, A.D. dates by positive numbers.

Throughout prehistory, antiquity, and the early Middle Ages, it is often difficult to place exact dates. Therefore, most of the dates in this book up to the year A.D. 1000 can be considered approximate. After A.D. 1000, dates can generally be considered exact unless marked with a "c." for "circa."

Birth and death dates have mostly been left out of the main text. However, the birth and death dates of many of the artists named in the timeline are included in the appendix.

B.C.

−43,000   At Panaramitee, Australia, humans make petroglyphs, rock engravings of circles, dots, arcs, and other nonrepresentational designs.   **SCULP**

−33,000   In France and other sites in Europe, beads, pendants, and other body ornamentation are fashioned from bone fragments and animal teeth.   **DECO**

−33,000–
−23,000   At Patna, India, and other sites in South Asia, ostrich eggshells, perhaps used as containers, are engraved with decorative, nonrepresentational patterns.   **DECO**

−30,000–
−20,000   In Germany and elsewhere in Europe, sculptures are made from stone, bone, ivory, antler, and horn. Some depict animals, some exaggerated female shapes called "Venuses," such as the four-inch Venus of Willendorf.   **SCULP**

−28,000   In Europe, flutes, the earliest known musical instruments, are made from bones.   **MUSIC**

−27,000   In Tanzania ocher fragments and ocher-stained palettes appear, evidence of the art of painting.   **PAINT**

−26,000   At the Apollo II cave in Namibia, Africa, artists paint stone slabs with black and red figurines of animals such as the zebra and black rhinoceros.   **PAINT**

−25,000–
−20,000   In the Pyrenees and Spain spears are decorated with grouped incisions and simplified animal carvings.   **DECO**

−25,000–
−18,000   Rock engravings are made in Arabia and India.   **SCULP**

−24,000   In Europe humans make huts as long-term dwellings. One example from Moravia probably consists of a low outer wall of clay and limestone with a timber superstructure and a roof of animal skins and brushwood.   **ARCH**

−23,000   An ivory Venus figurine's skirt of intertwined fibers, from the cave of Lespugue, France, introduces the beginnings of weaving.   **DECO**

MULTICULTURAL ROCK ART

W here were the first paintings produced? Most people who have any answer to this question will think of Europe, and the images of bison, horses, and deer painted on cave walls by the prehistoric people known as the Cro-Magnon. These paintings are well known from sites such as Lascaux, France (17,000 years old) and Altamira, Spain (14,000 years old), which were among the first examples of prehistoric art to be discovered. But Europe was no more the cradle of art than it was the cradle of humanity. Paleontologists now know that by about 40,000 to 30,000 years ago modern humans (Homo sapiens sapiens) were living in many parts of the world besides Europe. Whether modern humans evolved earlier in Africa or independently in several parts of the world is still a debated question. But wherever they traveled, they produced art, including engraving, sculpture, and painting.

The world's oldest known rock paintings come not from Europe but from southern Africa. In the Apollo II cave in Namibia, archaeologists have found slabs painted in black and red, dating from 26,000 to 19,000 years ago, portraying animals such as the zebra and black rhinoceros. Rock painting was also practiced in central East Africa. At Kisese, Tanzania, the remnants of painters' tools, ocher fragments, and palettes stained with ocher, have been found dating to 29,000 years ago.

By 13,000 years ago, rock painting was being practiced in such distant places as India and Australia; by 9,000 years ago, it was taking place in the Sahara plateaus of North Africa.

−20,000– −10,000	In France and Spain paintings are made on cave walls. Images include horses, bison, cattle, and nonrepresentational designs such as dots and lines, along with stenciled silhouettes of hands. **PAINT**
−20,000– −15,000	Animal sculpture becomes much more common in central and eastern Europe as artists carve ivory statuettes of felines, horses, and bison. **SCULP**
−20,000– −10,000	In France and Spain people decorate caves with realistic and abstract engravings and lifelike bas-relief animal sculptures. **SCULP**
−15,000	In Europe pierced staffs begin to feature finely engraved animal decorations. **DECO**
−15,000	Throwing sticks made of reindeer horn are frequently decorated with animal carvings or reliefs. **DECO**

Cave painting of a horse from the Lascaux Cave, Perigord, Dordogne, France.
(Giraudon/Art Resource)

−15,000   Artists in the Lascaux Cave in southern France paint lifelike animals on cave walls, using earth pigments such as ocher. Paint is applied with bundled grasses, reeds, or hands, or blown through hollow bones.   **PAINT**

−15,000   Two bison are modeled in clay in the cave of Le Tuc d'Audoubert, France.   **SCULP**

−13,000   In Mezhirich in eastern Europe huts are built from mammoth bones.   **ARCH**

−13,000   At the Wargata Mina cave, Tasmania, stenciled silhouettes of hands are rendered on cave walls by blowing pigment over human hands.   **PAINT**

−12,000   Crosshatching and shaded applications of color begin to enhance the modeling of cave engravings.   **SCULP**

−11,000   At Bhimbetka, India, animals and abstract figures are painted on rocks.   **PAINT**

−10,000   By now, across much of the inhabited world, in Europe, Asia, Africa, and the Americas, the art of building tents and huts from such materials as timber, animal bones, hides, and brushwood has become widespread. In some sites, notably in Australia, simple windbreaks made of branches are used as shelters. **ARCH**

−9000   In Japan *jomon* (cord-marked) pottery vessels are made, notable for their pointed bases and cord-marked patterns. **DECO**

−8000   The first cities appear in Iraq and elsewhere in the Near East, notably Jericho in Palestine. **ARCH**

−8000   Africans weave matting from palm fronds and other fibrous materials for use in bedding and walls. **DECO**

−8000   In Australia rock paintings of animals are made. **PAINT**

−7000   In Jericho mortar is invented for use with sun-dried brick. **ARCH**

−7000   Clay pottery appears in Turkey and the Near East. **DECO**

−7000   In the Saharan plateaus, which will begin to become a desert after 6000 B.C., animals are painted on rock walls, ushering in a long tradition of rock painting in the region. **PAINT**

−7000   The faces of human skulls from Jericho are individually reconstructed in tinted plaster with pieces of seashells for the eyes. These Neolithic "sculptured heads" point the way to Mesopotamian portrait sculpture. **SCULP**

−6000   Fertility goddesses made of baked clay appear in a number of religious shrines throughout Anatolia, in present-day Turkey. **SCULP**

−5900   In Mesopotamia the Ubaid culture begins to build temples consisting of a single mud-brick room with an altar and offering temple. **ARCH**

−5400–
−4300   During the Late Ubaid period in Mesopotamia, mud-brick houses are built on a tripartite plan, consisting of a large rectangular room in the center with rows of smaller rooms on either side. **ARCH**

−5000   In the Near East nuggets of gold, silver, copper, and other metals come into use as ornaments and trade goods. **DECO**

−5000   In China ritual jade objects are fashioned with abrasives. **DECO**

−5000   Near Eastern influences reach the Balkans with the creation of baked clay fertility goddesses in that region. **SCULP**

−4300–
−3100   In Mesopotamia during the Uruk period, elaborately decorated temples, raised on platforms, are built following the tripartite plan of houses of the Late Ubaid period. *See also* 5400–4300 B.C., ARCH. **ARCH**

−4000   In Iraq building bricks are fired in kilns. **ARCH**

−4000–
−3000   Eastern Europe becomes a major center of the potter's art and the clay modeling of free-standing figures. **MISC**

−4000	In Egypt rattles and clappers are used in ritualistic music to exorcise evil spirits. **MUSIC**
−4000– −2000	Artists from the settlement of Vinca in Serbia create hundreds of triangular clay heads with pierced ears to which can be attached hair, headdresses, or earrings. **SCULP**
−3500	In the Near East the Sumerians develop cuneiform, the system of pictograms wedged into clay tablets that is the earliest known form of writing. **LIT**
−3500	Sumerian sculptors from Uruk in the Near East create marble cult statues with heads inlaid with colored materials and topped with either gold or copper. **SCULP**
−3300	The pottery wheel is invented in Sumeria. By 3000 B.C., it is also developed in China, probably independently. **DECO**
−3100	The Egyptians invent an early form of hieroglyphics. **LIT**
−3100	At the beginning of the Egyptian First Dynasty, artists start to use bronze tools for carving. **SCULP**
−3000	Clothing dyes are in use in China and Egypt. **DECO**
−3000	Pottery and stylized stone figurines of humans are made in Ecuador. Independent pottery styles will develop elsewhere in the Americas, notably Mexico and Georgia, by 2400 B.C. **DECO**
−3000	Egyptian goldsmiths make fine jewelry from gold and precious and semiprecious stones. **DECO**
−3000	Harps of several designs are played in Mesopotamia. **MUSIC**
−3000– −2155	During the Old Kingdom in Egypt (First to Sixth Dynasties), wall paintings in tombs feature fractional representation, in which the shoulders and eyes are viewed frontally while the head and feet are in profile. Hierarchical scaling is also common, in which some figures are enlarged to illustrate their social prominence. **PAINT**
−3000	In Egypt, red earthenware statuettes of lions are produced, predecessors to the Great Sphinx. *See* 2500 B.C., SCULP. **SCULP**
−3000	With the political unification of Upper and Lower Egypt, artists aim to spread the image of a new society and the glory of the pharaoh. Bas-relief carvers use divided compositions and simplified human forms. **SCULP**
−3000	Hieroglyphic reliefs celebrating King Narmer's victory over Lower Egypt appear on a ceremonial slate palette. The palette demonstrates a break from prehistoric traditions as a strictly Egyptian style emerges, marked by a strong sense of order and clarity. **SCULP**
−2778– −2160	During the Third to Tenth Dynasties of the Old Kingdom, harps with small bow-shaped resonators, long vertical flutes, and double clarinets are played in Egypt. **MUSIC**

Pyramid of Zoser, Sakkara, Egypt. *(Egyptian Tourist Authority)*

–2650   The pyramid of Zoser in Egypt, the world's first large stone structure, is designed by Imhotep, physician, architect, and counselor to Zoser. Also called the Step Pyramid, it is almost 200 feet high. (Dates for this period are controversial. Some archaeologists will date the pyramid of Zoser as early as 2950 B.C., with the Great Pyramid of Giza as early as 2900 B.C., and the Great Sphinx as early as 2850 B.C.) *See* 2550 B.C., ARCH; 2500 B.C., SCULP.   **ARCH**

–2600   Sumerian sculptors create simplified and schematic groups of cylindrical marble figures representing gods and temple worshippers.   **SCULP**

–2550   The Great Pyramid of Giza is built under the supervision of the Egyptian pharaoh Khufu (Cheops). The pharaohs Khafre (Chephren) and Menkure (Mycerinus) will also build pyramids at Giza in, respectively, c. 2500 B.C. and c. 2470 B.C. *See also* 2650 B.C., ARCH.   **ARCH**

–2500   The cities of Mohenjo-Daro and Harappa arise in the Indus Valley. The houses are uniformly constructed of mud brick and laid out according to a plan.   **ARCH**

–2500   Glass ornaments are in use in Egypt.   **DECO**

-2500	Performances are given in temples in pharaonic Egypt. Coronation dramas are staged in which each scene is enacted at a different station along a given route. **DRAMA**
-2500	The oldest written story, the Sumerian *Epic of Gilgamesh*, is set into writing for the first time. It concerns the adventures of Gilgamesh and the "wild man" Enkidu. **LIT**
-2500– -2001	A five-tone scale is used in Chinese music. **MUSIC**
-2500	Egyptian sculptors create a more cubic and impersonal view of the human body for royal portrait statues to be placed in funerary temples and tombs. **SCULP**
-2500	Egyptian pharaoh Khafre (Chephren) supervises the building of the Great Sphinx at Giza. *See also* 2650 B.C., ARCH. **SCULP**
-2423	A decline in the quality of workmanship becomes apparent among Egyptian funerary stelae of the Sixth Dynasty. Sculptors ignore the old rules of human proportions and begin to enlarge the head and elongate the eyes and hands. **SCULP**
-2400	Limestone portrait busts begin to appear in Old Kingdom Egypt, perhaps echoing the Neolithic custom of keeping the head of the deceased separate from the rest of his body. **SCULP**
-2400	Egyptian sculptors focus more on observation rather than established conventions by creating painted limestone reliefs illustrating scenes of daily life for the tomb of Ti at Saqqara, Egypt. **SCULP**
-2340	At the beginning of his rule, Sargon sets up an imperial workshop in northern Mesopotamia to mass-produce monuments of royal victory to be sent throughout the empire. For the next two centuries, sculptors will work without variety or spontaneity but will achieve a technical perfection in the rendering of the human anatomy. **SCULP**
-2300	In Peru a monumental temple is built of stone and mud. **ARCH**
-2300	Near Eastern engravers of Akkad establish the iconography of classical Babylonia through detailed depictions of the gods and their attributes. **SCULP**
-2200	Sumerian sculptors complete reliefs illustrating Naram-Sin's victorious army on a large stone stele. It is the earliest known monument to honor a conqueror. **SCULP**
-2160– -1580	In the Egyptian Middle Kingdom (Eleventh to Seventeenth Dynasties), barrel-shaped drums, perhaps imported from sub-Saharan Africa, and asymmetrical lyres, imported from Asia, are played. Flute melodies probably move in large intervals. The long-neck lute appears toward the end of the period. **MUSIC**

–2160–
–1785   During the Middle Kingdom in Egypt, wall paintings in rock-cut tombs or in cliffsides feature more freely drawn figures and more foreshortening than in Old Kingdom images.   **PAINT**

–2160   A new type of capital featuring the sculpted head of the goddess Hathor on both sides appears at the start of the Eleventh Dynasty throughout Middle Kingdom Egypt.   **SCULP**

–2150   Sumerian ruler Gudea assembles a workshop of sculptors and has numerous diorite statues of himself placed in the shrines of the Sumerian city-state of Lagash.   **SCULP**

–2100   The Sumerians build the ziggurat at Ur. A pyramidal brick platform on top of which a temple is erected, the ziggurat is ascended by means of zigzag ramps. Some ziggurats reach nearly 300 feet in height.   **ARCH**

–2000   The palace of Minos at Knossos, Crete, is constructed. It features light and air shafts and interior bathrooms with a water supply. **ARCH**

–2000   Minoan sculptors of Crete create terra-cotta statuettes. The Mycenaeans of mainland Greece will also produce terra-cotta figurines 1400–1200 B.C.   **SCULP**

–2000   Egyptian sculptors at the beginning of the Twelfth Dynasty develop a new type of pharaonic portrait, known as the "pessimistic king," that features deep-set eyes and sad faces.   **SCULP**

–1900   As the Near Eastern kingdom of Ugarit prospers from its trade with Egypt, statuettes of gods and goddesses in the guise of warriors reveal an Egyptian influence which will grow steadily for several centuries.   **SCULP**

–1830   In Babylonia temple service music evolves from simple chanted hymns to a complete liturgical service, with five to twenty-seven selections interspersed with instrumental music. The practice of using a particular melody for a certain poem type develops.   **MUSIC**

–1760   Hammurabi, the founder of the Babylonian dynasty, has his law code inscribed in a diorite stele which features the ruler confronting the sun god Shamash.   **SCULP**

–1600–
–1100   Mycenaean citadels (fortified hilltop palaces) are constructed of stone blocks without mortar and are decorated with paintings and sculpture.   **ARCH**

–1600   In the Near East, glass is used to form objects and vessels and as a glaze for pottery.   **DECO**

–1600   The world's first purely phonetic alphabet is invented by the Phoenicians. Based on symbols for sounds, not things or syllables, it is the ancestor of all modern Western alphabets.   **LIT**

–1580–
–1085
The New Kingdom in Egypt (Eighteenth to Twentieth Dynasties) is marked by a surge in temple construction, including funerary temples and public temples to the sun god Amun-Ra, associated with the pharaoh. The buildings employ stone post-and-lintel construction with closely spaced columns. Examples include the temples at Karnak (c. 1280 B.C.) and Luxor (c. 1390 B.C.).   **ARCH**

–1580–
–1085
During the New Kingdom in Egypt, the papyruses of the *Book of the Dead*, a collection of spells related to the afterlife, are illustrated with images of the deceased appearing before the gods.   **GRAPH**

–1580–
–1085
The New Kingdom sees a great flowering of Egyptian music. Older instruments appear in new forms, often splendidly decorated. New instruments include double oboes, trumpets, short lutes, and the sistrum. Melodies move in smaller intervals and there is evidence of antiphonal and responsorial singing, men's and women's choruses, strophic songs, and liturgical music.   **MUSIC**

–1580
Egyptian sculptors of the New Kingdom create more slender and graceful human figures. This delicate rendering of the body and its features will continue to the end of the Eighteenth Dynasty, during the reigns of Tutankhamen and Haremhab.   **SCULP**

–1550
Artists from central Crete produce bronze votive figurines with a strong concave bend of the back to correspond to the customary Minoan ideal of prayer.   **SCULP**

–1550
Sculptors in the Tehuacán Valley of the southern Puebla region of central Mexico begin to make little clay figures. The figurine cult will soon spread throughout Mesoamerica, with distinct styles developing in different regions.   **SCULP**

c. –1523–
c. –1027
Artisans of the Shang dynasty in China produce ritual bronze vessels, many decorated with stylized animal heads.   **DECO**

–1500
The Shang palace complex at Anyang, China, consists of a south-facing rectangular hall within a courtyard rimmed by galleries That pattern will be adapted for palaces and temples throughout the Shang period (1523–1027 B.C.).   **ARCH**

–1500
The rebuilt Minoan palace at Knossos, Crete, is three stories tall with post-and-lintel construction, using stone lintels and pointed wooden columns tapering downward. The palace walls are painted with fresco decorations, including scenes of dolphins and youths leaping over bulls. *See* 2000 B.C., ARCH.   **ARCH**

–1500
Terra-cotta vessels in animal form become common in Cretan art and central to Minoan religious cults.   **DECO**

–1500
During the Shang dynasty (c. 1523 B.C.–c. 1027 B.C.), the Chinese develop a system of writing.   **LIT**

Lion Gate at Mycenae, Greece. *(Foto Marburg/Art Resource)*

-1480   The funerary temple of Queen Hatshepsut in Egypt is a rock-cut cliff sanctuary fronted by three terraced courtyards faced with colonnades. Long ramps lead from the valley to the temple.   **ARCH**

-1450   An upright harp as tall as a man, along with a kithara, are painted on the walls of the tomb of Paser in Egypt.   **MUSIC**

-1400–
-1200   The Mycenaeans of mainland Greece adapt many architectural elements of Minoan Crete, including decoration with frescoes.   **ARCH**

-1400   Sculptors in central Mexico make an important technical innovation by creating effigies that are partly or entirely hollow. This construction will allow greater size.   **SCULP**

-1379–
-1361   A temple to Aton, the sun-disk god, is erected by Egyptian pharaoh Akhenaton, who briefly introduces monotheistic worship to Egypt in his capital at Tell al-'Amarna. His reign, known as the Amarna period, also introduces short-lived innovations in art, including greater realism and emotion in depictions of people, along with exaggeration of some features and curvilinear contouring of bodies.   **MISC**

-1350   Silver and gold trumpets are buried in the tomb of Tutankhamen in Egypt.   **MUSIC**

-1250   Mycenaean architects build the Lion Gate, which uses post-and-lintel construction with corbeled arches. A great stone relief of two lions is carved over the doorway of the hilltop fortress. This new manner of integrating architecture with sculpture will be seen throughout ancient Greek temple construction.   **ARCH**

-1200   The Olmec civilization of Mesoamerica (Mexico and Central America) constructs pyramids and stone monuments.   **ARCH**

-1200   The dye known as Tyrian purple is invented by the Phoenicians. Obtained from a Mediterranean snail, it will be a favorite of the rich and powerful throughout antiquity.   **DECO**

-1200   The Egyptians weave linen from flax stalks.   **DECO**

-1200   Artists introduce the jaguar, the constrictor snake, the condor, and the eagle as the main iconographic sources of pre-Columbian temple art throughout the sculptures and reliefs at the temple of Chavín de Huantar in the northern highlands of Peru.   **SCULP**

-1100s   The oldest material in the Hebrew Bible, known to Christians as the Old Testament, begins to be compiled. Written in Hebrew in what is now Israel, these sacred scriptures will continue to be compiled until the second century B.C. The New Testament will be written in Greek in the first century A.D.   **LIT**

-1150   Sculptors of the Olmec culture in central Mexico create figures that combine realistic human and animal elements. This style will proliferate for centuries throughout Mesoamerica in the form of hollow ceramic figures, effigy axes, and stone relief sculptures.   **SCULP**

–1085– –945	In the Twenty-first Dynasty in Egypt, the ankh, a sacred hieroglyph symbolizing life, adorns many royal bracelets and ornaments. **DECO**
–1027– –256	The Chou dynasty is the classic period of Chinese civilization. The oldest collection of Chinese poetry, the *Shih Ching* (*The Book of Odes*), which mentions the existence of drums (ku) and bells (chung), and the use of music during agricultural festivals, is composed, as is the oldest Chinese historical work, *Shu Ching* (*The Book of Documents*), and the work of divination, *I Ching* (*The Book of Changes*). These are part of the *Wu Ching* (*Five Classics*), which is the core of Confucianism. Philosophers Confucius, Lao-tzu, Chuang-tzu, and Meng-tzu (Mencius) flourish. **LIT**
–1000– –612	Assyrian palace architecture employs brick arch-and-vault construction and ziggurats similar in design to those of the Sumerians, but smaller. **ARCH**
–1000	The Adena culture of the Ohio River valley in North America produces stone effigy pipes of standing male figures. **DECO**
–1000	Lightweight woven mats of reeds, willows, and cattails are made in North America. They are used for sitting, sleeping, and covering huts. **DECO**

....

"Praise him with the sound of the trumpet: praise him with
the psaltery and harp."
Praise him with the timbrel and dance: praise him with
stringed instruments and organs.
Praise him upon the loud cymbals: praise him upon the
high sounding cymbals.
Let every thing that hath breath praise the Lord."
—Psalm 150: 3-6, describing musical instruments of the
time of Israelite king David, tenth century B.C.

....

–1000	Bronze lures (horns) are made in Denmark using lost-wax (circe perdue) techniques. **MUSIC**
–1000	Rock gongs are used in Nigeria to make ceremonial music. **MUSIC**
–1000	The Olmec civilization of central Mexico creates colossal stone portrait heads at ceremonial precincts near the isthmus of Tehuantepec. **SCULP**
–900– –700	Abstract geometric patterns (the geometric style) predominate in Greek pottery painting. Some vases, such as the Dipylon amphora, are more than five feet high. **DECO**

Olmec jade ceremonial piece, Mexico. *(Giraudon/Art Resource)*

–900   The music in Solomon's temple in Jerusalem probably includes trumpets and choral singing accompanied by string instruments.   **MUSIC**

–900   The Nok culture of Nigeria produces a series of naturalistic, triangular terra-cotta heads. These heads represent the earliest Nigerian attempt at portraiture and will continue to appear through A.D. 200.   **SCULP**

–900   Artists of the Paracas culture from the south coast of Peru begin to model clay mummy masks and figurative spouted bottles with deeply incised sculptural decoration. This tradition will continue for six centuries.   **SCULP**

–800s   Greek poet Homer composes the epics *The Iliad* and *The Odyssey*, both based on legendary material concerning the Trojan War. Homer's influence will reverberate throughout the history of Western literature; literary descendants will include Virgil's *Aeneid* (19 B.C.), Dante's *Divine Comedy* (1321), John Milton's *Paradise Lost* (1667), and James Joyce's *Ulysses* (1922).   **LIT**

–883   At the beginning of his reign, Assyrian king Ashurnasirpal II is the first to introduce thematic sculpted wall decoration to the Near East, depicting court ceremonies at home and battles abroad.   **SCULP**

–870   Assyrian sculptors erect the "White Obelisk," which features a narrative relief that wraps around the monument from the bottom to the top. This practice will be seen again a thousand years later in Rome with the scenes on Emperor Trajan's column.   **SCULP**

. . . .

"Among all men on earth bards have a share of honor and reverence, because the muse has taught them songs and loves the race of bards."—Greek poet Homer on poet-singers or bards, **The Odyssey, Book VIII,** *line 479, ninth century* **B.C.**

. . . .

–858   Assyrian king Shalmaneser II dedicates monuments at Balawat featuring bronze friezes ornamented in relief with scenes of his conquests.   **SCULP**

–800   The Adena culture of the Ohio River valley builds circular, conical-roofed houses thirteen to thirty-two feet in diameter.   **ARCH**

–800   Egyptian coffins are painted on the outside with scenes of the deceased making offerings to the dead, and on the inside with extracts from the *Book of the Dead*.   **DECO**

-800–
-700

Babylonian music makes use of five-tone and seven-tone scales. **MUSIC**

-800–
-700

In Greece music is part of everyday life for all social classes. Professional bards (Rhapsodes) intone epics of war and adventure; choral and dramatic music also develop. **MUSIC**

-700s

In Italy, the Etruscans invent the true arch, as opposed to the corbeled arch used by the Greeks. **ARCH**

-700s

Greek poet Hesiod writes the *Theogony*, the oldest surviving account of the origin of the Greek gods, and *Works and Days*, advice on farming and moral life. **LIT**

-750

The Nubians build a temple to Amun-Ra at Jebel Barkal, influenced by Egyptian designs. **ARCH**

-750

Greek artists begin to look for what they consider to be the essential forms of objects to create simple bronze sculptures. The result will be a limited range in subject matter for most of Archaic Greek sculpture. **SCULP**

-750

Greek sculptors produce an ivory statuette of a nude goddess that incorporates an Eastern sculptural form with Greek details and an orderly construction of the human figure. This figure will serve as a precursor to later Archaic sculptural creations. **SCULP**

-725

The incorporation of ivory carvings and metalwork from Phoenicia or Syria, which reflects Mesopotamian as well as Egyptian styles, influences new motifs for Greek art. **SCULP**

-722–
-481

These years are the subject of the *Ch'un ch'iu* (*Spring and Autumn Annals*), a chronicle of the feudal state of Lu. **LIT**

-722

A long series of reliefs from the Assyrian palace of Sargon II at Dur Sharrukin, illustrating the conquests of the royal armies, is the first large-scale narrative to describe the progress of specific events in time. **SCULP**

-700–
-500

Etruscan architects in Italy design tombs with interiors resembling domestic settings, decorated with low reliefs and containing sarcophagi ornamented with terra-cotta figures. **ARCH**

-700–
-500

The basic building material for much Greek architecture is marble, a smooth limestone, or dolomite that can be cut to fit the definite lines of the building design. **ARCH**

-700–
-500

During the archaic period, the Greeks develop their basic temple structure: a rectangular stone post-and-lintel edifice with a pitched roof and fluted columns on all four sides. The Greek architectural orders are developed, systematizing temple proportions and ornamentation. The oldest order, the Doric, employs heavy baseless columns topped by plain capitals; the Ionic order uses slender columns with bases and carved spiral scrolls on the capitals; the Corinthian order is characterized by slender columns, bases, and capitals ornamented with carved acanthus leaves. The Doric order is named for the mainland Greeks, the Dorians; the Ionic for the Ionian tribes of the Greek islands and Asia Minor; and the Corinthian for the Greek city-state of Corinth. **ARCH**

-700–
-500

During the archaic period of Greek art, pottery painting incorporates both Mesopotamian motifs, such as hybrid animals, and Greek geometric designs. Narrative art concentrating on figures becomes increasingly common. **DECO**

-700

Low relief carving dominates the pre-Columbian sculptural repertory at Chavín de Huantar in the northern highlands of Peru. Chavín carvers begin to reduce anatomical details to straight lines and curves and execute details through engraving. **SCULP**

-700

Olmec artists in central Mexico shape votive axes out of light green jadeite, detailed with flaring eyebrows and cats' eyes in relief. These features will become more common in Chavín art of Peru than in Mesoamerica. **SCULP**

-600s

Archaic pottery painting in Greece employs the black-figured style, with black figures or designs painted on clay that becomes orange-red after firing. *See also* 500s B.C., DECO. **DECO**

-600s

In Mesoamerica the Zapotec invent a system of hieroglyphics that is the earliest known writing system in the western hemisphere. **LIT**

-600s

Sparta is a great center of music, drawing poet-musicians such as Alcman, Tyrtaeus, and the semilegendary Terpander. Religious festivals frequently include musical competitions. **MUSIC**

-675

Human-shaped pottery urns appear in Etruscan tombs. **DECO**

-669

Assyrian king Ashurbanipal begins to decorate his palace at Ninevah with a series of elaborate reliefs depicting his defeat of the Elamites in the battle at the Ulai. He will also adorn his palace with sculptures illustrating his lion hunt achievements. **SCULP**

-650

Artists in Crete make statues by nailing hammered sheets of bronze over a wood core. This sphyrelaton technique allows the creation of larger-sized bronze statues before the development of hollow bronze casting. **SCULP**

−650   The first truly free-standing stone images of the human form are created as votive offerings in Greece. These figures, known as kouros for male youths and korai for maidens, are produced in large numbers and reveal an Egyptian influence in the cubic character of the anatomy and a rigid, left leg forward stance. **SCULP**

−600– −500   Greek philosopher and mathematician Pythagoras is credited with developing the octave. **MUSIC**

−600– −500   The Greeks create groups of tones called modes, the forerunners of modern major and minor scales. **MUSIC**

−600– −500   The vina, the main melody instrument of India, develops. It is made of two hollow gourds connected by strings and bamboo reeds. **MUSIC**

−600   Greek artists begin to decorate stone temples with architectural sculpture in the pediment, free-standing terra-cotta figures above the pediment, and carved reliefs in the frieze below the pediment. **SCULP**

−600   High relief carvings decorate the pediment of the temple of Artemis at Corfu. The symmetrical arrangement of the composition within a confined zone recalls the Lion Gate at Mycenae as well as Sumerian ornamentation. **SCULP**

−500s   The audience hall of Darius and Xerxes and the palace at Persepolis are grand examples of Persian architecture. The audience hall's columns draw on Egyptian and Ionian Greek sources; the palace's double bull capital and column reflect Assyrian and Persian ornamental tradition. **ARCH**

−500s   In Greece the red-figured style of pottery painting emerges, in which backgrounds are painted black and the figures are the orange-red of clay that has been fired. *See also* 600s B.C., DECO. **DECO**

−500s   Chinese philosopher Lao-tzu founds the system of thought known as Taoism, expounded (probably in the fourth or third century B.C.) in the verse and prose work the *Tao-te ching*. **LIT**

−500s   Early this century Greek lyric poet Sappho, born in Lesbos, leads a group of women devoted to music and poetry. Her work will survive only in fragments. **LIT**

−580   The marble kouros figures of Kleobis and Biton from Delphi feature what will be known as the "archaic smile" which serves not as a display of emotion but as a symbol for a higher state of being. The "archaic smile" will fall out of use after 500 B.C. **SCULP**

−575   The François vase by Greek potter Ergotimos and potter and painter Cleitias is a two-foot-high krater decorated with five tiers of mythological scenes. Exekias is another skilled Greek potter and painter of the sixth century B.C., as seen in the Dionysus kylix, a wine cup from about 540 B.C. **DECO**

−570   A marble kore figure from the temple of Hera on the island of Samos relates the human body to drapery through a smooth, close-fitting, continuous flow of lines.   **SCULP**

−550   Relief carving of elongated human figures and glyphs becomes the predominant form of sculpture among the post-Olmec cultures of central Mexico for the next four centuries.   **SCULP**

−530   Artists from the Ionian island Siphnos produce marble sculpture for the facade of the treasury at Delphi.   **SCULP**

−525   Greek vase painter Psiax paints the forceful, compact scene *Herakles Strangling the Nemean Lion* on a black-figured amphora.   **DECO**

−525   Archaic Greek sculptors create kouros figures in the manner of the black-figure vase painter Psiax by rendering anatomical details and emphasizing the swelling curves of the human body.   **SCULP**

−522   Greek lyric poet Pindar, also known as the Dircaean Swan, is born (d. 438 B.C.). His works include *Epinicia* (*Odes of Victory*), *Encomia* (*Laudatory Odes*), *Scolia* (festive songs), *Hymns*, and *Choral Dithyrambs to Dionysus*.   **LIT**

−518   Darius I begins to decorate the double stairway leading up to the academic hall at his palace in Persepolis with low reliefs of marching figures. The repetitive and solemn nature of the subject matter will be typical of all Persian sculpture as sculptors ignore the tradition of Assyrian narrative.   **SCULP**

−500   Artists of the Alexander culture in the middle Tennessee River valley fashion pottery by separating the base, body, and rim into different decorative fields. This concept of pottery will influence ceramic development throughout the Gulf coast.   **DECO**

−500–   Actors in Greece perform plays in open-air theaters before a stage
−300   wall. The theaters are lit by natural light, there is no scenery, and the actors wear masks and long, decorated robes.   **DRAMA**

−500–   The sayings of the Chinese philosopher Confucius (551–479 B.C.)
−300   and anecdotes about him and his disciples are collected in the *Lun-yu* (*Analects*).   **LIT**

−500–   The primary Greek musical instruments are the aulos (the most im-
−450   portant wind instrument in ancient Greece), kithara, and lyre. **MUSIC**

−500–   Classical music proper is perfected by Greek lyric poet Pindar, who
−450   begins to write his orchestral odes, and by the new Athenian tragic and comic dramatists. Choral music is at its height.   **MUSIC**

−500   The Daima, an iron-using culture from the Nigeria-Cameroon border, begin to make clay figurines of cows, goats, sheep, and human beings.   **SCULP**

–500 Etruscan artists cast a large bronze statue of a she-wolf. Romans will place the statue in the temple of Jupiter on the Capitoline Hill as the wolf becomes the totemic animal of Rome. Bronze images of Romulus and Remus will be added in the Renaissance. **SCULP**

–490 The Greek pottery painter known as the Foundry Master paints *Lapith and Centaur* on the interior of a red-figured kylix (wine cup). **DECO**

–490 The Persian limestone relief carving of Darius and Xerxes from the treasury at Persepolis reveals Ionian Greek influences in the rendering of overlapping details. Persian carvings under the Achaemenids will be a synthesis of many diverse styles and will show a preoccupation with decorative effects. **SCULP**

–490 Relief carving is abandoned in favor of placing statues specifically designed to fit the triangular frame of the pediment at the temple of Aphaia in Aegina. For the first time, Greek sculptors soften the lines to create individual details of the musculature. **SCULP**

–480 Greek historian Herodotus is born (*d.* c. 425 B.C.). Known as the father of history, he will write the anecdotal and charming, if unreliable, *History of the Persian Wars*. **LIT**

–480 Greek sculptors begin to create statues that explore emotions and states of mind. This early classical or severe style will feature little ornamentation and focus on expressive, moody facial types. **SCULP**

–480 In Athens a marble statue of a standing youth, attributed to Critius, breaks the 150-year-old kouros stance by featuring contrapposto (positioning of the body to achieve a symmetrical balance). Contrapposto will allow sculptors to animate the human body in a more relaxed natural manner. **SCULP**

–472 Greek playwright Aeschylus's tragedy *The Persians* is produced. His *Seven Against Thebes* will be produced in 469 B.C. The first great playwright of ancient Athens, Aeschylus writes perhaps ninety plays, but only seven will survive. Over the course of his career, he moves from writing chorus- and dance-centered drama to actor/character-centered drama, helping to change the direction of Greek theater. **DRAMA**

–470 Greek historian Thucydides is born (*d.* 401 B.C.). He will write the somber, well-researched *History of the Peloponnesian Wars*, ending in 411 B.C., seven years before the wars ended with the defeat of Athens by Sparta. **LIT**

**–466–
–459** Aeschylus's tragedy *Suppliant Women* is produced. The production date of *Prometheus Bound* will not be known, and twentieth-century scholars will question whether Aeschylus actually wrote it. **DRAMA**

-461-   Pericles serves as leader of the Athenian democracy during the pe-
-429   riod of its greatest flourishing. A patron of the arts, he encourages
         the development of architecture, sculpture, painting, music, and
         drama.   **MISC**

-460   Greek sculptors produce marble pedimental sculpture for the tem-
         ple of Zeus at Olympia, depicting the victory of the Lapiths over the
         Centaurs under the aegis of Apollo. This compact group of inter-
         locking figures is typically severe as the narrative struggle is ex-
         pressed through facial emotions as well as gesture.   **SCULP**

-460   A large, free-standing nude bronze statue of either Poseidon or Zeus
         in motion is the most important achievement of early classical
         Greek sculpture in the severe style. The statue will be recovered
         from the sea near the coast of Greece in 1956.   **SCULP**

-458   Greek playwright Aeschylus's trilogy *Oresteia* is produced. It in-
         cludes the tragedies *Agamemnon*, *Choëphoroi* (*The Libation Bearers*)
         and *Eumenides*.   **DRAMA**

-450-   Greek red-figured vase painting incorporates several characteristics of
-400   Greek sculpture of the period, including implied movement and clas-
         sical contrapposto. The figures also become more naturalistic. **DECO**

-450-   During the classical period of Greek art, mural painting develops. It
-400   will be documented by later Roman copies, though no original ex-
         amples will survive. The Erechtheum in Athens is built to contain a
         picture gallery, the first known example of a room especially de-
         signed for displaying paintings. *See* 437–432 B.C., ARCH.   **PAINT**

-450   Greek sculptor Myron from Argos, working in Athens, creates his
         bronze statue of the *Discobolus* (*Discus Thrower*). Only a Roman
         marble copy will survive.   **SCULP**

-450   Greek sculptor Polyclitus executes the *Doryphorus* (*Spearbearer*) and
         the *Diadumenus* (*Youth Binding a Fillet on His Hair*). His views on
         mathematical proportions in sculpture will be highly influential. **SCULP**

-450-   Greek sculptor Phidias, the most famous sculptor of antiquity, pro-
-432   duces many of his greatest works, including the colossal statues of
         Zeus in the temple at Olympia and Athena in the Parthenon. Both
         statues are now lost; the former was considered one of the Seven
         Wonders of the World. His other works include the Lemnian
         Athena. *See also* 447 B.C., SCULP.   **SCULP**

-448   Aristophanes, who will become a great writer of Greek Old
         Comedy, is born. He will write about forty plays, eleven of which
         will survive. Most of his comedies will be parodies and satires fo-
         cused on public figures and social issues of his day. He will die c.
         388 B.C. *See also* 425 B.C., DRAMA; 411 B.C., DRAMA.   **DRAMA**

THE MULTIPURPOSE TEMPLE

*T*he greatest achievement of classical Greek architecture, the Parthenon, was originally erected as a place of worship. It remained a place of worship for thousands of years—but not to the same gods. Built in 447 to 432 B.C. on the Acropolis, the fortified sacred hill above Athens, the Doric temple was originally dedicated to the goddess Athena Parthenos—the virginal Athena, daughter of Zeus and namesake and patron of Athens. About a thousand years later, in the sixth century A.D., long after Greece had been absorbed into the Roman Empire and the Roman Empire had become Christian, the temple became a church, with the Virgin Mary taking the place of the virginal Athena. After another thousand years, following the conquest of Greece by the Ottoman Turks in the fifteenth century, the Parthenon became a mosque, with a minaret added for good measure.

Despite its service to three great religions, the ageless temple was nearly destroyed by being put to the service of the god of war. Used for storing gunpowder, the central section was demolished by an explosion during a siege in 1687.

−447– −432 Greek architects Ictinus and Callicrates design the Parthenon, the temple to Athena on the Acropolis in Athens. The greatest masterpiece of Greek architecture, it stands on a three-step stylobate and is surrounded by forty-six Doric columns. It contains numerous impressive sculptures. *See* 447 B.C., SCULP. **ARCH**

−447 Numerous artists, assembled from different parts of Greece and having different technical backgrounds, begin work on the Parthenon sculptures under the supervision of Phidias. The entire program of pedimental sculpture, metopes, and frieze will be completed c. 432 B.C. The Parthenon sculptors' concentration on graceful rhythms and the optical effects of light and shade will be known as the Phidian or high classical style and will dominate Athenian sculpture to the end of the fifth century. This style will become a standard for Western art in antiquity and modern times. **SCULP**

−441 Greek playwright Sophocles writes the tragedy *Antigone*. By now, he has also written the tragedies *Ajax* and *Trachiniae*. Of more than one hundred plays written by Sophocles, only seven will survive. His well-plotted tragedies feature incisive language and richly drawn characters facing moral dilemmas in the midst of crisis. **DRAMA**

ANCIENT PREQUELS

*I*n Hollywood parlance, a prequel is a sequel depicting events that happened before the previous film. Thus, Butch Cassidy and the Sundance Kid *(1969) was followed by* Butch and Sundance: The Early Days *(1979). Far from being a modern marketing ploy, this dramatist's technique is as old as ancient Athens.*

Sophocles's tragedy Antigone, *set in legendary Thebes and first staged in 441 B.C., concerned the courage of the title character in defying a royal order against burying her rebel brother, despite the penalty of death. The Theban material clearly interested the playwright, because the play was followed around 429 B.C. by* Oedipus the King. *This tragedy, set many years earlier, concerned Antigone's father Oedipus, who blinds himself in horror after unwittingly killing his father and sleeping with his mother. It ends with Antigone still a young girl, leading her father away.*

The playwright's last tragedy, Oedipus at Colonus, *produced after the author's death in 406 B.C., takes place after the second play but before the first. In it, Antigone leads her blinded father Oedipus to the vicinity of Athens, where he is exalted at his death by the gods. Thus, the first play in the cycle was followed by a prequel, which in turn was followed by a sequel, which was nevertheless another prequel relative to the first play. For clarity, Hollywood would most likely now label the cycle* Antigone I, II, *and* III.

–440	A marble statue of a dying Niobid carved for the pediment of a Doric temple is the earliest large female nude in Greek art. The sculptor positions the body in action commonly reserved for the male nude and displays a typically high classical feeling of pathos in the facial expression. **SCULP**
–438	The tragedy *Alcestis* by the Greek playwright Euripides is produced. Only nineteen of his ninety-two plays will survive. Most of his highly dramatic tragedies focus on individual passions and present a largely fatalistic view of life. His writing is unusually realistic for the day, employing colloquial language. **DRAMA**
–437– –432	The Propylaea, designed by Mnesicles, is constructed on the Acropolis in Athens. Serving as the western entry gate to the Acropolis, it includes both Doric and Ionic columns. **ARCH**
–431	Greek playwright Euripides's tragedy *Medea*, in which Medea revenges her husband Jason's infidelity by killing their two children and Jason's lover, is produced. **DRAMA**

Parthenon, Athens, Greece. *(Scala/Art Resource)*

−431   Greek historian Xenophon is born (*d.* 355 B.C.). He will write such works as *Anabasis, Memorabilia,* and *Cyropaedia.* **LIT**

−430– −428   The tragedy *Heraclidae (Children of Heracles)* by the Greek playwright Euripides is produced. **DRAMA**

−430   Greek sculptors begin to explore the decorative aspects of the "wind-blown" style of rendering drapery developed by the sculptors of the Parthenon. The resulting sculpture will stress grace, softness, and elegant flourishes. **SCULP**

−429   Greek playwright Sophocles writes the tragedy *Oedipus Tyrannus (Oedipus the King),* his most famous and perhaps his greatest play. The Greek philosopher Aristotle will view *Oedipus Tyrannus* as the ideal tragedy. **DRAMA**

−428   The tragedy *Hippolytus* by Greek playwright Euripides is produced. **DRAMA**

−427   Greek philosopher Plato is born (*d.* 348 B.C.). He will couch his philosophy in dialogues such as the *Crito, Euthyphro, Phaedrus, Republic,* and *Symposium* known for their literary quality as well as for their theoretical content. He will also write the *Apology,* an account of the defense made by Socrates at his trial for impiety and corruption of youth. **LIT**

−426	The tragedy *Hecuba* by Greek playwright Euripides is produced. **DRAMA**
−425	*The Acharnians*, a comedy by the Greek playwright Aristophanes, is produced. It will be followed by these Aristophanes comedies: *The Knights* (424 B.C.), *The Clouds* (423 B.C.), *The Wasps* (422 B.C.), *The Peace* (421 B.C.) and *The Birds* (414 B.C.). **DRAMA**
−421– −405	The Erechtheum on the Acropolis in Athens, possibly designed by Mnesicles, has three Ionic porticoes, including the Porch of the Caryatids, and sanctuaries to Athena, Poseidon, and the Athenian king Erechtheus. **ARCH**
−420	Greek sculptor Polyclitus executes a colossal gold and ivory statue of Hera for a new temple at the Argive Heraion. **SCULP**
−415	The tragedy *Trojan Women* by Greek playwright Euripides is produced. **DRAMA**
−414	The tragicomedy *Iphigenia in Tauris* by Greek playwright Euripides is produced. **DRAMA**
−413	The tragicomedy *Ion* and the tragedy *Electra* by Greek playwright Euripides is produced. **DRAMA**
−412	The high comedy *Helen* by Euripides is produced. **DRAMA**
−411	Aristophanes's *Lysistrata*, a comedy in which Greek women withhold sex to force the men to end a war, is produced. It will be followed by *Thesmaphoriazusae* (*Women at the Festival*) (410 B.C.), *The Frogs* (405 B.C.), *Ecclesiazusae* (*Women in Parliament*) (392 B.C.) and *Plutus* (*Wealth*) (388 B.C.). Eleven of his forty plays will survive. The greatest writer of Old Comedy, Aristophanes focuses his sharp satire on public figures and social issues of the day. **DRAMA**
−411– −409	The pageant play *Phoenician Women* by Greek playwright Euripides is produced. **DRAMA**
−410	Athenian sculptors create large numbers of marble grave stelae decorated with reliefs and exported throughout the Greek world. **SCULP**
−409	Greek playwright Sophocles writes the tragedy *Philoctetes*. He might have written his tragedy *Electra* shortly before. His tragedy *Oedipus at Colonus*, probably written near the end of his life, will be produced posthumously in 401 B.C. **DRAMA**
−408	The tragedy *Orestes* by Greek playwright Euripides is produced. The production date for his tragedy *Bacchae* is not known. **DRAMA**
−407	The marble figure of Nike from the balustrade of the Temple of Athena Nike shows the emergence of the carving of "wetlike" drapery that clings to the human body. **SCULP**
−400	The Moche people succeed the Chavín culture in the northern highlands of Peru and begin to produce modeled pottery and small objects of bone and shell. **DECO**

−400   The people of the Recuay-Vicus, a satellite of the Moche culture from the northern highlands of Peru, create large hollow vessels in a variety of figurative shapes.   **DECO**

−400   The late Adena culture of the Ohio Valley engrave designs composed of broad lines into simple, rectangular stone tablets. The tablets are not distributed but the iconography will spread throughout the eastern woodlands.   **SCULP**

−300s   The earliest known collection of Aesop's fables appears in print. The Greek fabulist is said to have lived around 600 B.C.   **LIT**

−390   Greek sculptors create marble images for the temple of Asclepius at Epidaurus depicting human suffering and experiences of pain. These sculptures will act as a precursor to a tradition of agonized faces in fourth century and Hellenistic art.   **SCULP**

· ·

"Criticism comes easier than craftsmanship."
—Greek painter Zeuxis, c. 400 B.C.

· ·

−384   Greek philosopher Aristotle is born (*d.* 322 B.C.). He will be considered an authority on nearly every area of human knowledge. His *Poetics* will be the cornerstone of Western literary criticism.   **LIT**

−372   Chinese philosopher Meng-tzu (Mencius) is born (*d.* 289 B.C.). His collection of teachings, *The Book of Mencius*, is a prime example of classical Chinese prose.   **LIT**

−369   Chinese philosopher Chuang-tzu is born (*d.* 286 B.C.). The work attributed to him, the *Chuang-tzu* (*Master Chuang*), is a classic both of Taoist thought and of Chinese literature.   **LIT**

−351   Demosthenes, the greatest Greek orator, writes his first *Philippic*, directed against Philip II of Macedon, military foe of Greece. Other *Philippics* will follow in 344 and 341 B.C.   **LIT**

−351   At the Mausoleum at Halicarnassus, Asia Minor, Greek sculptor Scopas completes his marble frieze illustrating the battle of the Greeks and Amazons. He also finishes his colossal portrait statue of Mausolus, the earliest Greek portrait to show a specific personal character. Individual likeness will soon play an important part in Hellenistic sculptural programs.   **SCULP**

−330   The figurative innovations of Greek sculptor Lysippus are evident in his bronze statue *Apoxymenos* (*Youth Scraping Himself with a Strigil*). Highly influential among Hellenistic sculptors, Lysippus develops a slenderer set of proportions than those of Polyclitus (*see* 450 B.C., SCULP) and, as court sculptor to Alexander the Great, develops the "personality portrait" genre.   **SCULP**

-325–
-100

During the Hellenistic period, Greek artistic styles spread throughout the Mediterranean world. The styles tend to be more sensual, emotional, and naturalistic than the classical ideal.   **PAINT**

· ·

"Tragedy is thus a representation of an action that is worth serious attention, complete in itself, and of some amplitude . . . by means of pity and fear bringing about the purgation of such emotions."—Greek philosopher Aristotle, Poetics, fourth century B.C.

· ·

-320

Greek philosopher Aristoxenus, pupil of Aristotle, writes on the musical theory of scales.   **MUSIC**

-316

Dyscolus (*The Bad-tempered Man*), a comedy by Greek playwright Menander, is produced. Out of more than one hundred plays written by him, it is the only one that will survive in complete form. The greatest writer of Greek New Comedy, he discards the topicality of Old Comedy to create comedies of manners. Their plots and stock characters will serve as models for Roman playwrights such as Plautus. Other plays of Menander include *Samia* (*The Girl from Samos*), *Perikeiromene* (*The Rape of the Locks*), and *Aspis* (*The Shield*). *See* 411 B.C., DRAMA; 254 B.C., DRAMA.   **DRAMA**

-300–
-250

The hydraulos, the organ of ancient Greece, is invented by Ctesibius of Alexandria. Its wind supply is provided with water instead of bellows and its keyboard mechanism will be rediscovered in the tenth century.   **MUSIC**

-300

Athenian sculptor Praxiteles creates the first completely nude cult image of the goddess Aphrodite. Influenced by the sculpture, female nudes will become a common form of statuary in Hellenistic and Roman times.   **SCULP**

-300

A marble statue of Apollo exhibits extreme Praxitelean qualities of soft modeling. This statue, known as the Apollo Belvedere, will become popular during the eighteenth and nineteenth centuries when Johann Winckelmann and Goethe find it to be the perfect embodiment of classical beauty. Numerous plaster casts of the Apollo will appear in museums, art academies, and colleges throughout the Greek revival of the eighteenth century.   **SCULP**

-300

Under the influence of Greek portraiture, individual likenesses begin to appear in Etruscan sculpture as heads on bronze statues.   **SCULP**

-200s   Lucius Afranius writes *Togata*, comedy based on daily life in ancient Rome. Several hundred fragments from forty-four of his plays will survive. It will be said that he introduced the subject of homosexuality into the theater.   **DRAMA**

-200s   Apollonius of Rhodes, librarian at Alexandria, Egypt, composes the *Argonautica*, an epic account of the voyage of Jason and the crew of the *Argo* in search of the treasured Golden Fleece.   **LIT**

-200s   In India the Sanskrit verse epic, the *Ramayana*, is composed, though some parts date from as early as 500 B.C. Ascribed to the poet Valmiki, it tells of exiled Prince Rama's efforts to rescue his wife and regain his kingdom.   **LIT**

-200s   Early this century Greek poet Theocritus, considered the inventor of the pastoral, writes his *Idylls*, of which thirty-two will survive.   **LIT**

-280   Sostratus of Cnidus constructs the lighthouse on Pharos near Alexandria, Egypt. Projecting light from concave mirrors, the 300-foot structure is one of the Seven Wonders of the World.   **ARCH**

-280   The Colossus of Rhodes, a 105-foot high statue of the sun god, Helios, that is one of the Seven Wonders of the World, is constructed.   **SCULP**

-254   Roman playwright Titus Maccius Plautus is born (*d.* 184 B.C.). He will write and produce about 130 verse comedies that Romanize the plots and characters of the Greek New Comedy and will long serve as a source of inspiration to comic playwrights in the West. His plays include *Menaechmi* (*The Twins*), *Aulularia* (*The Pot of Gold*), *Mercator* (*The Merchant*), *Asinaria* (*The Comedy of Asses*), *Cistellaria* (*The Casket*), *Mostellaria* (*The Haunted House*), *Pseudolus*, *Amphitruo* (*Amphitryon*), and *Casina*. See 316 B.C., DRAMA.   **DRAMA**

-239   Roman poet Quintus Ennius, known as the father of Latin literature, is born (*d.* 169 B.C.). His works will include the Roman historical epic *Annales*.   **LIT**

-234   Roman politician Marcus Portius Cato (Cato the Elder) is born (*d.* 149 B.C.). A spokesman for moral rectitude and military vigilance, he will be admired for his prose style, though only his treatise *De re rustica* (or *De agri cultura*) will survive.   **LIT**

· ·

"Grasp the subject, the words will follow."
—Roman politician Marcus Porcius Cato (the Elder)
on the art of writing, second century B.C.

· ·

-230   A Hellenistic bronze statue of a dying Gaul is dedicated to Attalus I of Pergamum in Asia Minor to celebrate his victories over the Gauls.   **SCULP**

-214   Emperor Shih Huang Ti (Cheng), founder of the Ch'in dynasty
              (221–207 B.C.), begins construction on the Great Wall of China. In time,
              it will stretch 1,500 miles from the Pacific Ocean to central Asia. **ARCH**

-206~   Performances mixing story dramatization, singing, and dancing are
A.D. 220   presented during the Han dynasty in China. **DRAMA**

-206–   During the Han dynasty in China, literature and the arts flourish,
A.D. 220   Confucian thought is systematized and becomes dominant, and the
              first historical annal, the *Shih chi*, is written. **MISC**

-200–   In India most of the encyclopedic Sanskrit epic the *Mahabharata* is
A.D. 200   composed, though some additions will be made as late as 600. The
              longest poem in world literature, the digressive work tells primarily
              of a royal dynastic struggle and includes the religious classic, the
              Bhagavad-Gita (*The Song of God*), which takes the form of a dialogue
              between Lord Krishna and Prince Arjuna. **LIT**

-200   The Chinese found an imperial bureau to establish an absolute sys-
              tem of pitch. **MUSIC**

-200   A marble statue of a winged Nike from Samothrace is carved as a
              victory monument. The figure displays a High Hellenistic style of
              animated and wind-blown drapery to create an active relationship
              with the surrounding space. **SCULP**

-100s   Rome conquers Greece, assimilating its artistic and intellectual tra-
              ditions. Roman painting, sculpture, drama, and poetry will be
              strongly influenced by the Greeks. Roman copies of Greek sculp-
              tures will survive to modern times, transmitting the image of origi-
              nals long since destroyed. **MISC**

-180   Hellenistic Greek sculptors carve a great marble frieze representing
              the Battle of the Gods and Giants to symbolize the victories of
              Attalus I for the Altar of Zeus at Pergamum. **SCULP**

-170   Lucius Accius, who will become a renowned playwright in ancient
              Rome, is born (*d.* 85 B.C.). The titles and some lines from about
              forty of his tragedies will survive. Some of his plays will be modeled
              on Greek dramas, and others will be wholly original. His work will
              often feature the melodramatic plots, exaggerated characters, and
              overblown rhetoric typical of Roman tragedy. **DRAMA**

-170   The scholars of Eumenes II of Pergamum in Asia Minor invent
              parchment, a writing material made from hides. It eventually re-
              places papyrus, an older vehicle for writing and illustrating. **GRAPH**

Figure on horseback. Earthenware with pigment, Han dynasty, China.
(Giraudon/Art Resource)

−106   Marcus Tullius Cicero, the greatest Roman orator, is born (*d.* 43
B.C.). His orations will include the orations against Catiline (63 B.C.),
the *Philippics* (directed against Marc Antony, 44 B.C.), and orations
in defense of Sestus, Plancius, and Milo (50s B.C.). He will also write
works of philosophy and rhetoric. He will be murdered by his political opponents, including followers of Antony and Octavius (later the
first Roman emperor, Augustus). *See also* 55 B.C., LIT; 54–51 B.C., LIT;
47-44 B.C., LIT.   **LIT**

−100   The Hopewell culture in southern Ohio creates stone platform pipes
in the form of animals, sculpted in the same degree of realism
found in Adena figures.   **SCULP**

−100   In Mesoamerica, classic Maya stelae are decorated with hieroglyph-
ic figures and low reliefs of costumed figures.   **SCULP**

−98   Roman poet Lucretius is born (*d.* 55 B.C.). He will be best known for
De rerum natura (*On the Nature of Things*), a didactic poem on the
nature of the universe based on the philosophies of Democritus and
Epicurus.   **LIT**

–90   The bronze statue of Aulus Metellus, also known as *L'Arringatore,* introduces the Roman gesture of address and salutation, which will reappear in hundreds of Roman statues.   **SCULP**

–84   Roman poet Catullus is born (*d.* c. 54 B.C.). Of his works, 116 poems will survive, including his love lyrics to Lesbia (pseudonym for Clodia), which will influence later love poets.   **LIT**

–75   Marble portraiture appears in Rome during the rule of Lucius Sulla. Portraits will depart from the expressive, psychological Hellenistic renderings by extending the antique tradition of preserving the face of the dead in wax to create detailed records of an individual's face.   **SCULP**

–59–   Roman historian Livy lives and composes the multibook history of
A.D. 17   Rome, *Ab urbe condita libri.*   **LIT**

–58–   Roman general and statesman Julius Caesar writes *Commentaries*
–44   *on the Gallic War,* a historical work famed for its clear, strong style. He also writes *Commentaries on the Civil War* in 45 B.C.   **LIT**

–55   Master of the Roman art of public speaking, Cicero writes his treatise on oratory, *De oratore.*   **LIT**

–54–   Roman orator Cicero writes *De re publica,* a six-book work on political
–51   cal philosophy.   **LIT**

–50   In Mesoamerica the Maya civilization develops a more refined system of writing than that used by the Zapotec. *See* 600s B.C., LIT.   **LIT**

–47–   Cicero writes several philosophical works, including *Tusculanae dis-*
–44   *putationes, De natura deorum, De divinatione, De senectute, De amicitia,* and his guide to Stoic morality, *De officiis.*   **LIT**

–40   In China *Li chi* (*The Book of Rites*) is composed, incorporating older material dealing with proper behavior and ritual.   **LIT**

–38   In China the octave is subdivided into sixty notes.   **MUSIC**

–37   Roman poet Virgil completes the *Eclogues,* or *Bucolics.* The collection of ten pastoral poems establishes his literary reputation.   **LIT**

–37–   Roman poet Virgil composes the agricultural poem, the *Georgics.*
–30   Written in four books, the poem celebrates farming and is patterned after Hesiod's *Works and Days.*   **LIT**

–23   Roman poet Horace composes his first notable collection of poems, *Odes,* or *Carmina.* In this year the first three of four books of odes appear.   **LIT**

–22   Roman poet Horace composes *Epistulae* (*Epistles*).   **LIT**

–20–   Roman poet Ovid is established as an important writer with his col-
–1   lections *Amores* and *Heroides.* The former is a book of love poems, the latter epistles from legendary women abandoned by men.   **LIT**

−20   Roman sculptors erect a marble statue of Augustus of Primaporta at the villa of his wife, Livia. The statue combines aspects of the divine ruler seen in Egyptian and ancient Near Eastern sculpture with an idealized head similar to Hellenistic portraits of Alexander the Great.   **SCULP**

−19   *The Aeneid*, Roman poet Virgil's epic poem on the founding of Rome by Trojan refugee Aeneas, is left unfinished upon his death. Drawing on Homer's *Iliad* and *Odyssey* (ninth century B.C.), the poem will influence Western writers through the ages, notably Dante in *The Divine Comedy* (1321 A.D.).   **LIT**

−13   Roman poet Horace composes *Ars poetica* (*The Art of Poetry*), in which he details the process of writing poetry.   **LIT**

−13   The Roman senate votes to have a monument known as the Altar of Peace (or Ara Pacis) constructed and set up on the Campus Martius in Rome. Roman sculptors decorate the wall screening the altar with a frieze depicting allegorical and legendary scenes as well as a procession led by Augustus. The entire sculptural program will be completed in 9 B.C.   **SCULP**

−4   Lucius Annaeus Seneca, who will become a philosopher, orator, statesman, and playwright in Rome, is born at Corduba (*d.* 65). Seneca's plays, the only dramas surviving in complete form from ancient Rome, will all be adaptations of Greek plays. The dramas may have been meant to be read aloud rather than staged. The tragedies of Seneca, for which dates are unknown, will include *Hercules Furens*, *Medea*, *Phaedra*, *Troades* (*Trojan Women*), *Agamemnon*, *Oedipus*, *Phoenissae* (*Phoenician Women*), and *Thyestes*. He will perhaps also be the author of *Hercules Oetaeus*. His work will have an influence on Shakespeare, evident in *Richard III* (*see* c. 1591–1594) and *Titus Andronicus* (*see* c. 1590–1592), and on Ben Jonson.   **DRAMA**

−3   Roman poet Ovid composes *Ars amatoria* (*Art of Love*).   **LIT**

A.D.

1   The Recuay culture in the valleys of northern Peru model thin-walled ceramics from a fine-textured white kaolin clay. Typical ceramics are large hollow vessels in a variety of shapes with a unique double spout arrangement.   **DECO**

THE BANISHED POET

*H*ow best to punish a sophisticated literary figure? Banish him to the provinces. That was what Roman emperor Augustus Caesar did to the poet Ovid in A.D. 8. Known for his witty, sensuous, amorous verse, he was the most illustrious living poet among Rome's literati when he slighted Augustus in ways that were never clearly defined. Perhaps Augustus, who was pursuing a campaign of moral reform, was offended by Ovid's Ars amatoria (Art of Love), a satiric manual in verse teaching readers of both sexes how to gain lovers. There were also unnamed charges of personal immorality. In any case, the fifty-year-old Ovid's "error" led to his exile to the Black Sea port of Tomis, now Constantsa, Romania. There, separated from his wife, his works banned from public libraries, he lived out the remaining ten years of his life.

For one accustomed to urban comforts and high culture, it was a dreadful punishment. At the far edge of the Roman Empire, the windswept outpost was only semi-Hellenized, severe in climate, and periodically attacked by barbarians. Ovid made the best of it, serving in Tomis's home guard, taking an interest in local politics, writing poetry in the local language, and warmly accepting the honors given him by the townspeople. Still, Rome was never far from his thoughts, as was attested to in Tristia and Letters from the Black Sea, both books of elegiacs lamenting his exile.

Even in his darkest moments, Ovid claimed that the emperor had no power over poetry. Indeed, despite Augustus's ban, Ovid's works have survived and influenced writers to the present day.

1   The marble group that will become known as the *Laocoön* is created by the sculptors Agesander, Polydorus, and Athenodorus of Rhodes. Admired in classical times as one of the greatest sculptures ever made, it will be rediscovered in Rome in 1506, when it will exert a profound influence on such Renaissance sculptors as Michelangelo. The group depicts the Trojan priest Laocoön and his two sons being crushed to death by snakes, as described in Book II of Virgil's *Aeneid. See* 19 B.C., LIT.   **SCULP**

1   The spread of Greek aesthetics throughout the Roman Empire produces a market for copies as sculptors begin to introduce the mechanical process of pointing. This method, originating in Athens, involves making plaster casts of originals and then preparing stone or bronze copies. In Rome, the demand will be for mass-produced marble versions of classical sculpture, which will need the addition of a support to make them stable.   **SCULP**

1   Roman sculptors in Tivoli erect a portrait statue of a general from the Late Republic. The pose and gestures are derived from statues of Hellenistic rulers.   **SCULP**

8   Roman poet Ovid composes the multibook collection of mythological tales, *Metamorphoses*.   **LIT**

23   Roman scholar Pliny the Elder is born (*d.* 79). His thirty-seven-volume *Historia naturalis* (*Natural History*) will become an important scientific work during the Middle Ages.   **LIT**

50–100   The books of the New Testament are written in Greek by members of early Christian communities in the Mediterranean region.   **LIT**

55   Roman historian Tacitus is born (*d.* 120). He will write *Germania*, a social history of Germany; *Annales*, a study of the Julian dynasty; and *Historiae*, a history of the years 69–96.   **LIT**

60   Roman satirist Juvenal is born (*d.* 140). He will write sixteen satires, primarily exposing vices of the age and empire.   **LIT**

65   Roman poet Lucan writes the *Pharsalia*, an epic on the civil war between Julius Caesar and Pompey.   **LIT**

69   Roman biographer and historian Suetonius is born (*d.* 140). He will write *De vita Caesarum* (*Lives of the Caesars*), a series of biographies of the Roman emperors from Caesar to Domitian.   **LIT**

79   Mount Vesuvius erupts near Naples, burying the towns of Pompeii and Herculaneum. The art and architecture of the buried towns, excavated in 1738, will spur the neoclassical movement of the eighteenth century.   **MISC**

79   Preserved at Pompeii are illusionistic frescoes by Roman artists that employ shading or modeling, foreshortening, overlapping, and atmospheric perspective.   **PAINT**

80   The Roman Colosseum is built. Seating 50,000 people, it is the largest public structure up to its time. Supported by an arch-and-vault system, it features three levels of arched openings decorated with Doric, Ionic, and Corinthian columns.   **ARCH**

81   Roman sculptors decorate a triumphal arch with marble relief panels commemorating the victories of the Emperor Titus. The sculptors successfully illustrate a crowd of figures in depth through different layers of relief.   **SCULP**

96   Spanish-born Roman rhetorician Quintilian publishes the influential
          educational treatise *Institutio oratoria* (*On the Training of an Orator*). **LIT**

100s   Early this century, the Pantheon in Rome is built, a domed, cylindri-
          cal temple 144 feet in diameter with an attached portico featuring
          Corinthian columns.   **ARCH**

100s   Sanskrit drama, encompassing both religious and secular themes,
          begins in India. It will flourish for the next millennium.   **DRAMA**

100s   *Ch'u tz'u* (*The Elegies of Ch'u*), a Chinese poetry anthology, is com-
          posed, though attributed to the fourth century B.C. Chinese poet
          Ch'ü Yüan.   **LIT**

100   Greek biographer Plutarch writes *Parallel Lives*, a series of paired bi-
          ographies of famous Greeks and Romans. The book will provide
          background for such Shakespeare plays as *Julius Caesar* (c. 1599). **LIT**

100   The Vicus culture along Peru's north coast creates a unique style of
          figurative sculpture. Artists shape compact bodies out of clay with
          shoulders that blend into an abstract form comprising both arms
          and legs.   **SCULP**

105   In China Ts'ai Lun invents paper, a writing and drawing surface that
          can be made more cheaply than papyrus or parchment. It will
          reach Europe in 1320.   **GRAPH**

113   Roman sculptors complete a continuous spiral band of relief begun
          in 106 that covers a column celebrating Emperor Trajan's victories
          against the Dacians. The scenes recount the history of the Dacian
          wars and are carved in a shallow relief that breaks the tradition of
          foreshortening and perspective. These stylistic aspects will domi-
          nate medieval art.   **SCULP**

121   Roman emperor Marcus Aurelius is born (*d.* 180). He will write the
          classic work of Stoic philosophy *Meditations*.   **LIT**

122   Hadrian's Wall, seventy-two miles long, is built by the Romans in
          Britain to defend against the Picts and other northern tribesmen. **ARCH**

125   Lucian of Samosata, Greek satirist, is born (*d.* 200). His satires will in-
          clude *The True History*, which describes a trip to the moon, *Dialogues
          of the Dead*, and the novel *Lucius; or, The Ass*. His biting, wide-ranging
          wit will influence later writers such as Jonathan Swift and Voltaire. He
          will be considered the inventor of satirical dialogue.   **LIT**

150   Hopewell culture centers in southern Ohio begin to direct their
          trade of flint, effigy platform pipes, and pottery toward the south
          and east.   **DECO**

161   Roman sculptors begin work on a bronze equestrian statue of
          Marcus Aurelius in the tradition of equestrian images established by
          Julius Caesar. The statue will be completed in 180.   **SCULP**

180	Roman sculptors begin to use the drill to create exaggerated details in the modeling of hair on marble portrait busts. **SCULP**
200s	Indian dramatist Bhāsa writes verse dramas that include *Svapnavasavadatta (The Dream of Vasavadatta)*. **LIT**
200s	Late this century, in the purge of Confucianism, the emperor of China orders all musical instruments destroyed. **MUSIC**
250	Stone masks become the predominant form of sculpture in the urban Mexican complex of Teotihuacán. Artists create simple, uniform masks inlaid with shells or small gems. **SCULP**
260	A relief of Shapur I triumphing over the Emperors Philippus the Arab and Valeria is carved in rock at Naksh-i-Rustam, the burial place of the Persian Achaemenid kings near Persepolis. The blending of Roman and Near Eastern elements will also be seen in Shapur's palace at Ctesiphon near Babylon. **SCULP**
300s	The art of Chinese scroll painting develops, typically depicting courtly life and landscapes. **PAINT**
300	The Nazca culture from the Peruvian Rio Grande Valley decorate vessel surfaces with two-dimensional polychrome scenes rather than with the type of modeling prefered in northern Peru. **DECO**
300	At the beginning of India's Gupta period, when the arts start to flourish under imperial patronage, sculpture takes on a new naturalism through a more refined system of aesthetics. The holy cities of Mathura and Sarnath will be the centers of sculptural production. **SCULP**
306	In Rome construction begins on the Basilica of Constantine or Maxentius, which employs concrete vaulting to reach vast dimensions—328 by 249 feet, with a central aisle 114 feet high. Basilicas, long civic halls with low side aisles and high central aisles or naves, were first developed in Hellenistic Greece and widely adopted by the Romans. **ARCH**
306	A colossal statue of Constantine will be built for the Basilica of Constantine or Maxentius, which is begun this year. The eight-and-a-half-foot-high head has enormous eyes in proportion to the face. **SCULP**
315	The Arch of Constantine near the Colosseum in Rome is decorated with sculpture taken from earlier Imperial monuments. Sculptors carve a frieze in a new Constantinian style that avoids all the devices developed since the fifth century B.C. to create spatial depth. The depiction of the emperor in a frontal pose surrounded by other figures is derived from Near Eastern art and will appear throughout Christian art compositions. **SCULP**

THE BUDDHA GOES EAST

*B*uddhism was introduced to China in the first century A.D., but it was not until the fourth century that it became a major force, beginning in northern China. The religion originated in India in the sixth and fifth centuries B.C. Merchants and monks then transported it along the Silk Road that ran from northern India to central Asia to northern China. The coming of Buddhism led to a burgeoning of creativity in the arts—sculpture, painting, and architecture—as fourth- and fifth-century artists sought to embody the new religious beliefs in concrete form. Among the most stunning works, adapted from central Asian models, were cave temples containing colossal statues of Buddha carved from the rock. Sitting or standing, sculptures at sites such as Yunkang and Lungmen towered more than forty or fifty feet in height.

The first great Chinese Buddhist shrine complex was Dunhuang, located in Kansu on the trade routes from India and central Asia. It contains more than 300 rock-cut shrines decorated with fresco murals and painted clay sculptures. Details such as elongated halos, columnar bodies, and exaggerated ripples in the hems of garments already began to add a distinctly Chinese identity to the borrowed images, an identity that would be fully realized by the sixth century.

320   Sculpture begins to play a secondary role in Early Christian art. The biblical prohibition of graven images is thought to apply to large cult statues worshiped in pagan temples. Sculpture develops in an antimonumental direction toward small-scale forms.   **SCULP**

333   Construction of Old St. Peter's Church begins in Rome. Though it will not survive to modern times, it will be remembered as a prominent example of early Christian basilicas, the design of which is based on Roman civic basilicas. The altar is located in an apse, or semicircular niche, at the eastern end, with the main entrance at the western end. An atrium, or courtyard, and a narthex, or entrance hall, precede entrance to the nave, or central aisle. The design will provide the model for church architecture in the West for centuries to come. *See* 306, ARCH.   **ARCH**

350   The Schola Cantorum, a school for church song, is founded in Rome.   **MUSIC**

350   Limestone stelae carved with scenes of Buddha leaving his family and the palace become a standard part of Indian Buddhist imagery.   **SCULP**

354	Christian philosopher St. Augustine of Hippo is born (*d.* 430). He will trace his conversion to Christianity in *Confessions* and present a defense of the religion in the multivolume *De civitate Dei* (*The City of God*). **LIT**
359	The Roman sarcophagus of Junius Bassus displays a mixture of Old and New Testament scenes carved in relief. Early Christian relief images are no longer intended to tell a story but to reflect a symbolic meaning. **SCULP**
370–800	During the migration period, invading Teutonic tribes such as the Visigoths, Ostrogoths, Vandals, Lombards, and Franks introduce new decorative art styles to Europe, particularly in gold objects such as fibulae and buckles. **DECO**
370	Roman poet Claudian is born (*d.* 404). He will write *Claudianus Major* and *Claudianus Minor*. **LIT**
375	Christ giving the law to Peter, or the Traditio Legis, becomes a very popular image in Early Christian tomb reliefs. Roman sculptors create a Theodosian style under Eastern influence by carving strong, well-rounded bodies. **SCULP**
380	Roman emperors, consuls, and high officials demonstrate a renewed interest in individual characterization by continuing the custom of erecting portrait statues of themselves in public places. **SCULP**
386	Hymn singing is introduced to the West by St. Ambrose, bishop of Milan, though Hilary, bishop of Poitiers (c. 315–366), has also been credited. Among the best known early hymns from this period is "*Te Deum laudamus*" ("We Praise Thee, O God"). **MUSIC**
390	The first "Alleluia" hymns are introduced in Christian churches. **MUSIC**
390	Ivory panels, designed for private ownership, display a more conservative style not found among the large official monuments sponsored by the church or state. **SCULP**
400s	A mosaic of the Good Shepherd is constructed at the mausoleum of Galla Placidia in Ravenna, depicting Christ as a young, beardless man surrounded by a flock of lambs. **DECO**
400s	In the Middle East, stamps are cut on wood for printing fabrics. **GRAPH**
400	Lake Woodland ceramics from western Florida feature elaborate ceremonial decoration consisting of incised geometric and floral motifs and modeled forms of birds and animals. **DECO**
400–700	Japanese music begins to flourish as it adopts styles and instruments from an eclectic variety of sources—Chinese ceremonial music (fifth century), Korean Buddhist song (sixth century), and Indian ceremonial dance (seventh century). New instruments, such as the zitherlike koto, will be introduced from China in the ninth and tenth centuries. **MUSIC**

400   Indian sculptors create an elegantly proportioned statue of Buddha standing with his right hand posed in a protective gesture. This image of Buddha will become the type most often represented in South Asian art.   **SCULP**

450   Germanic tribes Angles, Saxons, and Jutes, now overrunning Britain, introduce migration period styles in such portable objects as brooches and cloisonné ware.   **DECO**

450   Following Jewish and Byzantine tradition, Roman Catholic church services employ alternative singing between soloist and congregation.   **MUSIC**

477   Chinese sculptors of the northern Wei dynasty create a gilt bronze statue of Maitreya, the Buddha of the Future. It will be the largest and most important bronze statue made during the period.   **SCULP**

500s   The church of San Vitale is constructed in Ravenna, Italy. The domed, octagonal church has the central plan characteristic of Eastern (Byzantine) churches, as opposed to the longitudinal plan of Western churches. The church is decorated with mosaics, including *Emperor Justinian and His Attendants*.   **ARCH**

500s   By now, the Chinese have invented block books, a form of printing in which a woodcut block of text and illustrations is used to print an entire page. *See also* 1450, GRAPH.   **GRAPH**

500   Woodland population centers along the entire Gulf coast employ a variety of decorative techniques to produce an assortment of pottery styles. These styles feature both abstract designs and naturalistic animal forms.   **DECO**

500   Roman philosopher Boethius writes on musical theory in *De institutione musica*. His views that music is a corollary of mathematics and that it has a strong influence on character development will be widely held throughout the Middle Ages.   **MUSIC**

500   Sculptors from the ancient Gandhara region of northwest India and northern Pakistan produce small portable bronze images of Buddha standing on a pedestal. These Gandharan-style Buddhas will serve as prototypes for early Buddhist images and iconography throughout the Far East and South Asia.   **SCULP**

500   An ivory diptych depicting the archangel Michael from the eastern Roman Empire shows a classicism that recalls the winged Victories of Graeco-Roman art.   **SCULP**

524   While in prison awaiting execution for treason against the Ostrogoth ruler of Rome Theodoric the Great, Roman philosopher Boethius writes the meditative treatise *The Consolation of Philosophy*.   **LIT**

Ostrogoth ruler Theodoric is laid to rest in Theodoric's tomb in

Ravenna, an important example of migration period architecture. **ARCH**

OUTLAW WRITERS

*T*he association of the literary life with legal trouble spans eras and continents. In addition to Roman poet Ovid (see sidebar "The Banished Poet"), here are a few other famous writers who have had difficulties staying on the right side of the law:

- *Boethius—Roman philosopher, author of* The Consolation of Philosophy, *was imprisoned for treason by Theodoric the Great, Ostrogoth ruler of Rome, and was executed in 525.*
- *Miguel de Cervantes—Spanish novelist, author of* Don Quixote, *which he began writing in 1605 while serving a prison term for fraud while a government tax inspector.*
- *John Milton—English poet, author of* Paradise Lost, *was arrested in 1660 for advocating republican government just as King Charles II was being restored to power.*
- *Oliver Goldsmith—English poet, playwright, and novelist narrowly escaped arrest for debt when his novel* The Vicar of Wakefield *(1766) was sold on his behalf by his friend Samuel Johnson.*
- *Fyodor Dostoyevsky—Russian novelist, author of* Crime and Punishment, *was arrested in 1849 and served four years in a labor camp in Siberia for political crimes.*
- *O. Henry (William Sydney Porter)—American short-story writer, author of the short-story collection* The Four Million *(1906), began writing stories while serving a three-year sentence for embezzlement while a bank teller.*
- *Aleksandr Solzhenitsyn—Russian novelist, author of* The Gulag Archipelago, *served time in Soviet labor camps for political crimes and was deported in 1974, only to return to Russia in 1994 after the fall of the Soviet Union.*
- *Salman Rushdie—British writer, was condemned to death in 1989, not by his own government but by that of Iran, which called for his execution for blasphemy for writing the novel* The Satanic Verses. *He has been forced to live in hiding since.*

TIE-DYEING BEFORE ROCK CONCERTS

*T*he craft of tie-dyeing, associated with T-shirts, rock concerts, and counterculture since the 1960s, goes back much earlier—to the sixth century in India. Indian artisans developed the technique of producing patterns on cloth by tying portions of fabric with waxed thread or rags before dipping the cloth into a vat of dye. Skill in tying and folding the cloth resulted in a limitless number of patterns in a variety of colors, consisting of spots, small circles, transverse bands, or zigzags. This traditional craft, which was originally associated with muslin turbans, was known as bandhnu. From that Hindi word, by way of Portuguese traders, comes the modern term bandanna for a large, figured, brightly colored handkerchief. By a quirk of history, it is not uncommon for the sort of person who wears a tie-dyed T-shirt to accessorize the look with a bandanna around the head.

532–535   The church of Santa Sophia (now called Hagia Sophia) is constructed in Constantinople. Designed by Anthemius of Tralles and Isidorus of Miletus, it is the greatest masterpiece of Byzantine architecture. Its dome, 184 feet from the floor and 112 feet in diameter, appears to float on a cushion of sunlight entering through a ring of arched windows at the dome's base. **ARCH**

532–535   Sculptors carve new ornamental motifs derived from classical architecture for the moldings and capitals at the church of Santa Sophia in Constantinople. **SCULP**

537   In Canton, China, the Pagoda of the Temple of the Six Banyon Trees is built; it will be rebuilt in 1098. It is a prominent example of the pagoda, a type of Buddhist tower found in Nepal, China, and Japan. Pagodas will reach up to fifteen stories in height, and assume square, hexagonal, or octagonal shapes. **ARCH**

Eagle Fibulae. Visigothic Spain. Gilt, bronze, and gems.
(The Walters Art Gallery, Baltimore)

550	Veracruz artists along the Gulf Coast of Mexico fashion the sides of stone heads to resemble the thin blade of an axe or hacha. **SCULP**

590–604	Antiphonal Gregorian chant (plainsong) appears in the Roman Catholic Church, developed under Pope Gregory. **MUSIC**

600s　　　Islamic civilization begins to develop strong craft traditions in carpets, ceramics, enamel, and metalwork. **DECO**

600s　　　Because the Arabic language in which the Koran (*see* 651, LIT) is written is considered sacred, and because Islamic law forbids most kinds of representational images, great attention is paid in Islamic art to calligraphy, handwriting as an expression of beauty. **GRAPH**

600s　　　Indian poet Bhartrhari, perhaps the greatest Sanskrit lyric poet, lives. His works include *Renunciation, Passion of Love,* and *Good Conduct.* **LIT**

600　　　Pope Gregory reorganizes the Schola Cantorum in Rome, training singers and teachers throughout Europe. **MUSIC**

600　　　The crwth (also called crowd or chrotta), a Celtic stringed instrument reminiscent of the Greek kithara, develops. **MUSIC**

600   Statues of seated Buddhas are made in the dry lacquer technique
           during China's T'ang dynasty. Numerous layers of lacquer-soaked
           cloth are first molded over a wooden base, then the figure is paint-
           ed in gesso, polychrome, and gilt. **SCULP**

618–907   Rod puppets appear during the T'ang dynasty in China. Originating
           in Bengal, the puppets have also become popular in Bali, Java, and
           Thailand. **DRAMA**

618–907   The T'ang dynasty is the golden age of Chinese poetry, notable for
           such poets as Wang Wei, Li Po, Po Chü-i, and Tu Fu, and also the
           period when fiction becomes established in China. **LIT**

651   The teachings of Islam's founder Muhammad, believed by Muslims
           to be divinely revealed, are collected into the Koran (Qur'an), a sa-
           cred volume of 114 chapters. **LIT**

670   Old English poet and monk Caedmon writes hymns, of which only
           the first, known as "Caedmon's Hymn," will survive. **LIT**

690   Artists begin to create sandstone statues of Ganesha, the elephant-
           headed Hindu god of auspiciousness, during the pre-Angkor period
           in Southeast Asia. **SCULP**

691   The mosque of Omar at Jerusalem, known as the Dome of the
           Rock, is built, following a domed, octagonal Byzantine plan. **ARCH**

700s   Celtic and Germanic artists do not render well-proportioned human
           figures as they attempt to reproduce Early Christian compositions
           for bronze plaques to adorn book covers. **DECO**

700s   *The Lindisfarne Gospels* and *The Book of Kells* in Ireland are exam-
           ples of the Hiberno-Saxon style of illuminating manuscripts. The
           pages are illustrated with interlacing patterns of hybrid animals,
           people, and birds, as well as jewellike crosses. **GRAPH**

700s   The Old English narrative poem *Beowulf* is anonymously com-
           posed, recounting the adventures of the warrior Beowulf against
           Grendel and other monsters. **LIT**

700s   The xylophone is invented in Southeast Asia or Oceania. It will be
           introduced to Europe in the 1500s and to China in the 1700s. **MUSIC**

700   In China porcelain is invented, a form of pottery that will eventually
           spread to Europe under the popular name "china." **DECO**

700   Mayan sculptors in Mesoamerica create stelae bearing a single fig-
           ure in low relief and carvings full of symbolic motifs and hiero-
           glyphic elements. **SCULP**

701   Chinese poet Li Po (or Li T'ai-po) is born (*d.* 762). He will write
           some of the best known and most beautiful Chinese lyric poetry. **LIT**

Interior of the Mosque at Cordoba, Spain. (*Fratelli Alinari/Art Resource*)

725	In China during the T'ang dynasty, the court orchestra of Emperor Ming Huang (Li Lung-chi) employs a five-note scale without semitones, harmony, or polyphony. Gongs, drums, bells, and flutes are among the instruments used. **MUSIC**
726–843	An imperial Byzantine ban on religious images forces artists to use only abstract symbols, such as floral patterns and crosses, in Byzantine church decor. **DECO**
731	English scholar and historian the Venerable Bede publishes *Ecclesiastical History of the English People*. **LIT**
750	The Old English poem *The Dream of the Rood* is composed. **LIT**
750	Gregorian chant (plainsong) is practiced in Germany, France, and England. **MUSIC**
750	In western Europe, water organs are replaced by wind organs from Byzantium. **MUSIC**
750	A new style of stone sculpture is introduced in Mesoamerica as artists from Copán, Honduras, carve human and animal figures to heroic scale from three-dimensional models rather than drawings. **SCULP**
786–987	The mosque at Cordoba, Spain, is built. It is notable for its many interior columns and its system of round, horseshoe-shaped arches. **ARCH**

792–805	The Palatine (or Palace) Chapel of Charlemagne is built in Aachen, Germany, following a more monumental, massive design than the domed Byzantine churches on which it is based. **ARCH**
800s	The Great Mosque at Samarra, Iraq, is constructed. One of the largest mosques ever built, it is notable for its spiral minaret probably modeled on Mesopotamian ziggurats. **ARCH**
800s	Gregorian music is recorded with neumes, notes similar to the accent marks in Greek poetry from which they are believed to derive. **MUSIC**
800s	As Islamic civilization spreads, it contributes musical instruments to Europe, Southeast Asia, and Africa. In Africa, new varieties of drums, lutes, reed pipes, and long trumpets are introduced. In Europe, the Arabs introduce lutes, kettledrums, and trumpets. **MUSIC**
800–810	Frankish King Charlemagne's gospel book, the *Coronation Gospels*, employs classical elements in its illustrations, including foreshortening and modeling (shading). **GRAPH**
800	Charlemagne, Emperor of the West, following Pope Gregory's plan for unifying the church through a common music, orders all Gallican songbooks destroyed. **MUSIC**
800	Islamic law bans large-scale human or animal figures for public display. Images of living things are approved solely for small-scale or everyday objects. **SCULP**
800	A statue of a standing Maitreya from Nepal exhibits the influences of the art of India by depicting the tribhanga pose. This statue will be one of the country's largest bronzes. **SCULP**
800	For the first time in Nigeria, copper alloys are used artistically, in bronze funerary objects and figurines among the Igbo Ukwu culture east of the Niger River. **SCULP**
816–835	The *Gospel Book of Archbishop Ebbo of Reims* depicts the evangelists in energetic, emotional renderings. **GRAPH**
820s	Wooden animal heads carved with geometric patterns are created for posts on Scandinavian Viking ships. **DECO**
825	Carolingian artists of Charlemagne's court school begin to carve deeply layered ivory plaques of the four Evangelists. **SCULP**
850	Church modes, a system that will lead in the seventeenth century to major and minor scales, emerges. **MUSIC**
855	Polyphony, music that combines several simultaneous voice parts, begins with "vertical" broadening of Gregorian chant. **MUSIC**
855	Toltec rulers establish the city of Tollan and dominate Mesoamerican art with warrior motifs and images of death on columns and relief slabs. **SCULP**

Indian sculpture of Siva Nataraja. Bronze, Chola dynasty. *(The Metropolitan Museum of Art, Harris Brisbane Dick Fund, 1964)*

860   Toltec motifs change Maya carving styles in the Yucatán Peninsula. Sculptural detail will be either reduced or eliminated.   **SCULP**

863   The Cyrillic alphabet is invented by Macedonian missionary Cyril and his brother Methodius. It will become the alphabet of Russians and other eastern peoples.   **LIT**

868   The earliest known dated woodcut appears in China in the Buddhist scripture *Diamond Sutra*, the first printed book.   **GRAPH**

870   *Musica enchiriadis* (*Handbook of Music*), a musical manuscript using Latin letters for musical notation, is the earliest treatise dealing with polyphony (called organum).   **MUSIC**

900s   Liturgical dramas, biblical-themed plays chanted in Latin, are performed in European churches. Plays are usually matched to the season of the year. There is no scenery other than that provided by the interior of the church, and the actors—priests and choirboys and, later, possibly nuns—wear liturgical robes, sometimes with small additions to indicate gender and status. These dramas will continue to be performed for several hundred years.   **DRAMA**

900s   *Jongleurs* or *menestrels* (minstrels) perform from town to town in France, singing and playing *chansons de geste* and other secular songs.   **MUSIC**

900   Part song in fourths, fifths, and octaves begins to develop.   **MUSIC**

900   Artists of the Chola dynasty in South India cast bronze statues of Parvati, the consort of Siva, by the lost-wax process.   **SCULP**

· ·

**"There are Six Essentials in painting. The first is called spirit; the second, rhythm; the third, thought; the fourth, scenery; the fifth, the brush; and the last is the ink."
—Chinese painter and essayist Ching Hao, Notes on Brushwork, c. 925**

· ·

962–1024   During the Ottonian period (so called for Saxon king Otto I, crowned Holy Roman Emperor in 962), Germany leads Europe in sculpture, architecture, and manuscript illumination.   **MISC**

975   The Exeter Book is compiled, preserving such Old English poems as "The Wanderer," "The Seafarer," "The Phoenix," "Widsith," "The Whale," "Christ," "Deor," "Juliana," "Wulf and Eadwacer," "The Husband's Message," and "The Wife's Complaint."   **LIT**

975   An Ottonian sculptor rejects Byzantine tradition by carving a more monumental, expressive image of Christ for a wooden crucifix. The powerful realism the crucifix displays will become the strength of German art.   **SCULP**

980   Graeco-Roman iconography influences Byzantine styles as sculptors carve scenes of Greek mythology on ivory caskets intended for wedding gifts.   **DECO**

980   A 400-pipe organ is in use at Winchester Monastery, England.   **MUSIC**

991   Viking invaders and Saxon defenders clash near Maldon in Essex, England, in the incident recounted in the Old English poem "The Battle of Maldon," written shortly afterward.   **LIT**

1000s   The Kandariya Mahadeva temple at Khajuraho in north central India is constructed. Its many stone towers contribute to the effect of a single monumental tower; its curved projecting forms suggest sexuality.   **ARCH**

1000s   Africans construct the great wall and highly decorated buildings of the city of Zimbabwe, the ruins of which will be found by Europeans in 1870 in what is now the nation of Zimbabwe.   **ARCH**

1000s   A mosaic in the dome of the monastery church at Daphne, Greece, depicts Christ as Pantocrator, stern judge of humankind, an image frequently found in Byzantine churches of this period.   **DECO**

1000s   Anglo-Norman prelate Theobald writes the first medieval bestiary, the Latin *Physiologus*. The form, which presents allegorical and descriptive verses about animals real and imaginary, will be popular in the twelveth and thirteenth centuries.   **LIT**

1000s   In European church music, Gregorian chant (plainsong) gives way to polyphonic singing.   **MUSIC**

1000s   The jongleurs or minstrels of France organize into brotherhoods, which will evolve into guilds.   **MUSIC**

1000s   In China Fan K'uan is the northern Sung dynasty's greatest landscape painter.   **PAINT**

1000   In Germany, the illuminations of the *Gospel Book of Otto III* blend Carolingian and Byzantine elements. The book is made at the Reichenau Monastery, the period's greatest center of manuscript illumination.   **GRAPH**

....

"Anything whatsoever may become the subject of a novel, provided only that it happens in this mundane life and not in some fairyland beyond our human ken."—Japanese writer Murasaki Shikibu, Tale of Genji, c. 1000

....

1000   Japanese court lady and writer Murasaki Shikibu writes the novel *Tale of Genji*. Translated into English by Arthur Waley in 1925–1933, it will be considered by many the world's first novel.   **LIT**

1000   Italian music theorist and monk Guido d'Arezzo invents the musical staff.   **MUSIC**

1000   Neumes, early music notations, show more specific musical intervals, manner of performance, and pitch.   **MUSIC**

1000   In the Islamic world, arabesque, scrolling or interlacing plant ornamentation, becomes an important motif.   **PAINT**

African Equestrian Figure.
(*Manu Sassoonian/Art Resource*)

1000   The West African Djenne civilization in Mali creates ceramic statuettes of kneeling figures with crossed arms and hands placed on shoulders. Most Djenne figurative terra-cottas will feature this pose.   **SCULP**

1000   Artists of the Late Heian period in Japan produce a bronze statue of Zao Gongen, the tutelary deity of Mount Kimpu in the Yoshino Mountains. The statue's active pose will become conventional for the representation of Buddhist guardian figures.   **SCULP**

1001–1033   In Germany Hildesheim cathedral (St. Michael's), commissioned by Bernward, bishop of Hildesheim, is a prominent example of Ottonian architecture.   **ARCH**

1015   Bishop Bernward commissions a pair of bronze doors for the two entrances leading to the ambulatory in St. Michael's Church at Hildesheim. The doors will differ from Roman and Byzantine doors by featuring biblical scenes carved in high relief into individual, horizontal fields.   **SCULP**

1023	Construction begins on Durham cathedral in England. Its solidity of design makes it a prime example of Romanesque architecture. **ARCH**
1026	Italian music theorist and monk Guido d'Arezzo introduces solmization, a system of syllables used for designating degrees of the scale (do, re, mi, fa, sol, la, ti). **MUSIC**
1041	In China movable type made from clay blocks is used by printer Pi Sheng. **GRAPH**
1063	Construction begins on St. Mark's in Venice, a lavishly decorated Byzantine church that follows the plan of the Greek cross (a central dome with four projecting arms of equal length). **ARCH**
c. 1090	Sculptors decorate the pilgrimage church of St. Sernin at Toulouse in southern France with massive, Roman-style figures of the Apostles. **SCULP**
1100s	The anonymous French epic *Chanson de Roland* (*The Song of Roland*) is composed, telling of Charlemagne's paladin Roland and his heroic death at the Battle of Roncesvalles. **LIT**
1100s	The Middle English lyric "The Cuckoo Song" is written, which begins "Sumer is ycomen in, /Loude sing cuckou!" **LIT**
1100s	German monk Theophilus writes *De diversis artibus*, the most important extant treatise on medieval European arts and crafts. It makes mention of techniques for producing oil paint centuries before it will become the dominant medium for Western painting. *See* 1500s, PAINT. **PAINT**
1100s	The Yoruba from the eastern part of Benin and southwestern Nigeria cast portrait heads in the lost-wax technique. This method will become common to many West African metalwork traditions. **SCULP**
1100s	Sculptors in Tuscany revive an interest in Late Antique and Early Christian art for the carving of New Testament scenes on marble sarcophagi. **SCULP**
c. 1100–1200	The music school of the Abbey of St. Martial in Limoges applies the polyphonic style in sequences and sacred music. **MUSIC**
c. 1100–1400	During the southern Sung dynasty in China, landscape painting becomes less monumental than in the past and more intimate and poetic. **PAINT**
c. 1100	A more animated style of carving becomes characteristic of numerous Spanish Romanesque ivory plaques. **SCULP**
c. 1100	The portal sculpture of the abbey at Moissac north of Toulouse rejects earlier Romanesque stiffness. Sculptors decorate the trumeau and jamb with fluid, Moorish-influenced human and animal forms. **SCULP**

c. 1100   A wood and gold leaf guardian statue of Fudo Myo-O becomes the central icon of the Kuhonji Gomado during the Late Heian period in Funasaka, Japan, northwest of Kyoto.   **SCULP**

c. 1100   The Chancay people from Peru's central coast produce ceramic scenes illustrating the daily activities of village houses. They also produce wooden human figures and mummy masks.   **SCULP**

1113–1150   Khmer emperor Suryavarman II supervises the building of the temple complex Angkor Wat in Cambodia. Notable for its sculptural ornamentation, it will be sacked and abandoned in 1177.   **ARCH**

· ·

"Against the disease of writing one must take special precautions, since it is a dangerous and contagious disease."—French philosopher and theologian Peter Abelard to nun and former lover Héloïse, twelfth century

· ·

1118   French philosopher and theologian Peter Abelard consummates his affair with his student Héloïse. After he is later castrated by her irate uncle, he will become a monk and she a nun. Their exchange of letters will enter the literature of starcrossed love.   **LIT**

1125   In southern France poet-musicians called troubadours establish a tradition of songs in the vernacular. In the mid-twelveth century, the movement spreads to northern France (trouvères) and Germany (minnesingers).   **MUSIC**

c. 1125   Classical monuments influence the development of Romanesque style throughout Provence. Statues for church portals will be carved almost entirely in the round with rich details.   **SCULP**

1127   St. Bernard of Clairvaux denounces the sculptured decoration of churches as diversions that tempt churchgoers to read in marble rather than in books.   **SCULP**

c. 1135   English ecclesiastic and chronicler Geoffrey of Monmouth publishes the chronicle *History of the Kings of Britain* in Latin, one of the main sources of Arthurian legend drawn upon by later writers.   **LIT**

c. 1135   Northern Romanesque artists in Cologne choose walrus ivory over elephant ivory to carve scenes depicting the Infancy and Passion of Christ. The pricked drapery will become a hallmark of the Cologne style.   **SCULP**

1137   The abbey of St. Denis near Paris, designed by Abbé Suger, is the first major example of Gothic architecture. Distinctive features include flying buttresses, pointed ribbed vaults, light upright supports, and stained-glass windows, all contributing to an impression of interior openness and light.   **ARCH**

Interior of Chartres Cathedral. *(Bildarchiv Foto Marburg/Art Resource)*

1145   Sculptors begin to carve the portals of Chartres cathedral in an Early Gothic style that emphasizes order and clarity. The cathedral will be rebuilt after a fire in 1195. The new transept facades will receive three large and lavishly sculpted portals by 1220.   **SCULP**

c. 1150–   The period later called "ars antiqua" is represented by the musical
1250   forms organum, clausula, conductus, and most significantly, the motet. Its greatest advances are the use of three and four voice parts and the establishment of strict rhythm based on rules called the rhythm modes.   **MUSIC**

c. 1150   Formal and symmetrical polychromed-oak statues of the Virgin and Child enthroned become popular in the Auvergne region of France.   **SCULP**

1151   Léonin (Leoninus), French composer and master of the school of Notre Dame, composes for two-part organ in what will be called the "ars antiqua" style.   **MUSIC**

c. 1160–   The Arthurian romances of French poet Chrétien de Troyes include
1190   *Yvain, or the Knight of the Lion*, *Eric and Enide*, *Launcelot, or the Knight of the Cart*, and *Percival, or the Story of the Grail*.   **LIT**

c. 1160   A vigorously carved statue of the Annunciation to the Virgin is completed for the apse of the Romanesque church of San Martin in the village of Fuentidueña, north of Madrid.   **SCULP**

1163   Construction begins on the cathedral of Notre Dame de Paris, a major achievement of early Gothic architecture. Famous for its sculptures, portals, and rose window, it will be mostly completed by 1250, although additions will be made into the fourteenth century.   **ARCH**

c. 1170   German poet Wolfram von Eschenbach is born (*d.* c. 1220). His works include *Willehalm, Parzival,* and *Titurel*.   **LIT**

c. 1180   Italian sculptor and architect Benedetto Antelami attempts to recapture the classical contrapposto for his statue of David which will be placed on the facade of the Fidenza cathedral in Lombardy.   **SCULP**

1182   Persian artists from Khurasan, Iran, create a bronze incense burner in the shape of a stylized, smoke-breathing animal.   **DECO**

1184   The cathedral at Sens, France, designed by William of Sens, is an important example of early Gothic architecture.   **ARCH**

1193   Indigo is imported from India to Europe for use in dying fabrics.   **DECO**

1194   A fire destroys most of Chartres cathedral (begun in 1145), leading to a reconstruction that will be completed early in the thirteenth-century. Its graceful interior nave, masterful stained glass, and strong vertical orientation mark it as the first major example of High Gothic architecture.   **ARCH**

1200s	Caddoan workshops from the Mississippi River valley craft massive figurative pipes to be smoked on ritual occasions. **DECO**
1200s	The Mississippian culture of North America produces carved sandstone masks and stone ceremonial axes engraved with figurative and facial designs. This Mississippian effigy tradition will be carried by the Cherokee Indians in the making of stone pipes until the eighteenth century. **DECO**
1200s	Karagoz, shadow puppet shows, are presented throughout the Middle East. They will remain popular for centuries to come, especially in the Ottoman Empire. **DRAMA**
1200s	Mystery plays, depicting biblical events or the lives of saints, and morality plays, instructing through entertainment, are performed in Europe. Mystery plays derive from liturgical drama, but differ in several ways: words are spoken rather than chanted, the vernacular is used, and the plays are presented outdoors on portable wagons; in addition, the actors are often lay people and props are used. Morality plays, staged by preaching friars, will be popular for several centuries. **DRAMA**
1200s	The portative organ, a small portable organ, is used in Europe. It is played only with the right hand while a small bellows is operated with the left. A related instrument, the positive organ, is placed on a table and requires an assistant for the bellows. **MUSIC**
1200s	The Etowah culture from the Mississippi River valley sculpt images of their founding ancestors in stone and wood. These cult figures will be placed in shrine houses and will appear for nearly two centuries. **SCULP**
1200	In Germany Latin monastic songs are preserved in a collection called the *Carmina Burana*. They will be set to new music for voices and orchestra by Carl Orff in 1937. **MUSIC**
1200	Neumes take on a square shape, as they appear in the book of Roman Catholic Church chants today. **MUSIC**
1200–1400	Gothic painting in northern Europe is best represented by illuminations on manuscript pages, while in Italy painters turn to large-scale panels and frescoes. Painters of the period include Cimabue, Giotto, and Duccio. **PAINT**
c. 1200	Ateliers of Limoges in the Limousin region of France produce six plaques consisting of gilded figures attached to an enamel ground for the altar of the abbey of Grandmont. **SCULP**
c. 1210	German poet Gottfried von Strassburg writes the unfinished epic *Tristan und Isolde*. **LIT**
1212	In Japan Kamo Chōmei writes *Hojo-ki* (*An Account of My Hut*), a personal narrative infused with Buddhist attitudes. **LIT**

1220s   German masters trained in the sculptural workshops of the great French cathedrals transplant a new Gothic style throughout Germany. Most sculptural work in Germany will be done for church interiors rather than exteriors.   **SCULP**

1220–1260 Salisbury cathedral is constructed, a prominent example of early Gothic architecture in England.   **ARCH**

1220–1270 In France Amiens cathedral is constructed, an example of the refinement of Gothic architecture.   **ARCH**

c. 1225   Masters and workshops from various other building sites begin work on the vast sculptural program for Reims cathedral in France. The sculpture will be completed by 1245 in a High Gothic style that will echo the monumental classicism of large-scale Roman sculpture.   **SCULP**

c. 1240   Parisian masters working for the royal court create the "S-curve" design for figurative sculpture. This pattern will become standard in High Gothic sculpture.   **SCULP**

c. 1250   An anonymous English writer composes the only surviving Middle English bestiary.   **LIT**

1250   Franco of Cologne, regarded as the inventor of time signatures, writes on the notation of time values for musical notes. His system will remain in use until 1600.   **MUSIC**

1250   Pérotin (Perotinus), master of the school of Notre Dame and the foremost representative of French ars antiqua, composes organa in three and four parts. Some of Pérotin and his collaborator's short two-part compositions (clausulae) are transformed into motets.   **MUSIC**

c. 1250   The Naumburg Master completes his statues and reliefs for the choir screen at Naumburg cathedral in Germany.   **SCULP**

1257–1289 French sculptors carve the doorway decorations for the monastery church of Moutiers-St.-Jean in Burgundy in a typically High Gothic style.   **SCULP**

1260   Italian sculptor Nicola Pisano finishes the carving of his Roman-influenced narrative scenes for a marble pulpit in the baptistery of Pisa cathedral. Beginning in 1302, his son Giovanni will also do a marble pulpit for the cathedral but in the elegant, Gothic style of the French royal court.   **SCULP**

1265   Franco of Cologne and Pierre de la Croix develop the motet, a central form of early polyphonic music. Frequently a three-part composition, it flourished throughout the century.   **MUSIC**

1270   Chinese painter Mu-ch'i Fa-ch'ang paints *Six Persimmons*.   **PAINT**

c. 1280–
1290   Italian painter Bencivieni di Pepo, known as Cimabue, executes the panel painting *Madonna Enthroned with St. Francis*. His formal approach, incorporating both abstract Byzantine and some naturalistic elements, is known as neo-Byzantine style or the Greek manner. **PAINT**

1285   French musician and playwright Adam de la Halle's *Le Jeu de Robin et Marion*, regarded as the first comic opera, is written for the Anjou court in Naples. **MUSIC**

1285   Italian painter Duccio (Duccio di Buoninsegna) paints the *Rucellai Madonna* in Florence. **PAINT**

1290s   The unidentified Master of the St. Francis Cycle paints the frescoes on the life of St. Francis on the nave walls of the Upper Church of San Francesco in Assisi. The frescos are sometimes attributed to Giotto and dated as late as the 1320s, though these claims are controversial. **PAINT**

1290s   French sculptors carve groups of oak angels carrying either candlesticks or the instruments of Christ's passion to be placed on the tops of columns around church altars. **SCULP**

c. 1290   Italian poet Dante Alighieri composes *La vita nuova* (*The New Life*), a collection of poems and prose inspired by his love for Beatrice. Later important works will include *De vulgari eloquentia* (*On the Vernacular Tongue*, 1304–1306) and *De monarchia* (*On World Government* or *On Monarchy*, c. 1313). *See also* 1321, LIT. **LIT**

1296   Construction begins on Florence cathedral in Italy, which combines the pointed ribbed vaults of French Gothic architecture with a classical exterior. A dome will be added in the fifteenth century. **ARCH**

1300s   Major cycles of English mystery (or miracle) plays, which flourish this century, are the York Cycle, the Wakefield (or Towneley) Cycle, and the Chester Cycle. In the 1400s, the Coventry (or N Town) Cycle will be added. *See also* 1200s, DRAMA. **DRAMA**

1300s   Passion plays, dramas depicting the last days of Christ's life on earth, are staged in Europe. They will remain popular through the next century and will sometimes be performed after that. An elaborate passion play is still staged every ten years in Oberammergau, Germany. **DRAMA**

1300s   Lauda, religious performances involving choral singing, dialogue, and narration, become popular in Italy. **DRAMA**

1300s   The tradition of Nō, carefully structured performances including the recitation of stories from classical literature and rhythmic dancing, begins in Japan. A complete Nō performance consists of five plays, each with a different theme. **DRAMA**

1300s   Chinese novelist Lo Kuan-chung writes the sprawling historical novel *San Kuo chih yen-i* (*The Romance of the Three Kingdoms*). **LIT**

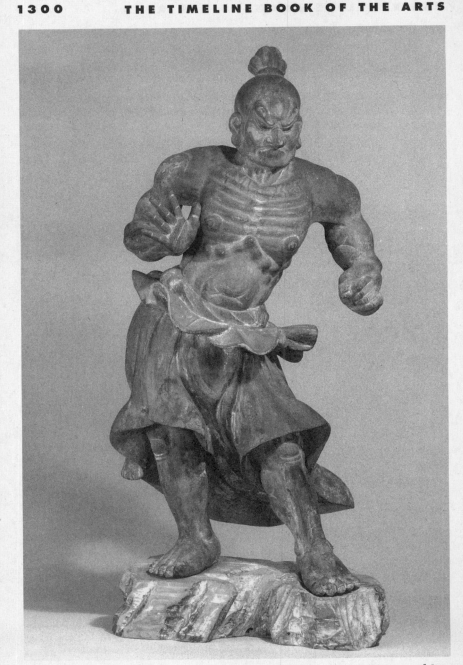

Japanese Temple Guardian, one of a pair. Wood. *(The Metropolitan Museum of Art, Gift of Mr. and Mrs. Samuel Josefowitz, 1964)*

1300s	The Virgin with Child becomes a frequent subject for votive statues in parish churches, cathedrals, oratories, and monastic chapels throughout France, Germany, and the Netherlands. **SCULP**
c. 1300	Artists from the Late Mississippian period create stone, terra-cotta, and wooden images depicting the deceased. These figures will guard the remains of the dead in temples. **SCULP**
1301	Italian sculptor Giovanni Pisano carves a marble lectern in the shape of an eagle for the pulpit of the church of Sant' Andrea in Pistoia. He will produce other eagles in Siena and Perugia. **DECO**
1304–1374	Italian poet Petrarch lives and composes the influential poems *Rime* or *Rime sparse* (*Scattered Lyrics*) and prose works *De viris illustribus* (*On Illustrious Men*) and *De vita solitaria* (*On the Solitary Life*). **LIT**
c. 1305–1306	Florentine painter Giotto (Giotto di Bondone) paints the fresco cycle in the Arena Chapel at Padua, a work that displays his skill at conveying narrative and emotion. Regarded as the father of modern Western painting, he introduces new naturalistic ideals and powerful, solid figures in marked contrast to earlier Byzantine conventions. **PAINT**
c. 1305–1310	Florentine painter Giotto is probably the creator of the unsigned panel painting *Ognissanti Madonna*. **PAINT**
1308–1311	In Italy Duccio paints the altarpiece *Maesta* (*Majesty*) for Siena cathedral. Duccio is an important innovator, reworking neo-Byzantine conventions. **PAINT**
c. 1310–1430	Ars nova, "new style art," is the term coined by French prelate Philippe de Vitry for the new, strongly contrapuntal style of music. **MUSIC**
1315	Italian painter Simone Martini, a follower of Duccio and major innovator in the international Gothic style, paints the large fresco of the *Maesta* in the Siena town hall, combining Byzantine and Gothic conventions. He will rework it in 1321. **PAINT**
1317	In Naples Italian painter Simone Martini paints an altarpiece of St. Louis of Toulouse, with predella (subsidiary) scenes presenting the most innovative use of perspective to date. **PAINT**
1321	Italian poet Dante Alighieri publishes the epic the *Divine Comedy*. Consisting of *Inferno, Purgatorio,* and *Paradiso,* it tells of the poet's journey through the worlds of the afterlife, guided by his master, the Roman poet Virgil. The epic begins, "In the middle of the journey of our life I came to myself within a dark wood where the straight way was lost." **LIT**
1322	Pope John XXII issues a decree at Avignon, banning the use of counterpoint in church music. **MUSIC**

| 1332-1357 | Gloucester cathedral is constructed, an example of High Gothic architecture in England, characterized by the Perpendicular style, which employs ceiling vaults with complex decorative networks of ribs. **ARCH** |

1333 Italian painters (and brothers-in-law) Simone Martini and Lippo Memmi paint the *Annunciation*. **PAINT**

1334 Florentine painter Giotto is appointed architect to Florence cathedral, although the design will be altered after his death in 1337. **ARCH**

•••

"To sit alone in the lamplight with a book spread out before you, and hold intimate converse with men of unseen sensations—such is a pleasure beyond compare." —Japanese poet and essayist Yoshida Kenkō, Essays in Idleness, c. 1340

•••

1340 French poet and composer Guillaume de Machaut, among the first to use music as a form of artistic expression, is the lead composer of the century and considered the bridge between ars antiqua and ars nova. His sacred and secular music will include twenty-three motets. **MUSIC**

1342 In Avignon serving the papal court, Italian painter Simone Martini paints *Christ Reproved by His Parents*. **PAINT**

c. 1350 Chinese influence is exhibited in painted images in Persian illuminated manuscripts, such as the *Summer Landscape* in *Album of the Conqueror* (Sultan Mohammed II). **GRAPH**

c. 1350-1400 The Middle English poetic romance *Sir Gawain and the Green Knight* is composed, as are the poems "Pearl," "Patience," and "Cleanness." **LIT**

1350-1352 Italian writer and poet Giovanni Boccaccio writes the *Decameron*, a collection of tales whose framing story is set in 1348, the year of the Black Death. **LIT**

1350-1400 English poet William Langland composes the allegorical poem *Piers Plowman*. **LIT**

1350-1400 The anonymous mystical treatise *The Cloud of Unknowing* is written in England. **LIT**

c. 1350-1550 The mastersinger movement in Germany is the middle-class continuation of the aristocratic minnesingers. **MUSIC**

1360s The Yoruban civilization of Ita Yemoo in Nigeria creates a series of small terra-cotta figures wearing crowns before casting them in bronze. **SCULP**

1360   The stringed keyboard instruments, the clavichord and cembalo (harpsichord), begin to develop.   **MUSIC**

1364   French poet and composer Guillaume de Machaut's Mass For Four Voices, the first to be written in four parts, is composed for the coronation of Charles V at Reims.   **MUSIC**

1369   English poet Geoffrey Chaucer writes the poem, *The Book of the Duchess*.   **LIT**

1372–1380   During this period, English poet Geoffrey Chaucer writes *House of Fame* and some lyric poems.   **LIT**

1375–1425   The international Gothic style, marked by fine naturalistic detail and aristocratic elegance, becomes common in painting, sculpture, and the decorative arts in northern Europe and Italy.   **MISC**

1378   As the papacy returns from the "Babylonian captivity" in Avignon, bringing its court musicians with it, Rome starts to become the center of European music.   **MUSIC**

1380–1386   During these years, English poet Geoffrey Chaucer writes the poems *Parlement of Foules*, *Troilus and Criseyde*, *Legend of Good Women*, some short poems, and the prose work *Boece*.   **LIT**

c. 1385   *The Second Shepherds' Play*, written by the anonymous Wakefield Master, is the finest English example of a mystery play. It is the second of two plays in the Wakefield (or Towneley) cycle depicting the shepherds' adoration of the infant Jesus.   **DRAMA**

1385–1393   Dutch sculptor Claus Sluter executes his elaborate sculptural program for the Chartreuse of Champmol while working for the Duke of Burgundy at Dijon. The project includes his powerful figures for the Well of Moses. Sluter's rendering of character type and expressive handling of drapery earn him the title of founder of the Burgundian school.   **SCULP**

c. 1387–1400   English poet Geoffrey Chaucer composes his unfinished Middle English masterpiece, *The Canterbury Tales*, a collection of poetic tales told by pilgrims who are journeying to Canterbury. It begins, "Whan that Aprill with his shoures soote."   **LIT**

c. 1387   English writer Thomas Usk writes *The Testament of Love*, an allegorical prose work.   **LIT**

1391–1392   English poet Geoffrey Chaucer writes the prose work *A Treatise on the Astrolabe*.   **LIT**

1391–1465   French poet Charles, duc d'Orléans, lives and writes "Oft in My Thought" and "My Ghostly Father," among other poems.   **LIT**

1394–1427   Japanese architects build the Kinkaku or Golden Pavilion in Kyoto. Like the Ginkaku or Silver Pavilion (c. 1500) in Kyoto, the edifice is built as a Zen center for meditation and recreation.   **ARCH**

1400s   Masque, a type of theatrical show involving music, poetry reading, and elaborate costumes and scenery, becomes popular in Italy and France. It will come into vogue in England in the sixteenth century.   **DRAMA**

1400s   Early this century, English mystic Margery Kempe writes the autobiographical work *The Book of Margery Kempe.*   **LIT**

1400s   The Early Renaissance period takes shape in Florence, with painters, sculptors, architects, and writers taking inspiration from Classical models to express a humanistic spirit. Prominent Florentine patrons of the arts include most notably the Medici, the ruling family of Florence and Tuscany for most of this period. Their most famous son is Lorenzo the Magnificent (1449–1492), himself a humanist poet. The century becomes known as the quattrocento (Italian "four hundred").   **MISC**

1400s   The simple three-part harmony known as *faux bourdon* (false bars) is used in English and continental music composition.   **MUSIC**

1400s   Early this century, Florentine architect Filippo Brunelleschi invents scientific perspective, a systematic, mathematically based method of representing depth on a flat surface. Put into practice by Masaccio, the technique will be essential to Western painting until the late nineteenth century. *See* 1425–1428, PAINT.   **PAINT**

1400s   Early Renaissance painters in Italy use fresco and tempera as their major media. Fresco, in which pigment is applied to a fresh lime-plaster ground, dates from Classical antiquity. Tempera, in which pigment is mixed with a gum or glue, especially egg, has been used in Europe since the early thirteenth century. Both media are water-based. *See also* 1500s, PAINT.   **PAINT**

1400s   The palette, a flat board with a hole for the thumb, used for arranging paints, first appears in Europe. Until now, individual containers have been used for mixing paints.   **PAINT**

1400s   Early this century, humanists and artists in Italy begin to collect ancient sculpture, especially small bronzes. Contemporary artists will produce portrait busts and bronzes of their own patterned after antique models.   **SCULP**

1400s   The Death of the Virgin becomes a popular subject in fifteenth-century art. Sculptural compositions will be based on the iconography of many Netherlandish (Flemish) paintings.   **SCULP**

c. 1400– 1425   The first extant European woodcuts are religious images, probably distributed at pilgrimage sites. Woodcut playing-cards appear by 1450.   **GRAPH**

c. 1400   Female English mystic Julian of Norwich writes the prose work *A Revelation of Divine Love.*   **LIT**

1402   Florentine sculptor Lorenzo Ghiberti wins a competition to decorate
                the doors for the Baptistery in Florence. He will complete a total of
                twenty-eight bronze panels for the doors in 1424.   **SCULP**

c. 1410   The anonymous Franco-Flemish manuscript illuminator known as
                the Boucicaut Master completes a Book of Hours that is a prime ex-
                ample of the international Gothic style.   **GRAPH**

1411–1413   Florentine sculptor Donatello, the greatest European sculptor of his
                century, executes the *St. Mark*, the first in a series of standing fig-
                ures in niches for Orsanmichele and Florence cathedral. The series
                will include the *St. George* (c. 1415–1417) and end with the *Zuccone*
                (probably 1436). Donatello's fresh conception of the human figure,
                drawing on classical models, helps to create Renaissance style. **SCULP**

1414   Florentine sculptor Nanni di Banco completes four marble statues
                of saints, the *Quattro Coronati*, for one of the niches on the exterior
                of Orsanmichele in Florence.   **SCULP**

1416   Flemish manuscript illuminators the Limburg (Limbourg) brothers,
                Herman, Jean (Jannequin), and Paul (Pol), die, probably from
                plague. Their most famous work, characteristic of international
                Gothic style, is the Book of hours *Très Riches Heures du Duc de
                Berry*.   **GRAPH**

1417   Florentine sculptor Donatello creates the bronze plaque of *St.
                George Slaying the Dragon*, illustrating a scene in depth with the illu-
                sion of perspective for the first time in carved relief.   **SCULP**

1420s   In northern Europe, especially Flanders, artists such as Robert
                Campin (the Master of Flémalle) and Jan and Hubert van Eyck begin
                to experiment with oil as a medium for panel painting. Campin
                paints the *Mérode Altarpiece*, with the Annunciation as his subject (c.
                1425–1430); the van Eycks paint the *Ghent Altarpiece* (c. 1425–1432),
                which uses atmospheric perspective. Its Adam and Eve are the first
                large-scale nudes in northern European panel painting.   **PAINT**

1420–1436   Florentine architect Brunelleschi gains fame as an architect for the
                enormous, double-shell dome he constructs for the Florence cathe-
                dral. He originates Renaissance architectural style through his cre-
                ative elaboration on Roman models.   **ARCH**

1421   Florentine architect Brunelleschi begins the San Lorenzo church,
                one of his several churches epitomizing the Early Renaissance ar-
                chitectural values of serene harmony and rational order.   **ARCH**

c. 1425   *The Castle of Perseverance* is a prime example of English medieval
                morality plays. It is the earliest in the collection known as the
                Macro Plays, which also include *Mankind* (c. 1473) and *Wisdom,
                Who Is Christ* (c. 1460). Morality plays depict human dilemmas
                through the use of allegorical figures such as Covetousness, Flesh,
                World, and Good Deeds. *See also* c. 1495, DRAMA.   **DRAMA**

1425–1428   Florentine painter Tommaso di Giovanni di Simone Guidi, known as Masaccio, paints the polyptych for the Carmelite church in Pisa. In Florence, he paints the fresco of St. Peter in the Brancacci Chapel, Santa Maria del Carmine, and the fresco *Trinity* in Santa Maria Novello. In his short life (1401–1428), he becomes highly influential by employing scientific perspective, using a single consistent light source, and applying to painting characteristics of Donatello's sculpture, particularly the clothed nude and contrapposto. Masaccio is also noted for drawing inspiration from Giotto in depicting grand, weighty figures.   **PAINT**

1425   Florentine sculptor Donatello makes a gilt bronze panel on the Feast of Herod for the baptismal font of San Giovanni in Siena, using Brunelleschi's system of linear perspective.   **SCULP**

1430   Florentine architect Brunelleschi begins the Pazzi Chapel.   **ARCH**

1430   The Burgundian school of music (centered in the duchy of Burgundy, including what will become the Netherlands, Belgium, and eastern France), is the center of European music. Its composers include Guillaume Dufay and Gilles Binchois.   **MUSIC**

c. 1430   Sienese sculptor Jacopo della Quercia rediscovers the ancient beauty of the nude in his marble relief *The Creation of Adam*. His nude figures will later influence Michelangelo's compositions.   **SCULP**

1430   Florentine sculptor Donatello completes his bronze statue *David*, the first life-size nude statue since antiquity to be completely free-standing.   **SCULP**

1433–1434   Flemish painter Jan van Eyck paints *Man in a Red Turban* (1433) and *Giovanni Arnolfini and His Bride* (1434).   **PAINT**

c. 1435   Florentine painter Tommaso di Cristoforo Fini, known as Masolino, paints the fresco *Baptism of Christ*.   **PAINT**

c. 1435   Flemish painter Rogier van der Weyden paints *Descent from the Cross*.   **PAINT**

c. 1435   Italian sculptor Luca Della Robbia carves his Cantoria, a variety of marble reliefs for the Florence cathedral. He will later concentrate on sculpture in terra-cotta and run a workshop to produce small Madonna panels and altarpieces for village churches.   **SCULP**

1436   Italian artist, architect, and art theorist Leon Battista Alberti writes on painting in *Della pittura*, which contains the first explanation of scientific perspective (credited to Brunelleschi). The most important art theorist of the Renaissance, Alberti will also write on architecture and sculpture.   **PAINT**

1437   Counterpoint in musical composition is developed by English composer John Dunstable.   **MUSIC**

1437	Florentine painter Fra Filippo Lippi begins painting the *Barbadori Altarpiece,* one of the first examples of the *sacra conversazione,* a depiction of the Virgin and Child with saints in a single scene. Fra Angelico, Domenico Veneziano, and others will also paint in this genre. **PAINT**
1440s	Florentine painter Fra Filippo Lippi helps to popularize tondi, paintings circular in shape. **PAINT**
1440s	Italian painter Domenico Veneziano paints the altarpiece for Santa Lucia dei Magnoli and the now-lost fresco cycle *Scenes from the Life of the Virgin.* **PAINT**
1440s	During the reign of Aztec king Montezuma I in Tenochtitlán, Mexico, a new style of sculpture emerges. Sculptors translate Aztec myths pictorially in relief. **SCULP**
1443–1453	Florentine sculptor Donatello works in Padua, where he produces the bronze monument of Gattamelata, the first life-size equestrian statue since antiquity. He also executes the sculptural decoration for the High Altar of the church of San Antonio. **SCULP**
1445–1460	The *Lochamer Liederbuch,* one of the earliest collections of German polyphonic songs, is compiled. It contains both monophonic melodies and three-part settings with tenor melody. **MUSIC**
1446–1451	Italian painter and writer Leon Battista Alberti builds the Palazzo Rucellai, which makes use of superimposed orders (classical orders placed one on top of another on the surface of a multistoried wall, as in the Roman Colosseum). He is also known for his churches, including San Andrea and San Sebastiano in Mantua. **ARCH**
1450s	Florentine sculptors revive the ancient Roman tradition of realistic portrait sculpture. **SCULP**
1450	In Europe block books are introduced, in which a woodcut block combining text and illustrations is used to print an entire page. By 1480, the time-consuming process will be made obsolete by Gutenberg's invention of movable metal type. *See* 1454, GRAPH. **GRAPH**
1450	The Chinese print pages using movable wooden type. **GRAPH**
c. 1450–1600	The Flemish school of composers (living in what is now Holland, Belgium, and northern France), gains dominance in western music. Its members include Jean d'Okeghem, Josquin Desprez, Jacob Obrecht, Adriaan Willaert, and Orlando di Lasso. **MUSIC**
c. 1450	Florentine sculptor and architect Bernardo Rossellino erects his marble tomb of Leonardo Bruno in the church of Santa Croce in Florence. His composition of a figure lying over a sarcophagus flanked by ornamented pilasters will become the prototype of the Renaissance monument. **SCULP**

The *Annunciation* by Rogier van der Weyden, Flemish, tempera and oil on wood.
(The Metropolitan Museum of Art, Gift of J. Pierpont Morgan, 1917)

c. 1452–1465   Italian painter Piero della Francesca paints the *Legend of the True Cross* frescoes in San Francesco in Arezzo. His style combines weighty grandeur in the tradition of Masaccio with an even more pronounced attention to geometric structure.   **PAINT**

1452–1466   Florentine painter Fra Filippo Lippi paints the fresco cycle on Saint Stephen and Saint John the Baptist in Prato cathedral. Lippi is remembered not only for his linear, decorative style but for the 1855 Robert Browning poem about him, "Fra Lippo Lippi."   **PAINT**

1454   Using movable metal type in a printing press of his own invention, Johannes Gutenberg of Germany prints his first 300 copies of the Bible in Latin. Now called the Gutenberg Bible, it is the first book in Europe to be printed with movable type.   **GRAPH**

· ·

"What a sweet mistress is this perspective!"—Florentine painter Paolo Uccello, famous for his fascination with perspective, when told by his wife to stop painting and come to bed, c. 1440s

· ·

c. 1455   Florentine painter Paolo Uccello demonstrates his passion for scientific perspective in the panel series *Battle of San Romano*.   **PAINT**

c. 1455   Italian painter Andrea Mantegna paints *Agony in the Garden* and the fresco *St. James Led to His Execution*. Working in Padua, Mantegna helps to bring Masaccio's use of perspective and clothed nudes from Florence to northern Italy.   **PAINT**

c. 1455   Flemish painter Rogier van der Weyden paints *Francesco d'Este*.   **PAINT**

c. 1460s   Italian painter Piero della Francesca paints the *Flagellation*.   **PAINT**

c. 1460s   Florentine painter Paolo Uccello paints *The Hunt in the Forest*.   **PAINT**

1460s   The Bellini family of painters, Jacopo Bellini and his sons Gentile and Giovanni, is active in Venice. Jacopo is best known for his experiments in perspective and composition, as recorded in the hundreds of drawings in his sketchbooks.   **PAINT**

c. 1460   Venetian painter Giovanni Bellini paints *Agony in the Garden*.   **PAINT**

c. 1466   Italian painter Andrea Mantegna paints *Dead Christ*, notable for its extreme foreshortening, the shortening of lines to produce the illusion of depth.   **PAINT**

1470s   Large wooden altar shrines carved in intricate detail characteristic of the Late Gothic, become popular in Germanic countries.   **SCULP**

Rhinoceros, woodcut by A. Dürer. German. *(The Metropolitan Museum of Art, Gift of Junius S. Morgan, 1919)*

c. 1470   Florentine painter and sculptor Andrea del Verrocchio reintroduces the putto, a chubby, often winged, nude child popular in classical art, to Early Renaissance sculpture as the center of his design for a bronze fountain for one of the Medici villas near Florence.   **SCULP**

1472   Italian painter and scientist Leonardo da Vinci is enrolled as a painter in the fraternity of St. Luke, Florence. He probably paints one of the angels in his master Verrocchio's *Baptism of Christ*. Other paintings from Leonardo's Florentine period (until c. 1481) include the *Annunciation* and the unfinished altarpiece *The Adoration of the Magi*.   **PAINT**

1473–1519   St. George's Chapel in Windsor is constructed.   **ARCH**

1474   After 425 years of construction, Winchester cathedral in England is completed.   **ARCH**

1474   The first book printed in English is *The Recuyell of the Historyes of Troye*, a prose romance by Raoul Lefèvre, translated from the French and printed by English printer William Caxton in Bruges, Belgium. Caxton will return to England to set up England's first printing press (1476–1477) and embark on an extensive publishing program.   **LIT**

1474   Italian painter Andrea Mantegna completes the fresco decoration of the Camera degli Sposi (Bridal Chamber) in the palace of the Gonzaga family in Mantua. The work resurrects classical Roman illusionistic painting of architecture, which appears to extend the space of the room, a motif soon adopted by other artists.   **PAINT**

c. 1475   Florentine painter, goldsmith, and sculptor Antonio del Pollaiuolo looks to action scenes on ancient painted vases to create a bronze, free-standing statue of Hercules and Antaeus posed in a violent struggle.   **SCULP**

c. 1476   Flemish painter Hugo van der Goes paints the *Portinari Altarpiece.*   **PAINT**

c. 1478   Italian painter Alessandro di Mariano Filipepi, known as Sandro Botticelli, paints the poetic allegory *Primavera*, which shows the influence of Fra Filippo Lippi in its linear, graceful style.   **PAINT**

c. 1480s   Leonardo da Vinci paints *The Lady with an Ermine.*   **PAINT**

c. 1480– 1495   Italian painter Andrea Mantegna paints the series *Triumph of Caesar.*   **PAINT**

c. 1480   Italian painter Sandro Botticelli paints the mythological work *The Birth of Venus*, reflecting Neoplatonic views of pagan myth as allegories of divine truth.   **PAINT**

c. 1480   Florentine painter Filippino Lippi, son of Fra Filippo Lippi, paints *The Vision of St. Bernard.*   **PAINT**

c. 1481   Italian architect Donato Bramante begins his first building, Santa Maria presso San Satiro in Milan.   **ARCH**

c. 1481   Leonardo da Vinci leaves Florence for Milan, where he stays until 1499. Among his works from this period are many drawings, including artistic sketches, scientific observations of nature, and technical plans for proposed machines.   **GRAPH**

1481–1482   Italian painters decorating the Sistine Chapel in the Vatican in Rome include Sandro Botticelli, Pietro Perugino, Domenico Ghirlandaio, and Cosimo Rosselli. *See also* 1508–1512, ARCH.   **PAINT**

1482   Portuguese explorers and missionaries come in contact with the Kongo tribes living along the lower Congo River. African sculptors will create brass crucifixes derived from early Portuguese prototypes to be used as power tokens by village chiefs.   **SCULP**

1484   Belgian music theorist and composer Johannes Tinctoris writes the treatise *De inventione et usu musicae.*   **MUSIC**

1484   Florentine painter Filippino Lippi completes Masaccio's fresco cycle in the Brancacci Chapel, Santa Maria del Carmine. *See* 1425–28, PAINT.   **PAINT**

1485   English prose writer Sir Thomas Malory's *Le Morte d'Arthur* is published posthumously. This collection of Arthurian romances will be
the principal vehicle through which the legends of King Arthur and
his knights will be perpetuated to future generations of readers.   **LIT**

c. 1485   Leonardo da Vinci paints the *Madonna of the Rocks*, which employs
a subtle form of chiaroscuro (strongly contrasting light and dark)
known as *sfumato* (Italian, "up in smoke"). Leonardo is considered
a pioneer of chiaroscuro, which will reach its height in the paintings
of Rembrandt in the seventeenth century. The painting exists in
two versions.   **PAINT**

1485   Venetian painter Giovanni Bellini paints the large oil *San Giobbe
Altarpiece*, depicting the Madonna and saints. The teacher of
Giorgione and Titian, Giovanni Bellini is the leader of Renaissance
painting in Venice.   **PAINT**

1486   Isabel of Castile commissions Spanish sculptor Gil de Siloé to create
an elaborate alabaster tomb for her parents, Juan II of Castile and
Isabella of Portugal. Gil de Siloé will employ other artists to help
carve many of the figures and complete the tomb in 1493.   **SCULP**

1487   Italian poet Matteo Maria Boiardo publishes the first two books of
his unfinished romantic epic *Orlando Innamorato* (*Roland in Love*),
which draws on the Carolingian legends shared by *The Song of
Roland* (1100s). *See also* 1532, LIT.   **LIT**

1488–1493   Florentine painter Filippino Lippi paints a fresco cycle on St.
Thomas Aquinas in the Carafa Chapel, Santa Maria sopra Minerva,
Rome.   **PAINT**

1489–1507   The Palazzo Strozzi in Florence is built.   **ARCH**

1490   Dance performances, the origins of ballet, are introduced at French,
Burgundian, and Italian courts for weddings, receptions for foreign
sovereigns, and other festive occasions. The loose sequences of
dances, based on steps of the conventional courtly repertory, are
performed in sumptuous costume and reflect the theme of the
occasion.   **DANCE**

c. 1490   Dutch painter Geertgen tot Sint Jans paints *Nativity*, notable for its strik-
ing use of light and shadow on the round heads of its figures.   **PAINT**

c. 1491–   Florentine sculptor, painter, and architect Michelangelo
1492   (Michelangelo Buonarroti) executes the marble relief of *The Battle of
the Lapiths and Centaurs*, while under the patronage of Lorenzo de'
Medici, who dies in 1492.   **SCULP**

1493   Holy Roman emperor Maximilian I makes Heinrich Isaac court
composer and Paul von Hofhaimer court organist.   **MUSIC**

c. 1495   The English morality play *Everyman* is first performed. The allegorical drama tells the story of Everyman's anxious search for companions to stand by him as he faces Death. In the end, only Good Deeds will accompany him.   **DRAMA**

1495   Leading French composer Josquin Desprez is appointed organist and choirmaster at Cambrai cathedral in France.   **MUSIC**

c. 1495   Italian artist Leonardo da Vinci paints the mural *Last Supper*, which soon begins to deteriorate due to the experimental medium the painter employed (a mixture of tempera and oil paint).   **PAINT**

c. 1495   Italian sculptor Tullio Lombardo carves a marble statue of Adam for the funerary monument of Doge Andrea Vendramin in the church of Santi Giovanni e Paolo. It will be the first large-scale classical nude since antiquity.   **SCULP**

1496   Venetian painter Gentile Bellini paints the large canvas *Procession of the Relic of the True Cross*.   **PAINT**

1496–1497   Italian sculptor, painter, and architect Michelangelo sculpts the *Bacchus*.   **SCULP**

1498   German painter and engraver Albrecht Dürer, the leading artist of the Renaissance in modern Europe, publishes the woodcut series *Apocalypse*, which raises the art of woodcut to a new height. He will also be famed for his engravings, drawings, watercolors, and oil paintings.   **GRAPH**

c. 1498–1499   While in his twenties in Rome, Italian sculptor, painter, and architect Michelangelo sculpts the *Pietà*, the greatest work of his early period.   **SCULP**

1499   Italian printer Aldo Mannucci (Aldus Manutius) publishes the illustrated book *Hypnerotomachia Poliphili*, which includes some of the most esteemed woodcuts from the period.   **GRAPH**

1499   English poet John Skelton publishes *The Bowge of Court*, a satirical dream-allegory on contemporary court life.   **LIT**

1500s   Benin artists in Nigeria produce art for the divine king and his court. Ivory pendant masks combining Benin symbolism with Portuguese figures are created to be worn by the king on his hip during funerary ceremonies.   **DECO**

1500s   Late this century, in England, theaters such as the Globe Theatre flourish. Most are open air and probably decorated, though there is no real scenery. The actors use props and, most likely, wear contemporary costumes whether or not it is appropriate to the play's setting. *See also* 1599, DRAMA.   **DRAMA**

Le Vierge, L'Enfant et St. Anne (*The Virgin, Child and St. Anne*), painting by Leonardo da Vinci. (*Louvre/Reunion des Museés Nationaux*)

1500s   Line engraving begins to supersede the woodcut as the preferred mode for printing illustrations. However, woodcuts will survive into the eighteenth century for popular items such as broadsheets and printers' decorations.   **GRAPH**

1500s   Emblem books, printed collections of symbolic images, become popular in Europe from now into the seventeeth century.   **GRAPH**

1500s   Chinese novelist Wu Ch'eng-en writes the comic fantasy novel *Hsi-yü chi* (*Monkey*), describing the magical adventures of a Buddhist priest in search of sacred scriptures in India.   **LIT**

1500s   Aztec conquests assure a supply of skilled artists and craftsmen to be brought to the capital to work and train Aztec apprentices. Aztec carvers will begin to create realistic sculpture in the round.   **MISC**

1500s   Late this century, art academies begin to appear in Italy as private associations of artists. These academies will become formal institutions that will take over the functions of the guilds.   **MISC**

1500s   Italian architects Giulio Romano and Michelangelo adapt the prevailing classical architectural style into the freer, more individualistic style known as mannerism.   **MISC**

c. 1500s   German religious reformer Martin Luther, founder of Protestantism, brings change and new life to ecclesiastical music. He encourages simple melodies and a return to the early Christian custom of communal singing. The chorale, or Lutheran hymn, develops and modern scales as we know them come into use.   **MUSIC**

1500s   Madrigals in new forms become popular in small Italian courts, composed for weddings and other ceremonies. Instrumental preludes and interludes (ritornellos, also found in motets), mark the beginnings of chamber music.   **MUSIC**

1500s   In Italy oil paint becomes the dominant medium for painting. Preferred in northern Europe since the fifteenth century, it will become the most important medium for Western painters to the present day. *See also* 1400s, PAINT.   **PAINT**

1500s   The Lamar culture of the Mississippian southeast reduce the diversity of sculptural imagery and concentrate on rendering rattlesnakes, panthers, thunderbirds, and death mask motifs.   **SCULP**

1500s   Late this century, the Counter-Reformation in Italy sees an increase in the literal sculptural depictions of the martyrdoms of saints. **SCULP**

1500   Antwerp cathedral, begun nearly 150 years earlier in 1352, is completed.   **ARCH**

1500   After his sojourn in Italy, French composer Josquin Desprez resides at the French court of Louis XII.   **MUSIC**

1500   Mastersingers' songs are reformed by Hans Folz of Nuremberg, and
              worldly subjects are now admitted.   **MUSIC**

c. 1500–   This period in Italy will become known as the High Renaissance, a
1520   time of great achievement in painting and sculpture, dominated by
              such artists as Leonardo da Vinci, Michelangelo, and Raphael. **PAINT**

1500   Italian painter Sandro Botticelli paints *Mystic Nativity*. Like many of
              his later paintings, it is more grave and intense than his earlier
              works.   **PAINT**

1500   Venetian painter Gentile Bellini paints the large canvas *Miracle at
              Ponte di Lorenzo*.   **PAINT**

1501   Italian printer Aldo Mannucci (Aldus Manutius) designs the typeface
              now called italic. Previous European volumes have used roman and
              gothic letters. Aldus also designs a Greek type.   **GRAPH**

1501   Ottaviano dei Petrucci of Venice uses movable type to print music,
              including *Harmonice Musices Odhecaton A*, a collection of ninety-six
              Franco-Flemish polyphonic chansons (popular songs).   **MUSIC**

c. 1501   Venetian painter Giovanni Bellini paints his best known portrait,
              Doge Leonardo Loredan.   **PAINT**

1501–1504   In Florence Michelangelo completes the monumental thirteen-foot
              nude marble sculpture *David*. Influenced by Hellenistic sculpture, it
              is notable for its sense of action in repose and of youthful defiance
              and restlessness.   **SCULP**

1502–1509   Italian architect Donato Bramante builds the classically inspired
              Tempietto in the cloister of the church of San Pietro in Montorio in
              Rome.   **ARCH**

1502–1516   French composer Josquin Desprez composes his three books of
              Masses.   **MUSIC**

1502–1507   Dutch painter Gerard David completes the triptych *St. John the
              Baptist*.   **PAINT**

1503   England's Canterbury cathedral, begun in 1070, is completed. **ARCH**

· ·

*"The Medici created and destroyed me."—Italian painter
and scientist Leonardo da Vinci, on the famous family of
patrons of the arts, c. 1508–1518*

· ·

1503   Italian painter and scientist Leonardo da Vinci paints the *Mona Lisa*,
              perhaps the world's most famous painting. The half-length portrait is
              noted for its enigmatic smile and deep, atmospheric tonalities. **PAINT**

1503   German painter Matthias Grünewald (Matthias Gothardt) paints *The
              Mockery of Christ*.   **PAINT**

1504	German painter and engraver Albrecht Dürer engraves the *Fall of Man*.　　**GRAPH**

1504　　　German painter and engraver Lucas Cranach the Elder paints *Rest on the Flight into Egypt*, an example of the attention to landscape characteristic of the Danube School, which also comprises Albrecht Altdorfer and Wolf Huber.　　**PAINT**

1504　　　Italian painter Giorgione completes his *Madonna* in Castelfranco cathedral.　　**PAINT**

1504　　　Italian painter Raphael paints *Marriage of the Virgin*, a stronger and more graceful work than that done by his master Perugino on the same subject. Aged twenty-one this year, Raphael is soon recognized as one of the greatest painters of his day.　　**PAINT**

1505–1506　Italian painter Raphael paints *Madonna with the Goldfinch*. The artist will become known for his many images of the Madonna.　　**PAINT**

PASSÉ SCULPTURE

*A*t any given time, the great classics of art seem eternal in their greatness. But in fact, all works of art are subject to decay—not only in their material composition, but even more fatally in critical estimation. Here are a few works of antiquity that were once considered essential to the canon of great sculpture but have since faded in importance:

Apollo Belvedere—*Roman marble copy of a Greek bronze of the god Apollo, discovered in the fifteenth century. Celebrated by neoclassical artists and critics as a pinnacle of ancient art, it dropped in reputation in the nineteenth century. In the twentieth century, art historian Kenneth Clark described it this way: "in no other famous work of art are idea and execution more distressingly divorced."*

Laocoön Group—*Hellenistic or Roman marble group executed probably in the first century and discovered in the sixteenth century. Praised by Michelangelo and having profoundly influenced baroque and neoclassical sculpture, it too fell in estimation in the nineteenth century. Twentieth-century art historian H. W. Janson commented that "its dynamism has become uncomfortably self-conscious."*

Medici Venus—*Roman copy of a Greek statue of Venus, discovered in the seventeenth century. Considered an enduring model of feminine beauty until the nineteenth century, it was described by twentieth-century art historian Martin Robertson as "among the most charmless remnants of antiquity."*

1505   Venetian painter Giovanni Bellini paints the San Zaccaria altarpiece,
              a remarkable example of *sacra conversazione*.   **PAINT**

1505–1506   German painter and engraver Albrecht Dürer paints a series of
              landscape watercolors.   **PAINT**

1505   Italian painter Giorgione paints the mysterious landscape with fig-
              ures *The Tempest*.   **PAINT**

1506   The reconstruction of St. Peter's Church, Rome, begins under the
              direction of Italian architect Donato Bramante, commissioned by
              Pope Julius II. Replacing the basilica erected eleven centuries earli-
              er, the new church will take over 150 years to complete. Other ar-
              chitects working on the project will include Raphael, Antonio da
              Sangallo the Younger, Michelangelo, Giacomo della Porta, Carlo
              Maderna, and Giovanni Bellini. *See also 333*, ARCH.   **ARCH**

1506   German painter and engraver Lucas Cranach the Elder executes the
              altarpiece *St. Catherine*.   **PAINT**

1506   The first century sculpture *Laocoön* is rediscovered in a vineyard in
              Rome. Its classical grandeur and expression of emotions will influ-
              ence artists in the Renaissance, baroque, and neoclassical periods.
              Among those influenced by the work is Michelangelo, who visits it
              at once.   **SCULP**

1506   German sculptor Tilman Riemenschneider completes the altar at St.
              Jakob's in Rothenburg.   **SCULP**

1507   Venetian painters Giorgione and Titian (Tiziano Vecellio) paint fres-
              coes for the exterior of the Fondaco dei Tedeschi.   **PAINT**

1508–1511   Italian architect Baldassare Peruzzi builds the Villa Farnesina in
              Rome.   **ARCH**

1508–1512   Italian sculptor, painter, and architect Michelangelo completes the
              painting of the Sistine Chapel in the Vatican. The ceiling features
              scenes of the Creation, Adam and Eve, and Noah, and images of
              prophets and sibyls foretelling Christ's birth.   **ARCH**

1508   The first chiaroscuro woodcut, a woodcut with tonal effects pro-
              duced by printing on one sheet from several blocks of different
              tone, is *The Emperor Maximilian on Horseback* by German painter
              and wood engraver Hans Burgkmair the Elder.   **GRAPH**

1508–1512   Venetian painter Lorenzo Lotto, known for his idiosyncratic style,
              works in Rome, painting works of *sacra conversazione*.   **PAINT**

1508   At age twenty-five, Raphael is summoned to Rome by Pope Julius II,
              where he will work until his death in 1520. In 1508–1511, he exe-
              cutes *The School of Athens* and the *Disputà*, frescoes in the Stanza
              della Segnatura, a papal room in the Vatican.   **PAINT**

1509   Dutch humanists and scholar Desiderius Erasmus composes the humanist satire *The Praise of Folly*.   **LIT**

1509   Florentine painter Andrea d'Agnolo, known as Andrea del Sarto, paints *Miracles of St. Philip*.   **PAINT**

1510   German painter and engraver Albrecht Dürer completes the print series *Great Passion* and *Life of the Virgin*.   **GRAPH**

c. 1510–
1515   Dutch painter Hieronymus Bosch paints the triptych *The Garden of Earthly Delights*, so called for its sensuous center panel. The left panel represents Eden, the right Hell. Bosch will be known for his fantastic, grotesque, richly symbolic style, as seen in paintings such as *The Temptation of St. Anthony* and *Ship of Fools*.   **PAINT**

1510   Venetian painter Sebastiano Luciani, known as Sebastiano del Piombo, paints *Salome*.   **PAINT**

c. 1512   Raphael designs the Chigi Chapel in Santa Maria del Popolo. His combination of architecture with sculpture, painting, mosaic, stucco work, and other forms of interior decoration exert a powerful influence in the baroque period.   **DECO**

1512–1517   German painter and engraver Hans Baldung Grien executes the altarpiece for Freiburg cathedral, including the center panel *Coronation of the Virgin*.   **PAINT**

1512   Florentine painter Andrea del Sarto paints *The Annunciation*.   **PAINT**

1512–1514   Raphael, renowned as a portrait artist, paints the portrait of Pope Julius II. During this period he also paints *The Sistine Madonna*, his most famous version of the Madonna and Child, and the fresco *Galatea*.   **PAINT**

1513–1520   Italian political philosopher Niccolò Machiavelli writes *La mandragola (The Mandrake)*, perhaps the best comedy of the Italian Renaissance.   **DRAMA**

1513–1514   German painter and engraver Albrecht Dürer engraves his master prints: *Knight, Death and the Devil*; *St. Jerome in His Study*; and *Melencolia I*.   **GRAPH**

1513   English poet John Skelton publishes *A Ballad of the Scottish King*.   **LIT**

c. 1513   Michelangelo sculpts two figures of *Slaves* for the tomb of Pope Julius II, though they are not included in the final monument when it is erected in 1545. The *Slaves* are now in the Louvre, Paris.   **SCULP**

1513   Renaissance patron of the arts Pope Julius II dies. His successor, Pope Leo X, begins the Vatican sculpture gallery.   **SCULP**

1513   German sculptor Tilman Riemenschneider completes the tomb of Emperor Henry II at Bamberg cathedral.   **SCULP**

MILITARY ETCHINGS

*T*he art of etching, used for making prints and book illustrations since the sixteenth century, began not as a printmaking technique but as a way of decorating armor. The first such example, dating from the late fifteenth century, is an Italian breastplate decorated using the basic principle of etching: biting a design into metal with acid.

The technique of etching requires the artist to cover the metal with a substance, such as beeswax, bitumen, or resin, that will resist the action of acid. The artist uses a steel needle to draw the design by cutting through the covering substance, or ground, and exposing the metal underneath. The metal is then immersed in a bath of dilute acid, such as nitric, which bites into the metal wherever it has been exposed. The image can be "stopped out," or shaded, by applying acid-resisting varnish to selected parts of the design before immersing, then reimmersing the plate as often as needed so that some parts of the design are bitten deeper than others.

As applied to armor, the result was a handsome chest engraving to impress foes in battle and courtiers at home. But by the early sixteenth century, graphic artists, such as the Germans Albrecht Dürer and Albrecht Altdorfer and the Swiss Urs Graf, were already applying the military technology to peaceful uses. By applying ink to the etched plate, any number of paper images could be produced, and a new graphic art technique was created.

1514	German painter and engraver Lucas Cranach the Elder, well known as a portraitist, paints the full-length portraits of the Duke and Duchess of Saxony. **PAINT**
1514	Italian painter Antonio Allegri, known as Correggio, paints his *St. Francis* altarpiece. **PAINT**
1514	Venetian painter Giovanni Bellini paints the mythological *Feast of the Gods*, which, after his death in 1516, will be altered by his pupil Titian. **PAINT**
1515	Raphael is named architect in chief of St. Peter's Church in Rome. **ARCH**
1515	German painter and engraver Albrecht Dürer uses the new technique of etching to produce the *Agony in the Garden*. **GRAPH**
c. 1515–1516	Michelangelo sculpts his *Moses* for the tomb of Pope Julius II. Of the forty large figures the artist at first envisioned for the tomb, it is the only sculpture of his that reaches the tomb. *See also* c. 1513, SCULP. **SCULP**

1515   German painter Matthias Grünewald paints the *Isenheim Altarpiece*, noted for its emotional intensity, brilliant color, and gruesome depiction of Christ's crucifixion.   **SCULP**

1516   English statesman and author Thomas More publishes *Utopia*, a Latin narrative about a visit to the fictitious ideal land of the title, which is taken from the Greek words for "no place" and "good place." The book will generate a tradition of utopian narratives in such works as Jonathan Swift's *Gulliver's Travels* (1726) and Samuel Butler's *Erewhon* (1872).   **LIT**

c. 1516   Italian painter Tiziano Vecellio, known as Titian, paints the allegory *Sacred and Profane Love* and his first great altarpiece *The Assumption*.   **PAINT**

1516   King Francis I invites Leonardo da Vinci to France.   **PAINT**

MOSES *ON THE COUCH*

*M*ichelangelo's statue of Moses *(c. 1515)*, admired as one of the world's great sculptures, represented only failure to the artist himself. He had planned to complete forty large figures for the tomb of Pope Julius II, which he was commissioned to construct in 1505; forty years later, when the much-scaled-down monument was finally unveiled, he had contributed only one finished sculpture, Moses. Despite this, the statue has had many admirers through the centuries, not least of them the Viennese founder of psychiatry, Sigmund Freud.

On his periodic visits to Rome, beginning in 1901, Freud made a point each time of scrutinizing Moses in the church of San Pietro in Vincoli. "In 1913," he wrote, "through three lonely September weeks, I stood daily in the church in front of the statue, studied it, measured it, drew it, until that understanding came to me that I only dared to express anonymously in the paper." The paper to which he referred, "The Moses of Michelangelo," published in 1914, laid out his theory that the statue represented a supreme moment of self-control, in which the subject held himself back from anger against the Israelites who had sinned in worshipping the golden calf. This he connected to Michelangelo's own desire to control his temper, to raise "himself with this self-criticism above his own nature." Indirectly, Freud alluded to his own struggle to control his anger against foes and estranged followers of his theory of psychoanalysis.

1516   Flemish painter Quentin Massys paints his portraits of Erasmus and Petrus Egidius as a gift for English humanist Sir Thomas More. The portraits establish the type of the scholar in his study.   **PAINT**

1517   Italian political philosopher Niccolò Machiavelli composes *Il principe* (*The Prince*), which will become an infuential work of political philosophy. Among his other works are *Discoursi* (*Discourses*, 1513–17).   **LIT**

1517   After Heinrich Isaac's death, Swiss composer Ludwig Senfl becomes court composer to Emperor Maximilian I.   **MUSIC**

1517   Florentine painter Andrea del Sarto paints the altarpiece *Madonna of the Harpies*.   **PAINT**

1517   Raphael paints the large composition the *Transfiguration*, which will stand above his bier at his funeral when he dies at age thirty-seven in 1520.   **PAINT**

1518   German painter Albrecht Altdorfer paints the altarpiece for St. Florian near Linz.   **PAINT**

1518   Raphael paints the portrait of Pope Leo X with cardinals.   **PAINT**

1518–1523   Italian painter Titian paints three mythological works for Alfonso d'Este: *Bacchus and Ariadne*, the *Worship of Venus*, and the *Bacchanal*.   **PAINT**

1518–1520   Italian painter Correggio undertakes his first large-scale commissions, the decoration of the abbess's room in the convent of San Paolo (c. 1518) and the dome for the church of San Giovanni Evangelista (1520).   **PAINT**

1519–1526   Italian painter Titian paints the Pesaro altarpiece (*Madonna of the Pesaro Family*), remarkable for its innovative diagonal composition.   **PAINT**

1520–1521   German painter and engraver Albrecht Dürer travels in the Netherlands, keeping a diary with drawings that is the first of its kind in art history.   **GRAPH**

1520   In Italy the period known as the High Renaissance (begun 1500) comes to an end as the mannerist period (ending 1600) begins. It will be marked by a reaction against the classical tendencies of the High Renaissance and by elaboration and innovation that will long be condemned by critics as artificial and decadent, though some in the twentieth century will come to view it more positively.   **MISC**

1521   Italian painter Jacopo Palma, known as Palma Vecchio or Il Vecchio, paints *Adoration*.   **PAINT**

1522   German painter and engraver Lucas Cranach the Elder creates woodcuts for the first German edition of the New Testament.   **GRAPH**

1522	Beginning this year with the poem *Colyn Cloute*, English poet John Skelton makes attacks on prelate-statesman Cardinal Wolsey that will also include *Speke, Parrot* (1521) and *Why come ye nat to Courte?* (1522–1523). **LIT**
1522–1523	Italian painter Girolamo Francesco Mazzola, known as Parmigianino, paints frescos in the cathedral in Parma. **PAINT**
1524	Michelangelo builds the Laurentian Library to house the Medici family's collection of books and manuscripts. **ARCH**
1524	Italian painter Parmigianino paints *Self-Portrait in a Convex Mirror*. **PAINT**
1525	The printing of English humanist William Tyndale's English translation of the New Testament begins at Cologne. His translation of this and other sections of the Bible will be banned and Tyndale will be executed for heresy in 1536, but his work will form the basis for the King James version in 1611. **LIT**
1525	Albrecht Dürer publishes the *Treatise on Measurement*, a theoretical study on proportion. **PAINT**
1525	Italian painter Palma Vecchio paints *Three Sisters*. **PAINT**
1526	Albrecht Dürer paints the two panels of the *Four Apostles*. **PAINT**
1526–1527	In Rome since leaving his native Parma in 1524, Italian painter Parmigianino paints *The Vision of St. Jerome*. He leaves Rome for Bologna in 1527 after Rome is sacked by German troops. **PAINT**
1526–1530	Italian painter Correggio paints the dome of Parma cathedral, which develops the illusionist motif of portraying a celestial scene as if it were taking place in the sky overhead. **PAINT**
1527	Flemish composer Adriaan Willaert becomes maestro di capella at St. Mark's, inaugurating the Venetian school of progressive, innovative Flemish and Italian composers. **MUSIC**
1527	German painter Hans Holbein the Younger, visiting in England (1526–1528), paints *Thomas More and His Family*, the first group portrait of full-length figures at home. **PAINT**
1528	Italian diplomat and writer Baldasarre Castiglione publishes *Il cortegiano* (*The Courtier*), a work in dialogue form concerning courtly manners and education. The book will be popular and influential across Europe. *See also* 1561, LIT. **LIT**
1528	*Four Books on Human Proportion* is published after the death of its author, German painter and engraver Albrecht Dürer, who dies this year. **PAINT**
1529	Italian sculptor and architect Jacopo Sansovino is appointed state architect of Venice. **ARCH**
1529	Martin Sohr, known as Martin Agricola, publishes *Musica instrumentalis deudsch*, an excellent account of contemporary instruments. **MUSIC**

1532   Italian poet Ludovico Ariosto publishes the final version of his mas-
        terpiece, the comic romantic epic *Orlando Furioso* (*Roland Mad*)
        (published in shorter form in 1516), which continues the story of
        Boiardo's *Orlando Innamorato. See also* 1487, LIT..   **LIT**

1532–1564 French writer François Rabelais composes the multibook satire
        about the search for the Oracle of the Holy Bottle, *Gargantua and
        Pantagruel.*   **LIT**

1533   German painter Hans Holbein the Younger paints the double por-
        trait *The Ambassadors.*   **PAINT**

1534   Regensburg cathedral in Germany, begun nearly three centuries
        earlier in 1275, is completed, while St. Basil's Basilica in Moscow is
        begun (completed 1561).   **ARCH**

1534   Michelangelo completes the tomb of the Medici and moves from
        Florence to Rome, where he works for the papacy for the rest of his
        life.   **ARCH**

1535   In Zurich Miles Coverdale publishes the first complete English trans-
        lation of the Bible.   **LIT**

c. 1535 Italian painter Parmigianino paints *Madonna of the Long Neck*, a re-
        fined, elegant work that is one of the standard examples of man-
        nerism. He also paints the erotic *Cupid Carving His Bow*.   **PAINT**

1536   German composer and master of the polyphonic Heinrich Finck's
        collection of songs, *Schöne Auserlesene Lieder*, is published
        posthumously.   **MUSIC**

1536–1541 Michelangelo paints the *Last Judgment* in the Sistine Chapel.   **PAINT**

1537   Italian sculptor and architect Jacopo Sansovino begins the Library of
        San Marco and the facade of the Doge's palace loggietta in Venice. **ARCH**

1537–1551 Italian architect Sebastiano Serlio publishes the six volumes of the
        influential architectural treatise *Tutte l'opere d'architettura*. Two
        more volumes will be published after his death (1554), one in 1575
        and one not until 1967. Used by craftsmen as a pattern-book, the
        work will spread Renaissance style across Europe.   **ARCH**

1537   The first conservatories of music are founded in Naples and
        Venice.   **MUSIC**

1537   Having settled permanently in England in 1532, German painter Hans
        Holbein the Younger executes the wall painting in Whitehall Palace of
        Henry VIII with his parents and third wife, Jane Seymour.   **PAINT**

1538–1540 During these years, Italian painter Titian paints the *Venus of Urbino*
        (1538), *A Young Englishman* (1540), and *Ecce Homo* (1543).   **PAINT**

1539   Flemish-born French painter Jean Clouet, court painter to King
        Francis I, is praised as the "equal of Michelangelo" by poet Clément
        Marot.   **PAINT**

c. 1540s   German painter and designer Hans Holbein the Younger executes numerous designs for decoration and produces miniature paintings. **DECO**

c. 1540   Spanish sculptor Alonso Berruguete completes his wood reliefs in an "anticlassical" Mannerist style for the choir stalls of Toledo cathedral. **SCULP**

1540   Italian architect Andrea Palladio builds the Villa Godi in Lonedo. **ARCH**

1541   François Clouet, son of Flemish-born painter Jean Clouet, succeeds his father as court painter to French king Francis I. **PAINT**

1542–1550   Michelangelo's last paintings, years before his death in 1564, include the frescoes *Conversion of St. Paul* and *Crucifixion of St. Peter* in the Cappella Paolina in the Vatican. **PAINT**

1543   Florentine goldsmith and sculptor Benvenuto Cellini creates a gold boat-shaped saltcellar for King Francis I of France. **SCULP**

1544   Italian painter and architect Francesco Primaticcio works with Florentine painter Giovanni Battista Rosso (Il Rosso Fiorentino) on the decoration of the royal palace at Fontainebleau, France. Their work will help establish the style of French mannerism associated with the school of Fontainebleau, a sensual, elegant style often combining mural painting with stucco ornament. **DECO**

1544   German painter and engraver Hans Baldung Grien completes *The Bewitched Stable Boy*, which presents erotic themes in allegorical fashion. **GRAPH**

• •

"He that will write well in any tongue, must follow this counsel of Aristotle, to speak as the common people do, to think as the wise men do; and so should every man understand him, and the judgment of wise men allow him."—English writer Roger Ascham, Toxophilus, 1545

• •

1545–1550   Italian architect Andrea Palladio builds the Palazzo Thiene in Vicenza. His symmetrical, classically inspired palaces and villas in or near Vicenza will greatly influence English architecture and decoration, leading to the movement called Palladianism in the eighteenth century. **ARCH**

c. 1545   The performance of commedia dell'arte, a form of improvised comedy which will remain popular in Italy through the early eighteenth century, is first recorded. **DRAMA**

1546   Michelangelo becomes architect of St. Peter's Church. The drum of the dome he designs will be nearly complete at the time of his death (1564); the dome will be completed afterward and a long nave will be added in the seventeenth century. *See also* 1506, ARCH. **ARCH**

1546   King Francis I commissions French architect Pierre Lescot to begin building the new Louvre palace in Paris. The Louvre will not be completed for more than a century.   **ARCH**

1546   German painter and engraver Lucas Cranach the Elder paints the portrait of Martin Luther.   **PAINT**

1546–1548   Portraits by Italian painter Titian during this period include that of Pope Paul III and his nephews (1546) and Charles V on horseback (1548).   **PAINT**

1547   Swiss humanist Heinrich Loris (Henricus Glareanus) publishes *Dodecachordon* on increasing church modal scales to twelve.   **MUSIC**

1548   Italian painter Jacopo Robusti, known as Tintoretto, paints *Miracle of the Slave*, a masterpiece of foreshortening.   **PAINT**

1549   English poet Sir Thomas Wyatt's first published collection is the posthumous *Certayne Psalmes*, a version of the penitential psalms.   **LIT**

1549   Adriaan Willaert, founder of the Venetian school of composers, combines Dutch and Italian musical styles in *Fantasie e Ricercari*.   **MUSIC**

1549   French sculptor Jean Goujon completes his reliefs for the Fontaine des Innocents in Paris. His figurative carving, combining classical details with a delicate slenderness, is the antithesis of contemporary Italian styles and will become traditional for French Renaissance sculpture.   **SCULP**

1550–1556   Suleiman's Mosque in Constantinople is built.   **ARCH**

1550–1570   Palladio builds the Palazzo Chiericati, Villa Rotunda, and Villa Barbaro in Vicenza.   **ARCH**

1550   Italian painter and art historian Giorgio Vasari publishes *Lives of the Artists*, which will long influence critical opinion and provide information on the lives of Italian Renaissance painters, sculptors, and architects.   **MISC**

1550   English composer and writer John Marbeck's *The Boke of Common Praier Noted* is the first musical setting of English liturgy.   **MUSIC**

1551   Italian composer Giovanni da Palestrina becomes director of music at St. Peter's in Rome.   **MUSIC**

1551   Italian painter Titian paints the portrait of *Philip II*.   **PAINT**

1551–1553   Flemish painter Pieter Brueghel travels to Italy through France, making landscape drawings of the Alps on his way back.   **PAINT**

1552   Italian natural philosopher Giambattista della Porta invents the convex lens and uses it to refine the camera obscura, an artist's tool for tracing invented by Roger Bacon three hundred years earlier.   **GRAPH**

1553   Italian painter Paolo Caliari, known as Veronese, paints the ceiling for the Doge's palace, Venice.   **PAINT**

Terracotta sculpture of the Buddha. Nepal. *(The Metropolitan Museum of Art, Purchase, 1962, Seymour Fund)*

1554–1557   English poet Henry Howard, Earl of Surrey, is the first to use blank verse (unrhymed iambic pentameter) in a published English work. He introduces what other publishers call "this strange meter" in his posthumously published translation of part of Virgil's *Aeneid* (Book IV, 1554; Book II, 1557). Blank verse will become a widely used verse form in English poetry, for example, in the plays of Shakespeare. **LIT**

1554   Italian composer Giovanni da Palestrina's *First Book of Masses* is dedicated to Pope Julius III, who honors him by making him a member of the Vatican's Sistine Choir.   **MUSIC**

1554   In England Dutch portrait painter Anthonis Mor paints the portrait of Mary Tudor. In England, he is known as Sir Anthony More; in Spain, as Antonio Moro. He will influence the development of royal and aristocratic portraits, especially in Spain.   **PAINT**

1554   Titian paints *Danaë, Venus and Adonis,* and *Perseus and Andromeda.*   **PAINT**

1555–1560   Gray's Inn hall in London is built.   **ARCH**

1555   Flemish composer Orlando di Lasso publishes his first collections of madrigals on poems by Petrarch, and madrigals and motets on Italian, French, and Latin texts.   **MUSIC**

1555   Tintoretto paints *St. George and the Dragon.*   **PAINT**

1557   An engraving of Brueghel's parable drawing *The Big Fish Eat Little Fish* is engraved and published by engraver Hieronymous (Jerome) Cock, who will execute many printed versions of Brueghel's drawings.   **GRAPH**

1557   In England printer Richard Tottel publishes an influential collection of poems known as *Songs and Sonnettes* or *Tottel's Miscellany.* It includes poems by Sir Thomas Wyatt, Henry Howard, Earl of Surrey, Nicholas Griswold, and others.   **LIT**

1558   Italian composer Gioseffo Zarlino's *Institutioni harmoniche* defines modern major and minor scales.   **MUSIC**

1558   Flemish painter Pieter Brueghel paints *Children's Games.*   **PAINT**

c. 1559–1575   Italian poet Torquato Tasso writes the romance *Gerusalemme liberata* (*Jerusalem Delivered*).   **LIT**

1559   The first edition of *A Mirror for Magistrates,* a collection of didactic poetry on fortune, wickedness, and the lives of great men, is published in English. Later editions and supplements will appear in 1563, 1574, 1578, 1587, and 1610.   **LIT**

c. 1560s   The first modern violins begin to be developed by Gasparo Bertolotti da Salò and Giovanni Paolo Maggini in Brescia, and the Amati brothers in Cremona, Italy.   **MUSIC**

1560   A new English translation of the Bible, written by Protestant English exiles in Geneva, is published. Known as the Geneva Bible, it becomes the most popular and influential English Bible until the King James version (1611).   **LIT**

1560   Orlando di Lasso becomes court Kapellmeister in Munich, where he is encouraged to produce a prodigious amount of music. His famous *Seven Penitential Psalms* (c. 1565) are included in the manuscripts at the Royal Library of Music, founded by Duke Albert. **MUSIC**

1560   Italian painter Tintoretto paints *Susannah and the Elders*. **PAINT**

1560   Italian painter and art historian Giorgio Vasari begins building the Uffizi in Florence for Duke Cosimo de' Medici. The principal public gallery of Florence, it will contain the world's greatest collection of Italian paintings. **PAINT**

1561–1565   Flemish architect Cornelis Floris builds Antwerp town hall, considered the most influential building in Flanders of the sixteenth century. **ARCH**

1561   Sir Thomas Hoby's English translation of Castiglione's *The Courtier* (1528) is published. Its content will influence courtly manners and political life in England; its literary style will influence Sir Philip Sidney, Edmund Spenser, and William Shakespeare. **LIT**

1562   The hall of the Middle Temple in London is built. **ARCH**

1562   In Venice Tintoretto paints *Christ at the Sea of Galilee* and Veronese paints *The Marriage at Cana*. **PAINT**

1563   The first true art academy, the Accademia del Disegno in Florence, is founded by Cosimo de' Medici at the urging of painter and art historian Giorgio Vasari. It is headed by Cosimo and Michelangelo. **MISC**

1563   English composer and organist William Byrd, age twenty, becomes organist at Lincoln cathedral. **MUSIC**

1563   French sculptor Germain Pilon develops his own style by taking elements from antiquity, Michelangelo, and the Gothic tradition for the carving of the tomb of Henry II in the abbey church of St. Denis in Paris. He will collaborate with architect Francesco Primaticcio and complete the monument in 1570. **SCULP**

1564   Italian composer Giovanni da Palestrina presents *Missa Papae Marcelli*, a mass named for Pope Marcellus II. **MUSIC**

1564   Michelangelo's last work, the last of his several sculptures of the *Pietà*, is left unfinished at the time of his death. **SCULP**

1565   Italian architect Andrea Palladio builds the Church of San Giorgio Maggiore in Venice, combining traditional basilican church form and classical detail. **ARCH**

1565   The lead pencil is in use in Europe. **GRAPH**

1565   Residing Brussels since 1563, Flemish painter Pieter Brueghel paints the series *The Months*, of which five will survive to the twentieth century, including *Hunters in the Snow*. **PAINT**

1565   Tintoretto paints *Flight into Egypt*. **PAINT**

1567	In Flanders Pieter Brueghel paints *Adoration of the Magi*. In Italy Titian paints *Jacopo de Strada*. **PAINT**
1568–1574	English architect Robert Smythson builds Longleat House in Wiltshire. **ARCH**
1568	Pieter Brueghel paints *The Faithlessness of the World* and *The Blind Leading the Blind* in his series based on proverbs. **PAINT**
1568	Spanish painter Juan Fernández de Navarrete, known as El Mudo because he is deaf and dumb, is appointed court painter to Spanish king Philip II. By his death in 1579, de Navarrete will have completed eight of the thirty-two altarpieces he was commissioned to execute. His eclectic style will help to disseminate Italian influence throughout Spain. **PAINT**
c. 1570	Vocal polyphonic a cappella style reaches its zenith with the composers Giovanni da Palestrina and Orlando di Lasso. **MUSIC**
1570	English goldsmith and painter Nicholas Hilliard is appointed Court Miniaturist and Goldsmith by Elizabeth I. Though best known for his miniature paintings, he will also paint full-size portraits of Elizabeth and others. **PAINT**
c. 1570	Florentine sculptor Battista Lorenzi erects a marble statue of Alpheus and Arethusa, illustrating a tale from Ovid, in a grotto at Alamanno Bandini's villa Il Paradiso. The figures' liveliness anticipates the Baroque. **SCULP**
1571	Italian architect Andrea Palladio builds the Loggia del Capitanio in Vicenza. **ARCH**
1572	English composer and organist William Byrd joins Thomas Tallis, an important composer of anthems and services with English texts, as organist at the Chapel Royal in London. **MUSIC**
1573	Having conquered Mexico, the Spanish begin to build the Mexico City cathedral, which will be completed in 1813. **ARCH**
1573	Italian painter Veronese is summoned before the Inquisition for including irreverent figures such as dwarfs and buffoons in a painting of the Last Supper. To pacify the authorities, the painting's name is changed to *The Feast in the House of Levi*. **PAINT**
1575	English composers and organists William Byrd and Thomas Tallis compose *Cantiones sacrae*, thirty-four motets dedicated to the queen. **MUSIC**
1576	The Theatre is built, England's first permanent structure for the performance of plays. **DRAMA**
1576	Spanish composer Tomás Luis de Victoria publishes *Liber primus*, a volume of masses and canticles. **MUSIC**

1576   Italian painter Titian dies, leaving his last work, *Pietà*, unfinished; it is completed by his pupil, Palma Giovane.   **PAINT**

1577   English author Raphael Holinshed publishes *Chronicles of England, Scotlande, and Irelande*, which will provide source material for many Shakespeare plays, including *King Lear*, *Macbeth*, and *Cymbeline*.   **LIT**

1577   The art academy Accademia di San Luca is founded in Rome.   **MISC**

1577   Spanish painter Doménikos Theotokópoulos, known as El Greco, paints the *Assumption of the Virgin*, an altarpiece in San Domingo el Antiguo, Toledo.   **PAINT**

1578   English writer John Lyly publishes the prose fiction work *Euphues, the Anatomy of Wit*, which introduces the ornate, exaggeratedly refined style known as euphuism. Tremendously popular, the book will generate a sequel by Lyly, *Euphues and His England*, in 1580.   **LIT**

1579   English poet Edmund Spenser publishes the first edition of his first major work, *The Shepheardes Calendar*, pseudonymously written under the name Immerito (unworthy). The popular collection consists of twelve pastoral poems, one for each month of the year.   **LIT**

1580   French essayist Michel Eyquem de Montaigne publishes his first two books of *Essays*, which introduce the literary form known as the personal essay.   **LIT**

1581   *Ballet comique de la Reine*, or court ballet, is organized by an Italian resident of France, Balthasar de Beaujoyeulx. Combining the features of French dances and masquerades with those of the pastorales and Italian interludes, it is often considered the starting point of ballet.   **DANCE**

1583   In Japan Toyotomi Hideyoshi begins construction of Osaka castle.   **ARCH**

1583   Flemish sculptor Giambologna (also known as Jean Bologne or Giovanni da Bologna) working in Florence, creates a larger-than-life marble group depicting the Rape of the Sabine Women. His sculpture is the first large marble composition intended to be seen from all sides.   **SCULP**

c. 1585–   *The Spanish Tragedy*, an extremely popular play by English drama-
1589   tist Thomas Kyd, is produced. Some will believe Kyd helped write Shakepeare's *Titus Andronicus*.   **DRAMA**

1585   Italian painter Veronese paints the *Triumph of Venice* on the ceiling of the Hall of the Great Council in the Doge's palace, Venice.   **PAINT**

1586   St. John Lateran in Rome is rebuilt.   **ARCH**

c. 1587–   *Tamburlaine the Great, Parts I and II*, dramas by English dramatist
1588   Christopher Marlowe, are produced.   **DRAMA**

1587–1588   Italian composer Claudio Monteverdi publishes eight books of madrigals.   **MUSIC**

THE FIRST BALLET

*T*he first ballet was the brainchild of a mother-in-law who was not above getting involved in her daughter-in-law's sister's wedding. The mother-in-law was Italian-born Catherine de Médicis (1519–1589), queen consort of French king Henry II, mother of three kings, generous patroness of the arts, and powerful political figure in France for much of the sixteenth century. In 1581, her son King Henry III was on the throne, and his wife, Queen Louise, had a sister who was getting married. Catherine, ever the matriarch, wanted to stage a lavish entertainment for the occasion. She commissioned court musician and dance master Baldassare di Belgioioso, known to the French as Beaujoyeulx, to design an appropriate spectacle. On October 15, 1581, at the Louvre, Beaujoyeulx staged the Ballet comique de la reine, often regarded as the first ballet.

Six hours in length, combining song, dance, pantomime, and poetry, the spectacle's narrative concerned the escape of Odysseus from the sorceress Circe. But more important was its original use of extended choreographed steps rather than free motion. Drawing on French and Italian court dance traditions, Beaujoyeulx sought to achieve the "geometrical arrangement of many persons dancing together under a diverse harmony of instruments."

Though it lacked many of the formal elements of classical ballet that would be codified by the nineteenth century, a new art form had been born. Catherine herself helped to spread the word about it, distributing reports of her spectacle throughout the continent.

1588   "My Mind to Me a Kingdom Is," a poem by English poet Sir Edward Dyer, is published.   **LIT**

1588   English composer and organist William Byrd's *Psalms, Sonets & songs of sadnes & pietie* attests to his mastery of expressive polyphony.   **MUSIC**

1588   *Musica Transalpina*, a collection of fifty-seven Italian madrigals provided with English texts is published by Nicholas Yonge in London, and leads to greater interest in England to the Italian style.   **MUSIC**

1589   Thoinot Arbeau (anagram for Jehan Tabourot), a French church dignitary from Langres, publishes *Orchésographie*, an important treatise on dancing.   **DANCE**

c. 1589–   English dramatist Christopher Marlowe writes the play *The Jew of*
1590   *Malta*. It will survive only in a version revised by someone else.   **DRAMA**

1589	English composer and organist William Byrd writes *Songs of sundrie natures*. **MUSIC**
1590s	English poet John Donne writes most of his great love poetry and his five *Satires*, though little of his poetry will be published until after his death in 1631. The first and most influential of the metaphysical poets, he will be known for his energetic, vigorous style and his use of conceits—ingenious, paradoxical, concentrated comparisons, often with a philosophical bent. *See* 1633, LIT. **LIT**
c. 1590–1592	The plays of English dramatist William Shakespeare begin to be produced. His earliest plays include the history plays *Henry VI Parts 1, 2,* and *3, The Comedy of Errors*, based principally on the *Menaechmi* of Plautus (*see* 254 B.C., DRAMA), and the tragedy *Titus Andronicus*. **DRAMA**
c. 1590	Until his death in 1619, Richard Burbage is one of the principal actors of his day, playing every major male role in Shakespeare's plays, including Richard III, Hamlet, Othello, and King Lear. He also performs in the plays of Ben Jonson and Beaumont and Fletcher. **DRAMA**
c. 1590	English dramatist Christopher Marlowe writes the drama *The Tragical History of Dr. Faustus*. Though it will survive only in a version adapted by others, it will be Marlowe's most frequently revived play. **DRAMA**
c. 1590	*The Old Wives' Tale*, a comedy by English dramatist George Peele, is written and produced. Peele's earlier comedy *The Arraignment of Paris* was probably produced in 1581. **DRAMA**
1590	A portion of English poet Sir Philip Sidney's prose romance *Arcadia* is published posthumously. Known as New Arcadia, it represents Sidney's revised version of the first three books of an earlier unpublished romance that is known as Old Arcadia. In 1593, the Countess of Pembroke will publish a hybrid of New Arcadia and the lost books of the unrevised Old Arcadia. **LIT**
1590	English poet Edmund Spenser publishes the first three books of *The Faerie Queene*, a monumental romantic verse epic originally intended to span twelve books. Though the work is never completed, three more books (IV-VI) will be added in the edition of 1596. The posthumous edition of 1609 will add the "Mutability Cantos." **LIT**
1590	Spanish painter El Greco paints *St. Jerome*. **PAINT**
c. 1591–1594	Shakespeare writes the history play *Richard III*. **DRAMA**
1591	English poet and playwright Robert Greene publishes *The Art of Conny-Catching*, a humorous, journalistic account of confidence games in London. **LIT**

1591   English poet Sir Philip Sidney's sonnet sequence *Astrophel and Stella* is published posthumously. It is the first great Elizabethan sonnet cycle.   **LIT**

c. 1592   Shakespeare writes the comedy *Two Gentlemen of Verona*.   **DRAMA**

c. 1592   English dramatist Christopher Marlowe writes the tragedy *Edward II*, chronicling the personal and political adversities faced by a homosexual king.   **DRAMA**

1592   English poet Samuel Daniel publishes the sonnet cycle *Delia*.   **LIT**

1592   English poet and playwright Robert Greene excoriates Shakespeare in his pamphlet *Groatsworth of witte bought with a million of Repentance*. He calls Shakespeare "an upstart crow, beautified with our feathers."   **LIT**

1592   Ludovico Zacconi publishes *Prattica di musica*, with extensive descriptions of instruments and directions for executing ornaments.   **MUSIC**

1592   Italian painter Tintoretto paints *The Last Supper*.   **PAINT**

c. 1593–   Shakespeare writes the comedies *The Taming of the Shrew* and
1594   *Love's Labour's Lost*.   **DRAMA**

1593   Shakespeare publishes a mythological narrative poem, *Venus and Adonis*.   **LIT**

1593   *The Phoenix Nest*, a poetic miscellany, is published in England, containing poems by Thomas Lodge, George Peele, Nicholas Breton, and possibly Sir Walter Raleigh.   **LIT**

1593   Italian writer Cesare Ripa's *Iconologia*, published this year, will become a standard reference on iconography for artists.   **MISC**

1593   El Greco paints *The Crucifixion* and *The Resurrection*.   **PAINT**

c. 1594–   Shakespeare writes the tragedy *Romeo and Juliet*. The archetypal
1596   story of starcrossed young lovers will be the basis for works in many media, including a Berlioz symphony (1839), a Gounod opera (1867), an orchestral piece by Tchaikovsky (1869, revised 1880), a ballet by Prokofiev (1938), the musical *West Side Story* with music by Leonard Bernstein and lyrics by Stephen Sondheim (1957), and movie versions by George Cukor (1936) and Franco Zeffirelli (1968).   **DRAMA**

c. 1594–   Shakespeare writes the history play *King John*.   **DRAMA**
1595

c. 1594–   Shakespeare writes the comedy *The Merchant of Venice*, in which
1598   the vengeful moneylender Shylock demands a pound of flesh in payment of Antonio's debt. In addition to "pound of flesh," phrases from the play that will enter the language include "Hath not a Jew eyes?" and "The quality of mercy is not strain'd."   **DRAMA**

1594	The Chamberlain's Men (known after 1603 as King's Men), an acting company, is started by William Shakespeare and several other performers. Shakespeare will write most of his plays for the group, and he will remain a member for about twenty years. In 1623, two members of the King's Men will publish all of Shakespeare's plays in folio form. **DRAMA**
1594	Shakespeare publishes the narrative poem *The Rape of Lucrece.* **LIT**
1594	English pamphleteer and dramatist Thomas Nash publishes *The unfortunate traveller*, perhaps the first picaresque novel in English. **LIT**
1594–1597	English theologian Richard Hooker publishes the first five books of his work *Of the Lawes of ecclesiasticall politie* (Books I-IV, 1594, Book V, 1597). Books VI and VIII (1648) and VII (1661), published posthumously, are of dubious authenticity. The apology for the organization of the English church is a masterpiece of theology and literary style. **LIT**
1594	Italian painter Michelangelo Merisi, known as Caravaggio, paints *The Musical Party*. **PAINT**
c. 1595–1596	Shakespeare writes the comedy *A Midsummer Night's Dream* and the historical play *Richard II*. **DRAMA**
1595	English poet Edmund Spenser publishes the sonnet sequence *Amoretti* and the marriage hymn *Epithalamion*. **LIT**
1595	English poet Michael Drayton publishes *Endimion and Phoebe*, an erotic mythological poem later revised as *The Man in the Moon* (1606, 1619). **LIT**
1595	English poet Sir Philip Sidney's critical treatise *An Apologie for Poetrie* is published posthumously in two editions, one under the title of *The Defence of Poesie*. **LIT**
1595	English poet Edmund Spenser publishes *Colin Clouts come home againe*, a pastoral poem based on a character in *The Shepheardes Calender* (1579). **LIT**
c. 1596–1598	Shakespeare's history plays *Henry IV Part 1* and *Part 2* introduce the rotund, high-living scoundrel Falstaff, companion of Prince Hal, who will become Henry V in the play of that title (c. 1599). Falstaff will also appear in the *Merry Wives of Windsor* (c. 1597–1601). **DRAMA**
1596	Edmund Spenser publishes *Four Hymns* and *Prothalamion*, a marriage poem. **LIT**
c. 1597–1601	Shakespeare writes the comedy *The Merry Wives of Windsor*. **DRAMA**
1597	English poet Michael Drayton publishes *Englands Heroicall Epistles*, modeled on Ovid's *Heroides*, earns him the title of "our English Ovid." **LIT**

1597   The first edition of English philosopher Francis Bacon's *Essays* is published. The first English essayist, his style is more formal and aphoristic than that of French essayist Michel de Montaigne, recognized as the founder of the genre. This edition contains ten essays; a second edition will contain thirty-eight (1612); a third fifty-eight (1625).   **LIT**

1597   *Dafne*, the first opera (now lost) written by Italian composer Jacopo Peri, is performed in Florence.   **MUSIC**

1597   English composer Thomas Morley publishes *A Plaine and Easie Introduction to Practicall Musick*, describing forms and compositional techniques.   **MUSIC**

1597   Italian composer Orazio Vecchi presents the madrigal-comedy *L'Amfiparnaso*.   **MUSIC**

1597   El Greco paints *St. Martin and the Beggar*.   **PAINT**

c. 1598–   Shakespeare writes the comedies *Much Ado About Nothing* and *As You Like It*.   **DRAMA**
1599

1598   *Every Man in His Humour*, the first popular comedy by English playwright Ben Jonson, is produced. William Shakespeare plays the part of Kno'well.   **DRAMA**

1598   *Hero and Leander*, a narrative poem by English dramatist Christopher Marlowe, is published posthumously.   **LIT**

1598   Flemish painter Jan Brueghel paints *Adoration of the Kings*.   **PAINT**

c. 1599   Shakespeare writes the history play *Henry V*.   **DRAMA**

c. 1599   Shakespeare writes *Julius Caesar*, a drama of the assassination of the Roman dictator that begins the period of his great tragedies.   **DRAMA**

c. 1599–   Shakespeare writes the tragedy *Hamlet*, which will be considered
1601   by many his greatest work and by some the greatest play ever written. The drama of the prince of Denmark's quest to avenge the murder of his father by his uncle Claudius includes the "To be or not to be" soliloquy (act 3, scene 1, lines 55-87), in which young Hamlet contemplates suicide. The play's sources include *Historica Danica*, 1514.   **DRAMA**

1599   The original Globe Theatre opens in London. It is the largest Elizabethan playhouse, and, over the next nine years, it will accommodate first productions of most of Shakespeare's best plays.   **DRAMA**

1599   "The Passionate Shepherd to His Love," a lyric poem by English dramatist Christopher Marlowe, is published posthumously. It begins with the famous lines "Come live with me and be my love,/And we will all the pleasures prove."   **LIT**

1599   A long-running pamphlet war between English pamphleteers Thomas Nash and Gabriel Harvey comes to an end in 1599 when church authorities order confiscation of their works.   **LIT**

1600s   Meddahs, storytellers expert in parody and satire, entertain in sultan's courts and coffeehouses in the Ottoman Empire.   **DRAMA**

1600s   Elaborate mourning ceremonies, in which dasteh (groups of mourners) flagellate and cut themselves while chanting, are performed in the streets of Iran. These ceremonies will grow larger and be performed more frequently by the nineteenth century.   **DRAMA**

1600s   Italian marionette shows are performed in London, and the character Punch is created. Punch will become the buffoon of nearly every British puppet show, and in the early 1700s, he will be joined by a wife, first named Joan, then Judy. By the 1800s, the two will have taken the form of hand puppets. Punch and Judy shows continue in England and abroad to the present day.   **DRAMA**

1600s   Kabuki theater develops into a stylized—and highly commercialized—art form. Wearing beautiful costumes and accompanied by music and clappers, actors perform historical and contemporary plays and dances. Crowd-pleasing material is chosen in order to compete effectively with *Jōruri* (*see* 1700s, DRAMA). Kabuki continues to be performed in Japan and abroad to the present day.   **DRAMA**

1600s   French artist and engraver Jean Berain creates elaborate, sometimes bejeweled costumes for actors performing the works of Molière and other playwrights at the court of Louis XIV.   **DRAMA**

1600s   Rome, Milan, and Turin each have theaters for puppet shows. Marionettes are popular in Italy and throughout Europe, as they will be through the nineteenth century.   **DRAMA**

c. 1600s Late this century, the overture emerges in two types: French, established by Jean-Baptiste Lully, and Italian, established by Alessandro Scarlatti.   **MUSIC**

1600s   Harps are used occasionally in Italian operas (e.g., Monteverdi's *L'Orfeo*) before falling out of use in orchestras.   **MUSIC**

c. 1600s Huge ancestral figures carved from volcanic rock are lined up on raised platforms on Easter Island in the Pacific.   **SCULP**

1600s   Akan cultures of southern Ghana and the Ivory Coast begin to modify traditional forms of wooden sculpture to produce commemorative terra-cotta heads and figures of the royal family.   **SCULP**

c. 1600 Shamba Bolongongo, king of the BaKuba people of what is now Zaire, Africa, is known as a patron of the arts. He welcomes representatives from craft guilds and introduces such innovations as embroidery and the weaving of raffia cloth.   **DECO**

c. 1600–
1602

Shakespeare writes the comedy *Twelfth Night*.   **DRAMA**

c. 1600

The Chinese novel *Chin p'ing mei* (*The Golden Lotus*) is written, known for its naturalism and erotic content.   **LIT**

1600

As mannerism comes to an end, baroque, originating in Rome, will become the dominant visual style in Europe until about 1750. It is characterized by vigorous movement, emotional intensity, and a concern for balance and wholeness.   **MISC**

1600

Italian composers Giulio Caccini's and Jacopo Peri's opera *Euridice* premieres in Florence. It becomes the earliest opera still extant.   **MUSIC**

1600

Italian composer Emilio de' Cavalieri's *La rappresentazione di anima e di corpo* is produced in Rome. Considered the first oratorio, its music consists almost exclusively of recitative and short choruses.   **MUSIC**

1600

The solo song with lute and viol accompaniment is popular in England, due in large part to the airs of John Dowland.   **MUSIC**

1600–1608

Flemish painter Peter Paul Rubens resides in Italy, where his personal style is formed and where he produces such works as *Marchesa Brigida Spinola-Doria*.   **PAINT**

c. 1601–
1604

Shakespeare writes the satiric tragedy *Troilus and Cressida*, based on the same legendary love affair that inspired Chaucer's poetic version (c. 1386). In the same period he writes the comedy *All's Well That Ends Well*.   **DRAMA**

1601

Lute songs by English poet and composer Thomas Campion are published in *A Book of Airs*, composed with Philip Rossiter. More books of airs will follow in about 1613 and 1617.   **MUSIC**

1601

English composer Thomas Morley publishes *Triumphs of Oriana*, a collection of madrigals in praise of Queen Elizabeth by twenty-five different composers.   **MUSIC**

1601

Caravaggio paints *The Conversion of St. Paul*.   **PAINT**

1602

The poem *The Burning Babe* by English poet Robert Southwell is published posthumously with several other of his works. Southwell (*b*. 1561), a Jesuit priest, died a Catholic martyr's death in England in 1595.   **LIT**

1602

English poet and composer Thomas Campion argues against rhyme and for classical meters in the treatise *Observations in the Art of English Poesy*. His arguments will be countered by Samuel Daniel's *Defence of Rime* in 1603.   **LIT**

1602	A new vocal style is introduced in the song collection *Nuove Musiche* by Italian composer Giulio Caccini, a major step in the development of the opera, oratorio, cantata, and baroque music in general. Caccini's work serves to counteract the Flemish emphasis on counterpoint and artful elaboration. The prevailing polyphonic a cappella style is replaced with accompanied solo song (aria, monody, recitative). **MUSIC**
1602	German composer Hans Leo Hassler publishes a collection of lieder, *Lustgarten.* **MUSIC**
c. 1603– 1604	Shakespeare writes the comedy *Measure for Measure* and the tragedy *Othello.* **DRAMA**
1603	Queen Elizabeth's death brings to an end the Elizabethan period of literature in England. It is followed by the Jacobean period under James II (1603–1625). **LIT**
1604	The sons of Flemish composer Orlando di Lasso publish 516 of his motets in the six volumes, *Magnum opus musicum.* **MUSIC**
1604	Italian painter Caravaggio paints *The Deposition.* **PAINT**
c. 1605	Shakespeare's tragedy *King Lear*, the drama of the legendary king of Britain whose decline begins when he divides his kingdom between his untrustworthy daughters Goneril and Regan while banishing his faithful daughter Cordelia. **DRAMA**
c. 1605– 1608	Shakespeare writes the tragedy *Timon of Athens.* **DRAMA**
1605	English philosopher Francis Bacon publishes the treatise *The Advancement of Learning*, which begins the project he refers to as *Instauratio Magna*, a proposal for educational and scientific reform based on a new vision of human knowledge, one that depends on experiment and observation. Bacon's ideas, expressed in a concise, masterful prose style, will contribute to the development of the scientific method. *See also* 1620, LIT. **LIT**
1605	The first of two parts of *Don Quixote de la Mancha*, a novel by Spanish novelist and playwright Miguel de Cervantes, is published. The second part of the comic saga of a man who feels called to set right the world's imperfections will be published in 1615. **LIT**
1605	Spanish composer Tomás Luis de Victoria's masterpiece, a Requiem Mass for Empress Maria, is his last published work. **MUSIC**
1605	English composer John Dowland composes *Lachrymae, or Seaven Teares in Seaven Passionate Pavans . . . set forth for the Lute, Viols, or Violins in five parts.* **MUSIC**
1605	Italian artist Annibale Carraci paints the frescoes in the Palazzo Farnese, Rome. **PAINT**

1606   The Grande Galerie of the Louvre in Paris is completed. *See* 1546,
             ARCH.   **ARCH**

c. 1606–   Shakespeare writes the tragedy *Macbeth*, the drama of the Scottish
    1608   nobleman who, with his wife Lady Macbeth, murders King Duncan
             in order to gain the throne. During this period he also writes the
             tragedy *Antony and Cleopatra* and the romance play *Pericles*. **DRAMA**

1606   *Volpone, or the Fox*, one of the best of English playwright Ben
             Jonson's comedies, is produced.   **DRAMA**

1606   English poet Michael Drayton publishes *Poems Lyric and Pastoral*,
             containing imitations of Horace's *Odes*.   **LIT**

1607-1614   Italian architect Carlo Maderna adds a nave and facade to St.
             Peter's Church, Rome, thus determining that the church will take
             the form of a Latin rather than a Greek cross.   **ARCH**

1607   Italian composer Claudio Monteverdi's opera *L'Orfeo* is produced in
             Mantua. It combines the archaic style of the earliest operas with
             greater expressiveness and dramatic impact.   **MUSIC**

c. 1608   Shakespeare writes the tragedy *Coriolanus* and the romance play
             Cymbeline.   **DRAMA**

1608   English writer Joseph Hall publishes *Characters of Vertues and Vices*,
             a collection of character sketches. This genre of writing, popular at
             this time, originated with the *Charakteres* of Greek philosopher
             Theophrastus in the third century B.C.   **LIT**

1608   Monteverdi composes his opera *L'Arianna*, a work now lost except
             for "Lamento d'Arianna."   **MUSIC**

1608   Italian composer Girolamo Frescobaldi, who advances the organ
             and its technique, is made organist at St. Peter's, Rome.   **MUSIC**

1608   Notable paintings include Italian painter Domenichino's *The
             Scourging of St. Andrew* and Spanish painter El Greco's *Golgotha* and
             Cardinal Taverna.   **PAINT**

c. 1609   English dramatists Francis Beaumont and John Fletcher's play
             Phylaster, or Love Lies Bleeding is produced, and their famous collab-
             oration begins. They will write six or seven plays together, including
             The Maides Tragedy (c. 1610) and *A King and No King* (1611), and
             their work will be popular with sophisticated audiences of the day.
             Each had written plays alone in the past, and Fletcher will do so
             again in the future.   **DRAMA**

1609   *Epicoene, or the Silent Woman*, a comedy by English dramatist Ben
             Jonson, is produced.   **DRAMA**

1609   Shakespeare's sonnets are published. The 154 sonnets, most of which were probably written before 1600, are dedicated to Mr. W.H., who may be either the Earl of Southampton or the Earl of Pembroke. Sonnets 1–126 are mainly about the poet's relationship with a youth, Sonnets 127–154 with a mistress known as the Dark Lady. Among the best remembered of the sonnets is Sonnet 18, "Shall I compare thee to a summer's day."   **LIT**

1609   English philosopher Francis Bacon publishes the Latin work on classical mythology *De Sapientia Veterum*, which will later be translated as *The Wisdom of the Ancients* (1619).   **LIT**

1609   Flemish painter Peter Paul Rubens paints his self-portrait with his wife, Isabella Brant.   **PAINT**

1610–1643   The Louis XIII style of interior decoration and architecture prevails in France. It marks a transition from Italian-influenced baroque style to French classicism. *See* 1643–1715, DECO.   **DECO**

c. 1610–1611   Shakespeare writes the romance plays *The Winter's Tale* and his last great work, *The Tempest*. The latter introduces the sorceror Prospero, the sprite Ariel, the monster Caliban, and Prospero's daughter Miranda, all of whom dwell in isolation on an island until they are visited by a crew shipwrecked in a tempest raised through Prospero's magic. Among the works inspired by *The Tempest* are Browning's poem "Caliban upon Setebos," Tchaikovsky's symphonic fantasy (1873), Huxley's novel *Brave New World* (1932), and the science fiction film *Forbidden Planet* (1956).   **DRAMA**

1610   English dramatist Ben Jonson's *The Alchemist* premieres. English poet and critic Samuel Taylor Coleridge will later call it one of the "three most perfect plots ever planned." *See* 1749, LIT.   **DRAMA**

1610   English poet John Donne publishes his most important prose work, *Pseudo-Martyr*, which encourages English Roman Catholics to become Anglicans.   **LIT**

1610   German composer Michael Praetorius publishes a collection of church hymns, *Musae sioniae*.   **MUSIC**

1610–1614   With the triptychs *Raising of the Cross* and *Descent from the Cross*, Flemish painter Peter Paul Rubens establishes himself as one of the most significant painters in northern Europe.   **PAINT**

1611   A new English translation of the Bible, authorized by King James I, is published. Known as the King James Bible or Authorized Version, it will have an enduring influence on English literary style. It is heavily dependent on previous English translations, including those of William Tyndale (1525), Miles Coverdale (1535), and the Geneva Bible (1560).   **LIT**

1611–1612   English poet John Donne writes two long poems, *The Anniversaries*, on the death of Sir Robert Drury's daughter Elizabeth.   **LIT**

1612   English dramatist John Webster's *The White Devil* is produced. His *The Duchess of Malfi* will be produced in 1614. Both are plays set in Renaissance Italy, and both will be seen as masterpieces of seventeenth-century English drama.   **DRAMA**

1612   The poem "What is our life?" by English poet Sir Walter Raleigh (or Ralegh) is printed in a madrigal setting. Raleigh is also known for "The Nymph's Reply to the Shepherd," a response to Christopher Marlowe's "Passionate Shepherd" (1599).   **LIT**

1612   English poet Michael Drayton publishes the first part of *Poly-Olbion*, a 30,000-line historical-geographical poem about the English countryside. The second part of this, his masterpiece, will appear in 1622.   **LIT**

c. 1613   Shakespeare's last play, which may have been coauthored by John Fletcher, is the historical drama *Henry VIII*.   **DRAMA**

1613   Italian composer Claudio Monteverdi is made maestro di cappella at St. Mark's, Venice, where he remains until his death in 1643.   **MUSIC**

1613   *Parthenia*, a collection of music for virginals (a type of harpsichord) by English composers William Byrd, John Bull, and Orlando Gibbons, is presented to Princess Elizabeth and Prince Frederick on their wedding.   **MUSIC**

1614   *Bartholomew Fair*, the last successful comedy by English dramatist Ben Jonson, is produced.   **DRAMA**

1615   Once a notorious rake and writer of love lyrics, English poet John Donne becomes an Anglican minister, reflecting his shift in recent years toward religious writing. He will compose religious verse and prose works, and more than 160 of his sermons will survive. His *Holy Sonnets* date from this decade.   **LIT**

1615   Adriano Banchieri founds Accademia de' Floridi in Bologna for the promotion of literature, science and the arts, including the cultivation of music.   **MUSIC**

1615–1619   Michael Praetorius writes his three-volume encyclopedia of music *Syntagma musicum*.   **MUSIC**

1616–1635   English architect Inigo Jones builds the Queen's House at Greenwich (1616–1635) and the Banqueting House in Whitehall (1619–1622). The latter includes a painted ceiling by Rubens. Jones's classical style is highly influential in England.   **ARCH**

1616   *Epigrams* and *The Forest*, verse collections by English dramatist Ben Jonson, are published.   **LIT**

1616   The musical society Collegium Musicum is founded in Prague.   **MUSIC**

1616   Dutch painter Frans Hals paints *Banquet of the Officers of the St. George Militia*, which sets a new standard for energetic, informal group portraits. In the 1620s and 1630s, Hals's group portraits will be in high demand by prosperous, ambitious members of the Dutch middle class.   **PAINT**

1617   Biagio Marini, one of the first great composers for violin, publishes *Musical Events*, sonata for solo violin, in Italy.   **MUSIC**

1617   German composer Johann Hermann Schein writes his dance suite, *Banchetto musicale* in Leipzig. The suite, as a composition in several movements and not merely a succession of pieces each in a particular mood and rhythm, is a German phenomenon.   **MUSIC**

1617   German composer Heinrich Schütz becomes Kapellmeister of the electoral chapel at Dresden until 1672.   **MUSIC**

1617   Flemish painter Peter Paul Rubens paints the dynamic and colorful mythological painting *The Rape of the Daughters of Leucippus*.   **PAINT**

1618–1625   Italian sculptor, architect, and painter Gian Lorenzo Bernini, the greatest artist of the Italian baroque era, executes four life-size sculptures: *Aeneas, Anchises, and Ascanius*, *The Rape of Proserpine*, *David*, and *Apollo and Daphne*. The dynamic vigor and emotion of the works represent a decisive break with late mannerism.   **SCULP**

1619   The most extensive and important collection of music for virginals, the *Fitzwilliam Virginal Book*, containing 297 compositions by nearly every composer of the virginalist school, is compiled in England by Francis Tregian.   **MUSIC**

1619   German composer Heinrich Schütz's *Psalms of David* reflects the opulent texture and coloration of the Venetian tradition.   **MUSIC**

1620s   While running a very prolific painting studio in high demand in Flanders, Peter Paul Rubens also designs tapestries, festival decorations, architectural decorations, and book illustrations.   **DECO**

1620s   Pedro Calderón de la Barca, one of the greatest playwrights of Spain's Golden Age and, from middle age on, a Roman Catholic priest, begins to have his work produced. He will write comedies, tragedies, histories, and *autos sacramentales* (religious allegories)— some 200 plays in all by the time of his death in 1681.   **DRAMA**

1620   English philosopher Francis Bacon writes the Latin work *Novum Organum* (*New Instrument*), which forms the second part of the *Instauratio Magna*, the program of educational and scientific reform begun in *The Advancement of Learning* (1605). The work seeks to add inductive reasoning to the tools of deductive inquiry that had been outlined in Aristotle's treatises of logic known as the *Organum*, or instrument.   **LIT**

1621   English writer Robert Burton publishes his only book, *The Anatomy of Melancholy*, a strange, seriocomic, paramedical study of melancholy, with many learned quotations and frequent digressions on religion, politics, and nearly everything else.   **LIT**

1621   Flemish painter Anthony Van Dyck travels to Italy, where he develops his elegant baroque style. His works there in the 1620s include portraits of Genoese nobility.   **PAINT**

1622–1625   Rubens paints a series of twenty-five paintings on the life of Marie de Médicis of France.   **PAINT**

1623   The first folio edition of Shakespeare's plays is published seven years after his death.   **DRAMA**

1624   English philosopher Francis Bacon publishes *Apophthegms New and Old*.   **LIT**

1624   Italian composer Claudio Monteverdi produces his madrigal opera in one act, *Il Combattimato di Tancredi e Clorinda*, in Venice.   **MUSIC**

1624   Dutch painter Frans Hals paints *The Laughing Cavalier*.   **PAINT**

1624–1638   For St. Peter's Church in Rome, Italian sculptor Bernini executes the baldacchino (canopy) over the High Altar and the statue of St. Longinus.   **SCULP**

1625   Italian sculptor, architect, and painter Bernini begins working at the Barberini palace, where he produces a series of technically superior portrait busts of Cardinal Scipione Borghese and others.   **SCULP**

1626   St. Peter's Church in Rome, the largest church in the Christian world, is dedicated by Pope Urban VIII. Construction of the church began in 1506. Bernini will make additions between 1629 and 1662 that include interior details and a forecourt with a piazza.   **ARCH**

1627   English playwright John Ford's drama *'Tis Pity She's a Whore*, considered provocative because of its depiction of incest, is produced.   **DRAMA**

1627   *The New Atlantis*, an unfinished Utopian fiction in Latin by English philosopher Francis Bacon, is published posthumously.   **LIT**

1627   German composer Heinrich Schütz presents *Dafne* (libretto by Martin Opitz), the first German opera, at Torgau. The music is later lost in a fire.   **MUSIC**

1627   French painter Simon Vouet is named court painter to King Louis XIII. The leading French artist of the first half of the seventeenth century, he has an eclectic style that combines classical and baroque tendencies.   **PAINT**

c. 1628   Dutch painter Frans Hals paints *The Jolly Toper*.   **PAINT**

c. 1628   In Rome French painter Nicolas Poussin paints the altarpiece *The Martyrdom of St. Erasmus* and the more personal work *Inspiration of the Poet*.   **PAINT**

1628	Dutch painter Rembrandt takes his first pupil, Gerrit Dou. Other painters taught by Rembrandt will include Carel Fabritius, Philips de Koninck, Nicolaes Maes, and Aert de Gelder. **PAINT**
1629	English poet John Milton writes his first great English lyric, "Ode Upon the Morning of Christ's Nativity." **LIT**
1630s	Pupils of Dutch painter Frans Hals now working in Holland include genre painters Adriaen Brouwer and Adriaen van Ostade. Two other pupils and genre painters, Judith Leyster (*see* 1630, PAINT) and Jan Miense Molenaer, are married in 1636 and share a studio. Genre painting, scenes of everyday life that often suggest a story, are a popular form in Dutch art of the seventeenth century. **PAINT**
1630–1648	The Taj Mahal is constructed in Agra, India, by Shah Jahan as a mausoleum in memory of his wife. **ARCH**
c. 1630	Spanish painter José de Ribera paints *Martyrdom of St. Bartholomew*. **PAINT**
1630	Dutch painter Judith Leyster paints *The Jolly Companion*, influenced by, but more complex than, her teacher Frans Hals's *The Jolly Toper* (c. 1628). **PAINT**
1632–1633	English sculptor and architect Nicholas Stone designs the three classical gateways in the Botanic Garden, Oxford. **ARCH**
1632–1634	Flemish painter Peter Paul Rubens paints the *Garden of Love*, noted for its lush color and brushwork. **PAINT**
1632	Rembrandt paints *The Anatomy Lesson of Dr. Tulp*, a radically dramatic group portrait. The artist paints nearly fifty portraits in 1632 and 1633. **PAINT**
1632	Flemish painter Anthony Van Dyck becomes court painter to King Charles I of England, a position he holds until his death in 1641. His portrait style strongly influences other English painters, including Thomas Gainsborough. **PAINT**
1633	English poet John Donne's *Collected Poems* is published, including *Songs and Sonnets* and *Divine Poems*. **LIT**
1633	Shortly after the death this year of English poet and divine George Herbert, his collection *The Temple* is published, containing about 160 poems. Centered on religious themes, they employ the technique of metaphysical conceits developed by John Donne. Among the best known poems are "Easter Wings" and "The Altar." **LIT**
1633	English poet Thomas Carew publishes *An Elegy Upon the Death of the Dean of Paul's, Dr. John Donne*. **LIT**
1634	The masque *Comus* by English poet John Milton is first performed. **DRAMA**

1634   English poet Thomas Carew's masque *Coelum Britannicum* is per-
            formed before King Charles I. He is one of a group of writers, also
            including Sir John Suckling and Richard Lovelace, known as the
            Cavalier poets because they flourished at Charles's court
            (1625–1649) before civil war brought about the king's dethroning
            and execution.   **DRAMA**

1635   French architect François Mansart completes the Hôtel de la
            Vrillière, an example of Renaissance classical architecture.
            Mansart's grand-nephew Jules Hardouin-Mansart will become the
            chief architect of the royal buildings for Louis XIV in 1699.   **ARCH**

1635   Italian composer Girolamo Frescobaldi writes *Fiori musicali di
            toccate*, which later influences German composer Johann Sebastian
            Bach.   **MUSIC**

1635   Rubens completes a series of paintings on the reign of King James I
            of England.   **PAINT**

1635   Dutch painter Frans Hals paints *Lucas de Clercq* and *Feyntje van
            Steenkiste*, notable for their monochromatic effects.   **PAINT**

1635–1636   French painter Claude Gellée, known as Claude Lorrain, after his
            birthplace, begins to compile his *Liber Veritatis* (*Book of Truth*), us-
            ing drawings to document his many paintings from that time on.
            One of the greatest landscape painters of all time, his work will in-
            spire the picturesque tradition in England.   **PAINT**

1635   Spanish sculptor Juan Martinez Montañes completes a gilt and poly-
            chromed wood statue of St. John the Baptist for the convent of
            Nuestra Señora de la Concepción in Seville.   **SCULP**

1636   French mathematician Marin Mersenne publishes his most impor-
            tant work, *Harmonie Universelle*, covering experiments on the phys-
            ical properties of sound and detailing contemporary musical
            instruments.   **MUSIC**

c. 1636   French painter Nicolas Poussin paints *Rape of the Sabine Women*,
            which exemplifies the artist's rational, linear style and his devotion
            to classical design and themes. Poussin, the most influential French
            painter of the seventeenth century, is the leading exponent of
            French classical style (sometimes called baroque classicism).
            Sources of his paintings during the 1630s include Roman mytholo-
            gy and the Old Testament.   **PAINT**

1636   Rembrandt paints *The Blinding of Samson*, notable for its turbulence
            and dramatic lighting, influenced by Caravaggio.   **PAINT**

1637   *Le Cid*, a tragicomedy by the French playwright Pierre Corneille, is
            produced in Paris.   **DRAMA**

1637   Teatro San Cassiano, the first public opera house, opens in Venice, with a paying clientele including all social classes. This transformation of opera from courtly entertainment to a public spectacle leads to changes in both music and libretto that will include more lavish staging, more characters, bolder musical effects, and more plot complications and burlesque comic episodes. Virtuoso soloists are featured and aria and recitative become two distinct forms.   **MUSIC**

1638   English poet John Milton publishes the elegy *Lycidas* in a volume of verses memorializing his deceased Cambridge classmate Edward King.   **LIT**

1639   *Chi soffre speri* by Marco Marazzoli and Virgilio Mazzocchi, the first comic opera, is presented in Rome.   **MUSIC**

1639   The opera *Adone* by Italian composer Claudio Monteverdi is produced at Teatro San Cassiano, Venice.   **MUSIC**

1639   French painter Nicolas Poussin paints *The Gathering of the Manna*.   **PAINT**

1640s   In the last decade of his life, Rubens paints *Hélène Fourment with Two of Her Children*, *The Judgment of Paris*, *Three Graces*, and *Venus and Adonis*.   **PAINT**

1640   *Horace*, a tragedy by French playwright Pierre Corneille, opens in Paris. *Cinna* and *Polyeucte*, also tragedies, will open in 1641 and 1642, respectively.   **DRAMA**

1640   Dutch painter Philips Wouwerman establishes his career by joining a painters' guild. A student of Frans Hals, he becomes known for his hilly landscapes, usually with horses.   **PAINT**

1640   French painter Nicolas Poussin, resident in Rome since the 1620s, returns to Paris briefly to oversee the decoration of the Grande Galerie of the Louvre and paint altarpieces. After unpleasant intrigues, he will return to Rome in 1642.   **PAINT**

1641   English poet John Milton publishes three anti-episcopal pamphlets, *Of Reformation in England, Of Prelatical Episcopacy,* and *Animadversions Upon the Remonstrant's Defence Against SMECTYMNUUS*.   **LIT**

1641   Claudio Monteverdi's first public opera *Il Ritorno d'Ulisse in patria* is produced in Venice.   **MUSIC**

1641   Dutch painter Frans Hals paints *Regents of the St. Elizabeth Hospital*, marking a shift to darker, more sober group portraits than his earlier work.   **PAINT**

1641   Italian sculptor, architect, and painter Bernini, skilled in creating portrait busts, executes the bust of Cardinal Richelieu, which earns him an invitation to work at the court of Louis XIV in Paris. He will sculpt the bust of Louis XIV in 1655.   **SCULP**

1642–1652　Italian sculptor, architect, and painter Bernini builds the Cornaro Chapel. With his marble group *Ecstasy of St. Theresa*, it exemplifies his ideal of joining sculpture, architecture, and painting in a harmonious whole. **ARCH**

1642　German painter and engraver Ludwig von Siegen of Utrecht invents the mezzotint, a method of engraving in tone. **GRAPH**

1642　English physician and writer Sir Thomas Browne publishes *Religio Medici* (*A Doctor's Faith*), a masterpiece of seventeenth century prose in which the author examines his own religious beliefs. **LIT**

1642　Monteverdi's opera *L'Incoronazione di Poppea* (the first on a historical rather than mythological subject), is given at Teatro di Santi Giovanni e Paolo in Venice, Europe's second public opera house. **MUSIC**

1642　Rembrandt paints *The Shooting Company of Captain Frans Banning Cocq*, also known as *The Night Watch*, his most famous group portrait. **PAINT**

1642　Spanish painter José de Ribera paints *The Clubfooted Boy*. **PAINT**

1643–1715　The Louis XIV (Louis Quatorze) style of decoration and architecture, with its classical rationality and formality, prevails in France. It extends to textile, furniture, and ornaments. **DECO**

1643–1645　English poet John Milton publishes a series of tracts advocating the legality of divorce on grounds of incompatibility. He writes these shortly after being abandoned by his wife Mary Powell; she will later return to him and bear him three daughters. During the same period he publishes *Areopagitica*, a classical oration in favor of freedom of the press, and the treatise *Of Education*. **LIT**

1643　Francesco Cavalli, the first popular opera composer in Venice, presents *Egisto*. **MUSIC**

....

"Art hath no enemy but ignorance."
—English pamphleteer John Taylor, To John Booker, translating a Latin proverb, 1644

....

1644–1911　During the Ch'ing (Manchu) dynasty in China, many encyclopedias, compendia, and works of literary and philological scholarship are composed. **LIT**

1645　English poet John Milton publishes a volume of his early poems, including *L'Allegro*, *Il Penseroso*, and *At a Solemn Music*. **LIT**

1645　French composer Jean-Baptiste Lully becomes violinist at the French court. **MUSIC**

1645   Cardinal Mazarin encourages the production of Italian operas in France. *La Finta Pazza* by Francesco Paolo Sacrati may be the first opera produced in Paris.   **MUSIC**

1646   English poet Richard Crashaw publishes *Steps to the Temple*, a collection of his devotional verses, influenced by contemporary Italian models and infused with the spiritual concerns that led him to convert to Catholicism.   **LIT**

1646   English physician and writer Sir Thomas Browne publishes *Pseudodoxia Epidemica* (*Vulgar Errors*), a compendium of delusive beliefs with Browne's refutations of them.   **LIT**

1647   English poet Abraham Cowley's *The Mistress*, a collection of witty metaphysical love lyrics, is published.   **LIT**

1648–1651   Italian sculptor, architect, and painter Bernini designs the *Fountain of the Four Rivers* in Rome.   **ARCH**

1648   English poet Robert Herrick publishes the collection *Hesperides*, which contains 1,200 poems heavily influenced by classical models and his association with poet Ben Jonson. A section called *Noble Numbers* includes poems on sacred themes. Among Herrick's best known works is "To the Virgins, to Make Much of Time," which begins, "Gather ye rosebuds while ye may."   **LIT**

1648   In France King Louis XIV establishes the Royal Academy of Painting and Sculpture, later reorganized by Jean-Baptiste Colbert (1663). French painter Charles Le Brun will become director in 1663 and issue a rigid curriculum of instruction in practice and theory.   **SCULP**

1649   English poet John Milton publishes *The Tenure of Kings and Magistrates* and *Eikonoklastes*, pamphlets attacking monarchy and justifying the execution that year of King Charles I. Milton is made Secretary of Foreign Tongues to English leader Oliver Cromwell's Council of State.   **LIT**

1649   English poet Richard Lovelace publishes the verse collection *Lucasta*, which includes "To Althea, from Prison" and "To Lucasta, Going to the Wars." A second *Lucasta* volume will be published posthumously in 1657.   **LIT**

1649   Italian composer Francesco Cavalli's opera *Giasone* is given in Venice.   **MUSIC**

1650   English metaphysical poet Henry Vaughan publishes *Silex Scintillans* (*The Fiery Flint*), a collection of devotional verses on the theme of the hard heart producing a spiritual flame when struck by divinely ordained afflictions. Influenced by George Herbert, the poems include "Peace," which begins, "My soul, there is a country/Far beyond the stars . . ."   **LIT**

1650	Spanish painter José de Ribera paints *The Adoration of the Shepherds*. **PAINT**

1651   English metaphysical poet Henry Vaughan publishes *Olor Iscanus* (*The Swan of Usk*), a collection of poems on his native Wales.   **LIT**

1651   By now, English poet John Milton is effectively blind, though he continues to write, producing such pamphlets as *Defensio Pro Populo Anglicano* (*Defence of the English People*), to be followed in 1654 by *Defensio Secunda* (*Second Defence*).   **LIT**

1651   English philosopher Thomas Hobbes publishes *Leviathan*, a treatise on political philosophy arguing that absolute obedience to supreme state authority when it is successful in maintaining the peace is needed to prevent people from destroying each other.   **LIT**

1651   English poet and dramatist Sir William Davenant publishes the verse epic *Gondibert*.   **LIT**

1652   The minuet, a French country dance, becomes fashionable at court when King Louis XIV is said to dance the first minuet composed by Jean-Baptiste Lully. It quickly spreads throughout Europe, superseding older types of dance, and establishing a new period of dance music.   **DANCE**

1652–1653   Perhaps the greatest etcher of all time, Rembrandt creates such etchings as *Christ Preaching* (1652) and *The Three Crosses* (1653). He will rework the latter in the 1660s. Rembrandt also becomes known for his drawings done with reed pen.   **GRAPH**

1652   *Carmen Deo Nostro* (*A Song to Our Lord*), a final collection of English poet Richard Crashaw's work, is published posthumously.   **LIT**

1652–1654   Englishwoman Dorothy Osborne writes letters to her fiancé, essayist and diplomat Sir William Temple. These will be published in 1888 and admired by such writers as Virginia Woolf.   **LIT**

1652   John Hilton publishes his famous collection of English catches, rounds, and canons, *Catch As Catch Can*.   **MUSIC**

1652   Dutch painter Carel Fabritius paints *The Goldfinch*.   **PAINT**

1653   English writer Izaak Walton publishes *The Compleat Angler*, the classic treatise on fishes and fishing.   **LIT**

1653   The elaborate masque, *Cupid and Death*, with music by Matthew Locke and Christopher Gibbons, is produced.   **MUSIC**

1653   Jean-Baptiste Lully becomes court composer for instrumental music for Louis XIV in France.   **MUSIC**

1653   Rembrandt paints *Aristotle Contemplating the Bust of Homer*.   **PAINT**

1653   Dutch painter Jacob van Ruisdael paints *Bentheim Castle*.   **PAINT**

1655   Now completely blind, English poet John Milton writes the sonnet "When I consider how my light is spent," which ends, "They also serve who only stand and wait." He also publishes the pamphlet *Pro Se Defensio/Defence of Himself.*   **LIT**

1655   Rembrandt paints *The Polish Rider* and *The Slaughtered Ox.*   **PAINT**

1656   The first English opera, *The Siege of Rhodes*, with libretto by Sir William Davenant and music by Matthew Locke and others, is produced at Rutland House in London.   **MUSIC**

1656   Spanish painter Diego Velázquez paints *The Maids of Honor*, remarkable for its fluid brushwork and rich color.   **PAINT**

1657   English poet Abraham Cowley's *Miscellanies*, published this year, includes his uncompleted epic poem, *Davideis*, and irregular odes in imitation of Pindar.   **LIT**

1657   Adam Krieger, master of German baroque lieder, presents *Deutsche Lieder*.   **MUSIC**

1658–1670   Italian sculptor, architect, and painter Bernini designs San Andrea al Quirinale church.   **ARCH**

1658   On October 24 French playwright Jean-Baptiste Molière and his troupe so impress King Louis XIV with performances of Corneille's *Nicomède* and Molière's own comedy *Le Docteur amoureux* (*The Doctor in Love*) that he grants them use of a Paris theater, launching Molière in his career as a writer.   **DRAMA**

1658   English physician and writer Sir Thomas Browne publishes *Hydriotaphia: Urne-Buriall*, a discussion of funeral practices that branches into a meditation on life and death, and *The Garden of Cyrus*, a treatise on the quincunx, a particular kind of five-spot pattern.   **LIT**

1659   Italian sculptor, architect, and painter Bernini begins the Palazzo Chigi-Odescalchi, which strongly influences baroque palace architecture.   **ARCH**

1659   French playwright Molière's comedy *Les Précieuses ridicules* (*The Affect Ladies*) is produced. It will be followed by Molière comedies *Sganarelle, ou Le Cocu imaginaire* (*Sganarelle, or the Imaginary Cuckold*, 1660), *L'École des maris* (*The School for Husbands*, 1661) and *Les Fâcheux* (*The Bores*, 1661).   **DRAMA**

c. 1660s   Dutch painter Jan Vermeer paints several genre paintings famed for their serenity, harmony, and exquisite lighting. Usually involving everyday activities in domestic settings, they include *Young Woman with Water Jug* and *Lady Reading a Letter*. His landscape *View of Delft* also dates from this period.   **PAINT**

1660   Women begin to act in plays in London. Previously, men had almost always performed both male and female roles. Women had begun to appear on stage in Italy and France somewhat earlier.   **DRAMA**

1660   In protest of the impending restoration of the English monarchy, John Milton publishes the pamphlet *The Ready and Easy Way to Establish a Free Commonwealth*. With the monarchy restored later this year, Milton's works are publicly burned and Milton himself is imprisoned, released only after payment of a large fine.   **LIT**

1660   English poet John Dryden celebrates the Restoration of King Charles II with the poem *Astrae Redux*.   **LIT**

1660–1669   English politician Samuel Pepys keeps his *Diary*. Active in the politics of the day, Pepys recreates a lively social tableau in his writings. Parts of the work will be first published in 1825.   **LIT**

1660   Italian composer Francesco Cavalli's opera *Serse* is performed for the marriage of Louis XIV in France.   **MUSIC**

c. 1660   Dutch landscape painter Jacob van Ruisdael paints *The Jewish Cemetery*.   **PAINT**

1661   French painter Charles Le Brun designs the Galerie d'Apollon at the Louvre.   **ARCH**

1661   In France Louis XIV founds the Académie Royale de Danse.   **MUSIC**

1661   English composer Matthew Locke becomes court composer to Charles II.   **MUSIC**

1661   French painter Charles Le Brun, known for his decorative classicism influenced by Poussin, paints *The Family of Darius Before Alexander*.   **PAINT**

1661   Dutch-born painter Sir Peter Lely, acclaimed as the "best artist in England," is named principal painter to the Restoration court of King Charles II. His works include *The Windsor Beauties*, *Flagmen*, and *The Family of the Earl of Carnarvon*.   **PAINT**

1662   King Louis XIV of France takes control of the Gobelins tapestry works. Under Jean-Baptiste Colbert and director of the works Charles Le Brun, Gobelins will produce lavish furnishings of all kinds for the royal palaces. Because of the king's financial troubles, it will return to making only tapestries after 1699.   **DECO**

1662   French playwright Molière's *L'École des femmes* (*The School for Wives*) is produced. *La Critique de l'École des femmes* and *L'Impromptu de Versailles*, both of which will be produced in 1663, will be Molière's humorous counterattacks on his critics.   **DRAMA**

1662   Rembrandt paints *The Syndics of the Cloth Guild*, often considered the apex of Dutch portait painting.   **PAINT**

1662   French painter Charles Le Brun becomes painter to King Louis XIV. Le Brun will dominate French painting, design, and artistic theory for decades.   **PAINT**

1663   Drury Lane, perhaps London's most famous theater, opens. There will be a second and third Drury Lane, and the fourth, which will open in 1812, continues in operation to the present day.   **DRAMA**

1663   English satirist Samuel Butler publishes the first part of *Hudibras*, a mock-heroic poem satirizing the Puritan regime recently unseated by the restoration of King Charles II. Part two will follow in 1664, part three in 1678.   **LIT**

1663   French politician Jean-Baptiste Colbert changes the focus of the Royal Academy of Painting and Sculpture to exercise central control over artistic theory, teaching, and exhibition. Painter Charles Le Brun serves as director of the academy, under Colbert's supervision. Colbert's program of patronage and strict domination of the arts helps to make France more important than Italy as Europe's artistic center. *See also* 1648, SCULP; 1662, DECO.   **MISC**

1664   Flemish painter Adam Frans van der Meulen moves to Paris, where he becomes an assistant to Charles Le Brun, making paintings and designs for tapestries, often depicting contemporary battles.   **DECO**

1664   *Le Mariage forcé* (*The Forced Marriage*) and *La Princesse d'Elide*, two comedies by French playwright Molière, are produced. Molière also produces the first three acts of *Tartuffe*, his controversial attack on religious hypocrisy. A revised version of *Tartuffe* will be performed once in 1667, but the play will be denounced and banned until 1669.   **DRAMA**

1664   *La Thébaïde, ou Les Frères ennemis* (*The Thebaid, or the Enemy Brothers*), the first play by French playwright Jean Racine, is staged by French playwright Molière. Racine's tragedy *Alexandre le Grand* (*Alexander the Great*) will be produced in 1665.   **DRAMA**

1664   German composer Heinrich Schütz's *Christmas Oratorio*, performed in Dresden, strikes a balance between Italianate style and solid contrapuntal Lutheran tradition.   **MUSIC**

1664   Dutch painter Frans Hals, now eighty-four, paints *The Governors of the Almshouse* and *Lady Regents of the Almshouse*, two moving group portraits that mark the climax of his career. Hals dies two years later.   **PAINT**

1665–1667   Italian architect Francesco Borromini designs San Carlo alle Quattro Fontane in Rome, the walls of which have a powerful sense of dynamic movement.   **ARCH**

1665   French playwright Molière's comedy *L'Amour Médecin* (*Love's the Best Doctor*) is produced. His comedies *Le Misanthrope* and *Le Médecin malgré lui* (*The Doctor in Spite of Himself*) will be produced in 1666, and *L'Avare* (*The Miser*) and *Amphitryon* will be produced in 1668. *The Miser* is derived from Plautus's *Aulularia* (*The Pot of Gold*).   **DRAMA**

1665   Dutch painter Rembrandt paints *The Jewish Bride*, notable for its psychological depth and flamelike color.   **PAINT**

1666   The great London fire this year forces rebuilding of many edifices. English architect Sir Christopher Wren redesigns many formerly Gothic churches in baroque style. *See* 1675–1710, ARCH.   **ARCH**

1666   English preacher and writer John Bunyan publishes his spiritual autobiography, *Grace Abounding to the Chief of Sinners*.   **LIT**

1666   Italian composer Antonio Cesti becomes Kapellmeister at the court in Vienna.   **MUSIC**

1666–1737 Italian violin maker Antonio Stradivari begins making violins. He will make more than 1000 instruments, including violins, violas, and cellos.   **MUSIC**

1667   English poet John Dryden's comedy *Secret Love* is performed.   **DRAMA**

1667   English poet John Milton publishes his masterpiece, *Paradise Lost*, a blank verse epic on the Fall of Man and the expulsion of Adam and Eve from Eden. Proposing to "justify the ways of God to men," the epic's form is modeled on the works of Homer and Virgil. A second edition in 1674, the year of Milton's death, will expand the poem from ten books to twelve. A companion work, *Paradise Regained*, will appear in 1671.   **LIT**

1667   English poet John Dryden publishes the poem *Annus Mirabilis* (*The Year of Wonders*).   **LIT**

1667   The French Royal Academy of Painting and Sculpture holds its first official annual exhibition, known as the Salon because of its location in the Salon d'Apollon in the Louvre.   **MISC**

1667   Italian composer Antonio Cesti's opera *Il Pomo d'oro* (*The Golden Apple*) is a hit in Vienna.   **MUSIC**

c. 1668   Mexican poet and nun Juana Inés de la Cruz's play *Amor es Mas Laberinto* (*Love is a Greater Labryinth*) is produced. She will write other plays on both religious and secular themes, as well as poetry and essays.   **DRAMA**

1668   English poet John Dryden's heroic tragedy *The Conquest of Granada* is performed.   **DRAMA**

1668   *Les Plaideurs* (*The Litigants*), the only comedy by French playwright Jean Racine, is produced.   **DRAMA**

1668   English poet Abraham Cowley's *Several Discourses by way of Essays, in Verse and Prose* is published posthumously.   **LIT**

1668   John Dryden becomes poet laureate of England and publishes *Essay of Dramatic Poesy*, a critical prose work.   **LIT**

1668   Danish composer Dietrich Buxtehude becomes organist at St. Mary's Church in Lübeck.   **MUSIC**

1669–1710   The palace of Versailles is constructed for King Louis XIV of France. The Garden Front, with its formal classical approach, is designed by French architects Louis Le Vau and Jules Hardouin-Mansart. The interior rooms feature lavish baroque decoration. The gardens, extending for miles, are designed in formal style by André Lenôtre. Charles Le Brun designs the Galerie des Glaces and the Great Staircase.   **ARCH**

1669   Pierre Perrini is granted a Royal patent for founding the Académie Royale des Operas in France, to produce operas in the French language similar to those given in Italy.   **MUSIC**

1669   In his final year Rembrandt paints his last two self-portraits, along with *The Return of the Prodigal Son* and the unfinished *Simeon with the Christ Child in the Temple*.   **PAINT**

1670   The colonnade of the Louvre, designed by Louis Le Vau and Claude Perrault, is completed in Paris.   **ARCH**

1670   *Le Bourgeois gentilhomme* (*The Bourgeois Gentleman*), one of French playwright Molière's finest and best known comedies, is produced. His *Les Amants magnifiques* (*The Magnificent Lovers*) is also produced.   **DRAMA**

1670   *Bérénice*, a tragedy by French playwright Jean Racine, is produced. *Bajazet*, *Mithridate* and *Iphigénie*, all Racine tragedies, will be produced in 1672, 1673, and 1674, respectively.   **DRAMA**

1670   English composer John Blow is organist at Westminster Abbey until 1680.   **MUSIC**

1671   John Milton publishes *Paradise Regained*, a four-book poem on the temptation of Jesus in the wilderness that serves as a companion to *Paradise Lost* (1667), and *Samson Agonistes*, a closet verse tragedy (not meant for performance) on Samson and Delilah.   **LIT**

1671   The opera *Pomone* by Robert Cambert is performed at the opening festivities for the Académie Royale de Musique in Paris and is a great success.   **MUSIC**

1671–1674   Italian sculptor, architect, and painter Bernini sculpts *The Blessed Lodovica Albertoni*.   **SCULP**

1672   Molière's satire *Les Femmes savantes* (*The Learned Ladies*) is pro-
            duced. *Le Malade imaginaire* (*The Imaginary Invalid*), Molière's final
            play, will be produced in 1673, and he will act in it on the night of
            his death.   **DRAMA**

1673   John Milton publishes *Of True Religion, Heresy, Schism, and
            Toleration*.   **LIT**

1673   The opera *Cadmus et Hermione*, by French composer Jean-Baptiste
            Lully, is produced.   **MUSIC**

1674   English poet John Milton dies the same year that the second, ex-
            panded edition of his epic poem *Paradise Lost* is published. *See*
            1667, LIT.   **LIT**

1675–1710   English architect Sir Christopher Wren rebuilds St. Paul's cathedral
            in London, combining classical style and baroque influences.   **ARCH**

1675   English dramatist William Wycherley's comedy *The Country Wife* is
            produced. It will be viewed as one of the masterpieces of
            Restoration drama, and it continues to be revived frequently to the
            present day. Wycherley's comedy *The Plain Dealer* will be produced
            in 1676.   **DRAMA**

1675   English composer Matthew Locke composes incidental music to
            Thomas Shadwell's *Psyche*.   **MUSIC**

1677   The tragedy *Phèdre*, generally seen as the greatest play by French
            playwright Jean Racine, is produced.   **DRAMA**

1677   English poet John Dryden completes *All for Love; or, the World Well
            Lost*, a Restoration tragedy that takes its plot from Shakespeare's
            Antony and Cleopatra. It will be considered by many his greatest
            play.   **DRAMA**

1678   English dramatist and novelist Aphra Behn's comedy *The Rover; or,
            the Banish't Cavaliers* is produced. The story of women who insist
            on sowing their wild oats the way men do, it will be seen as her
            best play. Behn will be the first woman in England to earn a living
            by writing.   **DRAMA**

1678   English preacher and writer John Bunyan publishes *The Pilgrim's
            Progress*, a masterpiece of Christian allegory written largely during
            his imprisonment for refusing to cease his Noncomformist preach-
            ing.   **LIT**

1678   In Hamburg the first German opera house is opened; two years later
            French ballets will be performed for the first time in Germany. **MUSIC**

1679   Italian composer Alessandro Scarlatti's first opera, *Gli equivoci nel
            sembiante*, opens in Rome.   **MUSIC**

Title page and frontispiece for *The Pilgrim's Progress* by John Bunyan.
(Photosearch, Inc.)

1680   La Comédie-Française, ultimately to become France's foremost theater, is founded by King Louis XIV. Run by its *sociétaires* (member actors), it continues to operate to the present day.   **DRAMA**

1681   The collection *Miscellaneous Poems* by English poet Andrew Marvell is published posthumously. Few of his poems have been published before this date, but his reputation will grow with the centuries. Among his best known works are "The Garden," "The Mower's Song," and "To His Coy Mistress," which begins, "Had we but world enough, and time . . ."   **LIT**

1681   English poet John Dryden publishes *Absalom and Achitophel*, a narrative poem in heroic couplets, using an Old Testament story to satirize contemporary politics.   **LIT**

1682   English poet John Dryden publishes his satirical attack on poet and playwright Thomas Shadwell, *Mac Flecknoe*. Shadwell had attacked Dryden in *The Medal of John Bayes* (also 1682). Dryden also publishes *Religio Laici*, a poem on his religious faith.   **LIT**

1682   Following a nearly two-month long captivity during King Philip's War, American Mary Rowlandson writes the immensely popular *Narrative of the Captivity and Restauration of Mrs. Mary Rowlandson.* It is likely the first Indian captivity narrative in print.   **LIT**

1682   French painter Claude Lorrain paints *Ascanius and the Stag.*   **PAINT**

1683   English composer Henry Purcell becomes court composer to King Charles II.   **MUSIC**

1683   French sculptor Pierre Puget completes his emotionally charged marble statue of Milo of Crotona. Puget's baroque style of expressive drama will not be accepted at the French court until after Colbert's death.   **SCULP**

1687   English poet John Dryden's *A Song for St. Cecilia's Day* is performed at a public concert. Dryden's second ode for St. Cecilia's Day, *Alexander's Feast*, will be performed in 1697.   **LIT**

1687   French sculptor François Girardon finishes a wax model derived from the equestrian *Marcus Aurelius* on the Capitoline Hill for an equestrian statue of Louis XIV. The final statue will be destroyed in the French Revolution.   **SCULP**

1688   English dramatist and novelist Aphra Behn publishes the prose romance *Oroonoko.*   **LIT**

1688   English composer Henry Purcell becomes organist at Westminster Abbey, following his teacher John Blow.   **MUSIC**

1689   English poet Andrew Marvell's political satire *The Last Instructions to a Painter*, written in 1667, is published posthumously. Marvell's other satires include *Clarindon's House-Warming* and *The Loyal Scot.*   **LIT**

1689   Japanese poet Matsuo Bashō writes *The Narrow Road to the Deep North*, a work interweaving travel sketches and haiku. He is the most important developer and practitioner of the three-line haiku verse form.   **LIT**

1689   English composer Henry Purcell's dramatic opera *Dido and Aeneas*, written for a fashionable girls' school, is performed.   **MUSIC**

1689   German-born painter Sir Godfrey Kneller and English painter John Riley are jointly named principal painters to William III and Mary II of England. The leading portraitist of his day, Kneller is known for his mass production of high society portraits, employing a large team of artists. Riley is better known for his portraits of ordinary people, including *The Scullion* and *Bridget Holmes.*   **PAINT**

c. 1690   Artists of China's Ch'Ing dynasty decorate porcelain figures in the famille verte palette of enamels that are applied directly onto the unglazed porcelain body.   **DECO**

1690   English composer Henry Purcell's stage music for *Dioclesian* premieres. He will write music for several productions that contain spoken dialogue, including *King Arthur* (1691), *The Fairy Queen* (1692), and *The Tempest* (1695).   **MUSIC**

1691   German organist and theorist Andreas Werckmeister's treatise *Musikalische Temperatur* suggests the octave be divided into twelve equal half-steps.   **MUSIC**

1693   *Teodora*, an opera by Italian composer Alessandro Scarlatti, opens.   **MUSIC**

···

"Music, the greatest good that mortals know,
And all of heaven we have below."
—English essayist and poet Joseph Addison,
"Song for St. Cecilia's Day," 1694

···

1695   *Love for Love*, a Restoration comedy of manners by the English dramatist William Congreve, opens in London.   **DRAMA**

1696   German composer Johann Kuhnau's *Fresh Fruit for the Clavier*, with the sonata as a piece in several contrasting movements, is a harbinger of the classical sonata.   **MUSIC**

···

"Music hath charms to soothe a savage breast,
To soften rocks, or bend a knotted oak."
—English dramatist William Congreve, opening
lines of The Mourning Bride, 1697

···

1697   English poet John Dryden's translation of Virgil's *Aeneid* is published.   **LIT**

1700s   The rich architectural styles of baroque and rococo become popular throughout Europe and reach a peak of expression in Germany and Austria, exemplified in designs such as the German Wurzburg Residenz.   **ARCH**

1700s   *Jōruri* puppet theater, which had existed for at least a century, reaches the height of its popularity in Japan. By now, the puppets are large, with movable eyes, fingers, and feet, and three performers manipulate each one to enact stories written by playwrights.   **DRAMA**

1700s   European actors wear powder makeup, usually mixed with some sort of liquid or grease before application, to help indicate the age and general appearance of the characters they are portraying. In the early 1800s, many will switch to wearing powder-based paint applied over a grease foundation.   **DRAMA**

1700s   The palette knife becomes popular for mixing and scraping paint.   **PAINT**

1700s   Early this century the European art of modeling wax is introduced to America. Colonial artists begin to create small wax portraits. **SCULP**

1700s   Early this century the bourgeoisie begins to build private collections of art. As a result, a market for drawing room figurines and statuettes emerges.   **SCULP**

1700   English dramatist William Congreve's *The Way of the World*, which is viewed by some as the greatest Restoration comedy, is presented.   **DRAMA**

1700   Published in the last year of his life, English poet John Dryden's last major work is *Fables, Ancient and Modern*, which is prefaced by a fine critical essay.   **LIT**

1700   German-born painter Sir Godfrey Kneller paints *Matthew Prior*, one of his first portraits.   **PAINT**

1701   Music publisher Henry Playford establishes a weekly series of concerts at Oxford.   **MUSIC**

1701   French painter Hyacinthe Rigaud paints the majestic state portrait of *Louis XIV*.   **PAINT**

1702   British novelist and journalist Daniel Defoe, a religious dissenter, publishes the satirical pamphlet *The Shortest Way with the Dissenters*, for which he is fined, imprisoned, and pilloried. Defoe will write more than 250 pamphlets.   **LIT**

1702   American clergyman Cotton Mather writes *Magnalia Christi Americana,* a wide-ranging ecclesiastical history of New England that sounds a clarion call for the renaissance of religious spirit in the colonies.   **LIT**

1702   Japanese painter Ogata Kōrin unites the Kano and Yamato imperial schools of painting.   **PAINT**

1703   French sculptor Pierre Le Gros breaks seventeenth-century tradition by placing his polychrome marble statue of St. Stanislas Kostka under the altar at the Convent of Sant'Andrea al Quirinale in Rome.   **SCULP**

1704   English clergyman and writer Jonathan Swift publishes *The Battle of the Books* and *A Tale of a Tub*, two powerful satires on intellectual corruption.   **LIT**

1704–1708   French painter Jean-Antoine Watteau begins his career studying under Claude Gillot, whose preference for theatrical subjects will be shared by Watteau in such paintings as *Love in the French Theater*.   **PAINT**

1705   German-born composer George Frideric Handel's first opera *Almira*, composed at age nineteen, premieres at the Hamburg - opera house.   **MUSIC**

1706–1710   German-born composer George Frideric Handel is in Italy, where his music becomes influenced by the leading musicians of Rome, Florence, Naples, and Venice.   **MUSIC**

1707   Irish playwright George Farquhar's comedy *The Beaux' Strategem* premieres. Farquhar's *The Constant Couple* and *The Recruiting Officer*, both comedies, had been produced in 1700 and 1706, respectively. *The Recruiting Officer* continues to be revived frequently to the present day.   **DRAMA**

1708–1709   The method of manufacturing porcelain is discovered in Europe at Meissen, Germany, near Dresden.   **DECO**

1708   German composer Johann Sebastian Bach becomes court organist, chamber musician, and concertmaster to the Duke of Weimar. **MUSIC**

1708   Bavarian sculptor Andreas Schlüter erects his bronze equestrian statue of Frederick William I in front of the royal palace.   **SCULP**

CRACKING PORCELAIN

*U*ntil the eighteenth century one of the best-kept secrets of the trade between China and the West was porcelain. Europeans loved the white, thin, strong pottery, miraculous for its translucent, shimmering quality. But because no European could figure out how to make it, porcelain in the West remained a rare and costly commodity from its introduction in the thirteenth century. In time, French, Italian, and English potters learned to make a handsome facsimile out of a mixture of clay and ground glass with a modified lead glaze. But this soft paste or artificial porcelain was still far from the real thing.

The secret of porcelain was finally cracked in 1708–1709 at Meissen, Saxony, by German chemist Johann Friedrich Böttger, who combined a clay base with ground feldspar. This mixture, it turned out, duplicated the Chinese formula which combined kaolin (china clay) and a ground feldspathic rock called petuntse. The Chinese monopoly was broken, and porcelain became increasingly available in Europe.

1709–1711	Under the pseudonym Isaac Bickerstaff (first used by Jonathan Swift), English essayists Sir Richard Steele and Joseph Addison publish the periodical *The Tatler*. Appearing three times a week, the paper presents urbane, reasoned views on entertainment, poetry, and society. **LIT**
1709	English poet Alexander Pope's first published work is *The Pastorals*. **LIT**
1709	The first pianoforte (later shortened to piano) is made by Bartolomeo Christofori of Florence. Unlike the earlier harpsichord, its strings are struck by hammers activated by keys, allowing the loudness of its sound to be varied by the touch of the fingers. By the end of the eighteenth century it becomes the principal keyboard instrument in Europe and America. **MUSIC**
1709	The oldest known portrait effigy from New England is a carved gravestone for Reverend Jonathan Pierpont in Wakefield, Massachusetts. **SCULP**
1710	German-born composer George Frideric Handel becomes music director at the electoral court at Hanover, Germany. **MUSIC**
1710	French sculptor Antoine Coysevox creates a marble statue of Marie-Adelaide of Savoy, the Duchess of Burgundy, portrayed as the goddess Diana. **SCULP**
1711	English clergyman and writer Jonathan Swift publishes the ironic *Argument Against Abolishing Christianity*. **LIT**
1711–1712	English essayists Joseph Addison and Sir Richard Steele publish the daily periodical *The Spectator*, the successor to *The Tatler* (1709–1711). Addison will revive it briefly in 1714. **LIT**
1711	English poet Alexander Pope publishes *Essay on Criticism*, a didactic poem in the manner of Roman poet Horace. **LIT**
1711	The clarinet is used for the first time in an orchestra. **MUSIC**
1711	The oratorio *Rinaldo*, by German-born composer George Frideric Handel, is a sensation when it premieres at London's Haymarket Theater. Handel will stay in England permanently as of 1712. **MUSIC**
1711	English trumpeter John Shore invents the tuning fork, an instrument used to indicate absolute pitch. **MUSIC**
1712	English poet Alexander Pope publishes the first version of his mock-epic poem *The Rape of the Lock*; an expanded edition will appear in 1714. **LIT**
1713	In England the Scriblerus Club is formed, an association of Tory writers and intellectuals, including Jonathan Swift, Alexander Pope, John Gay, Thomas Parnell, and John Arbuthnot. **LIT**
1714	German sculptor Balthasar Permoser collaborates with architect Mathäus Pöppelmann to decorate the Zwinger at Dresden. **SCULP**

1715–1723   Fine curved lines and bronze reliefs are characteristic of Régence style in France, named for the regency of Philippe II, duc d'Orléans.   **DECO**

c. 1715   Chinese novelist Ts'ao Hsueh-ch'in is born (*d.* 1763). His most famous work will be the psychologically subtle autobiographical work *Hung lou meng* (*The Dream of the Red Chamber*), about the fall of an aristocratic family.   **LIT**

1715–1720   English poet Alexander Pope publishes his translation of Homer's *Iliad* in heroic couplets. It is a great commercial success, as is his translation of *The Odyssey*, making him one of the first nondramatic poets to earn enough from writing to enable him to live independently.   **LIT**

c. 1715   In France the rococo style of painting, decoration, and architecture emerges, marked by grace, lightness, and refinement. Rococo decoration incorporates such motifs as flowers, shells, and scrolls. Great French rococo painters include Watteau, Boucher, and Fragonard. In architecture, Gabriel, and in sculpture, Falconet, embody rococo principles. Associated with Louis XV style, rococo will spread throughout eighteenth-century Europe. *See* 1723–1774, DECO.   **MISC**

1715   Vaudeville, popular musical comedies, appear in Paris.   **MUSIC**

1715   English painter and writer Jonathan Richardson writes *An Essay on the Theory of Painting*, a treatise on the seriousness of painting that influences painter Joshua Reynolds, among others.   **PAINT**

1717   David Garrick, who will become one of the greatest English actors, is born in Hereford, England (*d.* 1779). An extraordinarily versatile and creative performer, Garrick will do some of his best work playing Abel Drugger in Ben Jonson's *The Alchemist*, Archer in George Farquhar's *The Beaux' Strategem*, and the title character in Shakespeare's *Hamlet*.   **DRAMA**

1717   English poet Alexander Pope's *Collected Poems* is published, including "Ode for Music on St. Cecilia's Day," "Eloisa to Abelard," and "Elegy to the Memory of an Unfortunate Lady."   **LIT**

1717   The orchestral suite *Water Music* by German-born composer George Frideric Handel is performed.   **MUSIC**

1717   German composer Johann Sebastian Bach becomes concert master to Prince Leopold of Anhalt-Coethan, where he will write many instrumental compositions for solo and group performance.   **MUSIC**

1717–1718   Italian opera is fashionable in England. The Royal Academy of Music organizes to present operas to the London public.   **MUSIC**

1717   French painter Jean-Antoine Watteau paints *Embarkation for Cythera*, a work of sensuous brushwork and pastel tones that wins him admission to the Royal Academy. Watteau's style influences not only painting but fashion and garden design.   **PAINT**

1718–1721   The six Brandenburg Concertos, dedicated to Duke Christian Ludwig of Brandenburg, are composed by German composer Johann Sebastian Bach. They represent the artistic peak of the baroque concerto.   **MUSIC**

1719   English novelist and journalist Daniel Defoe publishes the novel *Robinson Crusoe*, based on the true story of shipwrecked sailor Alexander Selkirk.   **LIT**

1719   George Frideric Handel becomes director of the Royal Academy of Music, where he will write some of his most accomplished operas.   **MUSIC**

1720   Haymarket Theatre opens in London. It will be rebuilt in 1820 and will be London's leading theater in the mid-nineteenth century. It continues in operation to the present day.   **DRAMA**

1720   English painter and engraver William Hogarth begins working in London as an engraver of billheads and book illustrations.   **GRAPH**

1721   German composer Georg Philipp Telemann arrives in Hamburg as director of music.   **MUSIC**

1721   The Bishop of Toledo hires Spanish sculptor Narciso Tomé to execute a monument to the Blessed Sacrament for the Toledo cathedral. Tomé's Transparente Altar, which will combine polychrome marbles, gilt stucco work, and frescoes, will be completed in 1732.   **SCULP**

1722   *La Surprise de l'amour* (*The Surprise of Love*), a romantic drama by French playwright and novelist Pierre Carlet de Marivaux, is produced. The unusual sensitivity and subtlety of his dialogue can be seen here and will be evident in most of his many other plays, including *La Double Inconstance* (*The Double Inconstancy*, 1723).   **DRAMA**

1722   Novels published this year by prolific English novelist and journalist Daniel Defoe include *Moll Flanders, A Journal of the Plague Year,* and *Colonel Jack.*   **LIT**

1722   German composer Johann Sebastian Bach completes Book I of *The Well-Tempered Clavier* as teaching materials for his children. Book II will be completed in 1744.   **MUSIC**

1722   *Treatise of Harmony* by French composer Jean-Philippe Rameau is published in Paris. This landmark development in the theories of harmony shifts the emphasis away from counterpoint to a symphonic style using chords.   **MUSIC**

1722   Austrian sculptor Johann Lukas von Hildebrandt creates marble fig-
              ures to be used as pillars in the Hall of Atlantes at the Upper
              Belvedere Palace in Vienna. The sequence will influence eighteenth-
              century architects through its interaction of decorative and spatial
              volumes.   **SCULP**

1723–1774   The Louis XV (Louis Quinze) period of decoration and architecture
              prevails in France, characterized by rococo ornamentation and
              chinoiserie, decoration influenced by Chinese art. Chinoiserie in in-
              teriors, furniture, and textiles will influence the English cabinetmak-
              er Thomas Chippendale and become a popular feature of American
              colonial style.   **DECO**

1723   German composer Johann Sebastian Bach becomes cantor at St.
              Thomas's school in Leipzig, Germany, where he will write many of
              his cantatas and choral masterpieces.   **MUSIC**

1724   Irish-born English clergyman and writer Jonathan Swift earns fame
              as an Irish patriot when he publishes the *Drapier Letters*. Written
              under the pseudonym "M.B., Drapier," the public letters urge the
              populace not to accept debased coinage from England.   **LIT**

1724   The Three Choirs Festival, combining the choral forces of
              Gloucester, Hartford, and Worcester, is founded in England. **MUSIC**

1725–1775   Rococo, an artistic style characterized by frivolous elegance and
              luxury that began in France about 1700, spreads to Germany and
              Italy. Its musical counterpart, gallante style, emphasizing pleasant-
              nesses and prettiness, replaces the impressive grandeur of the
              baroque style.   **MUSIC**

1725   The Prague opera house (Standetheater) is founded.   **MUSIC**

1725   Four violin concertos by Italian composer Antonio Vivaldi, collec-
              tively known as *The Four Seasons*, are published.   **MUSIC**

1726   The Belgian ballerina Marie de Camargo debuts at the Paris
              Opera.   **DANCE**

1726   English clergyman and writer Jonathan Swift publishes his greatest
              work, *Gulliver's Travels*, a satirical account of Dr. Lemuel Gulliver's
              adventures in Lilliput, Brobdingnag, Laputa, Houyhnhnmland, and
              elsewhere.   **LIT**

1727   His Majesty's Admiralty Office in New England announces that
              carved motifs other than the lion may be used for ships' figure-
              heads. Human figures will begin to appear after 1750.   **DECO**

c. 1727–   Giovanni Battista Tiepolo, the greatest Italian painter of the eigh-
    1728   teenth century, paints the fresco cycle in the Archbishop's Palace in
              Udine. His work is rich, grand, and colorful in the tradition of Italian
              decorative painting.   **PAINT**

1728   English playwright John Gay's *The Beggar's Opera* is produced. The
            first ballad opera (a genre satirizing Italian opera that was to be-
            come popular at this time), it includes songs arranged by John
            Christopher Pepusch. Its tale of the highwayman Macheath will be
            the basis for Bertolt Brecht and Kurt Weill's *The Threepenny Opera*
            (1928).   **DRAMA**

1728   English poet Alexander Pope publishes the mock epic satire *The
            Dunciad*, in which he wittily and mercilessly attacks his literary ene-
            mies, especially critic Lewis Theobald and playwright Colley Cibber.
            An expanded edition will be published in 1743.   **LIT**

1728   French painter Jean-Baptiste-Siméon Chardin is received into the
            Royal Academy for his still life *The Rayfish*. Chardin is known for his
            naturalistic still lifes and simple, serious genre paintings, often set
            in kitchen interiors. His works also include *Benediction, Return from
            Market, Blowing Bubbles, Madame Chardin, Pipe and Jug,* and *The
            Young Governess*.   **PAINT**

1729   English clergyman and writer Jonathan Swift publishes the satirical
            pamphlet *A Modest Proposal*, which ironically advocates the eating
            of the Irish by the English.   **LIT**

1729–1766   American statesman and writer Benjamin Franklin purchases the
            weekly periodical *The Pennsylvania Gazette* from publisher Samuel
            Keimer and brings it to success, imprinting it with his views. The
            weekly will remain in print until 1815.   **LIT**

1729   The choral work *Passion According to St. Matthew* by German com-
            poser Johann Sebastian Bach premieres at St. Thomas's church in
            Leipzig on Good Friday.   **MUSIC**

1729   Spanish sculptor Pedro de Ribera mixes French, Italian, and native
            Spanish motifs in his stone decoration of the portal of the Hospicio
            de San Fernando in Madrid.   **SCULP**

1730s   Colonial American cabinetmakers and artisan carvers begin to copy
            the more elaborate models illustrated in European design books. **DECO**

1730s   Lavish stucco decorations appear on the facades of private houses
            throughout Bavaria.   **DECO**

1730   Scottish poet James Thomson publishes the collected edition of *The
            Seasons*, consisting of *Winter, Summer, Spring,* and *Autumn*. The
            work will remain popular throughout the eighteenth century.   **LIT**

1731   English clergyman and writer Jonathan Swift, still very much alive,
            publishes the ironic poem *Verses on the Death of Dr. Swift*.   **LIT**

1731–1735   English poet Alexander Pope's book of poems *Moral Essays* (or
            Ethics) is published.   **LIT**

1731   The first public concert on record in America is held in Boston,
            Massachusetts.   **MUSIC**

Music of the Cantata no. 112 by Johann Sebastian Bach. *(Pierpont Morgan Library, Mary Flagler Cary Music Collection, 1968)*

c. 1731   English painter and engraver William Hogarth paints the six scenes of *A Harlot's Progress*, a "morality play" in which a sequence of anecdotal pictures is used to make moral and satirical points. Having invented this form, Hogarth popularizes it with engravings of this sequence and later ones.   **PAINT**

1732   French writer François-Marie Arouet, known as Voltaire, writes *Zaïre*. Based on Shakespeare's *Othello*, it will generally be considered his dramatic masterpiece. However, most of his plays will not prove enduring, and he will be remembered for his writing in other genres.   **DRAMA**

1732–1757   American statesman and writer Benjamin Franklin publishes *Poor Richard's Almanack*, an annual compendium of practical information and plain philosophical thinking.   **LIT**

1732   *Sonate da Cimbalo di piano e forte*, probably the first compositions for modern piano, are published by Italian composer Lodovico Giustini.   **MUSIC**

1732   The Academy of Ancient Music is founded in London.   **MUSIC**

1732   The Covent Garden Opera House opens in London.   **MUSIC**

1733–1734   English poet Alexander Pope publishes the four poetic epistles of his *Essay on Man*, establishing him as a philosophical and ethical poet.   **LIT**

1733   English poet Alexander Pope publishes *Imitations of Horace*.   **LIT**

1735   The Imperial ballet school is founded at St. Petersburg, Russia.   **DANCE**

1735   English poet Alexander Pope publishes a complete version of *An Epistle to Dr. Arbuthnot* (an early version appeared in 1727). The poem will be regarded as Pope's most masterful rhetorical performance in the mode of Horace.   **LIT**

1735   The ballad opera *Flora* at Charleston, South Carolina, is the first musical theater presentation in the English colonies.   **MUSIC**

1735   English painter and engraver William Hogarth paints *The Rake's Progress* (eight scenes), his best known "morality play." *See also* c. 1731, PAINT.   **PAINT**

1735   English painter and engraver William Hogarth opens an academy in London, forerunner of The Royal Academy. Hogarth helps to establish a British style distinct from that of the continent.   **PAINT**

1737   Bavarian sculptor Johann Baptist Zimmerman completes his French-influenced stuccoes throughout the shooting lodge of Amalienburg in the park of Schloss Nymphenburg.   **SCULP**

1738   English critic and writer Samuel Johnson publishes the poem *London*, an imitation of Juvenal's tenth satire.   **LIT**

1738   Planned excavation begins at Pompeii and Herculaneum in Italy. The archaeological discoveries prompt a revival of interest in classical antiquity that spurs the neoclassical movement in art and architecture. *See* 79, MISC; 1760s, DECO.   **MISC**

1738   German composer Johann Sebastian Bach completes his *Mass in B minor*.   **MUSIC**

1738   French sculptor Nicolas-Sébastien Adam begins work on a minutely detailed marble figurine of Prometheus. It will be completed in 1762 and submitted to the Royal Academy.   **SCULP**

1739   The dramatic oratorio *Saul*, by German-born composer George Frideric Handel, is well received in London. It signals the start of his commitment to the English oratorio, which appeals to a middle-class audience uncomfortable with aristocratic Italian opera.   **MUSIC**

1740s   Stone portrait busts appear as grave markers from Massachusetts to South Carolina.   **SCULP**

1740   German architect Johann Balthasar Neumann decorates the grand staircase at the Schloss Augustusburg in Brühl with polychrome stuccoes and wrought-iron railings.   **DECO**

1740   American wood-carver Simeon Skillin opens his shop to create work for the furniture shops and shipyards of Boston. His sons, John and Simeon Jr., will work in the shop until 1778 and become New England's leading carvers.   **DECO**

1740   English novelist Samuel Richardson publishes the novel *Pamela: or Virtue Rewarded*, which will be parodied by Henry Fielding in *Shamela* (1741) and *Joseph Andrews* (1742).   **LIT**

1740–1780   Under the reign of Maria Theresa, the queen of Bohemia and Hungary who exercises power over the Holy Roman Empire, Vienna develops into an important center for music and the arts.   **MISC**

c. 1740   English painter and engraver William Hogarth paints *The Shrimp Girl* and *Captain Coram*.   **PAINT**

1740   French sculptor Robert Le Lorrain completes his stone decorative reliefs on the Hôtel de Rohan, Paris. Le Lorrain will play a leading role in the emergence of rococo sculpture.   **SCULP**

1740   The lead Basin of Neptune, by French sculptors and brothers Lambert-Sigisbert and Nicolas-Sébastien Adam, is added to Louis XIV's seventeenth-century ensemble in the gardens of Versailles. **SCULP**

1741   American theologian Jonathan Edwards publishes his sermon, *Sinners in the Hands of an Angry God,* which details his seminal ideas about the inadequacies of humans and the need for salvation from God. The work vividly describes the horrors of Hell for the unrepentant.   **LIT**

1742   German-born composer George Frideric Handel's oratorio *Messiah* premieres at the New Music Hall in Dublin. **MUSIC**

1742   English painter and engraver William Hogarth paints *Taste in High Life*. **PAINT**

1743   English painter and engraver William Hogarth paints the six-scene work *Marriage à la Mode*. **PAINT**

1743   At age eighty-seven, esteemed French painter Nicolas de Largillière is named director of the French Royal Academy. The artist has painted about 1,500 portraits, many of wealthy middle-class individuals. **PAINT**

1744   English critic and writer Samuel Johnson publishes the first of his biographies, the *Life* of his late friend, poet Richard Savage. Later biographies will include Sir Thomas Browne (1758) and Richard Ascham (1761). **LIT**

1744   The Madrigal Society is founded in London. **MUSIC**

1744   Spanish sculptor Ignacio de Vergara completes his marble decoration of the entrance to the palace of the Marqués de Dos Aguas in Valencia. **SCULP**

1745   Bohemian composer Johann Stamitz becomes conductor of the Mannheim School, a highly trained group of musicians who form the orchestra at the court of Mannheim, Germany. Stamitz's style of orchestral music and performance lays the foundation for the formal development of the sonata. **MUSIC**

1745   Italian painter Giovanni Battista Tiepolo paints the decorations in the Palazzo Labia in Venice, assisted by Gerolamo Mengozzi-Colonna. **PAINT**

1745   French sculptor Edme Bouchardon combines classical modeling with contemporary rococo details throughout his marble composition for the Fountain of the Seasons, to be placed along the Rue de Grenelle, Paris. **SCULP**

1745   Italian sculptor Nicola Salvi begins work on both the marble facade and statue of Neptune for the Trevi Fountain. It will be completed in 1762 and installed in the Piazza di Trevi, Rome. **SCULP**

1746   English poet William Collins, a favorite of later romantic poets, publishes *Odes on Several Descriptive and Allegorical Subjects*. **LIT**

1747–1748   English novelist Samuel Richardson publishes his masterpiece, the epistolary novel *Clarissa: or The History of a Young Lady*. The longest novel written in English, running to over one million words, it tells the tale of the seduction and rape of the unfortunate Clarissa Howe by the notorious libertine Robert Lovelace. **LIT**

1747   German-born composer George Frideric Handel composes the bibli-
            cal oratorio *Judas Maccabaeus*.   **MUSIC**

1748   The Royal Danish Ballet is founded in Copenhagen. It will be known
            for the delicacy of its productions.   **DANCE**

1748   French writer Voltaire writes the philosophical tale *Zadig, or la
            Destinée*. Later tales include *Micromégas*.   **LIT**

1748   A jury system of selection is introduced to the Salon, the French
            Royal Academy's regular official exhibition of painting and sculp-
            ture. *See also* 1667, MISC.   **MISC**

1749   *Irene*, the only play by English critic and writer Samuel Johnson, is
            produced by the actor David Garrick in London. It will run for only
            nine performances, but Johnson will earn more money from it than
            he will from any of his other writing.   **DRAMA**

1749   English novelist Henry Fielding publishes the novel *The History of
            Tom Jones*, a comic novel about a foundling who grows up into a
            high-spirited young man. Condemned by many for immorality, the
            novel has an intricate plot that will be called by English poet and
            critic Samuel Taylor Coleridge one of "the three most perfect plots
            ever planned" (along with Sophocles's *Oedipus Tyrannus*, 426 B.C.,
            and Ben Jonson's *The Alchemist*, 1610).   **LIT**

1749   English critic and writer Samuel Johnson publishes *The Vanity of
            Human Wishes*, his longest and best-known poem.   **LIT**

1749   Italian sculptor Antonio Corradini displays virtuoso carving in the
            rendering of drapery for his marble statue of Modesty in the
            Sansevero Chapel, Naples.   **SCULP**

c. 1750s   French painter François Boucher paints several portraits of Madame
            de Pompadour, mistress and confidante of King Louis XV.   **PAINT**

1750s   In England conversation pieces by such painters as Arthur Devis
            and Thomas Gainsborough are a popular form. In these group por-
            traits, two or more subjects converse or otherwise mix politely in a
            domestic or landscape setting.   **PAINT**

1750–1752   British critic and writer Samuel Johnson writes more than 200
            moral essays and commentaries for the twice-weekly periodical *The
            Rambler*.   **LIT**

1750   French sculptor Jean-Baptiste Pigalle allows the Sèvres manufactory
            to publish an altered version of his marble statuette *Child with
            Birdcage* in biscuit, an uncolored, ersatz marble.   **SCULP**

1751   The minuet becomes a fashionable dance in Europe.   **DANCE**

1751   *La locandiera* (*The Mistress of the Inn*), the masterpiece of Italian
            comic playwright Carlo Goldoni, is produced. In this and other plays,
            Goldoni challenges the traditions of commedia dell'arte.   **DRAMA**

1751   English poet Thomas Gray publishes "Elegy Written in a Country Churchyard."   **LIT**

1751   Scottish novelist Tobias George Smollett publishes *The Adventures of Peregrine Pickle*. Like his other comic adventure novels, including *The Adventures of Roderick Random* (1748) and *The Expedition of Humphrey Clinker* (1771), it is rich with characterization and satire. **LIT**

1751–1780   French encyclopedist and philosopher Denis Diderot and others compile the multivolume *Encyclopédie, ou Dictionnaire Raisonné des Sciences, des Arts et des Métiers*.   **LIT**

1751   French painter François Boucher paints *Reclining Girl*, one of his many playfully sensual paintings.   **PAINT**

1752   The invasion of Italian opera buffs in Paris divides the city into pro-Italian and pro-French music lovers, marking the end of French baroque opera and stimulating the development of the opéra comique. From 1750 to 1850 French music will be largely restricted to efforts to build up a new "grand opera."   **MUSIC**

1752   German-born composer George Frideric Handel composes the biblical oratorio *Jephitha*.   **MUSIC**

1752   Spanish artists Felipe de Castro and Luis Salvador Carmona establish the Academy of San Fernando to banish the substitution of extravagant French styles for native Spanish traditions. As a result, late 18th-century sculpture in Spain will reveal a mixture of Spanish naturalism with a closer study of the antique.   **SCULP**

1753   English painter and engraver William Hogarth publishes the aesthetic treatise *The Analysis of Beauty*.   **PAINT**

1753–1754   English painter Joshua Reynolds, who will be credited with raising the artist to a new position of respect in England, gains notice for his portrait *Commodore Keppel*, based on the *Apollo Belvedere*, a classical statue discovered in the late fifteenth century and greatly admired into the late eighteenth century.   **PAINT**

1753   French painter Claude-Joseph Vernet is commissioned by King Louis XV to paint a series of seaports. He is the founder of a painting dynasty that will include his son Antoine-Charles-Horace (Carle) Vernet and grandson Émile-Jean-Horace (Horace) Vernet.   **PAINT**

1755   European design books assist colonial wood-carvers in the decoration of the chancel of St. Michael's Church in Charleston, South Carolina. For the first time, American carvers employ classical motifs such as dentils, pilasters, and Corinthian capitals.   **ARCH**

1755   English critic and writer Samuel Johnson publishes *A Dictionary of the English Language*, a landmark of lexicography that he has compiled by himself over the course of eight years.   **LIT**

. . . .

"Whatever is fitted in any sort to excite the ideas of pain, and danger . . . or is conversant about terrible objects, or operates in a manner analogous to terror, is a source of the sublime; that is, it is productive of the strongest emotion which the mind is capable of feeling."
—English statesman and writer Edmund Burke on the role of fear in creating the sublime, in A Philosophical Enquiry into the Origin of Our Ideas of the Sublime and the Beautiful, 1756

. . . .

1756   English statesman and writer Edmund Burke publishes *A Philosophical Enquiry into the Origin of Our Ideas of the Sublime and Beautiful*. This work of aesthetics, with its emphasis on the sublime, will have a powerful influence on romantic artists and writers. **MISC**

1757   Italian painter Giovanni Battista Tiepolo decorates rooms in the Villa Valmarana near Vicenza. **PAINT**

1757   Genoese sculptor Francesco Queirolo captures the eighteenth century's obsession with allegory and its elaborate system of symbols in his marble sculpture of Count Antonio Sangro for the Sansevero Chapel in Naples. **SCULP**

1757   French sculptor Jean-Baptiste Lemoyne epitomizes the style of Louis XV with a long series of portrait busts designed to feature the king at every age. **SCULP**

1758–1760   English critic and writer Samuel Johnson publishes *The Idler*, a series of essays. **LIT**

1758   The first English manual on guitar playing is published. **MUSIC**

1759   English critic and writer Samuel Johnson publishes the philosophical romance *Rasselas*. **LIT**

1759   English poet, playwright, and novelist Oliver Goldsmith publishes *An Inquiry into the Present State of Polite Learning in England*. **LIT**

1759   French writer Voltaire composes the satirical novel *Candide, ou L'Optimisme*, an attack on Leibnitzian optimism built around the adventures of the naive title character and his tutor Dr. Pangloss. **LIT**

1759–1768   English novelist Laurence Sterne writes the comic novel *Tristram Shandy*. His later works include the unfinished *A Sentimental Journey Through France and Italy*. **LIT**

1760s   Scottish architect Robert Adam, working with his brother James Adam, designs and decorates Osterly Park (1761–1780) and Syon House (1762–1769) near London. Highly prolific, Robert Adam achieves an elegant, distinctive, influential blend of styles that encompasses architecture, furniture, and interior decoration.   **ARCH**

....

"[A]ll Paris is à la grecque. . . . Our ladies have their hair done à la grecque, our petits-maîtres would be ashamed to carry a snuffbox that was not à la grecque."—Baron Grimm reporting on the Greek taste, the fashion for Greek-inspired ornamentation, then sweeping France, 1763

....

1760s   The Greek taste, a fashion for ornamentation superficially inspired by classical Greek models, begins to hold sway in France and England. It will remain popular into the early nineteenth century, leaving its mark on furniture, decoration, and costume.   **DECO**

1760s   Neoclassicism takes shape in Germany in the writings of art historian Johann Winckelmann (*see* 1764, MISC) and the paintings of Anton Mengs. Inspired by the excavations of Pompeii and Herculaneum (*see* 1738, MISC), the movement in art and architecture spreads across Europe and the United States into the early nineteenth century. It seeks to recapture the heroic grandeur and civic ideals of ancient Greek and Roman art, as well as classical content and forms, marked by linearity and rationality.   **PAINT**

1760s   Swiss sculptor Franz Anton Bustelli produces immensely popular porcelain figures drawn from Italian comedy while working at the Nymphenburg manufactory near Munich.   **SCULP**

c. 1760   American painter John Singleton Copley paints such portraits as *Colonel Epes Sargent*.   **PAINT**

c. 1760   Italian painter Giovanni Battista Tiepolo paints *A Young Woman with a Macaw*.   **PAINT**

1760   While working in England French sculptor Louis-François Roubillac creates the French rococo marble tomb for Lady Elizabeth Nightingale to be placed in London's Westminster Abbey.   **SCULP**

1762–1763   Scottish biographer James Boswell keeps the private journal that will be published nearly two centuries later as *Boswell's London Journal* (1950).   **LIT**

1762   English poet, playwright, and novelist Oliver Goldsmith's *Letters from a Citizen of the World* is published, a collection of satirical essays on Britain from the point of view of a fictitious Chinese visitor.   **LIT**

Elijah in the Fiery Chariot, engraving by William Blake. *(The Metropolitan Museum of Art, Rogers Fund, 1916)*

1762	French philosopher Jean-Jacques Rousseau writes the philosophical treatise on government and the populace, *Du contrat social* (*The Social Contract*), and the philosophical romance *Émile, ou Traité de l'éducation*, about nature and child development. **LIT**
1762	French encyclopedist and philosopher Denis Diderot composes the satiric novel *Le Neveu de Rameau* (*Rameau's Nephew*). Among his later novels is *Jacques le fataliste* (1796). **LIT**
1762	Austrian composer Wolfgang Amadeus Mozart, age six, tours Europe as a musical prodigy. **MUSIC**
1763	On May 16 English critic and writer Samuel Johnson meets the young Scotsman James Boswell, who will become his biographer. *See* 1791, LIT. **LIT**
c. 1763	English painter Thomas Gainsborough paints *Mary, Countess Howe*, one of many elegant portraits that will make him a founding member of the Royal Academy in 1768. **PAINT**
1763	French painter Joseph-Marie Vien paints *The Cupid Seller*. **PAINT**

1764   French engraver Pierre-Simon Fournier develops the first system for measuring and naming sizes of type.   **GRAPH**

1764   English novelist Horace Walpole publishes the Gothic novel *The Castle of Otranto*.   **LIT**

1764   German archaeologist and critic Johann Winckelmann publishes his *History of Ancient Art Among the Greeks*, the first book to include the phrase "history of art" in the title. His theoretical treatises, which also include *Reflections on the Painting and Sculpture of the Greeks* (1755), analyze and praise Greek art, and are extremely influential in the development of both neoclassicism and the discipline of art history. *See* 1760s, PAINT.   **MISC**

1764   Austrian composer Wolfgang Amadeus Mozart, age eight, writes his first symphony. Four years later, he will have composed his first operas, *Bastien und Bastienne* and *La finta semplice*.   **MUSIC**

1765   English critic and writer Samuel Johnson publishes his eight-volume edition of Shakespeare's plays, noted for its critical preface.   **LIT**

c. 1765   Welsh painter Richard Wilson, one of the first British artists to concentrate on landscapes, paints *Snowdon from Llyn Nantlle*.   **PAINT**

1765   French painter Jean-Honoré Fragonard, influenced by François Boucher, is admitted to the Royal Academy for his painting *Coresus Sacrifices Himself to Save Callirrhoe*. His work is noted for its fluid brushwork, gaiety, whimsy, and charm. His specialty will be aristocratic love scenes. His works will include *Love's Vow, The Swing,* and *The Music Lesson*.   **PAINT**

COMMERCIAL ART

*S*ir Joshua Reynolds, eighteenth-century England's most important portrait painter and art theorist, was a businessman as much as a fine artist. By the late 1750s he was seeing 150 sitters a day and employing a large team of assistants and drapery painters. By the 1760s he was earning the handsome annual income of £6,000. This was in addition to his duties as first president of the Royal Academy (from 1768) and his delivery of the classic lectures known as Discourses on Art. So busy was his schedule that on the day he was knighted, April 21, 1769, he had to sandwich in his visit to the king between two sittings with paying subjects.

1765   French painter François Boucher, famed for his frivolous, artificially ele-
            gant style, becomes director of the Royal Academy and painter to King
            Louis XV. His body of work includes portraits, mythological allegories,
            decorations for such royal abodes as Versailles and Fontainebleau, and
            designs for stage settings and everyday objects.   **PAINT**

1765   American painter John Singleton Copley paints *The Boy with a
            Squirrel*, a portrait highly praised when exhibited in London.   **PAINT**

1766   English clergyman and writer Jonathan Swift's *Journal to Stella* is
            published posthumously. The letters to his beloved Esther Johnson
            (whom he called "Stella") were composed in the 1710s.   **LIT**

1766   English poet, playwright, and novelist Oliver Goldsmith publishes
            his only novel, *The Vicar of Wakefield*.   **LIT**

1766   Swiss painter Angelica Kauffmann moves to London, where she be-
            comes a founding member of the Royal Academy in 1768. She will
            adorn many interiors by architect and designer Robert Adam. *See*
            1760s, ARCH.   **PAINT**

1766   English sculptor Joseph Wilton is commissioned by Americans to
            create a marble statue of William Pitt out of gratitude for the repeal
            of the Stamp Act. The statue will·be erected on Sept. 7, 1770, at the
            intersection of Wall and William Streets in New York City.   **SCULP**

1767   In a forerunner to minstrel shows, a white actor named "Tea," his
            face blackened with cork, performs an early "Negro Dance" with
            the American Company in Philadelphia.   **DANCE**

1767   John Street Theater, the first permanent theater for the production
            of plays in New York City, opens on Dec. 7. It will operate until
            1798.   **DRAMA**

1769–1790   As first president of the Royal Academy, founded in 1768, English
            painter Joshua Reynolds delivers the lectures published as *Discourses
            on Art*. His exposition of neoclassical style, favoring idealized general-
            ization over observed particulars, is highly influential.   **MISC**

1769   English painter Joshua Reynolds is knighted. Throughout his career,
            he paints more than 2,000 portraits and history paintings, depicting
            such eminent Britons as Samuel Johnson and Edmund Burke.   **PAINT**

1770s   Wolfgang Amadeus Mozart's symphonies are influenced by Italian
            symphonists, especially his K. 81, 95, 112, 132, 162, and 182, while
            a new force, the music of Franz Joseph Haydn, is apparent in sym-
            phonies like K. 133. After his first tour of Italy, he composes his first
            symphonies that show something approaching a mastery of the
            symphonic form: two symphonies in A (K. 114 and 134) in
            1771–1772 and one in F (K. 130) in 1772.   **MUSIC**

1770s	French sculptor Claude Michel, known as Clodion, exemplifies the erotic side of rococo sculpture with his small terra-cotta statuettes of satyrs. **SCULP**

1770   English poet, playwright, and novelist Oliver Goldsmith's best known poem, *The Deserted Village*, is published. **LIT**

1770   English painter Thomas Gainsborough paints one of his most famous portraits, *The Blue Boy*. **PAINT**

....

"Neither a lofty degree of intelligence nor imagination nor both together go to the making of genius. Love, love, love, that is the soul of genius."—Attributed to Austrian composer Wolfgang Amadeus Mozart, late eighteenth century

....

1770–1771   In his third and fourth *Discourses*, English painter Joshua Reynolds propounds the grand manner of history and portrait painting, in which the subjects are elevated and idealized. The tradition is rooted in the work of such seventeenth-century artists as Poussin. **PAINT**

1770   American painter Benjamin West paints *The Death of Wolfe*, which takes the radical step in history painting of portraying figures in contemporary dress. **PAINT**

1770   English sculptor Joseph Wilton erects his lead equestrian image of King George III in New York City. Patriots will dismantle the statue in 1776. **SCULP**

1771–1790   American statesman and writer Benjamin Franklin writes but does not complete *The Autobiography of Benjamin Franklin*, taking it to the end of the 1750s. Its optimism and unadorned writing style mark it as a distinctly American work. **LIT**

1772   The first barrel organs are produced by Flight and Kelly, a London firm of organ builders. Barrel organs will enjoy great popularity in rural English churches into the nineteenth century. **MUSIC**

1772   American painter Benjamin West, in England since 1763, becomes historical painter to King George III. He is the first American painter to win a reputation in Europe. **PAINT**

1772   American sculptor Patience Lovell Wright leaves for England to create numerous portraits of the upper middle class and aristocracy. In 1781 she will model Benjamin Franklin's likeness in wax while in Paris. **SCULP**

1773   The waltz becomes fashionable in Vienna. **DANCE**

1773   The Bolshoi ballet school opens in Russia and will become one of the foremost purveyors of classical, realistic ballet in the world. **DANCE**

1773   English poet, playwright, and novelist Oliver Goldsmith's comedy *She Stoops to Conquer* is produced.   **DRAMA**

1773   American statesman and writer Benjamin Franklin publishes the *Edict by the King of Prussia*, a satire about England and Germany that reflects Franklin's stand against the Townshend Act. The piece was published in the *Philadelphia Public Advertiser*.   **LIT**

1773   In London American slave Phillis Wheatley publishes the collection *Poems on Various Subjects, Religious and Moral*. The book establishes her as the first female African-American poet.   **LIT**

1773–1774   The more than twenty symphonies Wolfgang Amadeus Mozart composes at Salzburg include his first two "masterwork" symphonies, no. 25 in G Minor (K. 183) and no. 29 in A (K. 201).   **MUSIC**

1774–1793   In France classical revival characterizes the Louis XVI (Louis Seize) style of decoration and architecture.   **DECO**

....

"No man but a blockhead ever wrote, except for money."—Prolific professional English critic and writer Samuel Johnson, c. 1770s

....

1774   German poet Johann Wolfgang von Goethe writes the short novel *The Sorrows of Young Werther*. Later works include the play *Iphigenia in Tauris* and the novel *Die Wahlverwandtschaften* (1809).   **LIT**

1774–1789   French painter Élisabeth Vigée-Lebrun paints many portraits of her friend, Queen Marie Antoinette, before the French Revolution sends the artist into exile (1789) and the queen to the guillotine (1793). **PAINT**

1774   French painter Jacques-Louis David, who, beginning in the 1780s, will become the dominant figure of French neoclassical painting, wins the Prix de Rome with *Antiochus and Stratonice*.   **PAINT**

1775   *The Rivals*, the enormously popular first play of Irish playwright Richard Brinsley Sheridan, is produced. It continues to be revived frequently to the present day. Sheridan's *St. Patrick's Day; or the Scheming Lieutenant*, a farce, and *The Duenna*, a comic opera, are also produced this year.   **DRAMA**

1775   English critic and writer Samuel Johnson publishes *A Journey to the Western Islands of Scotland*.   **LIT**

1776–1788   English historian Edward Gibbon publishes the six volumes of *The History of the Decline and Fall of the Roman Empire*.   **LIT**

1776–1783   American writer Thomas Paine publishes *Common Sense*, a pamphlet exhorting the need for American independence from England, and *The American Crisis*, a series of sixteen pamphlets written during and after the war for independence that begins with the words, "These are the times that try men's souls." **LIT**

1777   Richard Brinsley Sheridan's *The School for Scandal*, one of the greatest English comedies of manners, is produced. Sheridan's *A Trip to Scarborough* is also produced this year. **DRAMA**

1777   English painter Thomas Gainsborough, one of the first great English landscape artists, paints the landscape *The Watering Place*. **PAINT**

1777   American painter Benjamin West paints *Saul and the Witch of Endor*. **PAINT**

1777   French sculptor Jean-Jacques Caffiéri exhibits his neoclassical design for the monument to Major-General Richard Montgomery at the Paris Salon. The statue will not be erected until 1789 under the east portico of St. Paul's Chapel in New York City. **SCULP**

1778   German composer Ludwig van Beethoven, age eight, is presented by his father as a six-year-old music prodigy. **MUSIC**

1778   La Scala opera house opens in Milan, Italy. **MUSIC**

1778   Wolfgang Amadeus Mozart composes piano sonatas K. 310 in A minor, and 330–333, among his best known in the genre. **MUSIC**

1778   Wolfgang Amadeus Mozart composes Symphony in D (*Paris*, K. 297), among his most critically acclaimed works. **MUSIC**

1778   Settled in England since the American Revolution began, American painter John Singleton Copley turns to history painting, including *Brook Watson and the Shark*. **PAINT**

1779   At the time of his death English cabinetmaker Thomas Chippendale (*b.* 1718) has had a broad and lasting influence in his designs of chairs, cabinets, bookcases, mirror frames, and tables. His work has combined Queen Anne and Georgian styles with chinoiserie, rococo, and Gothic. **DECO**

1779   English novelist Fanny Burney (also known as Madame d'Arblay) writes the young woman's coming-of-age novel *Evelina, or The History of a Young Lady's Entrance Into the World*. Later novels include *Cecilia, or Memoirs of an Heiress* (1782) and *Camilla* (1796). **LIT**

1779   The opera *Iphignia in Tauris*, by German composer Christoph Willibald Gluck, premieres in Paris. **MUSIC**

1780s   Wolfgang Amadeus Mozart composes many great piano concertos. Among them: three in the spring of 1784, K. 450 in B-flat, K. 451 in D, and K. 453 in G. Three important concertos in 1784–1785 include K. 459 in F, K. 466 in D minor, and K. 467 in C. **MUSIC**

1780   The Spanish dance bolero is invented by dancer Sebastiano Cerezo.   **DANCE**

1780   The first modern pianoforte is made in Paris by Sébastien Érard.   **MUSIC**

1781   English critic and writer Samuel Johnson publishes *The Lives of the Poets*, a collection of fifty-two essays on individual poets, combining biography and criticism.   **LIT**

1781   Swiss-born painter Henry Fuseli paints the grotesque work *The Nightmare*.   **PAINT**

1782   French-born writer farmer Michel-Guillaume-Jean de Crèvecoeur publishes *Letters from an American Farmer*, which addresses the life of the land and the American character.   **LIT**

1782   French sculptor Étienne Falconet, working with portraitist Marie-Anne Collot, completes his bronze equestrian statue of Peter the Great to be placed in the Square of the Decembrists, St. Petersburg, Russia.   **SCULP**

1783   English actor John Philip Kemble successfully debuts in London in a distinctive portrayal of Hamlet. He will make his mark in classical tragic roles. His sister Sarah Siddons's stage career will flourish around the same time, and she will also excel in tragedy, giving her greatest performance as Lady Macbeth. John and Sarah's younger brother Charles will be a less accomplished actor, though ultimately he will do well in romantic and comic parts. Stephen, a fourth sibling, will be best known for putting his great circumference to use as Falstaff. Fanny Kemble, Charles's daughter, will give outstanding performances in a number of tragic and romantic roles, including Juliet.   **DRAMA**

1783   English poet George Crabbe publishes *The Village*, a realistic poem about rural life.   **LIT**

1783   English artist and poet William Blake publishes *Poetical Sketches*, his first book of poems.   **LIT**

1783   English painter Thomas Gainsborough paints *The Mall*, an example of the genre of fancy pictures, in which idealized peasants are depicted in rural settings.   **PAINT**

1783   American painter John Singleton Copley paints *The Death of Major Peirson*.   **PAINT**

1784   The Paris Conservatoire National de Musique opens.   **MUSIC**

1784   American artist Joseph Wright, son of Patience Lovell Wright, completes his wax bas-relief profile portrait of George Washington. Wright will be commissioned by the government to make designs for coins it will soon print.   **SCULP**

1785   American statesman and architect Thomas Jefferson designs the Virginia state capitol, notable for its neoclassical approach based on Roman models. **ARCH**

1785   English poet William Cowper publishes *The Task*, a meditative poem evoking English country life. **LIT**

1785   A year after the death of his friend Samuel Johnson, Scottish biographer James Boswell publishes an account of a voyage they took together in 1773, *The Journal of a Tour to the Hebrides*. **LIT**

1785–1786   While working on *Le Nozze di Figaro* (*The Marriage of Figaro,* K. 492), Wolfgang Amadeus Mozart composes three piano concertos. The first two are in a comparatively light mood, while the third (K. 491) in C minor is one of his great tragic creations. The C-major concerto of December 1786 (K. 503) is considered its triumphal counterpart. **MUSIC**

1785   French sculptor Jean-Antoine Houdon arrives in Philadelphia on Sept. 14 to study George Washington's features for a monumental sculpture commissioned by the Virginia assembly. The marble statue will be placed in the rotunda of the Virginia state capitol in 1796. **SCULP**

1786   Scottish poet Robert Burns publishes *Poems, Chiefly in the Scottish Dialect.* **LIT**

1786   Mozart's opera *The Marriage of Figaro* premieres in Vienna. **MUSIC**

. . . .

"Upon the whole, it seems to me, that the object and intention of all the arts is to supply the natural imperfection of things, and often to gratify the mind by realising and embodying what never existed but in the imagination."—English painter Sir Joshua Reynolds, Discourse XIII, 1786

. . . .

1786–1797   American painter John Trumbull paints the much-reproduced *The Declaration of Independence.* **PAINT**

1787   Scottish poet Robert Burns begins collecting and writing hundreds of songs, traditional and new, for *Scots Musical Museum*, including "Auld Lang Syne" and "A Red, Red Rose." **MUSIC**

1787   Mozart's opera *Don Giovanni* premieres in Prague. **MUSIC**

1787   French painter Jacques-Louis David paints *The Death of Socrates.* Like his other neoclassical paintings of the decade, including *The Oath of the Horatii* (1784) and *Brutus and His Dead Sons* (1789), it embodies a stern republican idealism and a commitment to classical aesthetic principles, against rococo frivolity and lightness. **PAINT**

1788   Among the last seven symphonies Wolfgang Amadeus Mozart composed while living in Vienna are three "great symphonies": E-flat (no. 39, K. 543), G Minor (no. 40, K. 550), and C Major *Jupiter* (K. 551). In this year he also composes the orchestral serenade *Eine Kleine Nachtmusik* (K. 525).   **MUSIC**

1789   Edmund Kean, who will become one of the greatest English stage actors, is born in London (*d.* 1833). He will give his best performances in Shakesperean roles, particularly Shylock, Macbeth, Richard III, and Iago.   **DRAMA**

1789   *The Power of Sympathy*, the novel believed to be the first written in the United States, is completed. The book's author was originally thought to be Sarah Wentworth Morton; William Hill Brown will come to be considered the probable writer.   **LIT**

1789   French painter Jacques-Louis David is active in the French Revolution, both through political activity and through his paintings, which embody republican principles.   **PAINT**

c. 1790–   Greek revival is an important movement in European and American
1840   architecture, drawing on models taken from ancient Greece.   **ARCH**

1790   English wood engraver Thomas Bewick publishes fine wood engravings in *A General History of Quadrupeds*. His other illustrated works of natural history will include *A History of British Birds* (1797, 1804). Bewick's finely detailed work will make wood engraving popular for book illustrations until the end of the nineteenth century.   **GRAPH**

1790   English artist and poet William Blake publishes his most important prose work, *The Marriage of Heaven and Hell*.   **LIT**

1790   English statesman and writer Edmund Burke publishes the conservative treatise *Reflections on the Revolution in France*. American writer Thomas Paine will reply to it in support of revolution in *The Rights of Man* (1791–1792).   **LIT**

1791   The waltz becomes fashionable in England.   **DANCE**

1791   Scottish biographer James Boswell completes *The Life of Samuel Johnson LL.D.*, perhaps the best-known biography in the English language.   **LIT**

1791   Scottish poet Robert Burns publishes the narrative poem *Tam O'Shanter*.   **LIT**

1791   French writer Donatien-Alphonse-François de Sade, known as the Marquis de Sade, writes *Justine, ou les Malheurs de la vertu*. Later works include *Juliette* (1797).   **LIT**

1791–1795   Austrian composer Franz Joseph Haydn composes his twelve London Symphonies, including the famous *Surprise Symphony* (no. 94), for the Salomon Concerts in London.   **MUSIC**

1791   Austrian composer Wolfgang Amadeus Mozart's last opera, *The Magic Flute* (K. 620), premieres in Vienna in the year of Mozart's death. **MUSIC**

1792   American painter Ralph Earl paints *Oliver Ellsworth and His Wife*.**PAINT**

1793   English poet William Wordsworth publishes the poem "An Evening Walk" and the collection *Descriptive Sketches*.   **LIT**

1793   *The Farmer's Almanac* is published for the first time by Robert Bailey Thomas. Still in publication, it is now called *The Old Farmer's Almanac*.   **LIT**

1793   Italian violin virtuoso Niccolò Paganini, age eleven, makes his debut in Genoa.   **MUSIC**

1793   French painter Jacques-Louis David paints *The Death of Marat*. **PAINT**

1794   English artist and poet William Blake publishes *Songs of Innocence and of Experience*, which includes the poems "The Lamb," "The Chimney Sweeper," "The Tyger," "The Garden of Love," "A Poison Tree," and "The Sick Rose." Like Blake's subsequent illuminated books, the volume is lavishly illustrated with etchings by the author.   **LIT**

1794   English novelist Ann Radcliffe publishes the Gothic novel *The Mysteries of Udolpho*.   **LIT**

1794   *Tammany, or The Indian Chief* by James Hewitt, an early American opera, is performed.   **MUSIC**

1794–1796   French painter Jacques-Louis David paints *Intervention of the Sabine Women*.   **PAINT**

1795–1796   American painter Gilbert Stuart paints a definitive series of portraits of first president George Washington. Of his three different types of Washington portraits, the most famous, the Athenaeum type, is used on the U.S. one-dollar bill.   **PAINT**

1796–1806   American statesman and architect Thomas Jefferson designs his home, Monticello, in Palladian style.   **ARCH**

1796   American wood-carver Samuel McIntire collaborates with furniture maker William Lemon to decorate a chest with European-influenced classical detail for Mrs. Elizabeth Derby.   **DECO**

1796   English novelist Matthew Lewis publishes the Gothic novel *The Monk*.   **LIT**

1796   English painter J. M. W. (Joseph Mallord William) Turner, perhaps the greatest landscape artist of the nineteenth century, completes *Fishermen at Sea*, his first oil painting to be exhibited at the Royal Academy.   **PAINT**

1797   German writer Ludwig Tieck writes the play *Der gestiefelte Kater* (*Puss in Boots*). Among his later works is the realistic short novel *Des Lebens Uberflub* (*Life's Overflow*, 1837).   **DRAMA**

1797	French painter Pierre-Narcisse Guérin wins the Prix de Rome, marking the beginning of a career that will include serving as teacher to romantic painters Eugène Delacroix and Théodore Géricault. **PAINT**

1798	German printer Aloys Senefelder invents lithography, a process for printing images based on the incompatibility of oil and water. It becomes a popular medium for fine and commercial artists. **GRAPH**

1798	English poets William Wordsworth and Samuel Taylor Coleridge publish the collection *Lyrical Ballads*, often regarded as the founding work of English romanticism. It includes Coleridge's "The Rime of the Ancient Mariner" and "The Nightingale" and Wordsworth's "The Idiot Boy," "The Thorn," "The Mad Mother," "Lines Written in Early Spring," and "Lines Composed a Few Miles Above Tintern Abbey." A second edition will appear in 1800 (with a famous preface by Wordsworth), a third in 1802. **LIT**

1798–1799	English poet William Wordsworth composes the "Lucy" poems and the first, two-part version of the autobiographical poem *The Prelude*. Revised throughout his life, *The Prelude* will not be published until 1850, after his death. **LIT**

1798	American novelist Charles Brockden Brown publishes the Gothic novel *Wieland*. **LIT**

1799	In Philadelphia English-born Benjamin Henry Latrobe, regarded as the first professional American architect, designs the Greek revivalist Bank of Pennsylvania, based on an Ionic temple. **ARCH**

1799	Spanish painter Francisco de Goya issues the series of engravings *Los Caprichos*. They display the grotesque, satirical, nightmarish elements that will become associated with his name. He will complete hundreds of etchings, lithographs, and drawings in addition to his hundreds of paintings. **GRAPH**

1799	American historian Hannah Adams publishes *A Summary History of New-England*. Adams is the first professional woman writer in the United States. **LIT**

1799	The oratorio *The Creation*, by Austrian composer Franz Joseph Haydn, premieres in Vienna. **MUSIC**

1799	Ludwig van Beethoven composes Symphony no. 1 in C Major and Piano Sonata Op. 13 (*Pathétique*.) **MUSIC**

1799	Swiss-born Henry Fuseli opens Milton Gallery in London, exhibiting dozens of his own paintings on literary subjects. He had previously contributed to John Boydell's Shakespeare gallery. **PAINT**

1800s   Costumes and scenery become increasingly realistic on stages in England and throughout Europe. More and more, historical research is undertaken to ensure accuracy in design. By the end of the century, actors are dressed largely as their characters would have been in real life, and plays are usually performed with sets that include appropriate furniture and accessories.   **DRAMA**

1800s   In China popular plays combine spoken dialogue with singing, dancing, and acrobatics. Most are histories or adaptations of legends or novels. There is usually no scenery other than a decorated backcloth, and the few props are mostly symbolic (for instance, a horsehair duster represents spirituality). Costumes and makeup can be elaborate, and the acting is highly stylized. This form of theater continues to the present day.   **DRAMA**

1800s   Historical dramas and pageant plays, many of them about Indians and frontiersmen, become popular in the United States. There are enough theaters that a number of American playwrights are able to support themselves through writing, though none produce works of lasting fame. Gas lighting is installed in theaters, improving illumination.   **DRAMA**

1800s   Western-style theater begins in Egypt, Syria, and Turkey. Translations of European plays and plays written by Middle Easterners are performed throughout the region.   **DRAMA**

1800s   Professional Parsi theater companies, presenting both South Asian plays and adaptations of work by Western playwrights, flourish in India. They will continue to be popular through the early twentieth-century.   **DRAMA**

1800s   Increasingly in Europe and America responsibility for all aspects of the production of a play is shouldered by an individual specifically hired for that purpose, and the profession of directing comes into being. Previously, playwrights, chief actors, and stage managers had supervised—sometimes in only a minimal way—the staging of plays. (Until 1956 directors will be called producers in England.)   **DRAMA**

1800s   The Maori of New Zealand carve representations of Mother Heaven and Father Earth on the fences of their fortified villages, meeting places, and storehouses. The sexual organs illustrating the union of the divinities will be removed during the Victorian period.   **SCULP**

1800s   Artists from the Tonga Islands create goddess figures of walrus ivory, bored with a hole so they can be suspended. Most Polynesian figure sculpture will be destroyed under early Western influence.   **SCULP**

1800s   White traders introduce metal carving tools to Northwest Coast settlements. Native Americans carve an abundance of monumental poles, grave markers, and doorposts to commemorate important tribal events.   **SCULP**

Original watercolor drawing for the White House, Washington, D.C., by Benjamin Latrobe. *(Library of Congress/Photosearch, Inc.)*

c. 1800–
1850

Japanese printmakers such as Andō Hiroshige, Katsushika Hokusai, and Kitagawa Utamaro create representative prints of the Ukiyo-e movement, portraying scenes from evanescent everyday life, with settings including theaters, brothels, and bathhouses. Japanese prints brought to Europe this century exercise a strong influence on avant-garde French artists.   **GRAPH**

1800–1900

Romanticism is the prevailing movement in modern music, characterized in music by subjective, emotional qualities and freedom of form, in reaction to the formalistic classical tradition. The movement's contributions will include the character piece for piano, the art song for voice, and the symphonic poem for orchestra.   **MUSIC**

c. 1800

Spanish painter Francisco de Goya paints the group portrait *Family of Charles IV* along with the erotic pair of portraits the *Clothed Maja* and *Naked Maja*.   **PAINT**

c. 1800

In Britain picturesque scenes, those with varied and irregular detail, are the favorite of landscape artists such as Thomas Girtin.   **PAINT**

1801

French novelist François-Auguste-René de Chateaubriand writes the novel *Atala*. His later works will include the romance *René* (1802) and *Le Génie du christianisme* (1802).   **LIT**

1801

Swiss-born painter Henry Fuseli publishes *Lectures on Painting*. **PAINT**

1801

French painter Jean-Auguste-Dominique Ingres wins the Prix de Rome with the history painting *Envoys from Agamemnon*.   **PAINT**

LORD ELGIN'S MARBLES

*F*ew art collectors have won as much fame—and notoriety—as British diplomat Thomas Bruce, seventh Lord Elgin, who obtained for Great Britain the group of sculptures known as the Elgin Marbles. Comprising most of the sculptures from the Parthenon in Athens, along with other classical Greek works, Elgin persuaded the Ottoman Turks to part with them in 1801–1803; they were sold to the nation in 1816, and are now in the British Museum. Given that the Turks were an occupying power who had no moral right to sell part of Greece's heritage, Elgin's deal sparked controversy then and now. But artists and critics in England were only too happy to get the chance to study the sculptures up close. Previously, art aficionados had been restricted for the most part to later Hellenistic and Roman copies, which lacked the classical purity of the originals. Painter Benjamin Robert Haydon, viewing the Elgin Marbles in 1808, was astonished by the combination of faithfulness to nature and idealized grandeur. He wrote:

> That combination of nature and idea which I had felt was so much wanting for high art was here displayed to midday conviction. My heart beat! If I had seen nothing else I had beheld sufficient to keep me to nature for the rest of my life. But when I turned to the [sculpture of] Theseus . . . the Ilyssus . . . and . . . the figure of the fighting metope . . . when I saw, in fact, the most heroic style of art combined with all the essential detail of actual life, the thing was done at once and for ever.

1801   English sculptor John Flaxman sculpts the monument to Lord Mansfield. Flaxman is known not only for his neoclassical monumental style but for his designs for potter Josiah Wedgwood (1775–1787) and his illustrations for works such as the *Iliad* and the *Odyssey* (1793).   **SCULP**

1802   *A Tale of Mystery*, a play by English playwright Thomas Holcroft that is generally considered the first melodrama produced in England, opens in London.   **DRAMA**

1802   English poet and critic Samuel Taylor Coleridge publishes "Dejection: An Ode," to which his friend William Wordsworth will reply in "Intimations of Immortality" (1807).   **LIT**

1802   French writer Anne-Louise-Germaine de Staël writes the early feminist novel *Delphine*. She later will write the novel *Corinne* (1807).   **LIT**

1802   Ludwig van Beethoven composes Symphony no. 2 in D Major, Op. 36, and Piano Sonata in C-sharp Minor, no. 2 (*Moonlight*).   **MUSIC**

1802   American painter Benjamin West paints *Death on a Pale Horse*.   **PAINT**

1803–1820   English artist and poet William Blake writes and engraves the illustrated poem *Milton*, which seeks to correct the moral and religious "errors" of John Milton's *Paradise Lost* (1667).   **LIT**

1803   Ludwig van Beethoven composes Sonata for Violin and Piano, Op. 47 (*Kreutzer*).   **MUSIC**

1804–1820   English artist and poet William Blake's *Jerusalem: The Emanation of the Great Albion* is the last of his prophetic books, incorporating his personal mythology.   **LIT**

1804   German composer Ludwig van Beethoven composes Symphony no. 3 in E-flat Major (*Eroica*). The "heroic symphony" is written in homage to Napoleon, but Beethoven withdraws the planned dedication when Napoleon takes the title of emperor.   **MUSIC**

1805–1818   American architect Benjamin Henry Latrobe designs the Roman Catholic cathedral in Baltimore, the first cathedral in the United States.   **ARCH**

1805   British poet and essayist Leigh Hunt, who will be considered a pioneer in dramatic criticism, begins writing about the theater. His work will continue to appear until at least 1821.   **DRAMA**

1805   Italian composer Niccolò Paganini begins touring Europe as a violin virtuoso.   **MUSIC**

1805–1807   As Napoleon's official painter, French artist Jacques-Louis David paints *Coronation of Napoleon*.   **PAINT**

1805   English painter J. M. W. Turner paints *Shipwreck*.   **PAINT**

1805   Italian sculptor Antonio Canova completes his neoclassical tomb for the Archduchess Maria Christina in Vienna's Church of the Augustinians. He will later produce a colossal nude statue of Napoleon and carve a marble portrait of Napoleon's sister, Pauline Borghese, as a reclining Venus in 1808.   **SCULP**

1806   Ludwig van Beethoven composes Symphony no. 4 in B-flat Major, Op. 60, and Violin Concerto, Op. 61.   **MUSIC**

1807   *Tears and Smiles*, a comedy of manners by American playwright James Nelson Barker, is produced in Philadelphia. Barker's *The Indian Princess; or La Belle Sauvage*, the first play about Native Americans to be staged in America, will be produced in 1808.   **DRAMA**

1807   William Wordsworth publishes *Poems in Two Volumes*, which includes "Intimations of Immortality from Recollections of Early Childhood" and "I Wandered Lonely as a Cloud."   **LIT**

1807 The Accademia di Belle Arti, the municipal picture gallery of Venice and one of Italy's major collections, is founded by order of Napoleon. **PAINT**

1808 English poet and critic Samuel Taylor Coleridge delivers eighteen lectures titled "On Poetry and the Principles of Taste" at the Royal Institute, the first of many lecture series he will deliver in the coming years. **LIT**

1808 British poet and essayist Leigh Hunt begins editing the radical weekly the *Examiner*, which will introduce poets John Keats and Percy Bysshe Shelley to the public. **LIT**

1808 Ludwig van Beethoven composes Symphony no. 5 and Symphony no. 6, (*Pastoral*). The descriptive title of the movements of the latter, each suggesting a different scene from life in the country, marks the beginning of nineteenth-century program music. **MUSIC**

1808 French painter Antoine-Jean Gros, Napoleon's official painter of battles, completes *Napoleon at Eylau*. **PAINT**

1808 French painter Jean-Auguste-Dominique Ingres paints *The Valpinçon Bather*, one of his many pictures of bathers. **PAINT**

• •

"Architecture in general is frozen music."
—German philosopher Friedrich von Schelling,
Philosophie der Kunst, 1809

• •

1809 American writer Washington Irving publishes the satiric overview of New York in *A History of New York, from the Beginning of the World to the End of the Dutch Dynasty, by Diedrich Knickerbocker*. The book establishes Irving as a writer; his character Knickerbocker will also appear in *The Sketch Book* (1819). **LIT**

1809 Dutch painter Wouter Johannes van Troostwijck paints *The Rampoortje*, a landscape of a gate in winter. **PAINT**

1810-1814 Spanish painter Francisco de Goya paints *The Disasters of War*, a horrific series of etchings depicting atrocities committed during Napoleon's invasion of Spain. **GRAPH**

1810 Scottish poet and novelist Walter Scott publishes the poem *The Lady of the Lake*. **LIT**

1811 English novelist Jane Austen publishes *Sense and Sensibility*. **LIT**

1811 With friend Thomas Jefferson Hogg, English poet Percy Bysshe Shelley publishes the pamphlet *On the Necessity of Atheism*, resulting in his expulsion from Oxford. **LIT**

1812   English chemist and physicist William Hyde Wollaston invents the camera lucida, a device that projects the image of an object onto a flat surface where a drawing can be traced.   **GRAPH**

1812   English poet George Gordon, Lord Byron, publishes the first two cantos of *Childe Harold's Pilgrimage*, which introduces the idea of the moody, rebellious, tempestuous Byronic hero. The third canto will appear in 1816, the fourth in 1818.   **LIT**

1812   The Gesellschaft der Musikfreunde is founded in Vienna. It will become the oldest and most important music society of Austria.   **MUSIC**

1812   Ludwig van Beethoven composes Symphony no. 7, Op. 92 and Symphony no. 8 Op. 93.   **MUSIC**

1813–1818   English writer William Hazlitt reviews plays for the *Champion*, the *Examiner*, the *Morning Chronicle*, and *The Times*.   **DRAMA**

1813   English novelist Jane Austen publishes the elegantly comic novel *Pride and Prejudice*, on the romance between Elizabeth Bennet and FitzWilliam Darcy.   **LIT**

1813–1814   English poet Lord Byron publishes the oriental tales, which include *The Giaour, The Corsair*, and *Lara*.   **LIT**

1813   English poet Percy Bysshe Shelley publishes his first major poem, *Queen Mab*.   **LIT**

1813   Swedish poet Esaias Tegnér publishes the collection *Hjälten*. His later collections will include *Frithiof's Saga* (1825), and *Nattvardsbarnen* (1820, tranlated into English by Henry Wadsworth Longfellow).   **LIT**

1813   The London Philharmonic Society is founded.   **MUSIC**

1814   English poet William Wordsworth publishes *The Excursion*, a philosophical poem in nine books.   **LIT**

1814   Scottish poet and novelist Walter Scott publishes the romance *Waverley*, his first in a series of "Waverley novels" set in Scotland that also include *Guy Mannering* (1815) and *Rob Roy* (1818).   **LIT**

1814–1815   German composer and writer E. T. A. (Ernst Theodor Amadeus) Hoffmann composes the collection of fantastic tales *Fantastiestücke* (*Fantasy-pieces*). He will also write the collection *Nachtstücke* (*Nightpieces*, 1817).   **LIT**

1814   German poet Friedrich Rückert publishes the collection of political poems *Geharnischte Sonette* (*Harnessed Sonnets*). Among his later works are *Kindertotenlieder* (*Songs on Children's Deaths*, 1872), set to music by Gustav Mahler.   **LIT**

1814   Austrian composer Franz Schubert begins his most prolific period of musical composition. By 1828 he will have written more than 600 German songs.   **MUSIC**

1814   German composer Ludwig van Beethoven presents the final version of his opera *Fidelio*.   **MUSIC**

1814   French painter Jean-Auguste-Dominique Ingres paints the *Grande Odalisque*, a picture of a harem slave done in neoclassical style.   **PAINT**

1814   Spanish painter Francisco de Goya paints *The Third of May, 1808*, an emotionally wrenching picture of Spanish citizens executed by Napoleon's troops in Madrid.   **PAINT**

1815   English poet Lord Byron publishes *Hebrew Melodies*, which includes the poem "She Walks in Beauty."   **LIT**

1816   English novelist Jane Austen publishes *Emma*.   **LIT**

1816   English poet and critic Samuel Taylor Coleridge publishes *Christabel and Other Poems*, which includes the fragment "Kubla Khan." **LIT**

1816   While spending the summer at Lake Geneva, Switzerland, English poet Percy Bysshe Shelley, his wife Mary Wollstonecraft Shelley, and their friend Lord Byron, engage in a ghost-story competition that results in Mary writing the novel *Frankenstein, or The Modern Prometheus*, which will be published in 1818. In the same summer, Percy Shelley writes the philosophical poems "Hymn to Intellectual Beauty" and "Mont Blanc."   **LIT**

1816   English poet Percy Bysshe Shelley publishes *Alastor, or The Spirit of Solitude*.   **LIT**

1816   American lawyer and linguist John Pickering writes an early study of the American language, *A Vocabulary, or, Collection of Words and Phrases Which Have Supposed to Be Peculiar to the U.S. of America*.   **LIT**

1816   English painter John Martin paints *Joshua Commanding the Sun to Stand Still*, typical of his spectacular, melodramatic scenes.   **PAINT**

1817   English poet and critic Samuel Taylor Coleridge publishes *Biographia Literaria*, an idiosyncratic compendium of critical theory, philosophy, and autobiography.   **LIT**

1817   English poet Lord Byron publishes the closet tragedy *Manfred*.   **LIT**

1817   English poet John Keats publishes *Poems*, his first collection.   **LIT**

1817   American poet William Cullen Bryant publishes the poem "Thanatopsis" in the *North American Review*.   **LIT**

1818   English novelist Jane Austen's *Northanger Abbey*, a satire of Gothic fiction, is published posthumously.   **LIT**

1818   English novelist Mary Wollstonecraft Shelley publishes the Gothic horror novel *Frankenstein, or The Modern Prometheus*. The story of the man who made a monster will become a fixture of popular literature and scholarly study. Twentieth-century audiences will come to know it through many movie versions, particularly James Whale's in 1931. *See* 1816, LIT.   **LIT**

1818   English poet Percy Bysshe Shelley publishes the political pamphlet
              The Revolt of Islam and the poem "Ozymandias," while fellow-poet
              John Keats publishes *Endymion: A Poetic Romance.*   **LIT**

....

**"We must have religion for religion's sake, morality for
morality's sake, as with art for art's sake . . . the
beautiful cannot be the way to what is useful, or to what is
good, or to what is holy; it leads only to itself."
—French art theorist Victor Cousin, foreshadowing the
art for art's sake movement at the end of the
nineteenth century, 1818**

....

1818–1819   French painter Théodore Géricault paints his most famous work,
              The Raft of the Medusa, renowned for its epic, grisly treatment of a
              controversial contemporary event, a shipwreck considered by some
              to be due to government incompetence.   **PAINT**

1819   Architecture courses are conducted for the first time at the École
              des Beaux Arts in Paris. Up until this time, the practice of being an
              architect did not require formal training and accreditation.   **ARCH**

....

**"Nobody can further art but the master. Patrons further
the artist."—German poet Johann Wolfgang von Goethe,
Sprüche in Prosa, 1819**

....

1819–1824   English poet Lord Byron publishes sixteen cantos of his unfinished
              satirical epic *Don Juan*, written in ottava rima.   **LIT**

1819   English poet Percy Bysshe Shelley publishes the poetic drama *The
              Cenci* and the poem "Ode to the West Wind."   **LIT**

1819   English poet John Keats writes most of his greatest poems, includ-
              ing the ballad "La Belle Dame Sans Merci," the sonnet "Fame," and
              the odes "On a Grecian Urn," "To a Nightingale," "On Melancholy,"
              "On Indolence," "To Psyche," and "Ode to Autumn." He also writes
              the poems "The Eve of St. Agnes" and "Lamia." Many of these
              works will be published in his collection of 1820, one year before
              his death.   **LIT**

1819   Scottish poet and novelist Walter Scott publishes his most popular
              novel, *Ivanhoe*, set in medieval England during the reign of Richard I. **LIT**

1819   Ludwig van Beethoven's Piano Sonata in B-flat, Op. 106
              (*Hammerklavier*), is published the year he becomes completely
              deaf.   **MUSIC**

THE OTHER DEAF ARTIST

German composer Ludwig van Beethoven's battle with deafness is well known. He began to lose his hearing around 1800, while entering his thirties, and was completely deaf by 1819. Though the incurable condition led him at one point to contemplate suicide, Beethoven went on to produce some of his greatest music, informed by his inner struggles and victories, culminating in the Ninth or Choral Symphony in 1824.

During the same years, another deaf artist was creating works of equal stature in a different medium. Spanish painter Francisco de Goya had been deaf since contracting a mysterious illness in 1792. Previously known for light rococo works, his period of convalescence led him to paint darker, more macabre pictures, in his words, "to occupy an imagination mortified by the contemplation of my suffering." For the rest of his career, his greatest works were predominantly grotesque, nightmarish scenes, including those in the etching series The Disasters of War (1810–1814) and the Black Paintings (1820s). The latter were painted in a country residence near Madrid he called the Quinta del Sordo—House of the Deaf Man.

Beethoven died in 1827. Goya, twenty-four years his elder, died the following year.

1820s	In what may be the first example of actual minstrel dancing, white actor Thomas Rice adapts for the stage a jig danced by a black man named Daddy Jim Crow. Using the stage name Daddy "Jim Crow" Rice, he becomes an immediate success and spawns a new form of entertainment. **DANCE**
1820s	Spanish painter Francisco de Goya paints the *Black Paintings*, a series of macabre images done principally in black, gray, and brown. **PAINT**
1820s	Artists in the Haida settlement in the Queen Charlotte Islands, British Columbia, create totem poles of argillite stone featuring prehistoric tribal motifs. Artists will begin to depict subjects favored by Western visitors to supply an active tourist market. **SCULP**
1820	English poet Percy Bysshe Shelley publishes his masterpiece, the poetic drama *Prometheus Unbound*. Among his other works this year are the political odes "To Liberty" and "To Naples," the political essay "A Philosophical View of Reform," and the lyric poems "The Cloud" and "To a Skylark." **LIT**
1820	Cuban poet José María Heredia publishes "En el teocalli de Cholula." Among his later poems will be "Niagara" (1824). **LIT**

1820–1825   British essayist Charles Lamb, writing under the name Elia, contributes a series of essays to *London Magazine*, collected in 1823 as *Essays of Elia* and 1833 as *The Last Essays of Elia*. They include "A Dissertation on Roast Pig" and "Blakesmoor in H—shire." **LIT**

1820   American writer Washington Irving publishes his best known work, *The Sketch Book of Geoffrey Crayon, Gent.*, which contains the tales of Rip Van Winkle and the Legend of Sleepy Hollow. **LIT**

1820   French poet Alphonse-Marie-Louis de Lamartine publishes the collection *Les Premières méditations*. Among his later collections are *Nouvelles méditations poétiques* (1823) and *Harmonies poétiques et religieuses* (1830). **LIT**

1820   Russian poet Aleksandr Pushkin publishes the poem *Ruslan i Lyudmila* (*Ruslan and Ludmilla*). Among his later works will be the verse novel *Eugene Onegin* (1833) and the Gothic-influenced story "The Queen of Spades" (1834). **LIT**

1820–1910   French photographer Gaspard-Félix Tournachon, known as Nadar, lives and becomes known for his romantic, pleasing portraits of the country's well-known figures, in works such as *Sarah Bernhardt* (1859). **PHOTO**

1821   English poet Percy Bysshe Shelley writes his best known prose work, the essay "The Defence of Poetry," though it will not be published until 1840, after his death. He also publishes *Adonais*, his elegy on the death of John Keats. **LIT**

1821   British poet Thomas Lovell Beddoes publishes the collection *The Improvisatore*. **LIT**

1821   British essayist Thomas De Quincey publishes *Confessions of an English Opium Eater*, along with numerous other pieces appearing in *London Magazine* from 1821 to 1824. **LIT**

1821   The romantic opera *Der Freischütz* by German composer Carl Maria von Weber premieres in Berlin. **MUSIC**

1821   French painter Théodore Géricault paints *Derby at Epsom*, one of several pictures with horse racing as the subject. **PAINT**

1821   Bristish painter John Constable paints the landscape *The Hay Wain*. His romantic approach to landscapes, with its broken color and careful observation of clouds and light, will influence such painters as Delacroix. **PAINT**

1822   English poet Lord Byron publishes the poem *The Vision of Judgement*, a satirical response to Robert Southey's poem *A Vision of Judgement* (1821), in the preface of which Southey had attacked the immoral attitudes in Byron's poem *Don Juan*. **LIT**

1822   English poet Percy Bysshe Shelley drowns in a boating accident, leaving his last poem, *The Triumph of Life*, unfinished. **LIT**

1822   French writer Comte Alfred-Victor de Vigny publishes the volume *Poèmes*. Among his later volumes will be *Poèmes antiques et modernes* (1826) and *Les Destinées* (1862).   **LIT**

1822   Polish poet Adam Mickiewicz publishes the volume of ballads and romances, *Ballady i romanse*. Among his later volumes will be *Pan Tadeusz* (1834), a historical poem about his native country.   **LIT**

1822   Hungarian composer and pianist Franz Liszt, age eleven, debuts as a child prodigy at the piano in Vienna.   **MUSIC**

· ·

"There is nothing ugly; I never saw an ugly thing in my life: for let the form of an object be what it may, —light, shade, and perspective will always make it beautiful."
—British painter John Constable, c. 1820s

· ·

1822   Ludwig van Beethoven's Missa Solemnis in D, Op. 123 and Franz Schubert's Unfinished Symphony are composed.   **MUSIC**

c. 1822   French painter Théodore Géricault paints *A Kleptomaniac*, one of several portraits of mental patients.   **PAINT**

1822   French painter Eugène Delacroix, perhaps the greatest French romantic painter, first comes to public attention with *The Barque of Dante*. Two years later he paints *The Massacre at Chios*. His works are remarkable for their color, brushwork, emotional intensity, and dramatic approach.   **PAINT**

1822   French inventor Joseph-Nicéphore Niepce creates the first permanent photographic representation. He will come to work with Louis Jacques Mandé Daguerre to make the first daguerreotype in 1839.   **PHOTO**

1823–1841   American novelist James Fenimore Cooper writes the novels known as the Leatherstocking tales. Featuring the character Natty Bumppo, they include *The Pioneers* (1823), *The Last of the Mohicans* (1826), *The Prairie* (1827), *The Pathfinder* (1840), and *The Deerslayer* (1841).   **LIT**

1824   The Shakers in Hancock, New York, design the first round barn. Characterized by divisions that form feeding stations, it will be popular with dairy farmers.   **ARCH**

1824   Italian poet Count Giacomo Leopardi publishes the volume *Canzoni*. Among his later volumes will be *Versi* (1826) and *Canti* (1836).   **LIT**

1824   The National Gallery is founded in London. It will move to its present site in Trafalgar Square in 1838.   **PAINT**

1824   French painter Jean-Auguste-Dominique Ingres completes the *Vow of Louis XIII* for the cathedral of Montauban. The work gains him a reputation as the leader of French neoclassicists. Other works by Ingres in this decade and the next include *The Apotheosis of Homer* (1827), *The Martyrdom of St. Symphorian* (1834), and *Antiochus and Stratonice* (1834–40).   **PAINT**

1825   Russian poet Aleksandr Pushkin writes the tragedy *Boris Godunov*, an exploration of the nature of power and resistance to tyranny modeled after Shakespeare's historical plays.   **DRAMA**

1825   English writer William Hazlitt publishes *The Spirit of the Age*, a collection of his essays.   **LIT**

1825   Symphony No. 9, *Choral*, by German composer Ludwig van Beethoven premieres. Perhaps his greatest achievement, it is the first choral symphony to achieve popularity and establishes the genre. It concludes with a magnificent setting of German poet Johann Friedrich von Schiller's "Ode to Joy."   **MUSIC**

c. 1825–
1875   In the United States, the Hudson River school of landscape painting flourishes, combining naturalism and grandeur in depicting wilderness areas such as the Hudson River valley and the Catskill Mountains. Leaders of the school include Thomas Cole, Thomas Doughty, and Asher B. Durand. Other members include Albert Bierstadt, John F. Kensett, Samuel F. B. Morse, and Frederick E. Church.   **PAINT**

1826   Landscape drawings by English painter J. M. W. Turner are published in *Picturesque Views of the Southern Coast of England*.   **GRAPH**

1826   Danish poet and novelist Bernhard Severin Ingemann publishes the historical novel *Valdemar Seier* (*Waldemar, Surnamed Seir, or the Victorious*). Other novels will include *Erik Menveds Barndom* (*The Childhood of King Eric Menved*, 1828) and *Kong Erik og de Fredløse* (*King Erik and the Outlaws*, 1833).   **LIT**

1826   German composer Felix Mendelssohn composes the orchestral overture *A Midsummer Night's Dream*, setting the standard for concert overtures of the period. It will be another seventeen years before he adds the incidental music, including the familiar "Wedding March."   **MUSIC**

1827   American poet and short-story writer Edgar Allan Poe anonymously publishes his first collection, *Tamerlane and Other Poems*.   **LIT**

1827   Italian novelist and poet Alessandro Manzoni publishes the historical novel *I promessi sposi*. Among his many Christian works are the essay *Osservazioni sulla morale cattolica* (1819) and the poetry collection *Inni sacri* (*Sacred Hymns*, 1822).   **LIT**

1827   German poet and journalist Heinrich Heine publishes the volume of poetry *Buch der Lieder* (*Book of Songs*). Among his later works will be *Französische Zustand* (*The Situation in France*, 1832) and *Zur Geschichte der Religion und Philosophie in Deutschland* (*On the History of Religion and Philosophy in Germany*, 1834).   **LIT**

1827   French painter Eugène Delacroix paints *Death of Sardanapalus*, based on a poem by Lord Byron.   **PAINT**

1829   French writer Prosper Mérimée publishes the novel *La Chronique du temps de Charles IX*. Among his later novels will be *Colomba* (1841) and *La Double Méprise* (1833).   **LIT**

1829   Polish pianist and composer Frédéric Chopin debuts in Vienna and is hailed as a "Young Mozart."   **MUSIC**

1829   The opera *William Tell*, by Italian composer Gioacchino Rossini, premieres in Paris.   **MUSIC**

1829   German composer Felix Mendelssohn revives interest in the works of Johann Sebastian Bach when he conducts a performance of *Passion According to St. Matthew* in Berlin, one hundred years after it was first performed in Leipzig.   **MUSIC**

1830   *Hernani*, a drama by the French writer and playwright Victor Hugo, opens at the Théâtre-Français, leading to a riot over the play's political content.   **DRAMA**

1830   British poet Alfred Tennyson (who will be made a lord in 1883) publishes *Poems Chiefly Lyrical*.   **LIT**

1830   British novelist Edward Bulwer-Lytton publishes the crime novel *Paul Clifford*, which begins memorably, "It was a dark and stormy night." Bulwer-Lytton, along with novelists such as William Harrison Ainsworth, specializes in Newgate novels, works of crime fiction often based on true cases and so-called in reference to Newgate Prison.   **LIT**

1830   French novelist Marie Henri Beyle, known as Stendhal, publishes *Le Rouge et le noir* (*The Red and the Black*). It and his future novel *La Chartreuse de Parme* (*The Charterhouse of Parma*, 1839) will be considered important milestones in the development of the modern realistic and psychological novel.   **LIT**

1830   French poet and novelist Théophile Gautier publishes the volume of poetry *Poésies*. Later examples of his finely wrought poetic works include *La Comédie de la mort* (1838) and *Émaux et camées* (1852).   **LIT**

1831   French writer Victor Hugo publishes the novel *The Hunchback of Notre Dame*, about the doomed love of Quasimodo for the beautiful Esmerelda. It will be the basis of memorable films in 1923 and 1939.   **LIT**

1832   *Le Roi s'amuse* (*The King Enjoys Himself*), a play by French writer Victor Hugo, is produced. It will be used as the libretto for Verdi's opera *Rigoletto*.   **DRAMA**

1832   French graphic artist Honoré Daumier, perhaps the greatest caricaturist of the nineteenth century, is imprisoned for his political cartoons lampooning the government of Louis-Philippe.   **GRAPH**

1832   American poet and editor William Cullen Bryant publishes the poem "A Forest Hymn."   **LIT**

1832   French novelist Amandine Dudevant, known as George Sand, publishes the controversial novel *Indiana*. Among her later works will be the novels *Consuelo* (1842) and *François le champi* (1847).   **LIT**

1832   Finnish poet and novelist Johan Ludvig Runeberg publishes the novel *The Elk Hunters*. Among his later prose works is *Tales of Ensign Stal* (1848, 1860), about his country's soldiers during the Russo-Finnish War.   **LIT**

1832   French composer Hector Berlioz's prototypical program symphony *Symphonie fantastique* premieres in Paris. It exhibits his idee fixe, a recurring theme in each movement, forerunner of the leitmotiv.   **MUSIC**

1832   American sculptor Horatio Greenough begins to carve a marble statue of George Washington derived from the classical Greek statue of Zeus. It will be completed in 1841 and stand outside the Capitol.   **SCULP**

1833   American builder Augustus Deodat Taylor invents the balloon frame house, which becomes popular for its sturdiness and ease of construction.   **ARCH**

1833   Scottish historian and essayist Thomas Carlyle publishes *Sartor Resartus*, a satirical, spiritual, wide-ranging philosophical work heavily influenced by German romanticism.   **LIT**

1833   American poet and short-story writer Edgar Allan Poe publishes the story "MS Found in a Bottle." A prize-winning entry in a Baltimore newspaper contest, it brings him fame as a writer of short stories.   **LIT**

1833   French novelist Honoré de Balzac publishes the novel *Eugénie Grandet*. Among his later novels will be *Le Père Goriot*; he will refer to his complete span of works as *La Comédie humaine* (*The Human Comedy*).   **LIT**

1833   The literary sketch "A Dinner at Poplar Walk" (later retitled "Mr. Minns and His Cousin") appears in the *Monthly Magazine* in December of this year, the first published writing of British novelist Charles Dickens. *See* 1836, LIT.   **LIT**

1833   German composer Robert Schumann helps found the leading music journal, *Die Neue Zeitschrift für Musik*. His articles establish the early reputations of such composers as Johannes Brahms, Louis-Hector Berlioz, and Frédéric Chopin.   **MUSIC**

1833   German composer Felix Mendelssohn's *Italian Symphony* premieres in London. **MUSIC**

1833   French sculptor François Rude combines neoclassical and romantic elements in his sculpture of *La Marseillaise* for the Arc de Triomphe in Paris. **SCULP**

1834   Austrian ballerina Fanny Elssler makes her debut at the Paris Opera. **DANCE**

....

"[O]n the day that my daughter was born I never left my studio and I went on working . . . in the intervals between labor pains."—Diligent French portrait painter Élisabeth Vigée-Lebrun, c. 1835–1837

....

1834   French poet and playwright Alfred de Musset writes *Lorenzaccio*, a historical drama which is probably his greatest work for the stage. Most of de Musset's other plays will be comedies such as *Le Chandelier* (*The Decoy*, produced in 1848) and *On ne Bandine pas avec l'amour* (*There's No Trifling with Love*, 1861). He was the lover of French writer George Sand and will become the lover of French actress Rachel. *See* 1838, DRAMA. **DRAMA**

1834   French sculptor Antoine-Auguste Préault exemplifies the physical and emotional violence of the romantic spirit in his bronze relief, *Slaughter.* **SCULP**

1835   French graphic artist Honoré Daumier begins drawing caricatures for the magazine *Charivari*. **GRAPH**

1835   Russian writer Nikolai Gogol publishes the short novel *Taras Bulba*. **LIT**

1835–1872   Danish writer Hans Christian Andersen publishes more than 150 fairy tales, including "The Little Match Girl," "The Red Shoes," "The Ugly Duckling," and "The Emperor's New Clothes." **LIT**

1836   French-born architect Augustus Pugin publishes *Contrasts*, which argues for the superiority of medieval over contemporary architecture. Pugin is a central figure in the Gothic Revival, which brings Gothic styles back into vogue in Europe and the United States, particularly in the building of churches. **ARCH**

1836   Russian writer Nikolai Gogol's satire *Revizor*, later widely known as *The Inspector General*, is produced. This send-up of bureaucracy—and the response of citizens to bureaucracy—will be seen by many, despite its comic exaggerations, as the best early example of Russian social realism. **DRAMA**

1836–1837   British novelist Charles Dickens publishes *Sketches by Boz*, a collection of descriptive essays, short stories, and character sketches originally published in magazines, often under the pseudonym "Boz." In the same period he publishes *The Posthumous Papers of the Pickwick Club*, his first novel. Like his later novels, it is issued in monthly numbers and subsequently published in complete form. **LIT**

1836   American essayist and poet Ralph Waldo Emerson publishes his first book, *Nature*. Its call for spiritual transformation arouses controversy among more conservative critics and thinkers.   **LIT**

1836   German composer Robert Schumann premieres his piano composition *Fantasia in C major*.   **MUSIC**

1836   Russian composer Mikhail Glinka's opera *A Life for the Tsar* premieres in St. Petersburg. It is the first popular opera in the Russian language and inaugurates the nationalist movement.   **MUSIC**

EMERSON AND THOREAU

When American transcendentalist Ralph Waldo Emerson gave his landmark 1837 Harvard commencement address "The American Scholar," the audience included one student who would come to embody his views in ways that made him a "more real" transcendentalist than Emerson himself: Henry David Thoreau.

Thoreau first became acquainted with Emerson's belief in the unity of nature and action earlier at Harvard, through the essay Nature (1836). During his adult years, his life became intertwined with Emerson's. He submitted writings to Emerson's periodical The Dial, tutored one of his relatives, and eventually was employed as a handyman at his estate. More important were the ways Emerson's views informed Thoreau's decisions throughout his life. As a young adult, Thoreau rejected the business world by not becoming part of the family manufacturing business (though he later became part of it). Later in his life he attempted his experimental existence at Walden Pond, refused to pay a poll tax that would support the Mexican War, and aided in helping fugitive slaves gain passage to Canada.

Through all these actions, Thoreau embodied Emerson's belief in the divinity of the commonplace, the need to "embrace the common . . . and sit at the feet of the familiar." His lifework also embraced Emerson's belief in the unity of human action and nature. Thoreau's life showed that "[a] right action seems to fill the eye, and to be related to all nature."

1836   American painter Thomas Cole, a founder of the Hudson River school paints the landscape *The Oxbow* and the historical series *The Course of Empire*. *See* c.1825–1875, PAINT.   **PAINT**

1837–1839   British novelist Charles Dickens publishes *The Adventures of Oliver Twist or, The Parish Boy's Progress*, his second novel.   **LIT**

1837   Scottish historian and essayist Thomas Carlyle publishes the history *The French Revolution*.   **LIT**

1837   American writer Nathaniel Hawthorne publishes the story collection *Twice-Told Tales*. Containing such stories as "The Minister's Black Veil," it establishes him as a noteworthy figure in American writing.   **LIT**

1837   American essayist and poet Ralph Waldo Emerson publishes his address to the Phi Beta Kappa Society at Harvard University, "The American Scholar." In it, he issues a clarion call for independence in American thought.   **LIT**

1837–1839   French inventor Hippolyte Bayard develops a method for making photographs and presents them publicly one month before Louis Daguerre displays his work in 1839. With support from the French government, Daguerre and his method will become the more well accepted.   **PHOTO**

1838   *Ruy Blas*, probably the best play of Victor Hugo, a French writer better known for his poetry and fiction, is produced.   **DRAMA**

1838   Rachel (Élisa Félix), who will become perhaps the greatest actress of nineteenth century France, makes her debut at the Comédie-Française, playing Camille in Corneille's *Horace*. During the next twenty years she will appear in many classical tragedies, attracting a huge following in France and abroad.   **DRAMA**

1838–1839   British novelist Charles Dickens publishes *The Life and Adventures of Nicholas Nickleby*, his third novel.   **LIT**

1838   American poet and short-story writer Edgar Allan Poe publishes the short novel *The Narrative of Arthur Gordon Pym*. The New England whaling tale had been serialized in the *Southern Literary Messenger* in 1837. Over the next decade Poe publishes several stories, including "The Fall of the House of Usher" (1839). "The Tell-Tale Heart" (1843), "The Masque of the Red Death" (1842), and "Murders in the Rue Morgue" (1841).   **LIT**

1838   American essayist and poet Ralph Waldo Emerson presents "The Divinity School Address" to the Harvard Divinity School. His comments on the divinity of Christ lead to great debate.   **LIT**

1838   Johanna Maria (Jenny) Lind, the "Swedish Nightingale," debuts in Carl von Weber's *Der Freischütz* in Stockholm.   **MUSIC**

1839–1842   Austrian ballerina Fanny Elssler tours the United States.   **DANCE**

BEFORE THE PHONOGRAPH

*L*ike present-day CD aficionados, music-lovers in the Victorian era shopped for disks with their favorite tunes to play at home. The instrument for playing these disks was the music box, a cabinet containing a mechanical device that could reproduce music automatically when activated by clockwork. Swiss watchmakers developed the music box early in the nineteenth century; the precisely arranged pins of its rotating cylinder would play musical tones when struck by the teeth of a metal comb. By 1835–1845 cylinder music boxes had reached such high quality that they could reproduce a variety of instrumental effects, including bells, drums, and chimes. Six or seven tunes could be set on one cylinder; some boxes had interchangeable cylinders, each with different tunes, so that listeners could load whatever cylinder suited their mood that evening. In the 1880s and 1890s, cylinders gave way to less cumbersome disks operating on the same mechanical principle.

At their peak, music boxes were handsome pieces of furniture, ranging in size from tabletop to free-standing, often made of fine wood lined with chromolithographic prints and inlaid with materials such as brass or mother of pearl. However, Edison's invention of the phonograph in 1877, and its commercial development in the early twentieth century, spelled the end of the music box era.

1839   Austrian composer Franz Schubert's Symphony in C Major, conducted by Felix Mendelssohn, premieres posthumously in Leipzig. **MUSIC**

1839   The first commercially viable photographic process, the daguerreotype, is developed by French inventor Louis Daguerre. In this technique, a direct positive image is made on a silver-coated plate. The same year British astronomer Sir John Herschel first uses the word *photography*, basing the term on the Greek words for light and writing. During his life he will also apply the terms "positive" and "negative" to the photographic process. *See also* 1837–1839, PHOTO. **PHOTO**

1840s   American settlers expanding into what is now the western United States after the Mexican War (1846–1848) encounter the arts of Native Americans of the region. Native Americans of the western plains weave baskets with complex geometric designs, make elaborately beaded costumes, and design ceremonial masks. The Hopi and Zuni (Pueblo) tribes of the Southwest are known for their ceremonial costumes, masks, and kachina (spirit) dolls, while the Navajo are known for sandpainting, the creation of temporary artworks made of colored sand, used as part of religious ritual. **DECO**

1840s   In France the Barbizon School of landscape painting flourishes, led by painter Théodore Rousseau and also including Charles-François Daubigny, Narcisse-Virgile Diaz de la Peña, and others.   **PAINT**

1840s   The possibilities of portrait photography are explored in the early studies of artists turned photographers such as D. O. Hill and Robert Adamson.   **PHOTO**

1840s   American photographers Albert Sands Southworth and Josiah Johnson Hawes become known for their distinctive daguerreotype portraits. They photographed important American figures of the day, including Ralph Waldo Emerson, Daniel Webster, and Oliver Wendell Holmes.   **PHOTO**

1840–1860   In London the Houses of Parliament are designed by Sir Charles Barry, with exterior and interior ornamentation by Augustus Pugin.   **ARCH**

1840–1841   British novelist Charles Dickens publishes *The Old Curiosity Shop*, his fourth novel.   **LIT**

....

"Artists are always young."
—American writer Margaret Fuller, 1842

....

1840–1844   American essayists and transcendentalists Ralph Waldo Emerson and Margaret Fuller establish the transcendentalist periodical *The Dial*.   **LIT**

1840   American poet and short-story writer Edgar Allan Poe publishes the collection *Tales of the Grotesque and Arabesque*, which contains the short story "The Fall of the House of Usher."   **LIT**

1840   Russian poet and novelist Mikhail Lermontov publishes the novel *A Hero of Our Time*. During his life he will publish several influential poems, including "Angel," "The Testament," and "Demon."   **LIT**

1840   Robert Schumann, a leading composer of romantic German lieder, writes more than one hundred songs during this year, in which he also marries pianist Clara Wieck.   **MUSIC**

1840   American painter Thomas Cole paints the allegorical series *The Voyage of Life*.   **PAINT**

1841   British novelist Charles Dickens publishes *Barnaby Rudge, A Tale of the Riots of Eighty*, his fifth novel. His first historical novel, it focuses on the anti-Catholic riots instigated by Lord George Gordon in 1780.   **LIT**

1841   Scottish historian and essayist Thomas Carlyle publishes *On Heroes, Hero-Worship and the Heroic in History*.   **LIT**

1841–1846   British poet Robert Browning publishes the series of poetic pamphlets entitled *Bells and Pomegranates*. The works include *Pippa Passes* (1841), *Dramatic Lyrics* (1842), *Dramatic Romances and Lyrics* (1845), and *Luria and A Soul's Tragedy* (1846). Poems from this series include "My Last Duchess," "Soliloquy of the Spanish Cloister," "The Pied Piper of Hamelin," and "The Bishop Orders His Tomb in St. Praxed's Church."   **LIT**

1841   American essayist and poet Ralph Waldo Emerson publishes the collection *Essays: First Series*, which includes his philosophical works "The Over-Soul" and "Self-Reliance."   **LIT**

1841   British physicist William Henry Fox Talbot invents a new photographic process, in which paper positives are printed from a paper negative (the calotype). The forerunner of modern photographic processes, the calotype process will displace that of Louis Daguerre. *See also* 1839, PHOTO.   **PHOTO**

1842   *Marriage*, a comedy by Russian writer Nikolai Gogol, is produced.   **DRAMA**

1842   British poet Alfred Tennyson publishes *Poems*, a highly acclaimed work that includes "Locksley Hall," "Ulysses," "The Lady of Shalott," and "The Lotos-Eaters."   **LIT**

1842   American poet Henry Wadsworth Longfellow publishes the mythic poem *Evangeline: A Tale of Acadie*. Among his other poems based on the early years of American life are "The Village Blacksmith" (1842), "The Wreck of the Hesperus" (1841), and "Paul Revere's Ride" (1863).   **LIT**

1842   Russian writer Nikolai Gogol publishes the short story "The Overcoat," which will be an influential work of realism for generations of writers. This year he will also publish the novel *Dead Souls*.   **LIT**

1842   English politician, historian, and poet Thomas Babington Macaulay publishes the poetry volume *Lays of Ancient Rome*. His later works will include the essay collection *Critical and Historical Essays* (1843) and *History of England from the Accession of James the Second* (1848–1861).   **LIT**

1842   The New York Philharmonic Society is founded by violinist Ureli C. Hill and other American musicians.   **MUSIC**

1842   Hungarian pianist and composer Franz Liszt becomes court music conductor at Weimar, making it the new European center for music.   **MUSIC**

1843   Scottish historian and essayist Thomas Carlyle publishes *Past and Present*.   **LIT**

1843 daguerreotype of John Quincy Adams by Philip Haas. *(The Metropolitan Museum of Art, Gift of Stokes and Hawes, 1937)*

1843   American poet and short-story writer Edgar Allan Poe publishes the short story "The Gold Bug," about a search for buried treasure. Originally published in *The Dollar Newspaper*, it appears in the collection *Tales* in 1845.   **LIT**

1843   British art critic John Ruskin publishes the first volume of *Modern Painters*; later volumes will follow in 1846, 1856, and 1860.   **PAINT**

1844   Spanish playwright José Zorrilla y Moral's drama *Don Juan Tenorio* is produced. Other works about the legend of Don Juan—who may never have existed—include Mozart's opera *Don Giovanni* (1787), Lord Byron's poem *Don Juan* (1819–1824), George Bernard Shaw's *Don Juan in Hell* (1907), and Edmond Rostand's *La Dernière nuit de Don Juan* (*The Last Night of Don Juan*, c. 1910).   **DRAMA**

1844   British novelist Charles Dickens publishes the long story *A Christmas Carol*, which introduces archetypal miser Ebenezer Scrooge, who is haunted on Christmas Eve by his deceased partner Jacob Marley and the Spirits of Christmas Past, Christmas Present, and Christmas Yet to Come.   **LIT**

1844   British novelist William Makepeace Thackeray publishes *Barry Lyndon*, recounting the adventures of an Irish scoundrel.   **LIT**

1844–1845   German poet Johann Ludwig Uhland publishes the collection *Alte hoch- und niederdeutsche Volkslieder* (*Old South and North German Folk-Songs*). Earlier works include *Ernst, Herzog von Schwaben* (*Duke Ernst of Swabia*, 1818).   **LIT**

1844   French novelist and playwright Alexandre Dumas père, publishes the swashbuckling novels *The Count of Monte Cristo* and *The Three Musketeers*. Among his later novels will be *The Black Tulip* (1895, published posthumously).   **LIT**

c. 1844   English landscape painter J. M. W. Turner paints *Rain, Steam, and Speed*. Like many of his later paintings, it portrays light, space, and elemental forces in increasingly abstract form.   **PAINT**

1844–1848   French painter Théodore Chassériau paints allegorical scenes of Peace and War for the Cour des Comptes in the Palais d'Orsay in Paris.   **PAINT**

1845–1846   American writer Margaret Fuller publishes two feminist works: *Woman in the 19th Century* (1845) and *Papers on Literature and Art* (1846).   **LIT**

1845   American poet and short-story writer Edgar Allan Poe publishes the poem "The Raven" in the periodicals *The American Review* and the *Evening Mirror* to immediate success.   **LIT**

1845   German composer Robert Schumann writes Concerto in A Minor.   **MUSIC**

1845   The first American grand opera, *Leonora*, by American composer William Henry Fry, premieres in Philadelphia.   **MUSIC**

1846   In Britain *Poems by Currer, Ellis and Acton Bell* is published. The names are pseudonyms for Charlotte, Emily, and Anne Brontë.   **LIT**

1846   British painter and poet Edward Lear publishes his first *Book of Nonsense*, a collection of limericks for children. Many books of nonsense will follow, and he will become famous for such poems as "The Owl and the Pussycat" and "The Jumblies."   **LIT**

1846   American novelist Herman Melville publishes his first novel, *Typee: A Peep at Polynesian Life*. Partly autobiographical, the book concerns two whalemen who abandon their ship to live with a South Seas tribe. The novel is a commercial success.   **LIT**

1846   American writer Nathaniel Hawthorne publishes the collection *Mosses From an Old Manse*, which includes the stories "Young Goodman Brown," "The Birthmark," and "Rappaccini's Daughter."   **LIT**

1846   American poet and short-story writer Edgar Allan Poe publishes "The Cask of Amontillado" in the periodical *Godey's Lady's Book*.   **LIT**

1846   The oratorio *Elijah*, by German composer Felix Mendelssohn, premieres in Birmingham, England.   **MUSIC**

1847   British novelist Charlotte Brontë publishes *Jane Eyre*, her sister Emily Brontë *Wuthering Heights*, and their sister Anne Brontë *Agnes Grey*.   **LIT**

1847–1848   British novelist William Makepeace Thackeray publishes his masterpiece, *Vanity Fair*, the novel that introduces the scheming Becky Sharp.   **LIT**

1847   American novelist Herman Melville publishes the novel *Omoo: A Narrative of Adventures in the South Seas*, a popular sequel to *Typee*.   **LIT**

1848–1850   British novelist William Makepeace Thackeray publishes *The History of Pendennis*, a semiautobiographical portrait of one of the "gentlemen of our age."   **LIT**

1848   British poet Arthur Hugh Clough publishes the verse-novel *The Bothie of Tober-na-Vuolich*.   **LIT**

1848–1858   Hungarian pianist and composer Franz Liszt composes twelve symphonic poems (orchestral music based on an extramusical idea).   **MUSIC**

1848   The Pre-Raphaelite Brotherhood is formed by British painters Holman Hunt, John Everett Millais, Dante Gabriel Rossetti, William Michael Rossetti, F. G. Stephens, James Collinson, and Thomas Woolner. The artists advocate a return to the artistic standards that prevailed before Italian Renaissance painter Raphael. They will influence such nineteenth-century artists and writers as William Morris and Edward Burne-Jones.   **PAINT**

1849   In New York City American inventor James Bogardus builds the first prefabricated homes.   **ARCH**

1849   British poet Matthew Arnold publishes *The Strayed Reveller and Other Poems*.   **LIT**

1849–1850   *The Personal History of David Copperfield*, the eighth novel by British writer Charles Dickens, is published.   **LIT**

1849   American writer Henry David Thoreau publishes the essay that will become known as "Civil Disobedience" in the periodical *Aesthetic Papers*. Titled in the magazine "Resistance to Civil Government," it is spurred by Thoreau's opposition to American involvement in the Mexican War. In the same year Thoreau publishes *A Week on the Concord and Merrimack Rivers*.   **LIT**

1849–1850   British painter Dante Gabriel Rossetti paints *The Annunciation*.   **PAINT**

1849   Stereophotography, which uses a double-lens camera to produce two views that together produce a three-dimensional view, is developed. It will remain popular over the next three decades.   **PHOTO**

1849–1851   Traveling to the Near East with French novelist Gustave Flaubert, French photographer and writer Maxime Du Camp takes a series of photographs of the land that establish him in the new practice of topographical photography.   **PHOTO**

1850s   Minstrel shows, featuring actors performing in blackface, become common in the United States. The shows will remain popular for two decades; the practice of performing in blackface will continue into the twentieth century.   **DRAMA**

1850s   Limelights—blocks of lime heated so that they give off a glow—come into general use as stage illuminators. By the 1890s most theaters will have electric lights but not necessarily electric stage lighting systems.   **DRAMA**

1850s   Music hall entertainment becomes popular in England. At first, mostly singers are featured, but over time, dancers, magicians, comedians, and acrobats will be added. These variety shows will flourish through the early twentieth century.   **DRAMA**

1850s   Inexpensive, tawdry paperbound novels called penny dreadfuls in Britain and dime novels in the United States become popular.   **LIT**

1850s   American novelists Nathaniel Hawthorne and Herman Melville meet in the Berkshires of New England. They come to affect each other's work significantly, notably in the cases of Melville's *Moby-Dick* and Hawthorne's *The House of Seven Gables*. Their meeting is recalled in Melville's "Hawthorne and His Mosses."   **LIT**

1850s   Inexpensive photographic portraits become available to all social classes, produced by large-scale photographic operations like that built by French photographer André Adolphe Eugène Disderi. The portraits measure four by two and a half inches; the process for making them will be patented in 1854.   **PHOTO**

1850s In France the possibilities for artistic expression are explored by members of the Société Française de Photographie, such as photographers Charles Marville, Charles Negre, and Gustave Le Gray. **PHOTO**

1850 German playwright Friedrich Hebbel completes *Herodes and Marianne.* **DRAMA**

1850 British philosopher and critic George Henry Lewes begins writing theater criticism. His work will appear in *The Leader*, a publication which he founded, for four years and later in other venues. He will become the companion of British novelist George Eliot. **DRAMA**

1850 Shortly after his death this year, William Wordsworth's autobiographical blank-verse poem, *The Prelude*, begun in 1798 and worked at throughout his life, is published for the first time. The fourteen-book poem will later be found to exist in a two-part version (1799) and a thirteen-book version (1805). **LIT**

1850 British poet Alfred Tennyson publishes *In Memoriam*, an elegy on the death of his friend Arthur Hallam, and succeeds William Wordsworth as Poet Laureate. **LIT**

1850 British poet Elizabeth Barrett Browning publishes *Sonnets from the Portuguese*, love poems written to Robert Browning before their secret marriage in 1846. It includes Sonnet 43, which begins, "How do I love thee? Let me count the ways." **LIT**

1850 British painter Dante Gabriel Rossetti's best known poem, "The Blessed Damozel," is published. **LIT**

1850 American essayist and poet Ralph Waldo Emerson publishes *Representative Men*, a book of essays. **LIT**

1850 *Cataline*, by Norwegian playwright Henrik Ibsen, premieres. **LIT**

1850 American writer Nathaniel Hawthorne publishes *The Scarlet Letter*, the story of Puritan sin and redemption as seen through the illicit love affair between Hester Prynne and the Reverend Dimmesdale, and the jealous actions of Roger Chillingsworth. It will become his best known work. **LIT**

1850 American composer Stephen Foster's "De Camptown Races (Gwine to Run All Night)" becomes popular in the United States. **MUSIC**

1850 The Swedish soprano Jenny Lind begins a highly successful two-year tour of America, under the direction of American entrepreneur Phineas T. Barnum. **MUSIC**

1850 The opera *Lohengrin*, by German composer Richard Wagner, is premiered in Weimar, Germany. **MUSIC**

1850 German composer Robert Schumann completes his Symphony no. 3 (*Rhenish*). **MUSIC**

1850   At the Salon of 1850 French painter Gustave Courbet exhibits *The Stonebreakers*, *The Burial at Ornans*, and *The Peasants at Flagey*, three works that establish him as the leader of the realist school of painting. *The Stonebreakers* will be lost in the firebombing of Dresden in World War II.   **PAINT**

1850   American painter George Caleb Bingham completes *Raftsmen Playing Cards*.   **PAINT**

1850   English Pre-Raphaelite painter Sir John Everett Millais completes *Christ in the Carpenter's Shop*.   **PAINT**

. . . .

"Painting is an art of sight and should therefore concern itself with things seen; it should, therefore abandon the historical scenes of the Classical school and poetic subjects from Goethe and Shakespeare favored by the Romantic school."—French painter Gustave Courbet on the school of realism in painting, c. 1850s

. . . .

1850   French realist painter Jean-François Millet completes *The Gleaners* and *The Sower*.   **PAINT**

1850   Pioneering American photographer Mathew Brady publishes a collection, *Gallery of Illustrious Americans*, to wide notice.   **PHOTO**

1851   The Crystal Palace, an eighteen-acre iron, glass, and wood building that will affect skyscraper design, is designed by British architect Sir Joseph Paxton.   **ARCH**

1851   British engineer William Cubitt builds King's Cross Station, in London.   **ARCH**

1851   American designer Thomas Walter is named the architect of the U.S. Capitol. He is responsible for building the dome of the U.S. House of Representatives building and wings in the U.S. Senate building.   **ARCH**

1851   Danish choreographer and dancer Auguste Bournonville presents the ballet *Kermesse in Bruges*, which like his earlier ballets, combines romanticism with a feeling for everyday life.   **DANCE**

1851   Austrian ballerina Fanny Elssler, definitive ballerina of the Romantic era, retires from the stage after more than twenty-five years of performances worldwide.   **DANCE**

1851   The cartoons of John Tenniel appear in the British periodical *Punch*.   **GRAPH**

1851   *The New York Times* is first published, under the editorship of American newspaperman Henry Raymond.   **LIT**

1851   American writer Nathaniel Hawthorne publishes *The House of Seven Gables*.   **LIT**

1851–1853   British art critic John Ruskin writes *The Stones of Venice*.   **LIT**

1851   German poet and critic Heinrich Heine publishes *Romanzero*.   **LIT**

··

"Remember that the most beautiful things in the world are the most useless: peacocks and lilies for instance."
—British art critic John Ruskin, The Stones of Venice,
1851-1853

··

1851   American novelist Herman Melville publishes his tragic tale of whaling, obsession, and redemption, *Moby-Dick; or, The Whale*. The daring novel earns little in royalties and elicits only limited critical appreciation.   **LIT**

1851   The opera *Rigoletto*, by Italian composer Giuseppi Verdi, premieres in Venice. Together with the operas *Il Trovatore* (1853) and *La Traviata* (1853), it represents a high point in Italian opera.   **MUSIC**

1851   The opera *Sappho*, by French composer Charles Gounod, is premiered in Paris.   **MUSIC**

1851   German composer Robert Schumann completes the rewriting of his 1849 *Manfred* Overture.   **MUSIC**

1851   German-born painter Emanuel Leutze, who spent many years in the United States, paints *Washington Crossing the Delaware*.   **PAINT**

1851   American painter George Caleb Bingham completes *The Trappers' Return*.   **PAINT**

1851   French painter Jean-Baptiste-Camille Corot completes *La Danse des Nymphes* (*The Dance of the Nymphs*).   **PAINT**

1851   The wet collodion process for developing photographs, which creates a negative image with the fine detail of a daguerreotype, is developed by British photographer Frederick Scott Archer.   **PHOTO**

1851   High-speed flash is used to capture movement in photographs.   **PHOTO**

1852   American mechanic Elisha Graves Otis patents the safety elevator. Operating by a system of rope, grips, and ratchets, the cagelike device will permit the development of skyscrapers.   **ARCH**

1852   Paddington Station in London is designed by Brunel and Wyatt.   **ARCH**

1852   The *Hungarian Dances*, a collection of twenty-one dances for piano by German composer Johannes Brahms, is published in four volumes.   **DANCE**

1852   *Masks and Faces*, by British playwrights Charles Read and Tom Taylor, premieres at the Haymarket Theatre in London.   **DRAMA**

1852   *La Dame aux camélias*, by French playwright Alexandre Dumas fils, premieres at the Théâtre du Vaudeville in Paris.   **DRAMA**

1852   The American comic periodical *Diogenes, Hys Lantern* publishes the first cartoon rendition of Uncle Sam, a character representing the United States.   **GRAPH**

1852   Five of Charles Dickens's long stories with a Christmas theme are collected in *Christmas Books*, containing *A Christmas Carol*, "The Chimes," "The Cricket on the Hearth," "The Battle of Life," and "The Haunted Man." *See also* 1844, LIT.   **LIT**

1852   British novelist William Makepeace Thackeray publishes his most elaborately planned novel, *The History of Henry Esmond*.   **LIT**

. . . .

"I have never seen angels. Show me an angel and I will paint one."—French painter Gustave Courbet on a request to depict angels in a church painting, c. 1850s

. . . .

1852   British critic and poet Matthew Arnold publishes *Empedocles and Other Poems*.   **LIT**

1852   American novelist Harriet Beecher Stowe publishes the antislavery novel *Uncle Tom's Cabin*, which becomes one of the best-selling books of the century. Traveling drama troupes that perform parts of the book will become popular in parts of the United States.   **LIT**

1852   British doctor and scholar Peter Mark Roget publishes the *Thesaurus of English Words and Phrases*.   **LIT**

1852–1853   British novelist Charles Dickens publishes his ninth novel, *Bleak House*, the story of the interminable lawsuit of Jarndyce and Jarndyce.   **LIT**

1852   French writer Prosper Mérimée publishes *Carmen*.   **LIT**

1852   American writer Nathaniel Hawthorne publishes *The Blithedale Romance*, based on his 1841 experience living in the utopian community Brook Farm.   **LIT**

1852   Russian writer Ivan Turgenev publishes the story collection *Sportsman's Sketches*, which establishes him as an important writer.   **LIT**

1852   The opera *Dmitry Donskoy*, with music by Russian court musician Anton Grigoryevich Rubinstein, premieres in St. Petersburg, Russia.   **MUSIC**

1852   British painter Ford Madox Brown paints *The Last of England*, an example of English realism.   **PAINT**

1852   French painter Gustave Courbet completes *Les Demoiselles de Village*.   **PAINT**

1852   British painter William Holman Hunt completes *The Light of the World*.   **PAINT**

1853   British designer P. C. Albert oversees the rebuilding of Balmoral Castle, in Scotland.   **ARCH**

1853   French designer Georges Haussmann oversees rebuilding the Paris boulevards and Bois de Boulogne.   **ARCH**

1853   The comedy *Die Journalisten*, by German playwright Gustav Freytag, is premiered in Breslau, Germany.   **DRAMA**

1853–1855   British novelist William Makepeace Thackeray publishes the panoramic social novel *The Newcomes*, subtitled *Memoirs of a Most Respectable Family*.   **LIT**

1853   British critic and poet Matthew Arnold publishes *The Scholar-Gipsy*, an elegy based on a legend about an Oxford student who becomes part of a group of gypsies.   **LIT**

1853   American writer Nathaniel Hawthorne publishes *Tanglewood Tales*.   **LIT**

1853   American novelist Herman Melville publishes "Bartleby the Scrivener," a short story about a clerk who "would prefer not to." The story will later appear in the collection *Piazza Tales* (1856) along with other well-known works including "Benito Cereno."   **LIT**

1853   British novelist Elizabeth Gaskell publishes *Cranford*. The domestic novel was first serialized in the magazine *Household Words* from 1851 to 1853.   **LIT**

1853   British novelist Charlotte Brontë publishes *Villette*.   **LIT**

1853   German-born Henry Steinway (born Heinrich Steinweg) begins to manufacture pianos with his three sons in New York. Over the years, the Steinway name will become known for high-quality piano manufacture; the firm will continue to retain facilities in New York.   **MUSIC**

1853   Italian composer Giuseppe Verdi completes the opera *La Traviata*. It and another of his operas, *Il Trovatore*, premiere this year.   **MUSIC**

1853   "My Old Kentucky Home, Good Night," which will become one of Stephen Foster's most beloved compositions, debuts in the United States in June. It is one of his several "plantation melodies."   **MUSIC**

1853   German composer Richard Wagner begins more than two decades of work on the four operas that comprise *Der Ring des Nibelungen* (*The Ring of the Nibelung*). The four works, with their dates of completion, consist of *Das Rheinold* (1854), *Die Walküre* (1856), *Siegfried* (1871), and *Götterdammerüng* (1874). *See also* 1876, MUSIC.   **MUSIC**

1853–1861   In the last decade of his life, French painter Eugène Delacroix (d. 1863) paints *Jacob and the Angel* and *Heliodorus Expelled from the Temple*.   **PAINT**

1853   French painter Rosa Bonheur completes *The Horse Fair*.   **PAINT**

1853–1854   London's Photographic Society and France's Société Française de Photographie are founded to promote the new scientific art internationally.   **PHOTO**

1854   *Bednost ne porok* (*Poverty Is No Crime*) by Russian playwright Aleksandr Nikolayevich Ostrovsky, premieres in Moscow.   **DRAMA**

1854   British novelist Charles Dickens publishes his tenth novel, *Hard Times*.   **LIT**

1854–1855   British novelist Elizabeth Gaskell publishes *North and South*, which centers on labor turmoil in the industrial north of England.   **LIT**

1854   American poet John Greenleaf Whittier publishes "Maud Muller," a narrative poem of unrequited love between a maid and a judge that ends with the rueful observation, "For all of the sad words of tongue or pen/The saddest of these: 'It might have been.'"   **LIT**

1854   British poet Alfred Tennyson publishes *Charge of the Light Brigade*, honoring Lord Cardigan and the Crimean War Battle of Balaclava.   **LIT**

1854   British novelist Charlotte Mary Yonge publishes *The Heir of Redclyffe*. It will establish her as a novelist of Victorian middle-class life.   **LIT**

1854   The antiliquor novel *Ten Nights in a Barroom and What I Saw There*, by American novelist Timothy Shay Arthur, is published, and serves as the source for a long-lived play adaptation by William Pratt (1858).   **LIT**

1854   The Astor Library, a precursor to the New York Public Library system, begins operation. At its opening, the library has 80,000 volumes.   **LIT**

1854   American writer Henry David Thoreau publishes the work *Walden*, a chronicle of his attempt to "live deliberately," based on his months at Walden Pond in Concord, Massachusetts.   **LIT**

1854   The Christmas Oratorio, *The Infant Christ*, by French composer Louis-Hector Berlioz, is premiered in Paris. His 1849 work, *Te Deum*, will be premiered in Paris the next year.   **MUSIC**

1854   American songwriter Stephen Foster's "Jeanie with the Light Brown Hair" debuts.   **MUSIC**

1854–1857   Hungarian pianist and composer Franz Lizst completes the tone poem *Préludes* and *A Faust Symphony*.   **MUSIC**

1854   British painter Dante Gabriel Rossetti completes *Found*.   **PAINT**

1854   French Romantic painter Eugène Delacroix produces *Christ on the Sea of Galilee*.   **PAINT**

1854   American painter James Abbott McNeill Whistler travels to Paris to study painting for four years. He will remain in Europe for the rest of his life.   **PAINT**

1854   French painter Gustave Courbet paints *The Winnowers* and *Bonjour, Monsieur Courbet*.   **PAINT**

1855   *Le Demi-Monde* by French playwright Alexandre Dumas fils, is staged.   **DRAMA**

1855   British poet Robert Browning publishes the poem *Childe Roland to the Dark Tower Came*. Its title comes from a piece of a song in Shakespeare's *King Lear*, Act 3, Scene 4.   **LIT**

....

"I greet you at the beginning of a great career, which yet must have had a long foreground somewhere for such a start."—American essayist and poet Ralph Waldo Emerson to poet Walt Whitman on the publication of the latter's Leaves of Grass, 1855

....

1855   In the same year, the *Daily News* is founded in New York, *The Daily Telegraph* begins publication in Britain, and *Leslie's Illustrated Newspaper*, founded by American publisher Frank Leslie, is started. *Leslie's* will be known for its liberal use of illustrations and its titillating stories, and within two decades *The Telegraph* will become the world's best-selling newspaper.   **LIT**

1855   British poet Robert Browning publishes the collection *Men and Women*, which contains, among other poems, "Fra Lippo Lippi" and "Andrea del Sarto."   **LIT**

1855   British critic and poet Matthew Arnold publishes the elegy, "Stanzas from the Grande Chartreuse."   **LIT**

1855   American poet John Greenleaf Whittier publishes "The Barefoot Boy," a poem about growing up in the countryside.   **LIT**

1855   American poet Henry Wadsworth Longfellow publishes *Hiawatha*, about the life and heroic works of the title character, a member of the Ojibway tribe.   **LIT**

1855–1857   British novelist Charles Dickens publishes his eleventh novel, *Little Dorrit*, about the effects of debtor's prison on the Dorrit family, particularly on Amy, or Little, Dorrit.   **LIT**

1855   *The Age of Fable* is published by American scholar Thomas Bulfinch. It provides an overview of the mythology of several countries and regions, and still remains a standard.   **LIT**

1855   American poet Walt Whitman publishes in limited edition his collection of poems, *Leaves of Grass*, which includes those now known as "Song of Myself" and "I Sing the Body Electric."   **LIT**

Photograph of Sarah Bernhardt in the title role of *Fedora* by Victorien Sardou. *(The Theater Museum, London/Photosearch, Inc.)*

1855   *Rip van Winkle*, by George Frederick Bristow, the first American grand opera on an American subject, premieres in New York City.   **MUSIC**

1855   "Listen to the Mockingbird" by American composer Richard Millburn and lyricist Alice Hawthorne (Septimus Winner) becomes popular.   **MUSIC**

| 1855 | Russian composer Mikhail Glinka completes *Festival Polonaise*. **MUSIC** |

1855   Russian composer Mikhail Glinka completes *Festival Polonaise*. **MUSIC**

1855   The opera *Les Vêpres Sicilennes*, by Italian composer Giuseppe Verdi, premieres in Paris. **MUSIC**

1855   Trio in B Major by German composer Johannes Brahms premieres in New York. **MUSIC**

1855   French painter Gustave Courbet organizes the *Pavillion du Réalisme* for the Paris World Fair. Among the realist works exhibited are his *The Painter's Studio*. **PAINT**

1855   American painter George Caleb Bingham completes *Verdict of the People*. **PAINT**

1855   The Crimean War is captured in photographs by British photographer Roger Fenton, who uses a wet collodion process to develop his work. It will be the first time a national war is extensively photographed. **PHOTO**

1856   Mauve, the first chemical dye, is discovered by British chemist William Henry Perkin. **DECO**

1856   British actress Ellen Terry, nine years old, makes her stage debut as Mamillius in Shakespeare's *The Winter's Tale*. Over the next fifty years, she will garner praise playing most of Shakespeare's major female roles and a variety of other parts. She will carry on a long correspondence with George Bernard Shaw (*see* 1856, LIT), and, late in life, deliver highly regarded lectures on Shakespeare. **DRAMA**

1856   British poet Elizabeth Barrett Browning publishes *Aurora Leigh*. **LIT**

1856   French novelist Gustave Flaubert publishes the novel *Madame Bovary*. The story of the bourgeois Emma Bovary will become known as a benchmark in the history of the novel. **LIT**

1856   The National Portrait Gallery, the national collection of portraits of famous Britons, is founded in London. **PAINT**

1857–1887   Urban park planner Frederick Law Olmsted designs Central Park in New York City, one of the earliest attempts to design a natural-looking public park in the United States. **ARCH**

1857   American lithographers Nathaniel Currier and James M. Ives enter into partnership in New York and begin a prolific career as the depictors of popular scenes of everyday urban and rural American life. Their business will run until 1907. **GRAPH**

1857   British novelist Anthony Trollope publishes *Barchester Towers*, one of his six novels set in the fictional county of Barsetshire. **LIT**

1857   Norwegian novelist, poet, and playwright Bjørnstjerne Bjørnson publishes the peasant novel *Synnøve Solbakken* (*Trust and Trial*). Among his later works will be the realist plays *Redaktøren* (*The Editor*, 1874) and *Over Aevne I* (*Beyond Our Power*, 1883,1895). **LIT**

1857   French poet Charles Baudelaire publishes the collection *Les Fleurs du mal* (*The Flowers of Evil*). It will become one of the best-known works of the symbolist poets.   **LIT**

1857   Pre-Raphaelite British artists William Morris, Dante Gabriel Rossetti, and Edward Burne-Jones work together on frescoes at the Oxford Union Society.   **PAINT**

1857   In Britain photographer Oscar Rejlander enjoys huge success with the allegorical multiphoto composition *The Two Paths of Life*. Influenced by *A Rake's Progress* by eighteenth-century English painter and engraver William Hogarth, it illustrates the good and ill paths a young man may choose.   **PHOTO**

1858   British artist William Morris publishes the poetry collection *The Defence of Guenevere and Other Poems*.   **LIT**

1858   Using the name Artemus Ward, American journalist Charles Farrar Browne publishes the first of his comic letters in the Cleveland *Plain Dealer*. The letters of the fictitious uneducated businessman spark a career in writing and lecturing that will continue until Browne's death in 1867.   **LIT**

1858   American jurist Oliver Wendell Holmes publishes *The Autocrat of the Breakfast Table*, a book collecting his *Atlantic Monthly* pieces on American society and topics of the day. Poems are also included. Several "Breakfast Table" sequels will follow until 1890.   **LIT**

1858   American poet Henry Wadsworth Longfellow publishes the poem "The Courtship of Miles Standish," which sells widely.   **LIT**

1858   The New York Symphony Orchestra gives its first public concert.   **MUSIC**

1858   Photographer Henry Peach Robinson establishes himself as a chronicler of the Victorian scene with his multiple-negative composition of a life near its end, *Fading Away*.   **PHOTO**

1859   British novelist Charles Dickens publishes his twelfth novel, *A Tale of Two Cities*. His second and last historical novel, it is set during the French Revolution and introduces the self-sacrificing Sydney Carton.   **LIT**

1859   British poet Alfred Tennyson publishes the first four books of *Idylls of the King*.   **LIT**

1859   British novelist and poet George Meredith publishes his first novel, *The Ordeal of Richard Feverel*.   **LIT**

1859   British poet and translator Edward FitzGerald publishes his free translation of *The Rubáiyát of Omar Khayyám*, based on the work of the twelfth-century Persian poet.   **LIT**

1859   French poet Frédéric Mistral publishes the work *Mirèio*. Among his later works will be *Lou Pouème Jóu Rose*. He will be the co-winner of the Nobel Prize in 1904.   **LIT**

1859   American sculptor Erastus Dow Palmer works directly from live models to create *White Captive*, his first attempt at an undraped neoclassical nude.   **SCULP**

1860s   Melodrama becomes popular on the American stage—and, with it, a melodramatic style of acting. Plays featuring adventure and romance, a number of them imports from France, are staged with histrionic performers. Melodrama will remain popular throughout the rest of the century, though, over time, it will be increasingly replaced by theater presenting serious subjects in realistic ways.   **DRAMA**

1860s   American photographer Alexander Gardner chronicles the U.S. Civil War in removed, unheroic compositions that become widely seen in mass periodicals of the day. The former assistant to American photographer Mathew Brady becomes important to the development of photojournalism.   **PHOTO**

1860s   Photographer Julia Margaret Cameron becomes known for her lyrical portraits of important men and women of the Victorian era.   **PHOTO**

1860s   In Europe stock photographs of city scenes, landscapes, and artworks become available through large stock houses. Among the more well-known of such firms are those run in England by Francis Firth and in Italy by the Alinari brothers.   **PHOTO**

1860s   American photographer William Henry Jackson becomes known for his photographs of Native Americans and the West. By the end of the next decade, after working with the Haden Geological Survey, he will begin his own photographic company.   **PHOTO**

1860   The golden era of wood carving begins in the Pacific Northwest. Artists will produce numerous examples of poles, masks, helmets, bowls, and rattles.   **DECO**

1860   British novelist Charles Dickens publishes the first edition of *The Uncommercial Traveller*, a collection of essays and sketches. Subsequent editions will appear in 1865 and posthumously in 1875.   **LIT**

1860–1861   British novelist Charles Dickens publishes his thirteenth novel, *Great Expectations*, which introduces the characters of Pip and Miss Havisham.   **LIT**

1860   British art critic John Ruskin publishes *Unto this Last*, a collection of essays on political economy that emphasizes the responsibilities of employers toward employees.   **LIT**

1860   American critic William Dean Howells writes one of his first books, *Lives and Speeches of Abraham Lincoln and Hannibal Hamlin*. The book about the presidential campaign yields Howells a political appointment as American consul to Venice.   **LIT**

1860   American writer Nathaniel Hawthorne publishes the novel *The Marble Faun*.   **LIT**

1860   Nationalism in music begins to gain strength as a reaction against the dominance of German music. The movement places strong emphasis on national elements and resources of music and is most popular in such "peripheral" European nations as Bohemia, Norway, Russia, Spain, and England.   **MUSIC**

1860   American sculptor John Quincy Adams Ward models his bronze *Indian Hunter* from sketches he made studying Native Americans in the Dakotas. He will enlarge the statue for another version to be placed in New York City's Central Park.   **SCULP**

1861   British artist William Morris cofounds a firm for the hand-manufacture of home decor, Morris, Marshall, Faulkner and Co. (reconstituted in 1875 as Morris and Co.). The firm sparks a revival in decorative arts, influenced by Morris's designs for wallpaper, embroideries, chintzes, tapestries, and carpets. The firm also becomes known for its stained glass, painted tiles, furniture, and stenciled mural decoration.   **DECO**

1861   British caricaturist Charles Samuel Keene begins a long association with the magazine *Punch*.   **GRAPH**

c. 1861   American poet Emily Dickinson writes poem 288, which begins, "I'm Nobody! Who are you?/Are you— Nobody—Too?" and 465, which begins, "I heard a Fly buzz—when I died—." They will become two of her best-known works.   **LIT**

1861–1862   British novelist William Makepeace Thackeray publishes his last completed novel, *The Adventures of Philip*.   **LIT**

1861–1865   American poet Walt Whitman serves as a volunteer nurse during the Civil War and visits many of the Army camp hospitals. The experience informs his 1865 collection of poems, *Drum-Taps*.   **LIT**

1861   Employing a team of several photographers, American photographer Mathew Brady begins systematic photographic coverage of the U.S. Civil War.   **PHOTO**

1862   British poet Christina Rossetti publishes *Goblin Market and Other Poems*.   **LIT**

1862   British novelist and poet George Meredith publishes his most important collection of poetry, *Modern Love*.   **LIT**

1862   American poet Emily Dickinson makes her first batch of poems public by sending them to Massachusetts clergyman Thomas Wentworth Higginson.   **LIT**

··

"So this is the little lady who made this big war."
—Attributed to U.S. president Abraham Lincoln, on meeting Harriet Beecher Stowe, author of the 1852 antislavery novel, Uncle Tom's Cabin, c. 1862

··

1862   French writer Victor Hugo publishes the novel *Les Misérables*, about the fate of peasant Jean Valjean after he steals a loaf of bread. The book will be the basis of a twentieth-century Broadway musical.   **LIT**

1862   A chronological catalogue of Austrian composer Wolfgang Amadeus Mozart's works, prepared by German music-lover Ludwig Köchel, is published. The Köchel or "K" numbers will be universally used to identify Mozart's compositions.   **MUSIC**

1862   French graphic artist Honoré Daumier paints *The Third Class Carriage*.   **PAINT**

1863   On November 19 American President Abraham Lincoln delivers his one-paragraph Gettysburg Address. It will become one of the best-known speeches in American literature.   **LIT**

1863   At the Salon des Refusés, an exhibition held in Paris to display creations rejected by the official Salon, artists represented include Édouard Manet, Paul Cézanne, Camille Pissarro, and James Whistler. Despite ridicule from many quarters, the event undermines the power of the official Salon, encouraging other independent exhibitions.   **PAINT**

1863   French painter Jean-Auguste-Dominique Ingres paints the *Turkish Bath*.   **PAINT**

··

"Insults are pouring down on me thick as hail."—French painter Édouard Manet telling poet Charles Baudelaire about criticism to his paintings, 1860s

··

1863   French painter Édouard Manet paints *Luncheon on the Grass*, which creates a scandal for its depiction of a female nude picnicking with two clothed men. Rejected by the official Salon, it is is presented at the Salon des Refusés. Manet's *Olympia*, depicting a nude prostitute in a pose drawn from Titian's *Venus of Urbino*, also creates controversy.   **PAINT**

1864   American actors Edwin Thomas, John Wilkes, and Junius Brutus
            Booth, three brothers, appear together for the only time in *Julius
            Caesar*. Edwin, particularly good in tragic roles, will become per-
            haps the greatest nineteenth-century American actor. John Wilkes,
            a less distinguished but still good performer, will go down in history
            as the assassin of President Abraham Lincoln (*see* 1865, DRAMA).
            Junius Brutus will do moderately well as an actor and a theater
            manager. The three men's father, Junius Booth, was a popular actor
            in England and America earlier in the century.   **DRAMA**

1864–1865   British novelist Charles Dickens publishes *Our Mutual Friend*, his
            fourteenth novel and the last he will complete.   **LIT**

1864   British poet Alfred Tennyson publishes a volume of poems that
            includes "Enoch Arden" and "Tithonus."   **LIT**

1864   British poet Robert Browning publishes *Dramatic Personae*, which
            includes the poems "Caliban Upon Setebos" and "Abt Vogler."   **LIT**

1864   British theologian John Henry Newman publishes *Apologia pro Vita
            Sua* (revised 1865), a defense of his conversion from Anglicanism to
            Roman Catholicism. Newman will be made a cardinal in 1879. He
            will also publish *The Grammar of Assent*, an argument for religious
            belief, in 1870.   **LIT**

1864–1869   Russian novelist Count Leo Tolstoy composes his epic novel of
            Russia during the invasion of Napoleon, *War and Peace*.   **LIT**

1864   French writer Jules Verne publishes the novel *Journey to the Center
            of the Earth*. This and subsequent works mark him as one of the
            founders of science fiction.   **LIT**

1864   Russian novelist Fyodor Dostoyevsky publishes the story "Notes
            from Underground." It will be considered a highly philosophical
            and psychological work.   **LIT**

c. 1865   Opera singer Ludwig Leichner invents grease paint. It will come
            into general use among actors over the next twenty-five years.
            Twentieth-century actors will continue to use grease paint, but they
            will also use liquid and "pancake" makeup.   **DRAMA**

1865   On April 14 American actor John Wilkes Booth assassinates
            President Abraham Lincoln during a performance of the British
            play *Our American Cousin* at Ford's Theatre in Washington, D.C. *See
            also* 1864, DRAMA.   **DRAMA**

1865   British critic and poet Matthew Arnold publishes *Essays in Criticism*,
            First Series, with its famous introduction, "The Function of
            Criticism at the Present Time." The Second Series will be published
            posthumously in 1888.   **LIT**

1865   British mathematician and writer Charles Dodgson, known as Lewis Carroll, publishes the children's book *Alice's Adventures in Wonderland*. Like its sequel, *Through the Looking-Glass*, it features illustrations by Sir John Tenniel.   **LIT**

1865   American poet Walt Whitman publishes his elegy to the late president Abraham Lincoln, "When Lilacs Last in the Dooryard Bloom'd." It will come to be considered the finest poem written about the assassinated president.   **LIT**

. . . .

"All books are divisible into two classes: the books of the hour, and the books of all time."—British art critic John Ruskin, Sesame and Lilies, 1865

. . . .

1865   American writer Samuel Langhorne Clemens, known as Mark Twain, publishes the yarn "The Notorious Jumping Frog of Calaveras County," the title character of which he heard about in his travels to mining camps in the western United States. The tall tale is widely reprinted and gains Twain much notice.   **LIT**

1865   French art theorist Hippolyte Taine publishes *Philosophie de l'art*, in which he articulates a positivist view of aesthetics.   **MISC**

1865   German composer Richard Wagner's opera *Tristan and Isolde* (completed in 1859) premieres in Munich. Its intensely dramatic style increases the expressive use of melody and chord.   **MUSIC**

1866   *Brand*, a verse play by Norwegian playwright Henrik Ibsen, is produced. *Peer Gynt*, also a verse play, will be produced in 1867. The two will be early critical and commercial successes for Ibsen. He will not write any subsequent verse plays.   **DRAMA**

1866   British critic and poet Matthew Arnold publishes the poem "Thyrsis," commemorating his friend and fellow poet Arthur Hugh Clough, who died in 1861.   **LIT**

1866   British poet Algernon Charles Swinburne publishes *Poems and Ballads*, which includes "Garden of Proserpine" and "Hymn to Proserpine."   **LIT**

1866   French novelist Pierre Loti (pen name of Louis-Marie-Julien Viaud) publishes the novel *Pêcheur d'Islande* (*An Iceland Fisherman*). Among his later novels will be *Mon Frère Yves* (1883) and *Matelot* (1893).   **LIT**

1866   French poet Paul Verlaine publishes the volume *Poèmes saturniens*. Among his later volumes will be *Fêtes galantes* (1869) and *Sagesse* (1881).   **LIT**

1866   French writer Alphonse Daudet publishes the story collection *Lettres de mon moulin* (*Letters from My Window*). Among his later works will be the novels *Le Nabab* (1877) and *Numa Roumestan* (1881).   **LIT**

1866   Russian novelist Fyodor Dostoyevsky publishes *Crime and Punishment*, a novel of guilt and redemption that introduces the scholar and axe-murderer Raskolnikov.   **LIT**

1867   British critic and poet Matthew Arnold publishes the poem "Dover Beach," which uses the metaphor of the ebbing of the sea as a metaphor for the waning power of faith in the modern world. Its closing lines are: "And we are here as on a darkling plain/Swept with confused alarms of struggle and flight,/Where ignorant armies clash by night."   **LIT**

1867–1868   French impressionist painter Frédéric Bazille paints *Family Reunion*.   **PAINT**

1868   American burlesque, a form of theatrical variety show including dancing by chorus girls, comes into being. Striptease acts will be added around 1920.   **DRAMA**

1868–1869   British poet Robert Browning publishes the poem *The Ring and the Book*.   **LIT**

1868–1870   British artist William Morris publishes the epic poem *The Earthly Paradise*.   **LIT**

1868   In *Overland Monthly* magazine, American humorist writer Bret Harte publishes the short story "The Luck of Roaring Camp," about the California Gold Rush.   **LIT**

1868   Russian novelist Fyodor Dostoyevsky publishes the novel *The Idiot*, which he will consider his favorite work.   **LIT**

....

"The pursuit of perfection, then, is the pursuit of sweetness and light. . . . He who works for sweetness and light united, works to make reason and the will of God prevail."—British critic and poet Matthew Arnold, Culture and Anarchy, 1869

....

1869   British critic and poet Matthew Arnold publishes *Culture and Anarchy*, a collection of essays that outlines his belief in the power of art, literature, and humanistic studies to improve individuals and society. The essays include "Sweetness and Light," "Barbarians, Philistines, Populace," and "Hebraism and Hellenism."   **LIT**

1869   British novelist Anthony Trollope publishes *Phineas Finn*, one of his six Palliser novels, noted for their depiction of Victorian politics.   **LIT**

1869   American writer Mark Twain publishes *The Innocents Abroad*, a col-
              lection of accounts of his journey overseas in 1867. The pieces,
              which had been published previously in newspapers, were intended
              to "suggest to the reader how he would be likely to see Europe and
              the East if he looked at them with his own eyes instead of the eyes
              of those who traveled in those countries before him."   **LIT**

1869   French novelist Gustave Flaubert publishes the novel *L'Education
              sentimentale*, about life during the reign of Louis-Philippe. During
              the decade he also published the novel *Salammbô*.   **LIT**

1869   Russian writer Ivan Turgenev publishes the novel *Fathers and Sons*,
              considered one of his finest works. Earlier in the decade he pub-
              lished the novel *A Nest of Gentlefolk* (1862).   **LIT**

1869   French sculptor Jean-Baptiste Carpeaux carves *The Dance*, derived
              from rococo compositions, for the facade of the Paris Opera.   **SCULP**

1870s   In England the aesthetic movement begins to gain strength, advo-
              cating the doctrine of "art for art's sake." Spokespeople for aestheti-
              cism include Walter Pater and Oscar Wilde.   **MISC**

1870   British novelist Charles Dickens's *The Mystery of Edwin Drood* is pub-
              lished, his fifteenth and final novel, left incomplete at his death.   **LIT**

1870   French writer Jules Verne publishes the science-fiction adventure
              novel *Twenty Thousand Leagues Under the Sea*.   **LIT**

c. 1870   American artist Winslow Homer paints *The Morning Bell*.   **PAINT**

1870   The Metropolitan Museum of Art, which has come to house one of
              the finest art collections in the world, is founded in New York City.
              It will move to its current site in Central Park in 1880.   **PAINT**

1871   British novelist Thomas Hardy, then an architect, publishes his first
              novel, *Desperate Remedies*.   **LIT**

1871   American poet Walt Whitman writes his critical prose work about
              American ideals, *Democratic Vistas*. Affected by the excesses of the
              Gilded Age, he attacks corruption in business and politics and chal-
              lenges Americans to reestablish their democratic ideals.   **LIT**

1871   French symbolist poet Arthur Rimbaud publishes the work *"Le
              Bateau ivre"* ("The Drunken Boat"). Among his later works will be
              the autobiographical *"Une Saison en enfer"* ("A Season in Hell,"
              1873).   **LIT**

1871–1893   French novelist Émile Zola publishes the multivolume series of nov-
              els, *Les Rougon-Macquart*. The series includes the novels *Germinal,
              Nana*, and *L'Assommoir*. Among his later works will be *"J'Accuse,"*
              the newspaper letter to the president of France concerning the
              Dreyfus affair.   **LIT**

1871–1872	Russian novelist Fyodor Dostoyevsky completes the novel *The Possessed*. **LIT**
1871	Société Nationale de Musique is founded in Paris by composer Camille Saint-Saens and Henri Bussine. The society encourages native composers by giving performances of their works, ushering in the French musical renaissance. **MUSIC**
1871	The Paris Commune, an insurrectionary government, appoints French painter Gustave Courbet as head of its arts commission. When the Commune falls later this year, Courbet is imprisoned and is later forced to flee to Switzerland for the remainder of his life. **PAINT**
1871	American artist James Abbott McNeill Whistler paints *Arrangement in Black and Gray: The Artist's Mother*. **PAINT**
1872	Swedish playwright August Strindberg writes *Mäster Olof*, his first major play. It will be produced in 1881. **DRAMA**
1872	*A Month in the Country*, generally seen as the finest play by Russian writer Ivan Turgenev, is produced. **DRAMA**
1872	French actress Sarah Bernhardt wins acclaim playing Cordelia in *King Lear* and the Queen in Victor Hugo's *Ruy Blas*. She will soon give a superb performance in Racine's *Phèdre*, and many will regard her as the greatest actress of her day. **DRAMA**
1872	American novelist Ned Buntline (pen name of Edward Zane Carroll Judson) publishes *The Scouts of the Plains*, one of more than 400 dime novels he is credited with writing. **LIT**
1872	British novelist Thomas Hardy publishes *Under the Greenwood Tree*. **LIT**
1872	British novelist Samuel Butler publishes the satirical dystopian novel *Erewhon*, to be followed by *Erewhon Revisited* in 1901. **LIT**
1872	American writer Mark Twain publishes *Roughing It*, a highly popular account of his travels cross-country to the West. **LIT**
1873	British essayist and critic Walter Pater publishes *Studies in the History of the Renaissance*. **LIT**
1873	American writers Mark Twain and Charles Dudley Warner collaborate on the novel *The Gilded Age*. The novel captures the post–Civil War era and provides its moniker. **LIT**
1873	German novelist Paul Heyse publishes the novel *Kinder de Welt* (*Children of the World*). He will win the Nobel Prize in 1910. **LIT**
1873–1876	Russian novelist Leo Tolstoy writes the tragic love story *Anna Karenina*. Among his later works is *The Death of Ivan Ilyich* (1886) and the essay on literary aesthetics, "What Is Art" (1897–1898). **LIT**
1873	French writer Jules Verne publishes the novel *Around the World in Eighty Days*, a romance about the winning of a bet by protagonist Phileas Fogg. It will be the basis of a film in 1956. **LIT**

CRITICS VS. ARTISTS

*I*n the mid- to late nineteenth century, British art critic John Ruskin was the preeminent arbiter of artistic culture. His support of artistic movements, such as the Pre-Raphaelites, established forms of artistic expression in the public eye. Throughout his career, his critical stance was consistent. While he believed in beauty for its own sake, he was even more attached to the idea that art must be linked to public morality: It should be a "visible sign of national virtue," he said.

Following these principles, Ruskin, in 1877, dismissed American painter James McNeill Whistler's impressionistic Nocturne in Black and Gold: The Falling Rocket. Ruskin accused Whistler of "flinging a pot of paint in the public's face" and complained about the painting's 200-guinea cost. The contentious and wild Whistler, who was well established in the European artistic community, sued Ruskin for libel. What resulted was one of the art world's most celebrated trials.

The trial surrounding the 1,000-pound lawsuit was marked by two elements: the absence of Ruskin, due to mental breakdowns, and Whistler's spirited defense of his artworks, some of which had been exhibited to the audience upside down.

In the end, the court sided with Whistler, the man who believed that art "should be independent of all claptrap—should stand alone, and appeal to the artistic sense of eye or ear, without confounding [it] with emotions entirely foreign to it, as devotion, pity, love, patriotism, and the like." But the court awarded him only a farthing's damages and ordered him to pay half of the court costs.

Owing to the trial, Whistler, previously a respected, successful painter, was diminished in the marketplace. He sold his house and was forced to declare bankruptcy in 1879. It would take several years and a different art form—etchings—before he would reestablish his place in the artistic community. Ruskin descended into the mental illness that first showed its signs during the trial. He spent the last years of his life in isolation and ceased writing.

1873   Russian composer Nikolay Rimsky-Korsakov's opera *Ivan the Terrible* premieres in St. Petersburg.   **MUSIC**

1873–1874   French painter Paul Cézanne paints *House of the Hanged Man*, characteristic of his impressionist period.   **PAINT**

1873   American photographer Timothy O'Sullivan makes the photograph *Ancient Ruins in the Canon de Chelle, N.M., in a Niche 50 Feet Above the Present*, an example of his pioneering landscape photography of the American West. Among other notable landscape photographers of the era are Carleton Watkins and William Henry Jackson. **PHOTO**

. . . .

"All art constantly aspires towards the condition of music."—British essayist and critic Walter Pater, Studies in the History of the Renaissance, 1873

. . . .

1874   British novelist Thomas Hardy publishes *Far From the Madding Crowd*, his first major commercial success and the first of several novels to use the name "Wessex" for the fictional region of England based on rural Dorchester, where he spent much of his early life. **LIT**

1874   Spanish novelist Pedro Antonio de Alarcón publishes the humorous work *El sombrero de tres picos* (*The Three-Cornered Hat*). Among his later works is the short novel *El capitán Veneno* (*Captain Venom*, 1881). **LIT**

1874   The bold and innovative Russian nationalist opera *Boris Godunov* by Russian composer Modest Mussorgsky premieres in St. Petersburg. Mussorgsky is considered the greatest of "The Mighty Five," a group of Russian nationalist composers that also includes Mily Balakirev, Aleksandr Borodin, César Cui, and Nikolay Rimsky-Korsakov. **MUSIC**

1874   The operetta *Die Fledermaus* by Austrian composer Johann Strauss premieres. **MUSIC**

c. 1874   American artist James Abbott McNeill Whistler paints *Nocturne in Black and Gold: The Falling Rocket*. **PAINT**

1874   In France, the term "impressionist" is coined derisively for a group of artists independently exhibiting their work this year. Committed to recording fleeting observations of reality with vivid color to capture an immediate impression, the group includes, or soon comes to include, Claude Monet, Pierre-Auguste Renoir, Edgar Degas, Camille Pissarro, Paul Cézanne, Berthe Morisot, Mary Cassatt, Armand Guillaumin, Alfred Sisley, and Frédéric Bazille. Among the impressionist works first exhibited this year is *Impression—Sunrise* by Monet, the artist most dedicated to the movement. **PAINT**

1875   British poet Gerard Manley Hopkins writes the poem "The Wreck of the *Deutschland*," which, like the rest of his poems, goes unpublished in his lifetime. *See* 1918, LIT. **LIT**

1875   American poet Sidney Lanier establishes himself as a poet with the publication of "Corn" in *Lippincott's Magazine*. **LIT**

Mary Cassatt, *Portrait of the Artist*, gouache. (*The Metropolitan Museum of Art, Bequest of Edith H. Proskauer, 1975*)

1875   French composer Georges Bizet's opera *Carmen* premieres in Paris. The violent love story is criticized as obscene and inappropriate for the stage, but will become one of the most popular operas ever written.   **MUSIC**

1875   American realist painter Thomas Eakins completes *The Gross Clinic*, a quietly forceful portrayal of surgery. It and similar paintings, like the 1889 *The Agnew Clinic*, generates conflict because of their honesty and lack of sentimentality.   **PAINT**

· ·

"Every artist was first an amateur."—American essayist and poet Ralph Waldo Emerson, Progress of Culture, 1875

· ·

1875   French sculptor Frédéric Auguste Bartholdi completes his final model of *Liberty Enlightening the World* as a gift from the French people to the United States in memory of French assistance during the War of Independence. He will collaborate with Gustave Eiffel to engineer an iron and steel framework to attach thin sheets of beaten copper. The Statue of Liberty will be inaugurated in the fall of 1886 in New York Harbor.   **SCULP**

1876   Russian composer Pyotr Ilich Tchaikovsky composes *Swan Lake*, one of the first ballets to make use of leitmotiv. It will become one of the most often produced ballets in dance history.   **DANCE**

1876   American writer Mark Twain publishes what will become one of his best-known works, *The Adventures of Tom Sawyer*. The episodic tale of Tom, his friend Huck Finn, Becky Thatcher, and Aunt Polly inspires three sequels, including *Huckleberry Finn* (1884).   **LIT**

1876   American novelist Henry James publishes the novel *Roderick Hudson*.   **LIT**

1876   *The Harvard Lampoon* magazine is founded by a group of Harvard students including Ralph Curtis and Samuel Sherwood.   **LIT**

1876   French symbolist poet Stéphane Mallarmé publishes the poem *L'Après-midi d'un faune* (*The Afternoon of a Faun*). The work will inspire French composer Claude Debussy to compose the musical work in its name (1894). Among Mallarmé's other works will be the poem "Le Cygne" ("The Swan," 1885).   **LIT**

1876   German archaeologist Heinrich Schliemann uncovers the Royal Shaft Graves at Mycenae. His discoveries will encourage the study of Bronze Age Greek art.   **MISC**

1876   The Bayreuth Festspeilhaus opens with the first complete performance of German composer Richard Wagner's *The Ring of the Nibelung*, a cycle of four operas. *See also* 1853, MUSIC.   **MUSIC**

AN UGLY DUCKLING CALLED SWAN LAKE

When Pyotr Ilich Tchaikovsky's ballet Swan Lake premiered in 1877 at the Moscow Imperial Bolshoi Theatre it was far from the respected work it is today. The work that the Russian composer hoped would broaden his range beyond symphonies was viewed instead as a mediocre evening of dance. Although Tchaikovsky's music was touted by critic Herman Laroche as the work of a master "at the height of his genius," the choreography and dancing were so uninspired that it led the critic to write, "I must say that I had never seen a poorer presentation on the stage of the Bolshoi Theatre."

Not until a decade later did Swan Lake begin to resemble the ballet performed and renowned today. Following an 1894 Tchaikovsky memorial in St. Petersburg that included portions of Swan Lake, Russian choreographers Lev Ivanov and Marius Petipa decided to restage the ballet. One of their changes was to elevate the quality of ballerina used for the ballet, hiring the respected Italian dancer Pierina Leganani for the part of the Snow Queen. A more complex change came in the choreography itself. In two of the ballet's acts the choreography was driven by the music rather than the strengths of the lead ballerina, as was the common practice.

The new adaptation of Swan Lake premiered in January 1895 in St. Petersburg, to great success. Over the years, this more organic approach to Swan Lake had profound effects on the choreography of twentieth-century ballet. Yet like the ugly duckling that becomes a graceful swan, Swan Lake had to undergo an artistic transformation to establish it as a groundbreaking work of modern ballet.

1876   German composer Johannes Brahms completes his Symphony in C Minor.
MUSIC

"What a terrifying spectacle is this of human vanity stretched to the verge of dementia. Someone should tell M. Pissarro forcibly that trees are never violet, that the sky is never the color of fresh butter, that nowhere on earth are things to be seen as he paints them."—Art critic in the French periodical Le Figaro critiquing the work of Camille Pissarro and other painters at the impressionist exhibition of 1876

1876   French painter Pierre-Auguste Renoir paints *Le Moulin de la Galette*, in which he applies impressionist principles to an outdoor group scene.   **PAINT**

1876   French painter Edgar Degas paints *The Glass of Absinthe* and *Prima Ballerina*.   **PAINT**

1877   Norwegian playwright Henrik Ibsen's *Pillars of Society*, a drama exploring hypocrisy, is produced.   **DRAMA**

1877   American novelist Henry James publishes the novel *The American*.   **LIT**

1877   French novelist Gustave Flaubert publishes the story collection *Trois Contes*, which includes the story "Un Coeur simple."   **LIT**

1877   Johannes Brahms's Symphony in D Major premieres.   **MUSIC**

1877   American inventor Thomas Alva Edison invents the phonograph, which will become the most important medium for recording music for most of the twentieth century.   **MUSIC**

1877   In a photo experiment, American photographer Eadweard Muybridge generates a series of twenty-four images of a horse in motion. The series of photos, taken as a horse travels along a track, becomes instrumental in the development of motion pictures. His work is influenced by the motion studies of French physiologist Étienne-Jules Marey.   **PHOTO**

1878   British novelist Thomas Hardy publishes *The Return of the Native*, the story of the unfortunate marriage between idealistic schoolmaster Clym Yeobright and the passionate Eustacia Vye.   **LIT**

1878   American novelist Henry James publishes *Daisy Miller*, the short novel about a young American woman disrupting European precedent. An ongoing debate about the satirical nature of James's portrait of the character will ensue, gaining the work wide publicity.   **LIT**

1878   Danish writer Karl Gjellerup publishes the novel *En Idealist*. Among his later works will be *Germanernes laerling* (1882) and *Der Pilger Kamanoto* (1906).   **LIT**

1878   Czech poet, novelist, and journalist Jan Neruda publishes the story collection *Povídky malostranské* (*Tales of the Little Quarter*) and the poetry collection *Pisně kosmické* (*Cosmic Songs*). His collection *Zpěvy páteční* (*Friday Songs*) will be published posthumously in 1896.   **LIT**

1878   German composer Johannes Brahms composes his Violin Concerto in D which takes its place alongside the works of Beethoven and Mendelssohn.   **MUSIC**

1878   French anthropologist and ethnographer Dr. Jules-Théodore-Ernest Hamy establishes the Musée de Trocadéro in Paris to house ritual objects and works of art brought in from the colonies of various scientific missions to America, Africa, and Oceania.   **SCULP**

1878   French sculptor Auguste Rodin, the most important sculptor of the late nineteenth century, executes his first major work, *The Age of Bronze*, which is controversial for its naturalistic depiction of a nude warrior.   **SCULP**

1879   *A Doll's House*, a realistic drama by Norwegian playwright Henrik Ibsen, is produced. In the next century it will be championed by feminists as a tale of a quest for female independence.   **DRAMA**

1879   British novelist and poet George Meredith publishes *The Egoist*.   **LIT**

1879–1882   American historian Henry Adams writes two biographies, *Life of Albert Gallatin* (1879) and *John Randolph* (1882).   **LIT**

1879–1880   Russian novelist Fyodor Dostoyevsky publishes the novel *The Brothers Karamazov*, the work of sin, religion, and psychology as seen through the lives of the four sons of Fyodor Pavlovich Karamazov. **LIT**

· ·

". . . [T]o make of Impressionism something solid and durable, like the art of the museums."—Stated goal of French painter Paul Cézanne, c. 1879

· ·

1879–1882   French painter Paul Cézanne paints *Still Life with Apples*, one of his many still lifes.   **PAINT**

1880s   European visitors to what is now Zaire, Africa begin to note the region's artistic forms, including elaborate masks used in initiation rites and public entertainment. Made of wood or basketry, they vary in design from grotesque to playful to naturalistic. The groups making the masks include the BaPende, BaYaka, BaSuku, and BaJokwe.   **DECO**

· ·

*"The history of art is the history of revivals."
—British satirist Samuel Butler, c. 1880s*

· ·

c. 1880s   Artists such as Paul Gauguin, Edvard Munch, and Felix Vallotton produce original woodcut illustrations, reviving a technology little used for artistic purposes since it was superseded by line engraving in the sixteenth century. In the twentieth century other artists, notably such German expressionists as Ernst Kirchner and Franz Marc, will also produce innovative woodcuts.   **GRAPH**

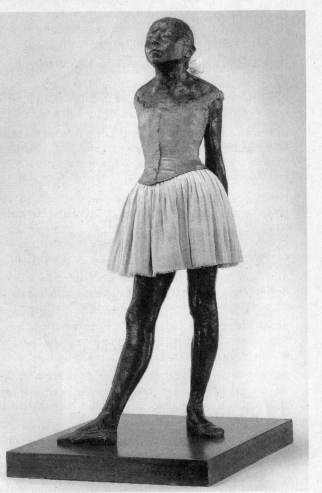

Ballet Girl: Statuette, by Edgar Degas, French. *(The Metropolitan Museum of Art,* Bequest of *Mrs. H. O. Havemeyer, 1929)*

1880s   The aesthetic movement in painting and literature comes into vogue in Britain, influenced by similar developments in France. Following the dictum of "art for art's sake," the movement's adherents include essayist and critic Walter Pater, writer Oscar Wilde, and poets Lionel Johnson and Ernest Dowson.   **MISC**

1880s   In France various post-impressionist styles arise that are informed by but in reaction against impressionism. The neo-impressionism of Georges Seurat is one example; Paul Cézanne, Vincent van Gogh, and Paul Gauguin are also considered post-impressionist artists.   **PAINT**

1880s	French physiologist Étienne-Jules Marey experiments with the artistic and scientific boundaries of photography in works such as *Walking in Front of a Black Wall* (c. 1884). **PHOTO**

1880   American writer Lewis Wallace publishes the novel *Ben Hur*.   **LIT**

1880   American historian Henry Adams's 1880 novel *Democracy*, about a U.S. senator who accepts a bribe of $100,000, captures the driving power of capitalistic pursuits during the Gilded Age.   **LIT**

1880   American writer Joel Chandler Harris publishes his first collection of Uncle Remus stories, *Uncle Remus: His Songs and Sayings*. Several sequels will follow, including *Uncle Remus and His Friends* (1892) and *Told by Uncle Remus* (1905).   **LIT**

1880   French sculptor Auguste Rodin is commissioned to make a bronze portal for the proposed Museum of Decorative Arts. His design, *The Gates of Hell*, is never completed, though its nearly 200 figures, worked on over a twenty-year period, provide the basis for numerous independent sculptures, including *The Thinker* (1889).   **SCULP**

1881   American Louis Comfort Tiffany establishes an interior decorating firm in New York that becomes famous for its glass vases, lamps, stained glass, and mosaics. *See also* 1890s, DECO.   **DECO**

1881   British actress Lillie Langtry makes her debut in Oliver Goldsmith's *She Stoops to Conquer*. Called "the Jersey Lily," she will be better known for her great beauty than her acting ability.   **DRAMA**

1881   Chinese writer Chou Shu-jen, known as Lu Hsün, is born (*d.* 1936). He will be considered China's greatest twentieth-century writer, known particularly for his short stories (translated into English in 1960 as *Selected Stories of Lu Hsün*).   **LIT**

1881   British painter Dante Gabriel Rossetti publishes the sonnet sequence *The House of Life*, which is severely criticized for its sensuality.   **LIT**

1881   American novelist Henry James publishes the novel *The Portrait of a Lady*. The story of young American Isabel Archer will become one of his best-known studies of European and American culture.   **LIT**

1881   French writer Anatole France (pen name of Jacques Thibault) publishes the novel *Le Crime de Sylvestre Bonnard* (*The Crime of Sylvester Bonnard*). Among his later works will be the novel *Le Lys Rouge* (*The Red Lily*, 1894) and *L'Île des pingouins* (*Penguin Island*, 1908).   **LIT**

1881   The French government withdraws official sponsorship from the annual exhibition known as the Salon, which then becomes run by a group of artists called the Société des Artistes Français.   **MISC**

1881   French painter Pierre-Auguste Renoir paints *Luncheon of the Boating Party*.   **PAINT**

1881	Photographer Frederic Ives produces the first color photograph. It will be decades later, in 1907, that a more practical process is developed for color photography. **PHOTO**
1882	*The Silver King*, a very popular melodrama by British playwrights Henry Arthur and Henry Herman, opens. **DRAMA**
1882	Cuban poet José Martí publishes the work *Ismaelillo*. Among his later works will be *Versos libres* (pub. 1913) and *Versos sencillos* (1892). **LIT**
1882	Russian composer Pyotr Ilich Tchaikovsky composes the *1812 Overture*. **MUSIC**
1882	The Berlin Philharmonic Orchestra is founded. **MUSIC**
1882	A year before his death, French painter Édouard Manet paints one of his greatest works, *A Bar at the Folies-Bergère*. **PAINT**
1883	James O'Neill, an Irish-born American actor, begins playing Edmond Dantès in a stage adaptation of Dumas's *The Count of Monte Cristo*, a role he will be seen in at least 6,000 times over the next thirty years. He will be the father of playwright Eugene O'Neill. *See* 1888, DRAMA. **DRAMA**
1883	Scottish novelist Robert Louis Stevenson publishes the pirate romance *Treasure Island*. **LIT**
1883	American writer Mark Twain publishes the autobiographical travel book, *Life on the Mississippi*. **LIT**
1883	Belgian poet Émile Verhaeren publishes the collection *Les Flamandes*. Among his later collections will be *Les Villes tentaculaires* (1895). **LIT**
1883	French short-story writer and novelist Guy de Maupassant publishes the novel *Une Vie*. By the end of his life he will also have written several well-known short stories, including "The Necklace," "Le Rendezvous," and "The Umbrella." **LIT**
1883	The Metropolitan Opera House opens in New York. **MUSIC**
1883–1884	French painter Georges Seurat paints *Bathers, Asnières*. **PAINT**
1884	Norwegian playwright Henrik Ibsen's drama *The Wild Duck* is produced. Realism is coupled with symbolism in this and subsequent Ibsen works, including *The Lady from the Sea* (1888). **DRAMA**
1884	George Bernard Shaw joins the Fabian Society. He will soon become a speaker for the group, lecturing on social and political reform. **DRAMA**
1884	The Lyceum Theatre School for Acting, which will become the American Academy of Dramatic Arts, is founded in New York City. Students will eventually include the actors Edward G. Robinson, Spencer Tracy, Lauren Bacall, Anne Bancroft, Ruth Gordon, Hume Cronyn, Jason Robards Jr., and Rosalind Russell. **DRAMA**

1884   American novelist Henry James publishes in *Longman's Magazine* his essay explaining his aesthetics of writing, "The Art of Fiction." The work will be collected in *Partial Portraits* in 1888.   **LIT**

1884   In France the Salon des Indépendants is established as a rival annual exhibition opposed to the official Salon, held since 1667.   **MISC**

1884   Johannes Brahms completes his Symphony in F Major.   **MUSIC**

1885–1887   American architect Henry Hobson Richardson designs the seven-story Marshall Field Wholesale Store in Chicago.   **ARCH**

1885   The first skyscraper, the Home Insurance Building, is built in Chicago. Designed by American architect William Jenney, it is a ten-story steel-framed marble building. Advances in iron technology and the invention of the elevator allow the skyscraper to become an important part of modern architecture.   **ARCH**

1885   *The Magistrate*, a farce by British playwright Arthur Pinero, premieres in London. Pinero's *The Schoolmistress*, *Dandy Dick*, and *The Cabinet Minister*—all successful farces—will be produced in 1886, 1887, and 1890, respectively.   **DRAMA**

1885   British novelist Henry Rider Haggard publishes the romance *King Solomon's Mines*. Other adventure novels by Haggard will include *She* (1887).   **LIT**

1885   American writer Mark Twain sees the U.S. publication of his boyhood-inspired novel, *The Adventures of Huckleberry Finn*. Over the years the story of Huck Finn and escaped slave Jim becomes a standard of American literature.   **LIT**

1885   American writer William Dean Howells publishes the realistic novel of morality, *The Rise of Silas Lapham*.   **LIT**

1885   Johannes Brahms completes his Symphony in E Minor.   **MUSIC**

1885   The operetta *The Mikado* by William S. Gilbert and Sir Arthur Sullivan premieres in London.   **MUSIC**

1885   In England Czech composer Antonin Dvořák composes the D minor symphony (no. 7), formerly referred to as no. 2.   **MUSIC**

1885–1887   French painter Paul Cézanne paints the *Mont Sainte-Victoire* series. **PAINT**

1885   Dutch painter Vincent van Gogh paints *The Potato Eaters*.   **PAINT**

1885–1895   French sculptor Auguste Rodin completes the monumental group *The Burghers of Calais*.   **SCULP**

1886   Russian novelist Count Leo Tolstoy writes *The Power of Darkness*, a play about the Russian peasantry. He will complete two more plays, *The First Distiller* and *The Fruits of Enlightenment*, over the next five years.   **DRAMA**

1886   British poet Alfred Tennyson publishes *Locksley Hall Sixty Years After*.   **LIT**

1886	British novelist Thomas Hardy publishes *The Mayor of Casterbridge*, which recounts the rise and tragic fall of grain merchant Michael Henchard. **LIT**
1886	Scottish novelist Robert Louis Stevenson publishes the horror novel *The Strange Case of Dr. Jekyll and Mr. Hyde* and the sea romance *Kidnapped*. **LIT**
1886	American novelist Henry James publishes the novel *The Bostonians*. **LIT**
1886	American painter Thomas Eakins is forced to resign from the Pennsylvania Academy of Fine Arts because of his use of nude models in art classrooms. **PAINT**
1886	In France neo-impressionist paintings by Georges Seurat, Camille Pissarro, and Paul Signac are exhibited at the final impressionist exhibition. Neo-impressionism employs an approach to light and color inspired by the impressionists but built on a systematic theoretical basis. The theory behind the movement is known as divisionism; the technique employed is pointillism, in which small dots of pure color are combined to create vivid, formal color effects. Among the works exhibited is *Sunday Afternoon on the Island of La Grande Jatte* by Georges Seurat, the work most associated with the movement. **PAINT**
1886–1891	French painter Paul Gauguin is the center of the Pont-Aven school of artists. Gauguin and Émile Bernard jointly develop the style of painting called synthetism or symbolism, in which forms are simplified into flat areas of unnatural color. **PAINT**
1886	French painter Edgar Degas paints *The Tub*. **PAINT**
1886	A halftone photo-engraving process, using multisized dots on the page, is invented by American Frederic Ives. **PHOTO**
1887	British novelist Thomas Hardy publishes the novel *The Woodlanders*. **LIT**
1887	British physician and novelist Arthur Conan Doyle publishes his first Sherlock Holmes story, the novel *A Study in Scarlet*. From now until 1927, Doyle will write a total of four novels and fifty-six short stories featuring the master detective. The other Holmes novels are *The Sign of Four* (1890), *The Hound of the Baskervilles* (1902), and *The Valley of Fear* (1915). **LIT**
1887	The tragic opera *Otello* by Italian composer Giuseppe Verdi premieres in Milan. **MUSIC**
1887	American inventor Thomas Alva Edison invents the first motorized phonograph. **MUSIC**
1888	Construction of the Washington Monument is completed. At a height of 553 feet, it is the tallest masonry building in the world. **ARCH**

1888   The Arts and Crafts Exhibition Society is founded in England. Drawing on the writings of John Ruskin and Augustus Pugin, the arts and crafts movement seeks to restore craftsmanship to the manufacture of household and workplace items, in revolt against mass produced, low-quality goods.   **DECO**

1888   Swedish playwright August Strindberg writes the drama *Fröken Julie* (*Miss Julie*). It will become his best-known and most frequently revived work. He also writes the drama *Creditörer* (*The Creditors*). He had written *Fadren* (*The Father*) in 1887.   **DRAMA**

1888   *Ubu-roi*, a parody by French poet and playwright Alfred Jarry, is produced as a marionette play. It will receive a live stage production in 1896, and it will be regarded by some as the first avant-garde play.   **DRAMA**

1888   British writer Thomas Hardy publishes the novel *Tess of the d'Urbervilles*, the story of a sensitive young woman driven to murder, for which she is eventually hanged. The same year Hardy begins to publish short stories with *Wessex Tales*. Other story collections will include *A Group of Noble Dames* (1891) and *Life's Little Ironies* (1894).   **LIT**

1888   American journalist and reformer Edward Bellamy publishes the novel *Looking Backward*, a look into how the future century may be corrupted by economic inequality.   **LIT**

1888   American novelist Henry James publishes the short novel *The Aspern Papers*, about one man's attempt to gain possession of the writings of a fictional romantic poet named Jeffrey Aspern.   **LIT**

1888–1891   French novelist and journalist Maurice Barrès publishes the novel trilogy *Le Culte du moi*. Among his later novels will be the series *Les Bastions de l'Est* (1905–1921).   **LIT**

1888   Swedish novelist and poet Verner von Heidenstam publishes his first poetry collection, *Vallfart och Vandringsår*. Among his later works is the collection *Dikter* (1895).   **LIT**

1888   Under the pseudonym "Phin," writer Ernest Lawrence Thayer publishes the baseball poem "Casey at the Bat," about the hapless at-bat of the hero of the Mudville team.   **LIT**

1888   Russian composer Pyotr Ilich Tchaikovsky's Symphony no. 5 in E Minor premieres in St. Petersburg.   **MUSIC**

1888   The symphonic suite *Scheherazade* by Russian composer Nikolay Rimsky-Korsakov, premieres in St. Petersburg.   **MUSIC**

1888   French painter Paul Gauguin paints *Vision After the Sermon* (*Jacob Wrestling with the Angel*), notable for its use of unnatural color and flat, curvilinear patterns.   **PAINT**

1888–1890   French painter Paul Cézanne paints *The Kitchen Table*.   **PAINT**

Femmes tahitiennes (Tahitian Women), painting by Paul Gauguin. *(Museé d'Orsay/Reunion des Museés Nationaux)*

1888	French painter Berthe Morisot paints *La Lecture (Reading)*.	**PAINT**

1888   French painter Berthe Morisot paints *La Lecture (Reading)*. **PAINT**

1888   Dutch painter Vincent van Gogh paints *Night Cafe*. **PAINT**

1888   American inventor George Eastman develops the low-cost, hand-held camera. It will expand the possibilities for photographic expression over the next several decades. **PHOTO**

1889   French architect Gustav Eiffel designs the Eiffel Tower. **ARCH**

1889   American architect Louis Henry Sullivan, whose basic principle is that "form follows function," designs his first skyscraper, the Wainwright Building. He is the leading figure in the Chicago School of architecture. **ARCH**

1889   Irish poet and dramatist William Butler Yeats publishes *The Wanderings of Oisin and Other Poems*; the title work is a mystical narrative poem based on Irish folklore. **LIT**

1889   Three years before his death, British poet Alfred Tennyson publishes a collection containing "Crossing the Bar," which at his request appears as the final poem in all collections of his work. **LIT**

1889   American writer Mark Twain publishes the satiric time-travel novel *A Connecticut Yankee in King Arthur's Court*. **LIT**

1889–1891   American historian Henry Adams publishes the nine-volume *History of the United States of America During the Administrations of Thomas Jefferson and James Madison.*   **LIT**

1889   The symphonic poem *Don Juan* by German composer Richard Strauss premieres at Weimar.   **MUSIC**

1889   After cutting off a piece of his left ear, Dutch painter Vincent van Gogh has himself committed to an asylum at St. Rémy near Arles. During his year here he creates 150 paintings, including *Starry Night* and *Yellow Cornfield.*   **PAINT**

1889   French sculptor Auguste Rodin completes his most famous work, *The Thinker.*   **SCULP**

1890s   The decorative style known as art nouveau emerges, emphasizing curvilinear patterns, often of plant and flower forms. It influences illustration and the graphic arts as well as the design of furniture, jewelry, and architectural ornamentation. Practitioners include Aubrey Beardsley in England and the Czech artist Alphonse Mucha in France, and Louis Comfort Tiffany in the United States. The style will flourish until the beginning of World War I.   **DECO**

1890s   The theater marquees on New York City's Broadway are electrified, and the street becomes known as "the Great White Way."   **DRAMA**

1890s   British illustrator Aubrey Beardsley becomes known for his sensuous black-and-white drawings, often on grotesque and erotic subjects. His illustrations include those for editions of Oscar Wilde's *Salome* (1894), Alexander Pope's *Rape of the Lock* (1896), and Ben Jonson's *Volpone* (1898).   **GRAPH**

1890s   Through his photographs of landscapes and churches, British photographer Frederick Henry Evans becomes known as a leader in the practice of artistic photography. He was part of the group known as the Linked Ring.   **PHOTO**

1890   *Sleeping Beauty*, by Russian composer Pyotr Ilich Tchaikovsky, is produced by the Kirov Ballet. The classical troupe will also become known for its production of *Swan Lake.* Its original name was the Imperial Russian Ballet.   **DANCE**

1890   *Hedda Gabler*, one of the greatest dramas by Norwegian playwright Henrik Ibsen, premieres.   **DRAMA**

1890   Irish writer Oscar Wilde publishes the novel *The Picture of Dorian Gray.*   **LIT**

1890   The *Literary Digest*, a current events periodical, is founded in New York City by I. K. Funk. With circulation reaching 2 million at its height, it will continue in publication until 1938. Eventually it becomes subsumed by the news magazine *Time.*   **LIT**

1890   American writer William Dean Howells publishes *A Hazard of New Fortunes*, a novel of social conscience and realism set in New York. **LIT**

1890–1891   French painter Claude Monet paints the series *Haystacks*. **PAINT**

1890   French painter Georges Seurat paints *Le Chahut* and *Woman Powdering Herself*, a year before his death of meningitis at thirty-one. **PAINT**

1890   Danish-born photographer and police reporter Jacob Riis publishes the sociological and photographic study *How the Other Half Lives*. His realistic photographs of New York City living conditions prompt a revision of tenement housing laws. **PHOTO**

1890–1930   Photographer Peter Henry Emerson champions naturalistic photography in his rural and landscape photos, such as *Haymaking in the Norfolk Broads* (c. 1890). His work is meant to contrast with the more obviously manipulated photographs of the time. **PHOTO**

1891   British artist William Morris founds the Kelmscott Press, which seeks to produce books of lasting beauty. He invents the Golden and Troy typefaces for this purpose. Among the press's finest works will be the folio Chaucer of 1896, with borders by Morris and illustrations by Edward Burne-Jones. **DECO**

1891   German actor and playwright Frank Wedekind's *Frühlings Erwachen* (*Spring Awakening*) is produced in Berlin. Given the subjects it explores—the sexual affair of two teenagers, abortion, homosexuality—and its antiauthoritarian stance, the play will prove extremely controversial. It continues to be revived to the present day. **DRAMA**

···

"It is the crown and flower of nineteenth-century magic, the crystallization of eons of groping enchantments. In its wholesome, sunny, and accessible laws are possibilities undreamed of by the occult lore of the east."—American filmmakers W. K. L. Dickson and Antonia Dickson on the first movie camera, the Kinetograph, 1891

···

1891   American inventors Thomas Alva Edison and W. K. L. Dickson patent the Kinetograph camera and Kinetoscope viewer, the world's first motion picture system. Edison's company will be an important force in the American film industry until 1917. **FILM**

1891   British novelist George Gissing publishes *New Grub Street*, an account of the struggles of writers in Victorian England. **LIT**

1891   British artist William Morris expounds his belief in a medieval-based socialism in the utopian novel *News from Nowhere*. **LIT**

1891   American writer William Dean Howells champions the new realism in *Criticism and Fiction*. He claims that realism will be more successful than romanticism in its shared aims "to widen the bounds of sympathy, to level every barrier against aesthetic freedom, [and] to escape the paralysis of tradition." **LIT**

1891   Swedish novelist and short-story writer Selma Lagerlöf publishes the novel *Gösta Berlings saga*. Among her later works is the story collection *Jerusalem* (1901–1902). **LIT**

1891   Italian novelist Matilda Serao publishes the work *Il paese di cuccagna*. **LIT**

....

"Art never expresses anything but itself."
—*Irish writer Oscar Wilde, The Decay of Lying, 1891*

....

1891–1895   French painter Claude Monet paints the *Rouen Cathedral* series, notable for its depiction of variations in lighting and seasonal conditions. **PAINT**

1891   French artist Paul Gauguin leaves France for Tahiti, where his painting will be influenced by the "primitive art" of indigenous peoples. **PAINT**

1891   French naive artist Henri Rousseau paints *Surprised!* (*Tropical Storm with a Tiger*). **PAINT**

1891   American painter Mary Cassatt paints *The Bath*. **PAINT**

1892   *The Master Builder*, one of the best works by Norwegian playwright Henrik Ibsen, premieres. It will be followed by Ibsen's *Lillie Eyolf* (produced in 1894), *John Gabriel Borkman* (1896), and *When We Dead Awaken* (1900). **DRAMA**

1892   *Lady Windermere's Fan*, a comedy by Irish writer Oscar Wilde, is produced at the St. James Theatre in London. *A Woman of No Importance* and *An Ideal Husband*, both Wilde comedies, will be produced in 1893 and 1895, respectively. **DRAMA**

1892   *Widowers' Houses*, the first play by Irish playwright George Bernard Shaw, premieres on Dec. 9. *The Devil's Disciple* will be staged in New York in 1897. **DRAMA**

1892   Irish poet and dramatist William Butler Yeats publishes *The Countess Kathleen and Various Legends and Lyrics*. Selected poems from this and his 1889 volume, *The Wanderings of Oisin and Other Poems*, will later be combined under the title *Crossways* and placed at the beginning of his collected *Poems*. Other poems from *Countess Kathleen* will be collected under the title *The Rose*, including "To the Rose Upon the Rood of Time," "Cuchulain's Fight with the Sea," and "The Lake Isle of Innisfree." **LIT**

1892   British writer Rudyard Kipling publishes the short-story collection *Soldiers Three* and the poetry collection *Barrack-Room Ballads and Other Verses*, both of which draw on his experiences in colonial British India. The poetry collection includes the ballad "Gunga Din," which includes the refrain, "You're a better man than I am, Gunga Din."   **LIT**

1892   Norwegian novelist and poet Knut Hamsun (pen name of Knut Pedersen) publishes the novel *Mysterier* (*Mysteries*). Among his later works will be *Pan* (1894) and *Victoria* (1898).   **LIT**

1892   Czech composer Antonín Dvořák becomes director of the National Conservatory of Music in New York City.   **MUSIC**

1892   French painter Henri de Toulouse-Lautrec paints *At the Moulin Rouge*, which vividly captures the spirit of the Paris nightclubs he frequents.   **PAINT**

1892   The first Nabis painting exhibition is held in Paris. Influenced by Gauguin, the Nabis, who include Paul Sérusier, Maurice Denis, Pierre Bonnard, and Édouard Vuillard, use color and line expressively.   **PAINT**

1892   In Berlin German graphic artist and painter Max Liebermann founds the Sezession (Secession), one of several groups of painters in Germany and Austria who want to break from artistic tradition and attempt more progressive exhibitions of their work. Sezession groups are also set up by other artists in Munich in 1892 and in Vienna in 1897.   **PAINT**

1893   *The Second Mrs. Tanqueray*, a drama by British playwright Arthur Pinero, is produced. Pinero's *The Notorious Mrs. Ebbsmith* will be produced in 1895.   **DRAMA**

1893   Czech composer Antonín Dvořák composes his ninth and last symphony in E minor *From the New World* (referred to as no. 5) while living in the United States. It incorporates African-American spiritual melodies.   **MUSIC**

1893   The symphony *Pathétique*, by Russian composer Pyotr Ilich Tchaikovsky, premieres.   **MUSIC**

1893   African-American painter Henry O. Tanner, a student of Thomas Eakins, paints *The Banjo Lesson*.   **PAINT**

1893–1894   American painter Mary Cassatt paints *The Boating Party*, which shows the influence of Japanese prints.   **PAINT**

1893   Norwegian painter Edvard Munch paints *The Scream*, in which swirling forms and unnatural color contribute to a sense of anxiety and despair.   **PAINT**

1894	Russian choreographer Lev Ivanov and French choreographer Marius Petipa adapt the book and choreography of Tchiakovsky's *Swan Lake*, turning it into a pioneering work of modern ballet. They will also be known for the choreography of *The Nutcracker* (1892), while Petipa choreographed *Sleeping Beauty* (1890). **DANCE**
1894	*Les Romanesques*, a satire by French playwright Edmond Rostand, is produced. The American musical *The Fantasticks* (*see* 1960, DRAMA) will take its story from the play. **DRAMA**
1894	British novelist George Du Maurier publishes *Trilby*, which introduces the sinister hypnotist Svengali. **LIT**
1894	British writer Rudyard Kipling publishes *The Jungle Book*, a collection of stories and poems centering on the boy Mowgli, who is raised by animals in the jungle. A sequel, *The Second Jungle Book*, will follow in 1895. **LIT**
1894	American writer Mark Twain publishes *The Tragedy of Pudd'nhead Wilson*, a novel of slavery and intolerance centering on a mulatto slave. **LIT**
1894–1897	In Britain the literary and art periodical *The Yellow Book* becomes the standard-bearer of fin-de-siècle decadence. **MISC**
1894	French composer Claude Debussy composes his symphonic poem *Prelude to The Afternoon of a Faun*. It is one of the first and most convincing realizations of musical impressionism. **MUSIC**
1895	Russian composer Pyotr Ilyich Tchaikovsky's ballet *Swan Lake* has its first complete performance in St. Petersburg. **DANCE**
1895	*The Importance of Being Earnest*, the comic play by Irish writer Oscar Wilde, is produced at the St. James Theatre in London. The play will close a few months later, following Wilde's arrest for "committing indecent acts" (engaging in homosexuality). **DRAMA**
1895	*Guy Domville*, the first of several unsuccessful plays by American novelist Henry James, is produced. **DRAMA**
1895	Swedish playwright August Strindberg begins his "Inferno Crisis," a period of mental illness that will last two years and include several psychotic episodes. **DRAMA**
1895	French inventors Louis and Auguste Lumière patent the Cinématographe, a combination camera-projector. Unlike Thomas Alva Edison's Kinetoscope, which exhibits movies peepshow-style, the Cinématographe is able to project movies onto a screen. *See also* 1891, FILM. **FILM**
1895	Polish novelist Henryk Sienkiewicz publishes *Quo Vadis?* **LIT**
1895	British novelist Joseph Conrad publishes his first novel, *Almayer's Folly*. **LIT**

1895   British novelist Thomas Hardy publishes *Jude the Obscure*, the tragic story of the illicit passion between stonemason Jude Fawley and his cousin Sue Bridehead. Readers and reviewers are outraged by what they consider the novel's immorality, and Hardy decides to write no further novels, turning instead to poetry.   **LIT**

1895   British novelist H. G. Wells publishes *The Time Machine*, the first of a group of science-fiction novels that will also include *The Island of Dr. Moreau* (1896), *The War of the Worlds* (1898), and *The First Men in the Moon* (1901).   **LIT**

1895   Twenty-four-year-old American novelist Stephen Crane publishes his masterwork *The Red Badge of Courage*. The tale of coming of age during the Civil War was originally serialized in the *Philadelphia Press* in 1894. Crane had no war experience before writing the book.   **LIT**

1896   *Salomé*, the last play by Irish writer Oscar Wilde, is produced in Paris by the French actress Sarah Bernhardt (*see* 1872, DRAMA). It will later be used as the libretto of an opera by the German composer Richard Strauss.   **DRAMA**

1896   *The Seagull*, a tragic drama by Russian playwright Anton Chekhov, is produced.   **DRAMA**

1896   British artist William Morris publishes the prose romance *The Well at the World's End*.   **LIT**

1896   British poet A. E. Housman publishes the collection *A Shropshire Lad*, which includes "To an Athlete Dying Young" and "Terence, This Is Stupid Stuff."   **LIT**

1896   American poet Paul Laurence Dunbar publishes the collection *Lyrics of Lowly Life*, which will become the best-known work of the pioneering African-American artist. It begins with an introduction by American historian William Dean Howells.   **LIT**

1896   American novelist Sarah Orne Jewett publishes her spare New England–based novel, *The Country of Pointed Firs*.   **LIT**

1896   The opera *La Bohème* by Italian composer Giacomo Puccini premieres in Turin.   **MUSIC**

1897–1898   German graphic artist Käthe Kollwitz creates the series of etchings *Weavers' Revolt*; with *Peasants' War* in 1902–1908, it will establish her reputation as an artist of social protest.   **GRAPH**

1897   British novelist Joseph Conrad publishes *The Nigger of the "Narcissus."*   **LIT**

1897   British writer Rudyard Kipling publishes the novel *Captains Courageous*, the tale of a spoiled rich boy's education at sea.   **LIT**

Aubrey Beardsley illustration of "The Peacock Skirt"
from *Salomé* by Oscar Wilde, 1896. *(Photosearch, Inc.)*

1897   American novelist Henry James publishes the novels *The Spoils of Poynton* and *What Maisie Knew.*   **LIT**

1897   American poet Edwin Arlington Robinson publishes the poem "Richard Cory," about the "gentleman from sole to crown" who ". . . one calm summer night,/Went home and put a bullet through his head."   **LIT**

1897   German composer Gustav Mahler becomes conductor at the Vienna State Opera, a positon he will hold until 1907. During this period of his greatest activity, he composes Symphony no. 4 in G Major (1899–1900), no. 5 in C-sharp Minor (1901–1902), no. 6 in A Minor (1903–1905), no. 7 in E Minor (1904–1905), and no. 8 in E-flat Major (1907). He also composes the *Kindertotenlieder* for voice and orchestra (1901–1904) and the five Rückert songs for voice and orchestra (1901–1902).   **MUSIC**

COUNT IRVING

*V*ampire folklore and Gothic horror fiction played a part in inspiring Bram Stoker's 1897 novel Dracula. But the personality of Count Dracula may owe as much to a real-life acquaintance of Stoker: British actor and theater manager Sir Henry Irving.

The first actor to be knighted (in 1895), Irving, born John Henry Brodribb, was well known for performing Shakespeare and staging popular melodramas, often concerning the supernatural. The productions at his Lyceum Theatre in London were marked by spectacular costumes and sets. A commanding, egotistical, difficult figure, he was identified with roles such as Mephistopheles in Faust and was held to have a Svengali-like influence over his wife, actress Ellen Terry. Among those who came into his circle of power was Stoker, who served as acting manager of the Lyceum during the time that he was writing Dracula.

It has been speculated that Stoker partly based his supernaturally dominating vampire on Irving, and that he perhaps hoped that Irving would play Count Dracula in a stage version. If so, his hopes were dashed: Irving showed no interest in the property. A staged reading was held at the Lyceum around the time of the book's publication, but Irving stayed out of the cast. Legend has it that the great actor caught a few moments of the show on his way to his dressing room. Asked what he thought as he parted, his one-word answer, loud enough for all to hear, was "Dreadful!"

1897   French composer Vincent d'Indy presents the opera *Fervaal* in Brussels.   **MUSIC**

1897   American composer Scott Joplin writes the ragtime song "Maple Leaf Rag." Named for the social club above the saloon in Missouri where he played piano, it will usher in the age of ragtime and give Joplin the moniker "King of Ragtime writers."   **MUSIC**

1897   French painter Henri Rousseau paints *The Sleeping Gypsy*.   **PAINT**

1897–1917   French painter Edgar Degas, his eyesight failing, lives in nearly complete seclusion and devotes himself to his art.   **PAINT**

1897   French sculptor Auguste Rodin's plaster cast statue of French novelist Honoré de Balzac is completed but rejected as too radical by those who commissioned it, the Society of Men of Letters. It will not be cast in bronze and set up until 1939, twenty-two years after Rodin's death in 1917.   **SCULP**

1898	The Moscow Art Theater is founded by Russian actor and director Konstantin Stanislavsky and Russian playwright and director Vladimir Nemirovich-Danchenko. All of Anton Chekhov's major plays will be produced there, as will plays by Shakespeare, Tolstoy, Gogol, and many others. The theater will serve as a training center in which actors will learn Stanislavsky's new methods of acting. *See* 1936, DRAMA. **DRAMA**
1898	*Cyrano de Bergerac*, a romantic comedy by French playwright Edmond Rostand, is produced. Rostand's most famous play, it continues to be revived frequently. **DRAMA**
1898	*Trelawny of the 'Wells,'* a comedy by British playwright Arthur Pinero, is produced. This tale of life in the mid-Victorian theater world will be Pinero's most enduring play. **DRAMA**
1898	British novelist Thomas Hardy publishes *Wessex Poems and Other Verses*, which includes "Hap," a meditation on fate and chance. **LIT**
1898	American novelist Stephen Crane writes the model short story "The Open Boat" based on his experiences covering a Cuban revolution in 1896 for a newspaper syndicate, during which he escapes a sinking ship by joining four other passengers in an open boat. **LIT**
1898	American novelist Henry James publishes the psychological ghost tale, "The Turn of the Screw," about the relation of two children to their former governess. **LIT**
1898	American journalist Finley Peter Dunne publishes the first collections of his popular satiric columns for the Chicago *Post* featuring the fictional character Mr. Dooley. The books, *Mr. Dooley in Peace and War* and *Mr. Dooley in the Hearts of His Countrymen* lead to several sequels. **LIT**
1898	Swedish poet Erik Karlfeldt publishes the collection *Fridolins visor*. His later works will include *Fridolins lustgård* (1901) and *Hösthorn* (1927). In 1918 he will win and refuse the Nobel Prize. **LIT**
1898	German poet Arno Holz publishes the collection *Phantasus*. The next year he will publish the collection *Revolution of Lyric Poetry*. **LIT**
1898	German painter Paula Modersohn-Becker joins the colony of landscape painters at Worpswede, which also includes her husband Otto Modersohn (married 1901). She later comes under the influence of Paul Gauguin. **PAINT**
1898–1905	French painter Paul Cézanne paints *The Bathers*. **PAINT**
1898–1927	French photographer Eugène Atget practices photography, recording simple, everyday elements and occurrences in Paris. His uncluttered, haunting work will be championed by Picasso and Man Ray, among other modern artists. **PHOTO**
1898	French sculptor Auguste Rodin completes *The Kiss*. **SCULP**

ABBOTT AND ATGET

*F*renchman Eugène Atget, now perhaps the most highly esteemed photographer of the nineteenth century, labored in relative obscurity during his lifetime. The master of the unadorned photograph remained little known until he was reintroduced to the world by a young twentieth-century American photographer. When Berenice Abbott was apprenticing in France with American artist Man Ray, she came to know the works of Atget. Although Atget made his living as a documentary photographer who took photos of Paris, his work was purchased by leading modern artists, including Abbott's teacher Man Ray.

Over the years, as the direct style of photojournalism became the dominant photographic aesthetic, Abbott set herself to inform the artistic world of Atget's defining role in its development. Her efforts were collected in The World of Atget *(1964)*. By the time of the book's reprinting in 1979, Atget had been established as the central photographer of his century.

1899   *Uncle Vanya*, a drama by Russian playwright Anton Chekhov, is produced.   **DRAMA**

1899   Irish poet and dramatist William Butler Yeats publishes the collection *The Wind Among the Reeds*, which includes the poems "The Song of Wandering Aengus," "The Valley of the Black Pig," "The Secret Rose," and "He Wishes His Beloved Were Dead."   **LIT**

1899–1900   American writer Mark Twain completes the short story, "The Man That Corrupted Hadleyburg," a dark tale about the limits of a town's self-proclaimed honesty.   **LIT**

1899   Polish novelist Wladyslaw Reymont publishes *Ziemia obiecana* (*The Promised Land*) about the effects of the industrial age on modern society. Among his later novels are *Chlopi* (*The Peasants*, 1904–1909) and the trilogy *Rok 1794* (1913–1918). He wins a Nobel Prize in 1924.   **LIT**

1899   Finnish composer Jean Sibelius presents the solidly romantic Symphony no. 1 in E Minor.   **MUSIC**

1899   German composer Richard Strauss presents the last of his successful symphonic poems *Ein Heldenleben* (*A Hero's Life*), in Frankfurt.   **MUSIC**

1899   French painter Claude Monet begins the *Waterlilies* series, which he will continue until near the end of his life in 1926. The subject of the paintings is his water garden at Giverny.   **PAINT**

1899   French painter Henri Matisse begins experimenting with bright, strongly contrasting colors. *See also* 1905, PAINT.   **PAINT**

1899   African motifs decorate some of the pavilions at the opening of the Universal Exhibition in Paris.   **SCULP**

1900s   The cakewalk, a dance of African origin, sweeps the United States. It is originally popularized by American black entertainers Egbert Williams and George Walker.   **DANCE**

1900s   The syncopated dance style called buck and wing, brought to the American stage by dancer James McIntyre, is now being referred to as tap dancing.   **DANCE**

1900s   The BaJokwe people of central Africa develop a chief's chair that shows European influence in its broad design but purely African characteristics in its ornamentation, which takes the form of human and animal figures. The BaJokwe people also become known internationally for stylized female masks used in ritual dances. The mask, called *mwana po*, is worn by a male dancer impersonating a female spirit.   **DECO**

1900s   Comic troupes perform partly preplanned, partly improvised shows, which sometimes include music and dance, in Iran and Turkey. They often make fun of authority figures and use sexual themes in humorous skits.   **DRAMA**

THE BIRTH OF THE CAKEWALK

*T*he influence of African-American dance forms on American popular dance saw its beginnings in the nineteenth century with entertainment known as minstrel shows and extended to the social dance with the craze for the cakewalk. A centuries-old slave dance, the cakewalk had originally become popular before the Civil War among Southern plantation owners. Afterward, it experienced minor success in jazz clubs. It was not until years later, when black entertainers Egbert Williams and George Walker introduced the dance in their stage performances that it entered high society and took the country by storm. Savvy promoters Williams and Walker fueled public interest by challenging nineteenth-century millionaire William K. Vanderbilt to a cakewalk contest. This was the impetus the two entertainers needed to make the cakewalk the rich man's dance of choice for years to come.

1900s	In the Western world plays are usually staged with realistic costumes and scenery, but increasingly, especially with avant-garde works, symbolic and abstract designs are introduced. With technological advances, stage lighting systems become more sophisticated, and lighting begins to play a greater role. **DRAMA**
1900s	Theater in Africa is used both to help mollify people unhappy with colonial rule and to propagate anticolonialism and marshal support for independence. **DRAMA**
1900s	Artists from Bamana villages near Bougouni and Dioica in southern Mali, Africa, create large wooden figures to appear in celebrations of the Jo society, a separate association of initiated men and women. **SCULP**
1900s	The Fang people of the rain forests of Gabon, Equatorial Guinea, and southern Cameroon carve wooden heads or figures to mount on top of reliquary boxes containing the skulls of ancestors. **SCULP**
1900s	The Asmat people from southern Irian Jaya (or New Guinea) carve mbis poles to display in front of the men's ceremonial house during funerary rituals. **SCULP**
c. 1900	In the mountainous Maprik district of New Guinea, the Abelam people build elaborate ceremonial houses, decorated with painting and sculpture. These cult houses are used to shelter artists and store ceremonial objects. **ARCH**
c. 1900	In the Micronesian islands Western explorers collect examples of highly developed crafts, including jewelry, ornaments, basketry, matting, decorated fabrics, and finely made tools and weapons. **DECO**
c. 1900	Artists in the Massim district of New Guinea decorate everyday objects such as blades and dugout canoes with elaborate spirals, scrolls, openwork, figures of people and animals, and other ornamentation. The style extends to the nearby Trobriand Islands. **DECO**
1900	British novelist Joseph Conrad publishes *Lord Jim*. **LIT**
1900	British novelist H. G. Wells publishes *Love and Mr. Lewisham*, one of several realistic novels drawn on his experiences growing up in the lower middle classes. Others of these novels include *Kipps: The Story of a Simple Soul* (1905) and *Tono-Bungay* (1909). **LIT**
1900	American poet and scholar William Vaughan Moody publishes his well-received political poem, "An Ode in Time of Hesitation," about the tumultuous dedication of the Saint Gaudens monument to Col. Robert Gould Shaw, the head of the first enlisted African-American regiment, which was active during the Civil War. **LIT**
1900	American writer Booker T. Washington publishes *Up From Slavery*, an autobiography of his move from Southern slave to the cofounding of Tuskegee Institute. **LIT**

1900   American writer L. Frank Baum publishes *The Wonderful Wizard of Oz*, a children's story about the journey of Dorothy and her dog Toto to the land of Oz. In 1939 it will be made into a film that will later become a staple of television.   **LIT**

1900   French novelist Sidonie-Gabrielle Colette, known simply as Colette, publishes the first of the four Claudine novels, *Claudine à l'école*. The novels will be published under the pseudonym Willy. Among her later works is the coming-of-age novel *Gigi* (1944).   **LIT**

1900   Italian writer Gabriele D'Annuzio publishes the novel *Il fuoco* (*The Flame of Life*). Among his works is the play *La gioconda* (1898). Both will be based on his relation with actress Eleonora Duse.   **LIT**

1900   Brazilian novelist and poet Joachim Maria Machado de Assis publishes his best known work, the comic novel *Don Casmurro*.   **LIT**

c. 1900   Impressionism in music reaches its height in the late nineteenth and early twentieth centuries, chiefly represented in the works of French composer Claude Debussy. Its vague, intangible style, a re-action against such "German" achievements as the sonata, symphony, thematic material, and developmental techniques, introduces various devices antithetical to the features of classical and romantic harmony.   **MUSIC**

1900   Italian composer Giacomo Puccini's opera *Tosca* opens in Rome. **MUSIC**

1900–1910   A form of jazz music called ragtime becomes popular in the United States. In New Orleans a form of jazz that comes to be known simply as New Orleans jazz also develops.   **MUSIC**

1900   French painter Paul Gauguin publishes the book *Noa Noa*, a memoir of his experiences in Tahiti.   **PAINT**

1900–1904   In his blue period Spanish Pablo Picasso, who will become the best-known artist of the twentieth century, produces such works as *La Vie* (1903) and the engraving *The Frugal Repast* (1904). His characteristic subjects in this period, painted in blue tones, are the socially downtrodden.   **PAINT**

c. 1900   The secession movement in photography, represented by artists such as Alfred Stieglitz and Edward Steichen, argues for recognition of photography as an art form on the level of painting.   **PHOTO**

1901   American architect Frank Lloyd Wright completes the lecture *The Art and Craft of the Machine*, detailing his ideas about modern architecture.   **ARCH**

1901   *Three Sisters*, a drama by Russian playwright Anton Chekhov, is produced. It tells the story of the Prozorov sisters and their desire to escape country provincialism for the worldliness of Moscow.   **DRAMA**

1901   Swedish playwright August Strindberg writes the dramas *Dödsdansen* (*The Dance of Death*) and *Kronbruden* (*The Crown Bridge*). Two years earlier, he completed four historical dramas that will be popular only in Sweden.   **DRAMA**

1901   British writer Rudyard Kipling publishes his masterpiece, the novel *Kim*, a tale of India that explores, through the eyes of a military orphan, the clash between British dedication to action and a Tibetan Lama's contemplative quest.   **LIT**

1901–1903   American novelist Frank Norris writes *The Octopus* (1901) and *The Pit* (1903), two naturalistic, muckraking novels of a projected trilogy about the place of wheat in modern lives. The first explores the conflicts between the railroad trust and the wheat farmer; the second the conflicts between farmers and wheat traders.   **LIT**

1901   German novelist Thomas Mann publishes the saga of a declining upper-class family, *Buddenbrooks*. Among his later works are *Death in Venice* (1912) and the tale of European decline as seen through the experiences of ailing Hans Castorp, *The Magic Mountain*.   **LIT**

1901   Czech composer Antonin Dvořák's opera, the tragic fairy tale *Rusalka*, opens in Prague.   **MUSIC**

1901   Russian composer Sergey Rachmaninoff presents his Piano Concerto no. 2 in C Minor, reportedly written with the aid of a psychoanalyst who was treating him at the time.   **MUSIC**

1901   Norwegian painter Edvard Munch completes the painting *Girls on the Bridge*.   **PAINT**

1901   On Dec. 21 Italian engineer Guglielmo Marconi broadcasts radio waves from England to Newfoundland, marking the invention of radio.   **TV&R**

1902   *The Lower Depths*, a realistic drama by Russian playwright Maksim Gorky (pen name of Aleksey Peshkov), is staged by the Moscow Art Theatre. The play depicts the sufferings of Moscow's poorer citizens.   **DRAMA**

1902   British playwright George Bernard Shaw's *Mrs. Warren's Profession*, a play exploring both prostitution and the role of the New Woman, is produced. His *Caesar and Cleopatra* will be performed in both Berlin and New York in 1906.   **DRAMA**

1902   French filmmaker Georges Méliès, a pioneer of film fantasy and special effects, makes his best-known work, *A Trip to the Moon*.   **FILM**

1902   American novelist Owen Wister publishes *The Virginian*, which sets the style for future Western novels.   **LIT**

Frank Lloyd Wright highback dining room side chair from the Ward W. Willets House, Highland Park, IL. *(Metropolitan Museum of Art*, Purchase, Mr. and Mrs. David Lubart Gift, 1978*)*

1902   British novelist Joseph Conrad publishes the novel *Youth* and the short novel *Heart of Darkness*. The latter tells the story of seaman Marlow's encounter with the mad ivory trader Kurtz, whose memorable last words are "The horror! The horror!"   **LIT**

1902   British novelist Thomas Hardy publishes *Poems of the Past and Present*, which includes "Lausanne" and "The Darkling Thrush."   **LIT**

1902   British writer Rudyard Kipling publishes the story-and-poem collection *Just So Stories*, illustrated by the author.   **LIT**

1902   American novelist Henry James publishes the novel *The Wings of the Dove*.   **LIT**

1902   American novelist Edith Wharton publishes *The Valley of Decision*, a period novel that will become one of her early successes.   **LIT**

1902   French novelist and thinker André Gide publishes the novel *L'Immoraliste* (*The Immoralist*). Among his later works will be *La Porte étroite* (*Strait Is the Gate*, 1909) and the story *La Symphonie pastorale* (*The Pastoral Symphony*, 1919).   **LIT**

1902   English composer Edward Elgar composes the first of his five *Pomp and Circumstance* marches for orchestra. No. 5 will be completed in 1930.   **MUSIC**

1902   Photographer Edward Steichen's work *Rodin With His Sculptures "Victor Hugo" and The "Thinker"* exemplifies the photo-secessionist movement, which opposes realism and fosters the idea of art for art's sake. The movement includes Gertrude Kasebier, Clarence White, Alvin Langdon Coburn, Frederick Henry Evans, and Alfred Stieglitz.   **PHOTO**

1903–1908   In Europe and the United States, American modern dance pioneer Isadora Duncan performs her dances informed by Greek art. They will be marked by stylization, including her appearance in bare feet and her use of scarves. Her work, demeanor, and way of life will influence the development of modern dance.   **DANCE**

1903–1932   The Wiener Werkstätte (Viennese workshops) are in operation in Vienna, providing space for artists and craftspeople to follow their goals of combining utility with high quality. Products include jewelry and items of home decoration, many reflecting the influence of art nouveau.   **DECO**

1903   *In the Shadow of the Glen*, a drama by Irish playwright John Millington Synge, is produced. Synge had previously written the play *When the Moon Has Set*—probably in 1901—but it had not been produced.   **DRAMA**

1903   American filmmaker Edwin S. Porter completes the influential films *The Life of an American Fireman* and *The Great Train Robbery*. *Fireman* is notable as the first known film to use intercutting. *Train Robbery* is important for its use of narrative and its influence on the genre of film westerns.   **FILM**

1903   Irish poet and dramatist William Butler Yeats publishes the collection *In the Seven Woods*, which includes the poems "The Folly of Being Comforted" and "Adam's Curse."   **LIT**

1903–1908   British novelist Thomas Hardy publishes the three parts (1903, 1905, 1908) of the epic verse-drama *The Dynasts*.   **LIT**

1903   A year after his death, British novelist Samuel Butler's masterpiece is published, the satirical, semiautobiographical novel *The Way of All Flesh*.   **LIT**

1903   American novelist Henry James publishes the short novel *The Beast in the Jungle*. He also publishes the novel *The Ambassadors*, which he will call "frankly, quite the best all round" of his works.   **LIT**

1903   American scholar and teacher W. E. B. Du Bois publishes *The Souls of Black Folk: Essays and Sketches*, a collection of profiles of African-American people and events.   **LIT**

1903   English composer Frederick Delius composes his masterpiece *Sea Drift*.   **MUSIC**

1903   German composer Anton Bruckner's unfinished Symphony no. 9 in D Minor premieres posthumously in Vienna.   **MUSIC**

1903   French sculptor Camille Claudel exhibits her piece, *Maturity*, an allegory of her break with Auguste Rodin, in the Salon of French artists.   **SCULP**

1904   The Abbey Theatre, dedicated to presenting Irish drama, opens in Dublin. Its directors include Lady Gregory and William Butler Yeats. Yeats's *On Baile's Strand* is the first play performed there.   **DRAMA**

1904   *The Cherry Orchard*, a drama by Russian playwright Anton Chekhov, is produced.   **DRAMA**

1904   Scottish novelist and playwright James Barrie's children's play *Peter Pan* premieres. Barrie had adapted the play from his novel *The Little White Bird*. His comedy *The Admirable Crichton* had been produced in 1902.   **DRAMA**

1904   *The King's Threshold*, a poetic play by Irish playwrights William Butler Yeats and Lady Gregory, is produced. The two also collaborated on *The Unicorn from the Stars* (1908). Yeats also has written and will write a number of plays alone—some of them in verse, some in prose, including *The Hour-Glass* (1914) and *The Words upon the Window Pane* (1934).   **DRAMA**

1904   *Riders to the Sea*, a one-act tragedy by Irish playwright John Millington Synge, is produced at the Abbey Theatre in Dublin. Synge's comedy *The Well of the Saints* will be produced in 1905.   **DRAMA**

1904   The Royal Academy of Dramatic Art is founded in London.   **DRAMA**

1904–1907   Ten plays by British playwright George Bernard Shaw are performed in repertory over three seasons at the Royal Court Theatre in London. They are *Candida*, *John Bull's Other Island*, *How He Lied to Her Husband*, *You Never Can Tell* (which premiered in 1900), *Man and Superman* (without Act III, which is produced separately as *Don Juan in Hell* in 1907), *Major Barbara*, *The Doctor's Dilemma*, *Captain Brassbound's Conversion*, *The Philanderer* (which was previously performed in a private theater club production), and the one-act *The Man of Destiny*. This huge undertaking establishes Shaw as a highly respected playwright.   **DRAMA**

1904   Uruguayan playwright Florencio Sánchez's drama *La gringa* (*The Foreign Girl*) is produced. His *Barranca abajo* (*Down the Gully*) will be produced in 1905. These works will be regarded as Sánchez's masterpieces, and he will be seen as one of South America's greatest playwrights.   **DRAMA**

1904   The first formal movie theater is opened near Pittsburgh, Pennsylvania. Among its first films is a French version of *Potemkin*.   **FILM**

1904   British novelist Joseph Conrad publishes *Nostromo*, a tale of revolution and moral decay set in the fictitious South American republic of Costaguana.   **LIT**

1904   Greek poet Constantine Cavafy (pen name of Konstantinos Kaváfis) publishes the pamphlet *Poems*, revised in 1910. His works, including "Ithaca" and "Waiting for the Barbarians," will gain the respect of such writers as T. S. Eliot and W. H. Auden.   **LIT**

1904   American novelist Henry James publishes the novel *The Golden Bowl*.   **LIT**

1904   American journalist Lincoln Steffens publishes *The Shame of the Cities*, a collection of his muckraking studies of the corruption of American cities. The articles first appeared in *McClure's* magazine.   **LIT**

1904   Italian composer Giacomo Puccini's opera *Madame Butterfly*, set near Nagasaki, Japan, opens in Milan.   **MUSIC**

1904   The London Symphony Orchestra gives its initial concert.   **MUSIC**

1904   Czech composer Leoš Janáček's opera *Jenůfa* opens in Brno. It will bring him renown when it comes to Prague and Vienna in 1916.   **MUSIC**

1904   The first of American composer George M. Cohan's major works, *Little Johnny Jones*, debuts on Broadway. It generates a number of song standards, including "Give My Regards to Broadway" and "Yankee Doodle Boy." Although most of Cohan's best-known songs will be written for the stage, one of his most famous will not: "Over There," the patriotic World War I song.   **MUSIC**

1904   Having settled in Paris, Spanish painter Pablo Picasso is in his rose period, when pink and gray tones are dominant and his favorite subjects are acrobats, dancers, and harlequins. He also begins sculpting in this period.   **PAINT**

1904–1905   French painter Henri Matisse completes *Luxe, calme et volupté*, a painting influenced by the neo-impressionist movement. It is shown at the Salon des Indépendents in 1905.   **PAINT**

1904   American photographer Edward Steichen takes the photograph "The Flatiron." This view of the new three-sided New York building is taken during daylight hours but later will be printed so as to appear a nighttime composition.   **PHOTO**

1905–1907   Spanish architect Antoni Gaudí designs the Casa Mila in Barcelona. Its fluid appearance embodies art nouveau principles.   **ARCH**

1905   American actress Ethel Barrymore appears as Nora and her brother John is Dr. Rank in Norwegian playwright Henrik Ibsen's *A Doll's House*. For the next several decades, Ethel will perform in both classical and modern roles, doing some of her best work—such as her 1940 portrayal of Miss Moffat in Emlyn Williams's *The Corn is Green*—late in life. John will have a similarly distinguished career, with his 1922 Hamlet being perhaps his greatest theatrical performance. But he will leave the stage in 1926 to work primarily in film. Ethel and John's brother Lionel will also gain success as a stage actor, often appearing with John, but like John, will leave the theater to work in film.   **DRAMA**

1905   Pioneering American cartoonist Winsor McCay develops the early comic strip, "Little Nemo in Slumberland." It is the first of several comic strips he creates over the next several years.   **GRAPH**

1905   Irish writer Oscar Wilde's extended prison letter *De Profundis* is published posthumously.   **LIT**

1905   The group of writers, artists, and thinkers known as the Bloomsbury group begins to meet in Bloomsbury, London. The group, which includes Virginia and Leonard Woolf, Vanessa and Clive Bell, Lytton Strachey, and E. M. Forster, will continue to exist until Virginia Woolf's suicide in 1941.   **LIT**

1905   British novelist E. M. Forster publishes his first novel, *Where Angels Fear to Tread*.   **LIT**

1905   American novelist Edith Wharton publishes *The House of Mirth*, a social satire of marriage in the upper levels of New York society that centers on the efforts of an outsider to acquire a society husband.   **LIT**

1905	German poet Rainer Maria Rilke publishes the collection *Das Stunden-Buch* (*The Book of Hours*). Later works include the series *Duineser Elegien* (*Duino Elegies*, 1923) and the cycle *Die Sonette an Orpheus* (*The Sonnets to Orpheus*, 1923). **LIT**
1905	Claude Debussy's symphonic poem *La Mer* premieres in Paris, representing the culmination of impressionist pictorialism and technique. **MUSIC**
1905	German composer Richard Strauss's intensely emotional opera *Salomé*, including the popular "Dance of the Seven Veils," opens in Dresden. **MUSIC**
1905	In France the Salon d'Automne exhibits the work of the fauves (French for "wild beasts"), a group of artists led by Henri Matisse who employ bright, pure, nonnaturalistic colors disconnected from traditional representation. Other fauvists include André Derain, Raoul Dufy, Georges Braque, Albert Marquet, Georges Rouault, and Maurice de Vlaminck. **PAINT**
1905–1906	French painter Henri Matisse paints *The Joy of Life*, an archetypal fauvist work. **PAINT**
1905	French painter Georges Rouault paints the violently expressive *Head of Christ*. **PAINT**

VACATIONING WITH FRANK LLOYD WRIGHT

*A*s with the work of any artist, the best way to appreciate an architect's work is to view it in person. Foremost twentieth-century American architect Frank Lloyd Wright worked in so many styles and parts of the United States that a survey of his work would require a cross-country tour. With that in mind, a Frank Lloyd Wright vacation itinerary might look like this:

New York City—Guggenheim Museum (designed 1942; completed 1959)

Bear Run, Pennsylvania—Fallingwater (1937–1939); an example of international modern house design

Chicago, Illinois—Robie house (1908); example of his prairie school houses

Oak Park, Illinois—Unity Church (1906)

Racine, Wisconsin—Johnson Wax Company factory complex (1936–1950); an example of organic architecture

Spring Green, Wisconsin—Taliesin (1911; burned and rebuilt in 1915; burned and rebuilt in 1925); his home and studio

Bartlesville, Oklahoma—skyscraper (1955); an example of his later work

Paradise Valley, Phoenix, Arizona—Taliesin West (1938–1959); his winter home

1905   In Dresden German expressionism emerges as a powerful artistic movement, in which color and shape are primarily used to express feeling rather than to represent nature. It has much in common with fauvism and cubism in France, though the latter are more concerned with structure and harmony, while German expressionism is more concerned with intense feeling and tortured psychological states. Die Brücke (the Bridge) is a German expressionist group founded in Dresden this year by Ernst Ludwig Kirchner, Emil Nolde, and other artists; the group will last until 1913. *See also* 1908, PAINT.   **PAINT**

1906   American architect Frank Lloyd Wright designs Oak Park Unity Temple near Chicago.   **ARCH**

1906   The novel *Sister Carrie* by American novelist Theodore Dreiser is published in the United States after six years of controversy over its alleged "immorality."   **LIT**

1906   American short-story writer William Sydney Porter, known as O. Henry, publishes the story collection *The Four Million*. The accessible collection, titled to contrast the actual population of New York with the number of high society members believed by some to be the only people of importance, contains the story "The Gift of the Magi."   **LIT**

1906   French painter André Derain paints *London Bridge*.   **PAINT**

· ·

"Art. This word has no definition."—American writer Ambrose Bierce defining art, The Devil's Dictionary, 1906

· ·

1906–1909   Now in his Negro period, Spanish painter Pablo Picasso creates increasingly abstract forms. A characteristic work is *Les Demoiselles d'Avignon* (1907), influenced by Cézanne's post-impressionist paintings and by African masks.   **PAINT**

1906   American painter John Sloan, who will be a member of the ashcan school, paints *Dust Storm, Fifth Avenue*.   **PAINT**

1907   *Une Puce à l'oreille* (*A Flea in Her Ear*), a farcical comedy by French playwright Georges Feydeau, premieres. Feydeau will eventually write more than sixty farces.   **DRAMA**

1907   *The Playboy of the Western World*, a comedy that is widely seen as the greatest play by Irish playwright John Millington Synge, is produced at the Abbey Theatre in Dublin. It leads to rioting in the theater. Synge's comedy *The Tinker's Wedding*, also a controversial work, will be produced in 1909 in London.   **DRAMA**

1907   The first daily comic strip, "Mr. Mutt," appears in the *San Francisco Chronicle*. Created by Bud Fisher, it will later be renamed "Mutt and Jeff."   **GRAPH**

1907   British novelist Joseph Conrad publishes *The Secret Agent*.   LIT

1907   Irish writer James Joyce publishes *Chamber Music*, a collection of poetry.   LIT

....

"With the single exception of Homer, there is no eminent writer, not even Sir Walter Scott, whom I can despise so entirely as I despise Shakespeare when I measure my mind against his. . . . It would positively be a relief to me to dig him up and throw stones at him."—British playwright George Bernard Shaw, Dramatic Opinions and Essays, 1907

....

**"Mr. Shaw is (I suspect) the only man on earth who has never written any poetry."
—British writer G. K. Chesterton critiquing playwright George Bernard Shaw, Orthodoxy, 1909**

....

1907   In England the Fabian Arts Group, with financial help from George Bernard Shaw, begins publication of the modernist journal *The New Age*, which will publish work by Ezra Pound, Edwin Muir, T. E. Hulme, and Katherine Mansfield.   LIT

1907   The cowboy hero Hopalong Cassidy makes his first appearance in the novel *Bar 20* by American writer Clarence E. Mulford. Several Hopalong Cassidy books followed, as well as more than sixty Cassidy movies, beginning in 1935 and starring William Boyd.   LIT

1907   Russian writer Maksim Gorky publishes the novel *Mother*. Among his other works will be the autobiographical trilogy *Childhood* (1913–1914), *My Apprenticeship* (1916), and *My Universities* (1923).   LIT

1907   German composer Gustav Mahler's Symphony no. 8 in E-flat Major (*The Symphony of a Thousand*) is presented.   MUSIC

1907   Hungarian composer Franz Lehár's operetta *The Merry Widow* opens in New York to great success.   MUSIC

1907–1908   Austrian painter Gustav Klimt paints *The Kiss*.   PAINT

1907   The first exhibition of cubist works is held in Paris. Spearheaded by Spanish painter Pablo Picasso and French painter Georges Braque, the movement uses abstract geometric shapes to represent subjects. Other cubist painters will include Juan Gris, Fernand Léger, Roger de La Fresnaye, and Robert Delaunay. The cubist movement will end with World War I.   PAINT

1907   American painter and illustrator Rockwell Kent paints *Winter,*
          Monhegan Island.   **PAINT**

1907   American photographer Alfred Stieglitz demonstrates his "straight,"
          modern approach in the photograph *The Steerage*, from a trip to
          Europe. He will also become known for his hundreds of pho-
          tographs of his wife, American painter Georgia O'Keeffe.   **PHOTO**

1908   The plastic Bakelite is developed by American L. H. Baekeland. First
          commercially manufactured in 1909, it will become a popular base
          for jewelry over the next several years.   **DECO**

1908   British novelist Ford Madox Ford founds the journal *The English*
          Review, which publishes work by Thomas Hardy, Henry James,
          D. H. Lawrence, Wyndham Lewis, and H. G. Wells.   **LIT**

1908   British novelist E. M. Forster publishes *A Room With a View*.   **LIT**

1908   American novelist Henry James publishes the novel *The Princess*
          Casamassima.   **LIT**

1908–1923 American essayist and journalist H. L. Mencken coedits the national
          periodical *The Smart Set* and establishes a journalistic reputation
          throughout the United States.   **LIT**

1908   The ashcan school of artistic realism is founded in Philadelphia by
          American artist Robert Henri, with colleagues George Bellows,
          William Glackens, George Luks, Everett Shinn, and John Sloan. It
          will be popular until World War I.   **PAINT**

1908   The building of the Musée Royal de l'Afrique Centrale is completed
          in Tervueren, Belgium, just outside of Brussels. It will contain the
          greatest collection of Congolese artifacts for artists to study.   **SCULP**

1909   The opera-ballet *The Golden Cockerel* by Russian composer Nikolay
          Rimsky-Korsakov is posthumously produced in Moscow.   **DANCE**

1909   Russia's Sergey Diaghilev premieres his Ballet Russe in Paris, intro-
          ducing the Russian tradition to the United States and Europe, and
          ushering in modern ballet.   **DANCE**

1909   Swedish playwright August Strindberg writes the autobiographical
          drama *Stora Landsvägen* (*The Great Highway*), his last play.   **DRAMA**

1909–1915 American composer Charles Ives writes Piano Sonata no. 2,
          Concord, Mass. 1840-1860. Key and time signatures and bar lines
          are omitted in parts of the piece, which includes four movements
          named for New England authors, "Emerson," "Hawthorne," "The
          Alcotts," and "Thoreau."   **MUSIC**

1909   The opera *Elektra*, by German composer Richard Strauss, a story of
          hate and murder set to brutal and violent music, opens in
          Dresden.   **MUSIC**

1909   Austrian-born composer Arnold Schoenberg composes his atonal
       Three Piano Pieces, Op. 11.   **MUSIC**

c. 1909–   Austrian painter Oskar Kokoschka paints "psychological" portraits
  1910   that reflect the subject's inner being while also producing highly
       original lithographs and posters.   **PAINT**

1909   Italian writer Filippo Thommaso Marinetti publishes the *Futurist
       Manifesto*, in which he advocates a new kind of Italian art celebrat-
       ing modern mechanization, dynamism, and speed. Painters associ-
       ated with futurism will include Umberto Boccioni, Carlo Carrà,
       Giacomo Balla, Luigi Russolo, and Gino Severini. A futurist exhibi-
       tion will be held in Paris in 1912.   **PAINT**

1909–1914 French painter Maurice Utrillo is in his white period, characterized
       by light tones in his paintings and considered by many his most
       fertile period.   **PAINT**

1909   Spanish artist Pablo Picasso leaves the Bateau-Lavoir and settles in
       a studio on the Boulevard de Clichy. There he will make his first cu-
       bist sculptures, including a bronze portrait of his companion
       Fernande Olivier.   **SCULP**

1909–1910 Romanian sculptor Constantin Brancusi and Italian sculptor
       Amedeo Modigliani work together in Paris. Influenced by African
       and Asian carving styles, dedicated to simple, almost abstract form,
       Brancusi will influence later artists, not least by reviving the physi-
       cal art of carving.   **SCULP**

1910s   In the United States and Europe, the South American dance called
       the tango gains popularity.   **DANCE**

1910s   Tin Pan Alley, the New York base for popular songwriting and pub-
       lishing, begins to thrive. Its denizens, including Irving Berlin,
       Sammy Cahn, and Jerome Kern, will dominate American popular
       music for half a century.   **MUSIC**

1910s   German sculptor Wilhelm Lehmbruck combines elements of Gothic
       elongation with Rodin's expressive energy for a series of looming
       monumental figures.   **SCULP**

1910   Russian composer Igor Stravinsky's ballet *The Firebird* meets with
       enthusiastic response when it premieres in Paris. **DANCE**

1910   *Chantecler*, the last produced play by French playwright Edmond
       Rostand, is produced. Some critics regard it as his finest work. **DRAMA**

1910   *Justice*, a drama critical of England's prison system by British novelist
       and playwright John Galsworthy, premieres. *Loyalties*, a Galsworthy
       play exploring anti-Semitism, will be produced in 1922. **DRAMA**

1910   *The Guardsman*, a play by Hungarian playwright Ferenc Molnár, premieres. It will be revived frequently in the years to come. Molnár's *Lilies* had been produced in 1909; it will serve as the basis for the American musical *Carousel* (1945). **DRAMA**

1910   American cartoonist John Randolph Bray patents the cel process for film animation. **FILM**

1910   Irish poet and dramatist William Butler Yeats publishes the collection *The Green Helmet and Other Poems*, which includes "No Second Troy," "The Fascination of What's Difficult," and "The Coming of Wisdom with Time." **LIT**

1910   British novelist E. M. Forster publishes *Howards End*, memorable for its epigraph, "Only connect . . ." **LIT**

c. 1910–   Expressionist music, written in a deeply subjective and introspec-
1929   tive style, reaches its height in the works of such Austrian composers as Arnold Schoenberg and Alban Berg. **MUSIC**

1910   British composer Ralph Vaughan Williams presents the orchestral work *Fantasia on a Theme by Thomas Tallis* for strings, and the choral work *A Sea Symphony*. **MUSIC**

1910   Operas of the year include Italian composer Giacomo Puccini's *The Girl of the Golden West* and French composer Jules Massenet's *Don Quichotte*. **MUSIC**

1910   American composer Victor Herbert writes his best-known score, for the Broadway show *Naughty Marietta*. Many of its songs, including "Tramp, Tramp, Tramp," and "Ah, Sweet Mystery of Life" will become musical standards. **MUSIC**

1910   French painter Henri Rousseau paints *The Dream*. **PAINT**

1910–1913   Russian painter Wassily Kandinsky completes the first entirely abstract, or nonrepresentational, paintings: *Compositions*, *Improvisations*, and *Impressions*. Abstract art will become a major force in twentieth-century painting. **PAINT**

1910–1912   British critic and painter Roger Fry introduces Britain to the works of prominent modern painters Paul Cézanne, Henri Matisse, and Vincent van Gogh, among others, at post-impressionist exhibitions in British galleries. **PAINT**

1910   German ethnographer Leo Frobenuis discovers a number of lifelike terra-cotta sculptures in the Yoruban center of Ife in Nigeria. **SCULP**

1911   American architect Frank Lloyd Wright designs his home, Taliesin, in Spring Green, Wisconsin. It will be rebuilt twice. **ARCH**

1911   Russian composer Igor Stravinsky's ballet *Pétrouchka* opens in Paris. Its novel rhythm and harmony, vivid colors, and subtle characterization contribute to its impact. **DANCE**

Pencil sketch of a dancer in the *Polovtsian Dances* from *Prince Igor* by Vaslav Nijinsky. *(The Theater Museum, London/Photosearch, Inc.)*

1911   British dancer Vernon Castle marries American dancer Irene Foot, thus entering into a dance partnership that will spawn several popular dances, including the Castle walk and the hesitation waltz. **DANCE**

1911   British playwright George Bernard Shaw's satire *Fanny's First Play* is produced. A send-up of several contemporary British drama critics, it is Shaw's first significant commercial success. *Androcles and the Lion* will follow in 1913.   **DRAMA**

1911   British novelist Joseph Conrad publishes *Under Western Eyes*.   **LIT**

1911   American novelist Theodore Dreiser publishes the controversial novel *Jennie Gerhardt*, about the conflicts faced by a young German immigrant woman who becomes pregnant out of wedlock.   **LIT**

1911   American novelist Edith Wharton publishes *Ethan Frome*, the tragedy of the married couple Ethan and Zenobia Frome and Zenobia's cousin Mattie.   **LIT**

1911–1913   German composer Anton Webern, a follower of Schoenberg, composes his strictly atonal *Five Orchestral Pieces*, Op. 10, with the longest piece lasting a minute and the shortest being fewer than seven measures. Webern's works become the basis for later serial music.   **MUSIC**

1911   German composer Gustav Mahler's *Das Lied von der Erde* (*The Song of the Earth*) is presented posthumously in Munich.   **MUSIC**

1911   German composer Richard Strauss's comic opera *Der Rosenkavalier* (*The Knight of the Rose*) opens in Dresden.   **MUSIC**

1911   Prolific American composer Irving Berlin (born Israel Baline) writes his first international song success, "Alexander's Ragtime Band." His first published song was "Marie from Sunny Italy" in 1907.   **MUSIC**

1911   The German expressionist group Der Blaue Reiter (The Blue Horseman) is founded in Munich by Wassily Kandinsky, Franz Marc, Paul Klee, and August Macke; it will be dissolved by 1914.   **PAINT**

1911   French painter Georges Braque paints the cubist work *The Portuguese*, the first painting to incorporate stenciled lettering.   **PAINT**

1911   French painter Henri Matisse paints *The Red Studio*.   **PAINT**

1911–1912   Dutch painter Piet Mondrian completes *Flowering Apple Tree*, a series of paintings in which the subject becomes less representational, reflecting the artist's interest in abstract art and cubism.   **PAINT**

1911   German sculptor Ernst Barlach travels to Russia and studies the simple forms of the preindustrial age. He decides not to carve his *Man Drawing a Sword* completely free from a massive block of wood.   **SCULP**

1912   Gerhart Hauptmann, considered the preeminent playwright of German naturalism, is awarded the Nobel Prize for Literature. His dramas include *Vor Sonnenaufgang* (*Before Dawn*, 1889) and *Die Weber* (*The Weavers*, 1892).   **DRAMA**

1912   In the United States film attendance reaches 5 million patrons daily.   **FILM**

1912   African-American poet and novelist James Weldon Johnson publish-
              es the novel *The Autobiography of an Ex-Coloured Man*, about a light-
              skinned African-American who passes for Caucasian. The book is
              originally published anonymously.   **LIT**

1912   American publisher Harriet Monroe founds the literary magazine
              Poetry in Chicago. It will grow to have wide influence in the literary
              community.   **LIT**

1912   American poet Robinson Jeffers publishes his first collection of po-
              ems *Flagons and Apples*. Later collections will include *Dear Judas*
              (1929), *Such Counsels You Gave to Me* (1937), and *Be Angry at the
              Sun* (1941).   **LIT**

1912   Indian writer Rabindranath Tagore publishes the poetry collection
              Gitanjali. The prolific author's works include poetry, philosophy, fic-
              tion, drama, and essays.   **LIT**

1912   Austrian-born composer Arnold Schoenberg's melodramatic song
              cycle *Pierrot Lunaire* for singing narrator and chamber orchestra, is
              presented in Berlin.   **MUSIC**

1912–1938   British-born conductor Leopold Stokowski becomes chief conductor
              of the Philadelphia Symphony Orchestra. During his final two sea-
              sons, he will share his position with Eugene Ormandy.   **MUSIC**

1912   Synthetic cubism supersedes the earlier phase of cubism, known as
              analytic cubism. Unlike the earlier phase, which concentrated on
              geometric form rather than color, the new phase, typified by
              Spanish painter Juan Gris (pseudonym of José González), makes use
              of color, decorative shapes, and collage.   **PAINT**

1913   Designed by American architect Cass Gilbert, the Woolworth Building
              in New York City is constructed. The 792-foot building celebrates the
              five-and-ten cent store empire of Frank W. Woolworth.   **ARCH**

1913   Russian composer Igor Stravinsky's ballet *Le Sacre du printemps*
              (*The Rite of Spring*) is produced in Paris. With its harsh sound and
              wild rhythms, it causes a storm of indignation at its first
              performance.   **DANCE**

1913   Indian writer Rabindranath Tagore is awarded the Nobel Prize for
              Literature, the same year that his play *Dakaghan* (*The Post Office*) is
              produced. Tagore's *Visarjana* (*Sacrifice*) was produced in 1890. **DRAMA**

1913   British novelist Joseph Conrad publishes *Chance*.   **LIT**

1913   British novelist D. H. Lawrence publishes the autobiographical novel
              Sons and Lovers.   **LIT**

1913   In London British social reformers Sidney and Beatrice Webb found
              the political periodical *The New Statesman*, which will become high-
              ly influential in the coming decades.   **LIT**

Self-Portrait of Enrico Caruso, Italian. *(Music Division, The New York Public Library)*

1913   American novelist Willa Cather publishes the novel *O Pioneers!* about Swedish settlers, primarily Alexandra Bergson, and their experiences in the new land of Nebraska.   **LIT**

1913   American poet Joyce Kilmer publishes the poem "Trees" in *Poetry* magazine. The poem gains wide popularity; it is the center of his collection *Trees and Other Poems* (1914).   **LIT**

1913   American novelist Henry James publishes the historical essay *Mont-Saint-Michel and Chartres*, a study of the unity of the medieval world as seen through Chartres cathedral and the Abbey Church at Mont-Saint-Michel. The book was printed privately in 1904.   **LIT**

1913–1920   American poet Vachel Lindsay establishes himself through the publication of several collections during the decade: *General William Booth Enters into Heaven and Other Poems* (1913); *The Congo and Other Poems* (1914); *The Chinese Nightingale and Other Poems* (1917); and *The Golden Whales of California and Other Rhymes* (1920).   **LIT**

1913–1927   French novelist Marcel Proust publishes the novel *À la recherche du temps perdu* (*Remembrance of Things Past*) about the nature of time and memory.   **LIT**

1913   Spanish philosopher and writer Miguel de Unamuno y Jugo publishes the meditative treatise *Del sentimiento trágico de la vida en los hombres y los pueblos* (*The Tragic Sense of Life*). Among his novels is *Niebla* (*Mist, A Tragicomic Novel*, 1914).   **LIT**

1913   French painter Georges Braque invents papier collé, a variety of collage in which pieces of decorative paper are incorporated into a painting.   **PAINT**

1913   Italian futurist painter and sculptor Umberto Boccioni paints *Dynamism of a Cyclist*.   **PAINT**

1913   French painter Marcel Duchamp completes his second version of *Nude Descending a Staircase*, combining elements of cubism and futurism.   **PAINT**

1913   The Armory Show in New York City introduces post-impressionist and cubist works to the American audience.   **PAINT**

1913   Italian futurist painter and sculptor Umberto Boccioni attempts to represent the motion of the human form and not the figure itself in his bronze sculpture *Unique Forms of Continuity in Space*.   **SCULP**

1914–1917   The Lincoln Memorial is designed by American architect Henry Bacon and built in Washington, D.C. It houses a massive statue of President Lincoln designed by American sculptor Daniel Chester French.   **ARCH**

1914   British playwright George Bernard Shaw's play *Pygmalion* is produced. It will form the basis for the popular American musical *My Fair Lady* (*see* 1956, DRAMA). Shaw's *Heartbreak House* will be produced in 1920.   **DRAMA**

1914   Irish poet and dramatist William Butler Yeats publishes the collection *Responsibilities*, which includes the poems "The Grey Rock," "The Hour Before Dawn," "The Magi," "The Dolls," and "A Coat."   **LIT**

| 1914 | British novelist Thomas Hardy publishes *Satires of Circumstance, Lyrics and Reveries*, which includes the elegiac "Poems of 1912–1913" written in memory of his wife Emma.   **LIT** |

1914   British novelist Thomas Hardy publishes *Satires of Circumstance, Lyrics and Reveries*, which includes the elegiac "Poems of 1912–1913" written in memory of his wife Emma.   **LIT**

1914   Irish writer James Joyce publishes *Dubliners*, an evocative collection of short stories about life in and around his native Dublin.   **LIT**

1914   American poet Robert Frost publishes the collection *North of Boston*, which contains such well-known poems as "Mending Wall," "Home Burial," and "Death of the Hired Man."   **LIT**

1914   In *Poetry* magazine American poet Carl Sandburg publishes what will come to be his most famous poem, *Chicago*, ode to the "Hog Butcher for the World."   **LIT**

1914   Chilean poet Gabriela Mistral (pen name of Lucila Godoy Alcayaga) publishes the collection *Sonetos de la muerte*. Her later works will include *Ternura* (1924) and *Tala* (1938).   **LIT**

1914   British composer Ralph Vaughan Williams composes *A London Symphony* (Symphony no. 2), which combines the extroverted energy of Edward Elgar with poetic contemplation.   **MUSIC**

1914   The American Society of Composers, Authors and Publishers (AS-CAP) is founded by American composer Victor Herbert for the purpose of protecting copyright and performing rights.   **MUSIC**

1914–1917   Popular World War I songs include George M. Cohan's "Over There," Ivor Novello's "Keep the Home Fires Burning," and Jack Judge's "Tipperary."   **MUSIC**

1914   American composer William Christopher (W. C.) Handy publishes his song "The St. Louis Blues." It will become the best-known blues song of its era and will help to define the blues as a musical genre.   **MUSIC**

1914   Spanish painter Juan Gris, a pioneer of synthetic cubism, uses papier collé in *The Sunblind*.   **PAINT**

1914   Italian painter Giorgio de Chirico, inventor of metaphysical painting, which emphasizes dream imagery and irrationality, paints *The Mystery and Melancholy of a Street*.   **PAINT**

1914   Following a trip to Tunisia, Swiss painter Paul Klee decides to abandon most of his work in black and white and pursue work in color, writing that "Color and I are one."   **PAINT**

1915   The Imperial Hotel in Tokyo, Japan, is designed by American architect Frank Lloyd Wright.   **ARCH**

1915   The Cleveland Play House, which in the 1920s will become America's first nonprofit professional regional theater, opens in Cleveland, Ohio.   **DRAMA**

THE FIRST MOVIE STAR

*T*he first American movie star to be known to the public by name is today hardly remembered. Florence Lawrence (1886–1938) of Ontario, Canada, became a popular favorite in U.S. films by D. W. Griffith and others produced by the Biograph Company. But despite lead roles in such features as Salome, The Zulu's Heart, The Viking's Daughter, An Awful Moment, and Antony and Cleopatra (all 1908), she was known to audiences only as the Biograph Girl. Movie studios of that era declined to identify actors by name lest they demand higher wages.

In 1910 upstart movie producer Carl Laemmle, who later founded Universal Pictures, lured Lawrence from Biograph to his own studio, IMP (Independent Motion Picture Company of America). In a publicity stunt, Laemmle circulated rumors that the Biograph Girl was dead, then debunked the story himself, stating in an advertisement that "enemies" of IMP were responsible for the tale. The ad reported that Florence Lawrence, formerly the Biograph Girl, was not only alive but was now the "Imp Girl," soon to star in her first IMP picture, The Broken Oath.

With one actress having been given a name, there was no going back. It became common practice for movie performers to be known by name, and silent film stars such as Mary Pickford, Douglas Fairbanks, and Charlie Chaplin were soon commanding enormous salaries, just as the studios had feared.

As for Florence Lawrence, her star faded when she was seriously hurt in a movie stunt in 1914 and forced to withdraw from movies for several years. A comeback attempt in the early 1920s failed, and by the 1930s she was working only as an extra. She died a suicide at age fifty-two.

1915   The Civil War epic *The Birth of a Nation* is released to great success. Directed by D. W. Griffith, the film is based on the Thomas Dixon work *The Clansman* and stars Lillian Gish. The film's racist message and its exaltation of the Ku Klux Klan make it perenially controversial, yet its masterful handling of the film medium is highly influential and helps to establish filmmaking as a serious art.   **FILM**

1915   British novelist Joseph Conrad publishes *Victory*.   **LIT**

1915   British novelist D. H. Lawrence publishes *The Rainbow*, which is banned for indecency but becomes known as perhaps his greatest novel.   **LIT**

1915   British poet Rupert Brooke's five war sonnets, including "The Soldier," are published.   **LIT**

1915   British novelist Ford Madox Ford publishes the novel *The Good Soldier*.   **LIT**

1915   British novelist Virginia Woolf publishes her first novel, *The Voyage Out*.   **LIT**

1915   American poet Edgar Lee Masters publishes *Spoon River Anthology*.   **LIT**

1915–1916   American poet Robert Frost publishes the poem "The Road Not Taken." Over time the poem will become known for its final lines, "I took the one less traveled by/And that has made all the difference."   **LIT**

1915–1923   American poet Wallace Stevens writes the poem "Sunday Morning." The sensual and complex poem about a woman at breakfast on Sunday morning will become one of Stevens's most praised works.   **LIT**

1915   Austrian novelist and short-story writer Franz Kafka writes the story "The Metamorphosis," about a man, Gregor Samsa, who awakens to find himself turned into a cockroach. Among his later works are the novels *The Castle* (1922) and *The Trial* (1925).   **LIT**

1915   English novelist and short-story writer W. (William) Somerset Maugham publishes the novel *Of Human Bondage*. Among his later novels will be *The Moon and Sixpence* (1919), *Cakes and Ale* (1930), and *The Razor's Edge* (1944). His short story "Miss Thompson" (1921) will introduce the character of loose woman Sadie Thompson.   **LIT**

1915   The neoclassical German composer Max Reger composes *Mozart Variations*.   **MUSIC**

1915   A vorticist exhibition is held in Britain. The avant-garde British arts movement, influenced by Italian futurism, has writer Wyndham Lewis as its principal spokesperson. Painters associated with it include C. R. W. Nevinson and William Roberts.   **PAINT**

1915   French painter Marc Chagall paints *The Birthday*.   **PAINT**

1915   The Dadaist movement is founded in Zurich and New York by a group of disillusioned American and European artists, including Romanian poet Tristan Tzara and French painters Hans Arp and Marcel Duchamp. Rooted in the cynicism of the First World War, Dada is devoted to the pursuit of antiart and illogic. The word *Dada* is French for hobby horse.   **PAINT**

1915   Romanian sculptor Constantin Brancusi sculpts *Le Nouveau-Né*.   **SCULP**

1916   *Theatre Arts*, a periodical which will run serious articles on a variety of theater-related topics, is founded in Detroit. It will merge with *The Stage* in 1948 and the resulting publication will be in business until 1964.   **DRAMA**

1916   Notable films include D. W. Griffith's *Intolerance*, Charlie Chaplin's *The Pawn Shop*, and Thomas Ince's *Civilization*.   **FILM**

1916   Irish writer James Joyce publishes the autobiographical novel *A Portrait of the Artist as a Young Man*. It was first published in Ezra Pound's journal *The Egoist* in 1914 and 1915.   **LIT**

1916   A year before his death in combat during World War I, British critic, biographer, and nature writer Edward Thomas publishes his first book of poetry. Like his posthumous volumes published in 1917 and 1918, it is well received for its subtlety and intensity.   **LIT**

1916–1951   American poet Carl Sandburg publishes a number of collections of expressive, inclusive American poetry: *Chicago Poems* (1916); *Cornhuskers* (1918); *Smoke and Steel* (1920); *Slabs of the Sunburnt West* (1922); *Good Morning, America* (1928); *The People, Yes* (1936); and *Collected Poems* (1951).   **LIT**

1916   Spanish novelist Vicente Blasco Ibáñez publishes *The Four Horsemen of the Apocalypse*.   **LIT**

1916   Spanish composer Manuel de Falla debuts his symphonic impressions, *Noches en los jardines de España* (*Nights in the Gardens of Spain*) in Madrid.   **MUSIC**

1916   British composer Gustav Holst composes the programmatic suite *The Planets* for orchestra, organ, and women's chorus.   **MUSIC**

1916–1937   French painter Georges Rouault paints *The Old King*, the color shapes and black outlines of which reflect his early training in making stained glass.   **PAINT**

1917   Spanish painter Pablo Picasso and French designer Jean Cocteau design costumes and scenery for the Diaghilev ballet *Parade*, one of several Diaghilev works to which they will contribute.   **DANCE**

c.1917   Dutch architect Gerrit Thomas Rietveld designs a chair that appears light and dematerialized.   **DECO**

1917–1921   German-born artist George Grosz completes a series of satirical drawings, *The Face of the Ruling Class*.   **GRAPH**

1917   American-born British poet T. S. (Thomas Stearns) Eliot publishes "The Love Song of J. Alfred Prufrock," a meditation on, among other subjects, the futility of existence in modern times.   **LIT**

1917   American poet Edna St. Vincent Millay publishes what will become one of her most noteworthy poetry collections, *Renascence*.   **LIT**

1917–1948   American poet Ezra Pound publishes the first three *Cantos*, a series of poems that he will continue to write and publish through the 1960s. *A Draft of XXX Cantos* will be published in 1933, *Eleven New Cantos* in 1934, and *Pisan Cantos, LXXI to LXXXV* in 1948.   **LIT**

1917   French symbolist poet Paul Valéry publishes the work *La Jeune Parque*. Among his later works will be the monologues "Le Cimetière Marin" and "Fragments du Narcisse," collected in the book *Charmes* (1922).   **LIT**

1917   German composer Hans Pfitzner's opera *Palestrina* is produced in Munich.   **MUSIC**

1917   Russian composer Sergey Prokofiev composes *Classical Symphony* no. 1 in D.   **MUSIC**

1917   French composers Georges Auric, Louis Durey, Arthur Honegger, Darius Milhaud, Francis Poulenc, and Germaine Tailleferre form the group eventually known as Les Six. Reacting against the vagueness of impressionism, they endorse the simplicity and clarity of the neoclassical movement.   **MUSIC**

1917   Dutch painters Piet Mondrian and Theo van Doesburg cofound the arts magazine and movement *De Stijl*. Mondrian begins to paint his works in geometric shapes and a mix of primary colors, black, white, and gray. He names the artistic theory behind his compositions neo-plasticism.   **PAINT**

1917   Marcel Duchamp sends a urinal listed as "an enameled pottery piece called *Fountain*" to the first exhibit of the Society of Independents in New York. The jury will reject Duchamp's submission. He will continue to exhibit manufactured objects of "ready-mades" as an intellectual challenge to traditional concepts of painting and sculpture. Such actions will help define the "antiart" character of the Dada movement.   **SCULP**

1917   In the United States, amplitude modulation (AM) radio is pioneered through the development of a superheterodyne circuit by Army Signal Corps officer Edwin Armstrong.   **TV&R**

1918   American architect Frank Lloyd Wright designs the Robie house in Chicago, a classic example of his prairie style, conceived in terms of low horizontal lines and abstract blocks.   **ARCH**

1918   In Germany architect Walter Gropius founds the Bauhaus, a school that seeks to unify the arts within the world of architecture in the service of the mass-production needs of the modern age. He will leave the Bauhaus in 1928.   **ARCH**

1918   The Yiddish Art Theatre opens in New York City. Through the late 1930s, it will present high quality Jewish theater.   **DRAMA**

1918	Notable films include Abel Gance's *The Tenth Symphony*, Charlie Chaplin's *A Dog's Life*, and Ernst Lubitsch's *Carmen*. **FILM**	

1918   American cartoonist Winsor McCay creates what may be the first feature-length animated film, *The Sinking of the Lusitania*. Notable McCay shorts of the time include *Gertie the Dinosaur* (1914) and *Little Nemo* (1911). **FILM**

1918   British poet and editor Robert Bridges publishes a collection of his late friend Gerard Manley Hopkins's poetry. Unpublished in Hopkins's lifetime, the poems, which include "Pied Beauty," "God's Grandeur," "The Windhover," and "That Nature Is a Heraclitean Fire" gain praise from modernist critics and poets and come to exercise a wide influence. **LIT**

1918   American novelist Willa Cather publishes *My Antonia*, a novel about Czech settlers in the middle United States, particularly a woman named Antonia Shimerda. **LIT**

1918   American historian Henry Adams publishes *The Education of Henry Adams*. Written in the third person, it is as much a search for a unified vision of the age as an ironic examination of his life. The chapter "The Dynamo and the Virgin" will become accepted as a standard for the comparison of the unity of the past and the incomprehensible disarray of the modern age. The book was privately printed in 1907. **LIT**

1918   Hungarian composer Béla Bartók's one-act opera *Bluebeard's Castle*, opens in Budapest. **MUSIC**

1918   French composer Erik Satie writes his serious symphonic drama *Socrate*. **MUSIC**

1918   In the midst of World War I, the New York Philharmonic Society bans compositions by living German composers. The German conductor of the Boston Symphony Orchestra, Karl Muck, is arrested as an enemy alien. **MUSIC**

c. 1918   Russian painter Kasimir Malevich paints *White on White*, a series characteristic of suprematism, a Russian movement related to cubism. **PAINT**

1918   Swiss architect Charles-Édouard Jeanneret, known as Le Corbusier, and French painter Amédée Ozenfant publish *Après le cubisme*, a treatise decrying the deterioration of synthetic cubism. The work is tied to the founding by the two men of the artistic movement of purism. **PAINT**

1919   *Le Bourgmestre de Stilmonde*, perhaps the finest drama by Belgian poet and playwright Maurice Maeterlinck, is produced. Maeterlinck had won the Nobel Prize for Literature in 1911. **DRAMA**

1919   The German horror film *Das Cabinett des Dr. Caligari* (*The Cabinet of Dr. Caligari*) opens. Directed by Robert Wiene, it draws from the German expressionist movement to define the aesthetic world of the horror film for decades to come.   **FILM**

1919   Irish poet and dramatist William Butler Yeats publishes the collection *The Wild Swans at Coole*, which includes the title poem along with such works as "An Irish Airman Foresees His Death," "Upon a Dying Lady," "Ego Dominus Tuus," and "The Double Vision of Michael Robartes."   **LIT**

1919   British novelist Virginia Woolf publishes the influential essay "Modern Fiction."   **LIT**

1919-1948   American journalist and essayist H. L. Mencken publishes *The American Language*, a pioneering reference work and study of the differences between the English and American tongues. The work will see supplements in 1945 and 1948.   **LIT**

1919   American novelist Sherwood Anderson publishes *Winesburg, Ohio*, a novel of linked tales about the repressed inhabitants of the title town.   **LIT**

1919   The Los Angeles Orchestra offers its first concert.   **MUSIC**

1919   American jazz music becomes popular in Europe, with tours by jazz musicians like Paul Whiteman and Jelly Roll Morton and long-term engagements by Duke Ellington to follow in the coming decade.   **MUSIC**

c.1919   Italian painter Amedeo Modigliani paints *Reclining Nude*.   **PAINT**

1919   French painter Fernand Léger paints *The City*, a work influenced by synthetic cubism.   **PAINT**

1919   French Dadaist painter Marcel Duchamp creates *L.H.O.O.Q.*, a reproduction of Leonardo da Vinci's *Mona Lisa* with a mustache and goatee on its face.   **PAINT**

1919   More than 300 works of Swiss painter Paul Klee are exhibited in Germany by Munich art dealer Goltz. The exhibition establishes Klee as a painter of international importance.   **PAINT**

1919   American painter George Bellows completes the portrait *Mrs. Chester Dale*.   **PAINT**

1919   Romanian sculptor Constantin Brancusi strives to visualize abstract form in the bronze *Bird in Space*.   **SCULP**

1920s   The Cotton Club becomes a popular night spot in New York's Harlem. Featuring top black musical talent, it is open only to whites.   **DANCE**

1920s   The Lindy hop, a fast-moving social dance named for American aviator Charles Lindbergh, becomes popular in the United States.   **DANCE**

1920s   Latin American theater becomes more experimental and technical-
               ly sophisticated. Though it still follows European trends, it focuses
               increasingly on themes and styles developed internally.   **DRAMA**

1920s   American journalist and essayist H. L. Mencken edits the *American
               Mercury*, one of the most respected and influential periodicals of its
               day.   **LIT**

1920s   Little magazines such as *Poetry*, *Story*, and *transition* are popular
               methods of introducing and nurturing new literary talent, and gain
               a wide readership.   **LIT**

1920s   Several students at Vanderbilt University, including John Crowe
               Ransom, Allen Tate, Cleanth Brooks, and Robert Penn Warren, com-
               prise an influential American literary circle that will become known
               as the fugitives, agrarians, or Nashville group.   **LIT**

c. 1920s   The neoclassical movement in music fosters a return to aesthetic
               ideals and formal methods of the seventeenth and eighteenth cen-
               turies, recast in modern idioms. It is represented by the works of
               such composers as Igor Stravinsky, Béla Bartók, and Paul
               Hindemith.   **MUSIC**

THE LAW OF "STAR DUST"

"Star Dust," one of the most widely recorded romantic ballads of the
twentieth century, was written not by a weepy writer locked in a
garret but by an eager law student noodling on a piano in a law
school lounge. In 1927 Indiana University law student Hoagy Carmichael
was taking a break from his studies at a meeting place called the Book Nook
when he conjured up a haunting tune on the lounge's old upright piano. The
melody lacked a name until his friend Stuart Gorrell called it "Star Dust"
because it played like "dust from stars drifting down through the summer
sky."

Though Carmichael was already a working composer, with "Riverboat
Shuffle" to his credit, it would take a decade and several musical incarna-
tions to establish "Star Dust" as a standard. Originally recorded in 1927 as
an up-tempo number, it was reborn as a ballad in 1930 by Isham Jones and
his orchestra. In this form it became the basis for two definitive big band
recordings in 1936—one by Tommy Dorsey, one by Benny Goodman. They,
along with the 1940 rendition by Artie Shaw and his orchestra, made it one
of the signature romantic ballads of the Swing Era.

1920s	Popular songs of the day include "Tea for Two," "Barney Google," "Bye, Bye Blackbird," "I Found a Million-Dollar Baby in the Five-and-Ten Cent Store," "Yes, We Have No Bananas," "Show Me the Way to Go Home," "Blue Skies," "Ol' Man River," "Makin' Whoopee," "Star Dust," and "Singin' in the Rain." **MUSIC**
1920s	French painter Raoul Dufy is active in popularizing modern art for larger audiences. **PAINT**
1920s	Beginning in this decade, American photographer Edward Steichen gains wide exposure as a portrait photographer for mass-market periodicals. Among his more well-known portraits will be *Greta Garbo*, taken for *Vanity Fair* (1928), which captures her elusive appeal. **PHOTO**
1920s	American photographer James Van Der Zee becomes a leading artist of the Harlem Renaissance with his telling, stately portraits of African-Americans. **PHOTO**
1920s	Hungarian-born constructivist painter and photographer László Moholy-Nagy experiments with expressions of time, space, and imagination through the creation of photograms, which involves removing the camera lens before exposing the photographic paper to light. **PHOTO**
1920s	American artist Man Ray creates the Rayogram, a collage of objects placed onto photographic paper and exposed to light. **PHOTO**
1920s	Blackfoot artist Hart Merriam Schultz, working under his Native name Lone Wolf, is one of the first modern Native American artists to produce sculpture. **SCULP**
1920	French composer Maurice Ravel completes the dance poem for orchestra *La Valse*, which uses the waltz form to portray the transition from pre-World War I social elegance to postwar decline. **DANCE**
1920	Russian composer Igor Stravinsky's ballets *Pulcinella* and *Le Chant du rossignol* (*The Song of the Nightingale*) are produced at the Paris Opera. **DANCE**
1920	In Los Angeles American dancer Ruth St. Denis and her husband, dancer Ted Shawn, form the influential Denishawn school of dance. **DANCE**
1920	*El maleficio de la mariposa* (*The Butterfly's Curse*), the first full-length play by Spanish poet and playwright Federico García Lorca, is produced. Lorca's historical drama *Mariana Pineda* will be produced in 1927. His comedy *La zapatera prodigiosa* (*The Shoemaker's Amazing Wife)* will be produced in 1930. **DRAMA**
1920	*Beyond the Horizon*, the first full-length play by American playwright Eugene O'Neill, is produced on Broadway. It will win the Pulitzer Prize. O'Neill's *The Emperor Jones*, a drama featuring a black protagonist, will also be produced this year. **DRAMA**

1920   Notable films include Paul Wegener and Carl Boese's *The Golem* and Paul Powell's *Pollyanna*, starring Mary Pickford.   **FILM**

1920   British novelist D. H. Lawrence publishes *Women in Love*. Like *The Rainbow* (1915), it explores human relationships with great psychological and poetic power.   **LIT**

1920   A collection of British poet Wilfrid Owen's poems is published posthumously, following his death in combat during World War I.   **LIT**

1920   American poet Ezra Pound publishes the influential poem about war and art, "Hugh Selwyn Mauberley."   **LIT**

1920   American novelist Sinclair Lewis publishes his satire of middle-class Midwestern existence, *Main Street*.   **LIT**

1920   American novelist F. Scott Fitzgerald publishes his first novel, *This Side of Paradise* and first collection of short stories *Flappers and Philosophers*. This year he marries Southern beauty Zelda Sayre. The two will become one of the most talked-about literary couples of the twentieth century.   **LIT**

1920   American novelist Edith Wharton publishes *The Age of Innocence*, a novel of manners set in upper-class New York in the 1870s that tells of the unfulfilled love between Newland Archer and Countess Ellen Olenska. The book will win the Pulitzer Prize.   **LIT**

1920–1922   Norwegian novelist Sigrid Undset publishes the saga *Kristin Lavransdatter*. Her later works will include *The Snake Pit*.   **LIT**

c.1920   The German word *kitsch*, meaning "vulgar trash," gains use to denote inauthentic or highly commercial artistic creations from souvenirs to paintings.   **PAINT**

1920   In Canada the association of painters known as the Group of Seven is formed. The members, who will develop Canada's first distinctive national movement in painting, include Franklin Carmichael, Lawren Harris, A. Y. Jackson, Frank Johnston, Arthur Lismer, J. E. H. Macdonald, and Frederick Varley. Their work is heavily influenced by the expressionist movement.   **PAINT**

1920–1970   Hungarian-born photographer André Kertész practices photography. His work, such as *Blind Musician* (1921) will be highly informed by the photos of Eugène Atget.   **PHOTO**

1920   Soviet painter and sculptor Vladimir Tatlin completes his model for a monument to the Third International that is meant to have a height of more than 1,300 feet. Though the monument is never built, Tatlin's ambitious model, combining painting, sculpture, architecture, and technology, represents the high point of the constructivist movement that he founded in 1913.   **SCULP**

1920	On November 2 KDKA in Pittsburgh, Pennsylvania, becomes the first radio broadcasting station in the world. Developed by Westinghouse engineer Frank Conrad, its first broadcasts are the result of the 1920 U.S. presidential election, in which Warren G. Harding is elected. **TV&R**
1921	*Shuffle Along*, the first all-black Broadway musical, opens to critical acclaim. The show helps to usher in the period of black artistic flowering known as the Harlem Renaissance. **DANCE**
1921	*Sei personaggi in cerca d'autore (Six Characters in Search of an Author)* by Italian playwright Luigi Pirandello is produced in Rome. It will become his most famous play. **DRAMA**
1921	*The Circle*, perhaps the best play by British novelist and playwright W. Somerset Maugham, premieres. Other notable plays of his will include *The Constant Wife* (produced in 1926), *The Sacred Flame* (1928), *The Breadwinner* (1930), and *For Service Rendered* (1932). **DRAMA**
1921	Sir John Gielgud, one of the greatest British actors of the twentieth century, makes his debut at the Old Vic. The grandnephew of actress Ellen Terry (*see* 1856, DRAMA), he is best known for his Shakespearean roles—especially Hamlet, probably his best role of all—and for his performances as Trigorin in Chekhov's *The Seagull* (1956), as Raskolnikoff in an adaptation of Dostoyevsky's *Crime and Punishment* (1946), and in Harold Pinter's *No Man's Land* (1975). He will also be a director and a repertory company manager, and appear memorably as a character player in films. **DRAMA**
1921	*Anna Christie*, a feminist drama by American playwright Eugene O'Neill, is produced. The story of a prostitute and a crude sailor transformed by their love for one another, it will earn O'Neill his second Pulitzer Prize. **DRAMA**
1921	Notable films include Charlie Chaplin's *The Kid*, D. W. Griffith's *Dream Street*, and Rex Ingram's *Four Horsemen of the Apocalypse*. **FILM**
1921	Irish poet and dramatist William Butler Yeats publishes the collection *Michael Robartes and the Dancer*, which includes the title poem along with such works as "Easter, 1916," "A Prayer for my Daughter," and "A Meditation in Time of War." Also included is the poem "The Second Coming," from which come the lines, "Things fall apart; the centre cannot hold" and "And what rough beast, its hour come round at last,/Slouches toward Bethlehem to be born?" **LIT**
1921	British novelist D. H. Lawrence publishes the nonfiction work *Psychoanalysis and the Unconscious*. **LIT**
1921	American novelist Willa Cather publishes a novel of World War I, *One of Ours*. Based on a family war death, the book will win the Pulitzer Prize. **LIT**

1921–1961   American poet Marianne Moore publishes her first collection of po-
             etry, *Poems*. Subsequent collections include *Observations* (1924),
             What Are Years? (1941), and *Collected Poems* (1951), for which she
             will win the Pulitzer Prize.   **LIT**

1921   Austrian playwright, novelist, and poet Franz Werfel completes the
             play *Bocksgesang* (*Goat Song*). His later works will include the play
             Juarez (1924) and the novel *The Song of Bernadette* (1941), which
             will be the basis of a film.   **LIT**

1921   Russian composer Sergey Prokofiev's farcical opera *The Love for
             Three Oranges*, produced in Chicago, is his first great operatic
             success.   **MUSIC**

1921   Italian conductor Arturo Toscanini opens the remodeled Teatro alla
             Scala, Milan.   **MUSIC**

1921   Spanish painter Pablo Picasso paints the synthetic cubist work
             Three Musicians.   **PAINT**

1921   French cubist painter Georges Braque completes *Still Life with
             Guitar*. One of his many still life paintings, it is an early example of
             his post-World War I aesthetic variance from friend and colleague
             Pablo Picasso, with whom he founded cubism.   **PAINT**

1921   Norwegian painter Edvard Munch completes *The Kiss*.   **PAINT**

1921–1924   German painter Max Ernst paints *The Elephant Célébes*, a work that
             will be regarded as surrealist after the founding of that movement
             in 1924.   **PAINT**

1921   American photographer Lewis Hine takes the photograph *Steamfitter*,
             one of his many photos of children and adults at work.   **PHOTO**

1922   The comedy *Abie's Irish Rose* by American playwright Anne Nichols
             begins its long run (2,327 performances). The play's title refers to
             an interfaith (Jewish-Christian) marriage.   **DRAMA**

1922   *Trommeln in der Nacht* (*Drums in the Night*), a drama by German
             playwright Bertolt Brecht, is produced. Brecht's *Im Dickicht der
             Städte* (*The Jungle of the Cities*) and *Mann ist Mann* (*A Man's A Man*)
             will be produced in 1923 and 1926, respectively.   **DRAMA**

1922   *Enrico IV* (*Henry IV*), a tragedy by Italian playwright Luigi Pirandello,
             is produced.   **DRAMA**

1922   *Back to Methuselah*, considered by British playwright George
             Bernard Shaw his finest work, is produced.   **DRAMA**

1922   *The Hairy Ape*, an expressionistic drama exploring class conflict by
             American playwright Eugene O'Neill, is produced.   **DRAMA**

1922   Notable films include F. W. Murnau's *Nosferatu*, D. W. Griffith's
             Orphans of the Storm, and Robert Flaherty's landmark documentary
             Nanook of the North, which sets a standard for the genre.   **FILM**

1922   Banned as obscene in England and America, Irish writer James Joyce's *Ulysses* is published in Paris. The most prominent example of stream-of-consciousness technique, the novel details the adventures of Leopold Bloom and Stephen Dedalus in Dublin on a single day, June 16, 1904 (now called "Bloomsday"). It alludes throughout to Homer's epic poem *The Odyssey* (ninth century B.C.), the central character of which, Odysseus, is known in Latin as Ulysses. **LIT**

1922   British novelist D. H. Lawrence publishes the novel *Aaron's Rod* and the short-story collection *England, My England*. **LIT**

1922   British novelist and playwright John Galsworthy completes the sequence of novels known as *The Forsyte Saga*, which began in 1906 with *A Man of Property*. **LIT**

1922   British novelist Virginia Woolf publishes *Jacob's Room*, her first experimental novel employing stream of consciousness and the first to be published by Hogarth Press, founded with her husband Leonard Woolf. **LIT**

1922   British poet T. S. Eliot publishes *The Waste Land*. The complex epic poem will be considered by many his most accomplished work. **LIT**

1922   American novelist Sinclair Lewis publishes the novel *Babbitt*, a satiric indictment of the American businessman. Following publication of the novel the word "Babbitt" came to be part of the American lexicon. **LIT**

1922–1928   American poet Edwin Arlington Robinson is awarded the Pulitzer Prize three times during the 1920s: for *Collected Poems* (1922), *The Man Who Died Twice* (1925), and *Tristram* (1928). **LIT**

1922   Under the guidance of American editors DeWitt and Lila Acheson Wallace, the *Reader's Digest* begins publication. It is meant to serve as a portable collection of articles from prominent periodicals. **LIT**

1922   English novelist Rebecca West publishes *The Judge*. Her later works will include *The Thinking Reed* (1936), *The Fountain Overflows*, and the nonfiction work *Black Lamb and Grey Falcon* (1942), an examination of Yugoslavia. **LIT**

1922   German poet and novelist Hermann Hesse publishes the novel *Siddhartha*. Among his later works will be *Steppenwolf* (1929) and *Magister Ludi* (1943). **LIT**

1922   The International Society for Contemporary Music (I.S.C.M.) forms at Salzburg. Its headquarters are established in London in 1923. **MUSIC**

1922   American jazz musician Louis Armstrong joins King Oliver's Creole Jazz Band in Chicago. He will join the Fletcher Henderson orchestra in 1924 and will make his first record, "Everybody Loves My Baby." **MUSIC**

1922   Swiss artist Paul Klee paints *Twittering Machine*. **PAINT**

1922	An international Dadaist exhibition is held in Paris, bringing together many European and American Dada artists. **PAINT**
1923	The Chicago Tribune building is designed by architect Raymond Hood. **ARCH**
1923	*L'Uomo del fiore in bocca* (*The Man with a Flower in His Mouth*), a one-act drama about a cancer patient by Italian playwright Luigi Pirandello, is produced. His *Come tu mi vuoi* (*As You Desire Me*) and *Quando si è qualcuno* (*When One Is Somebody*) will be produced in 1930 and 1933, respectively. **DRAMA**
1923	*The Shadow of a Gunman*, the first play by Irish playwright Sean O'Casey, is produced at the Abbey Theatre in Dublin. **DRAMA**
1923	*Saint Joan*, a historical play by British playwright George Bernard Shaw, is produced. Some critics see this treatment of the legend of Joan of Arc as Shaw's finest play. **DRAMA**
1923	American actors Alfred Lunt and Lynn Fontanne, married since 1922, appear together for the first time in American playwright Paul Kester's *Sweet Nell of Old Drury*. Later joint performances will include Ferenc Molnár's *The Guardsman* (1924) and Noel Coward's *Design for Living* (1933). **DRAMA**
1923	*The Adding Machine*, an expressionistic fantasy play by American playwright Elmer Rice, is produced. His *Street Scene*, a realistic depiction of poverty, will be produced in 1929, and will win the Pulitzer Prize. **DRAMA**
1923	Notable films include Harold Lloyd's *Why Worry*, Cecil B. De Mille's *The Ten Commandments*, and Allan Dwan's *Robin Hood*, starring Douglas Fairbanks. **FILM**
1923	The Eastman Kodak Company introduces 16mm movie film for amateur use. It will become the favorite medium for student, industrial, and educational films. **FILM**
1923	Syrian writer Kahlil Gibran publishes *The Prophet*, an often translated and reprinted work of inspiration. **LIT**
1923	American publisher Frank Gannett founds the Gannett Company, which unites four upstate New York newspapers and over the years will come to encompass many dozens more. **LIT**
1923	American writer of the Harlem Renaissance Jean Toomer publishes *Cane*, a multigenre exploration of modern African-American life. **LIT**
1923	American poet Robert Frost publishes the poem "Stopping by Woods on a Snowy Evening," about a traveler who has stopped to view the snow while remembering that he has "miles to go before I sleep." **LIT**

1923   American poet Wallace Stevens publishes the poem "The Anecdote of the Jar," about a jar left on a hill in Tennessee. Employed for most of his life at a Connecticut insurance company, Stevens will publish a vast number of collections: *Harmonium* (1923); *Ideas of Order* (1935); *Owl's Clover* (1936); *The Man with a Blue Guitar and Other Poems* (1937); *Parts of a World* (1942); *Notes Toward a Supreme Fiction* (1942), and others.   **LIT**

1923   American poet William Carlos Williams publishes the four-stanza sixteen-word poem "The Red Wheelbarrow." It will become one of his best-known works.   **LIT**

1923   American poet e. e. cummings publishes his first collection of poetry, *Tulips and Chimneys*. Subsequent volumes will include *XLI Poems* (1925), *5* (1926), and *No thanks* (1935).   **LIT**

1923   The weekly newsmagazine *Time* is published for the first time on March 3 by American reporters Henry Luce and Briton Hadden. It will form the basis for a publishing empire and will set a standard for weekly news periodicals.   **LIT**

1923   Austrian-born composer Arnold Schoenberg demonstrates his twelve-tone technique in *Five Piano Pieces*, Op. 23, and the *Serenade for Seven Instruments and Bass Voice*, Op. 24.   **MUSIC**

1923   French composer Arthur Honegger debuts his symphonic poem *Pacific 231*, inspired by the movement of a locomotive.   **MUSIC**

1923   German composer Paul Hindemith composes the song cycle *Das Marienleben* (*The Life of Mary*) for piano and soprano.   **MUSIC**

1923   Spanish artist Pablo Picasso completes the paintings *Lady With a Blue Veil*, *Melancholy*, and *Women*.   **PAINT**

· ·

"A house is a living-machine."—Swiss architect Le Corbusier, Vers une architecture, *1923*

· ·

1924   Dutch architect Gerrit Thomas Rietveld designs Schroeder house in Utrecht. Its rectangular shapes and primary colors are characteristic of the De Stijl movement. *See* 1917, PAINT.   **ARCH**

1924   American historian and critic Lewis Mumford completes *Sticks and Bones*, a history of architecture.   **ARCH**

1924   The realistic tragedy *Juno and the Paycock*, the first major work by Irish playwright Sean O'Casey, is produced in Dublin.   **DRAMA**

1924   A department of drama is established at Yale University, with George Pierce Baker as its head. It will become a separate graduate school in 1955, which many will come to view as America's best theater training center.   **DRAMA**

1924   *All God's Chillun Got Wings* and *Desire Under the Elms*, two contro-
              versial dramas by American playwright Eugene O'Neill, are
              produced.   **DRAMA**

1924   German-born actress Katharine Cornell, who will be respected as much
              for her character as for her great acting ability, stars in the title role of
              George Bernard Shaw's *Candida*. Later she will portray Elizabeth Barrett
              in Besier's *The Barretts of Wimpole Street* (1931).   **DRAMA**

1924   Notable films include John Ford's *The Iron Horse*, F. W. Murnau's *The
              Last Laugh*, Jean Renoir's *Nana*, and Raoul Walsh's *The Thief of
              Baghdad*, starring Douglas Fairbanks.   **FILM**

1924   British novelist E. M. Forster publishes *A Passage to India*, his last
              and greatest novel, though he lives until 1970.   **LIT**

1924–1933   With drama critc and editor George Jean Nathan, American journal-
              ist and essayist H. L. Mencken founds and edits the influential peri-
              odical *American Mercury*.   **LIT**

1924   American writer Ernest Hemingway debuts with the story collec-
              tion *In Our Time*. The stories are based on Hemingway's early life in
              Michigan.   **LIT**

1924   American novelist Herman Melville's short novel *Billy Budd, Sailor*,
              is published posthumously. This tale of Budd and master-at-arms
              Claggart, written late in Melville's life, confronts the author's con-
              cerns with good and evil.   **LIT**

1924   Chilean poet Pablo Neruda (born Neftalí Ricardo Reyes Basualto)
              publishes the collection *Veinte poemas de amor y una canción deses-
              perada*. Later collections will include *Residencia en la tierra*
              (1932–1935) and *The Selected Poems of Pablo Neruda* (1970). **LIT**

c. 1924   Russian scientist Leo Theremin invents the earliest electronic musi-
              cal instrument, the theremin.   **MUSIC**

1924   Russian-American conductor Serge Koussevitzky becomes the con-
              ductor of the Boston Symphony Orchestra, a position he will hold
              until 1949. He will be known for his support of modern music. **MUSIC**

1924   Spanish painter Juan Gris paints *Violin and Fruit Dish*.   **PAINT**

1924   In France André Breton publishes the *Surrealist Manifesto*, herald-
              ing the founding this year of surrealism, which works with dream
              and fantasy imagery and the irrational. Salvador Dalí, René
              Magritte, Max Ernst, André Masson, and Joan Miró are among the
              best known surrealist painters. The movement will last until World
              War II.   **PAINT**

1924   Spanish painter Joan Miró completes the surrealistic work *Catalan
              Landscape*.   **PAINT**

1924   American painter George Bellows paints *The Dempsey-Firpo Fight*, which shows fighter Jack Dempsey being knocked through the ropes in a 1923 bout with Luis Firpo. Dempsey came back to win the fight.   **PAINT**

1924   The first successful 35mm camera, the Leica, is developed in Germany. It will become a standard for both professional and amateur photographers.   **PHOTO**

1924   Romanian sculptor Constantin Brancusi sculpts *Le Commencement du monde*.   **SCULP**

1924   There are 2.5 million radios in U.S. households, signaling the immense popularity of the new form of communication.   **TV&R**

· ·

"Millions are to be grabbed out here and your only competition is idiots. Don't let this get around."—American screenwriter Herman J. Mankiewicz encouraging writer Ben Hecht to join him in Hollywood, c. 1925

· ·

1925   The Charleston, a fast-paced social dance, sweeps U.S. and European dance halls and clubs.   **DANCE**

1925   *Hay Fever*, a comedy by British actor and playwright Noel Coward, is produced in New York and London. *Private Lives* and *Design for Living*, both sophisticated comedies, will be produced in 1930 and 1933, respectively.   **DRAMA**

1925   Notable films include Harold Lloyd's *The Freshman*, Charlie Chaplin's *The Gold Rush*, and King Vidor's *The Big Parade*.   **FILM**

1925   Russian director Sergey Eisenstein's *The Battleship Potemkin* is exhibited. Over the years, this film about the 1905 Russian revolution will become known as a film classic for its powerful use of montage and its epic filming of the attack on the Odessa steps.   **FILM**

1925   British novelist Virginia Woolf publishes *Mrs. Dalloway*, as well as the collection of essays *The Common Reader*, to be followed in 1932 by *The Second Common Reader*.   **LIT**

1925   American novelist Theodore Dreiser publishes *An American Tragedy*, a novel inspired by the murder case of Chester Gilette and his victim Grace Brown. The book is an immediate success.   **LIT**

1925   African-American poet Countee Cullen establishes himself as a literary force with his first collection, *Color*. Among his later collections will be *Copper Sun* (1927) and *Brown Girl* (1928).   **LIT**

1925   American novelist Sinclair Lewis publishes *Arrowsmith*, his satire of the medical profession as seen through the experiences of Dr. Martin Arrowsmith.   **LIT**

1925   American novelist F. Scott Fitzgerald publishes *The Great Gatsby*, about the promises of the 1920s as seen through the misplaced dreams of the title character. The book will become known as Fitzgerald's finest work.   **LIT**

1925–1929   American poet Marianne Moore serves as editor of the literary magazine *The Dial*.   **LIT**

1925   Irish novelist and short-story writer Liam O'Flaherty publishes the novel *The Informer*, which will be made into an Academy Award–winning film. Other works will be collected in *The Stories of Liam O'Flaherty* (1956).   **LIT**

1925   Austrian composer Alban Berg's atonal opera *Wozzeck* is produced in Berlin.   **MUSIC**

1925   Russian composer Dmitry Shostakovich's Symphony no. 1, composed as a nineteen-year-old graduate student at the Leningrad Conservatoire, debuts to critical acclaim.   **MUSIC**

c. 1925   American painter George Luks paints *Boy with Baseball*.   **PAINT**

1925   On March 3 the U.S. Congress authorizes Gutzon Borglum to carve a colossal memorial of the busts of Washington, Jefferson, Lincoln, and Theodore Roosevelt on the face of Mount Rushmore in the Black Hills of South Dakota. The project will be finished in 1941 by Borglum's son Lincoln.   **SCULP**

....

"The worst tragedy for a poet is to be admired through being misunderstood."
—French writer and filmmaker
Jean Cocteau, 1926

....

1926   The buildings of the Bauhaus at Dessau, designed by German architect Walter Gropius, are prominent early examples of the international style, which takes a formalistic, simplified approach emphasizing austere skeletons and large areas of glass. Other proponents of the style in the 1920s include Le Corbusier and Mies van der Rohe. The style will become dominant in the building of skyscrapers in the 1950s and 1960s.   **ARCH**

1926   Hungarian composer Béla Bartók's expressionist ballet *The Miraculous Mandarin* is produced in Cologne. The ballet is widely banned for its erotic and violent subject.   **DANCE**

1926   The Civic Repertory Company is founded in New York City by American actress and director Eva Le Gallienne. The company will provide serious theater at inexpensive ticket prices for the next seven years.   **DRAMA**

1926   *Exiles*, the only play by Irish writer James Joyce, has its London premiere. Its 1970 and 1971 revivals by British playwright Harold Pinter will be considered more successful than the original production. **DRAMA**

1926   Irish playwright Sean O'Casey's drama *The Plough and the Stars* is produced at Dublin's Abbey Theatre. This play about the Easter Rising of 1916 leads to a riot. **DRAMA**

1926   *The Great God Brown*, a complex drama by American playwright Eugene O'Neill, is produced. The play's actors wear elaborate masks at certain times. **DRAMA**

1926   Notable films include Fritz Lang's *Metropolis*, F. W. Murnau's *Faust*, and Alan Crosland's *Don Juan*, the first film to be shown with Vitaphone music and sound effects. **FILM**

1926   International film heartthrob Rudolph Valentino dies following completion of the movie *The Son of the Sheik*. **FILM**

1926   American poet Carl Sandburg publishes the first part of his biography of Abraham Lincoln in two volumes entitled *Abraham Lincoln: The Prairie Years*. The second part, in four volumes entitled *Abraham Lincoln: The War Years*, will be published in 1939 and will win a Pulitzer Prize. **LIT**

1926   American writer Ernest Hemingway publishes *The Sun Also Rises*, about the aimless post–World War I existence of American Jake Barnes and his love affair with Lady Brett Ashley. **LIT**

1926   American poet Langston Hughes publishes his first collection of poems, *The Weary Blues*. Later volumes will include *The Dream-Keeper* (1932) and *Montage of a Dream Deferred* (1951). **LIT**

1926   British playwright A. A. (Alan Alexander) Milne publishes the children's book about the bear with "very little brain," *Winnie-the-Pooh*. Milne will later write a companion volume, *The House at Pooh Corner* (1928). **LIT**

1926   Italian composer Giacomo Puccini's opera in three acts *Turandot* is produced posthumously at La Scala in Milan. **MUSIC**

1926   British composer William Walton's Suite no. 1, *Façade*, with its music-hall influences, is an immediate success. **MUSIC**

1926   Belgian surrealist painter René Magritte paints *The Menaced Assassin*. **PAINT**

1926–1934   British painter Stanley Spencer paints a series of oil murals for the Sandham Memorial Chapel at Burghclere in England, which, by depicting the life of a soldier who died in Macedonia, serves to honor all soldiers. **PAINT**

1926   American painter Georgia O'Keeffe completes one of her trademark works, *Black Iris*, an enlarged, sensuous view of a flower.   **PAINT**

1926   Spanish painter Joan Miró paints *Dog Barking at the Moon* and *Person Throwing a Stone at a Bird*.   **PAINT**

1926   American radio entrepreneur David Sarnoff founds NBC, the National Broadcasting Company, a network of nine radio stations.   **TV&R**

1927   In Europe and the United States the slow and simple foxtrot becomes a fashionable social dance.   **DANCE**

1927   *The Royal Family*, by American playwright George S. Kaufman and American playwright and novelist Edna Ferber, is produced. Kaufman and Ferber will later write the plays *Dinner at Eight* (1932) and *Stage Door* (1936), each of which will be made into a popular movie.   **DRAMA**

1927   Notable films include Clarence Brown's *Flesh and the Devil* and Cecil B. De Mille's *King of Kings*.   **FILM**

1927   The first feature film with extended sound sequences, Alan Crosland's *The Jazz Singer*, premieres. The musical drama of family travail about the career decisions of a cantor's son (Al Jolson) ushers in the end of the silent era and the beginning of sound films.   **FILM**

1927   American writer Ernest Hemingway publishes *Men Without Women*, a collection of fourteen short stories, which contains the classic "The Killers," concerning the fatalistic resignation of ex-boxer Ole Andreson to his impending execution by gangsters.   **LIT**

1927   British novelist Virginia Woolf publishes the novel *To the Lighthouse*.   **LIT**

1927   American journalist Don Marquis publishes *archy and mehitabel*, a prose collection about a cat and a cockroach who live in the New York *Sun* newspaper building where Marquis works. The amusing characters will spark many sequels.   **LIT**

1927   American novelist Willa Cather publishes the novel *Death Comes to the Archbishop*, about two Catholic clergymen in New Mexico. It will become one of her most highly regarded novels.   **LIT**

1927   Irish novelist Elizabeth Bowen publishes *The Hotel*. Among her later works will be *The House in Paris* (1935) and *The Heat of the Day* (1949).   **LIT**

1927   French novelist François Mauriac publishes the novel of sin and marriage, *Thérèse Desqueyroux*.   **LIT**

1927   French composer Maurice Ravel composes the sinuous orchestral piece *Boléro*, his best-known work.   **MUSIC**

1927   American jazz musician Bix Beiderbecke joins the Paul Whiteman orchestra. An influential songwriter and performer, his compositions and music will help shape American jazz.   **MUSIC**

1927   American modernist painter Edward Hopper completes *Manhattan Bridge*.   **PAINT**

1927   American painter John Sloan paints *The Lafayette*.   **PAINT**

1927   Television is demonstrated for the first time in the United States by AT&T executive Walter Gifford, who broadcasts images of Secretary of Commerce Herbert Hoover from Washington, D.C., to New York. **TV&R**

1928   British architect Elisabeth Scott designs the Shakespeare Memorial Theatre at Stratford-upon-Avon.   **ARCH**

1928   German playwright Bertolt Brecht achieves his first great success when *Die Dreigroschenoper* (*The Threepenny Opera*), his adaptation of John Gay's *The Beggar's Opera*, is produced in Berlin. The show includes music by German-born composer Kurt Weill, and Brecht and Weill will collaborate on several operas, including *Happy End* (1929).   **DRAMA**

1928   *Strange Interlude*, a nine-act drama by American playwright Eugene O'Neill, is produced. This unusually long play features asides in which the actors address the audience directly. It will net O'Neill his third Pulitzer Prize. O'Neill's *Lazarus Laughed*, a play about the resurrection of Lazarus, is also produced this year.   **DRAMA**

1928   Notable films include René Clair's *The Italian Straw Hat*, G. W. Pabst's *Pandora's Box*, Sergey Eisenstein's *October*, and Carl Dreyer's *The Passion of Joan of Arc*.   **FILM**

1928   American animated filmmaker Walt Disney's first Mickey Mouse cartoons, "Plane Crazy," "Gallopin' Gaucho," and "Steamboat Willie," are shown. The third marked the first sound Mickey Mouse cartoon.   **FILM**

1928   The first color motion pictures are shown in Rochester, New York, by American inventor George Eastman.   **FILM**

1928   Irish poet and dramatist William Butler Yeats publishes the collection *The Tower*, which includes the title poem along with such works as "Sailing to Byzantium," "Leda and the Swan," "Among School Children," "A Man Young and Old," and "All Souls' Night."   **LIT**

1928   British novelist Dorothy L. Sayers publishes *The Unpleasantness at the Bellona Club*, one of her many detective novels featuring Lord Peter Wimsey.   **LIT**

1928   British novelist Thomas Hardy's posthumous poetry collection *Winter Words in Various Moods and Metres* is published.   **LIT**

1928   British novelist D. H. Lawrence publishes a two-volume collection of his poetry and his last novel, the notorious *Lady Chatterley's Lover*. **LIT**

1928   British novelist Virginia Woolf publishes her most commercially successful work, the fantastic novel *Orlando*, the story of an androgynous person who lives through four centuries. Woolf also publishes the essay *A Room of One's Own*, a classic of feminist literary criticism.   **LIT**

1928   American poet and playwright Steven Vincent Benét publishes the epic poem that spans much of the Civil War, *John Brown's Body*. The poem will win the Pulitzer Prize.   **LIT**

1928   American poet Archibald MacLeish publishes the poem *The Hamlet of A. MacLeish*, about the despair of the modern age.   **LIT**

1928–1940   Russian novelist Mikhail Sholokhov publishes *Tikhiy Don* (*And Quiet Flows the Don*, English translation, 1934), the first half of his four-volume novel *The Quiet Don*. The second half, *The Don Flows Home to the Sea*, will be published in 1940. The novel, concerning the impact of the Bolshevik revolution on life in Russia's Don Cossack region, is considered the greatest work of early Soviet literature.   **LIT**

1928   Spanish poet Federico García Lorca publishes the collection *Romancero Gitano*. Among his later works will be *Poeta en Nueva York* (1929, pub. 1940) and *Llanto por Ignacio Sánchez Mejías* (1935).   **LIT**

1928   Italian conductor Arturo Toscanini leaves his position as musical director at La Scala in Milan and becomes principal conductor of the New York Philharmonic Symphony Orchestra. He will remain there until 1936, when he will depart to conduct the NBC Symphony (1937–1954).   **MUSIC**

1928   American painter Charles Demuth paints *The Figure 5 in Gold*.   **PAINT**

1928   Station WGY in Schenectady, New York, makes the first scheduled television broadcasts in history.   **TV&R**

1929–1930   Swiss architect Le Corbusier designs Villa Savoye at Poissy, France. His 1923 book *Towards a New Architecture* has already established him as a spokesperson for modern architecture.   **ARCH**

1929–1931   On the former site of the Waldorf-Astoria Hotel in New York City, the Empire State Building is constructed. At 1,250 feet and 102 stories, it will be the tallest building in the world for decades. *See* 1972, ARCH; 1973, ARCH.   **ARCH**

1929–1933   The Palace of the League of Nations in Geneva, Switzerland, is constructed.   **ARCH**

1929   American dancer Martha Graham founds her own dance troupe. Over the next several decades it will be a seminal force in modern dance, with productions that include the Aaron Copland work *Appalachian Spring* (1944).   **DANCE**

1929   British playwright George Bernard Shaw's play *The Apple Cart* is produced. *Too True to Be Good* (1932), *Geneva* (1938), and *In Good King Charles' Golden Days* (1939) will follow.   **DRAMA**

1929   *The Silver Tassie*, a pacifist drama about World War I by Irish playwright Sean O'Casey, is produced in London and New York. O'Casey's *Within the Gates*, *The Star Turns Red*, and *Red Roses for Me* will premiere in 1934, 1940, and 1943, respectively.   **DRAMA**

1929   The Academy of Motion Picture Arts and Sciences, founded two years earlier, presents its Academy Awards for the first time. In a ceremony at the Hollywood Roosevelt Hotel, Best Picture honors go to *Wings*, with Best Actor to Emil Jannings for *The Last Command* and *The Way of All Flesh*. The Best Actress award goes to Janet Gaynor and the Best Director to Frank Borzage, both for *Seventh Heaven*. Gaynor's Best Actress award also reflects her work in *Street Angel* and *Sunrise*.   **FILM**

. . . .

"I've been to Paris, France, and I've been to Paris, Paramount. I think I prefer Paris, Paramount."
—German-born American director
Ernst Lubitsch, c. 1930s

. . . .

1929   Notable films include Ernst Lubitsch's *The Love Parade* and Harry Beaumont's *Broadway Melody*.   **FILM**

1929   American mystery writer Ellery Queen (pen name of Frederic Dannay and Manfred Lee) publish *The Roman Hat Mystery*, the first of the series of novels starring the detective Ellery Queen.   **LIT**

1929   American mystery novelist and former private detective Dashiell Hammett publishes his first novel, *Red Harvest*. The innovative "hard-boiled" style exhibited in this and future detective novels, including *The Maltese Falcon* (1930) and *The Thin Man* (1934), will prove highly influential.   **LIT**

1929   British poet, novelist, and critic Robert Graves publishes the memoir *Goodbye to All That*.   **LIT**

1929   American writer Ernest Hemingway publishes the novel *A Farewell to Arms*, about the disillusionment caused by World War I as seen through the experiences of American ambulance driver Frederic Henry.   **LIT**

1929   American novelist Sinclair Lewis publishes *Dodsworth*, a critique of the spoiled, self-involved American woman as embodied by Fran Dodsworth.   **LIT**

1929   American novelist William Faulkner publishes *The Sound and the Fury*, a complex work about the aristocratic but decaying Compson family in Mississippi. He also publishes the novel *As I Lay Dying*. **LIT**

1929   American humorist James Thurber and essayist E. B. White cowrite the parody of modern sexual psychology, *Is Sex Necessary?* **LIT**

1929   German novelist Erich Maria Remarque publishes the World War I novel *All Quiet on the Western Front*. Among his later works is the novel *A Time to Love and a Time to Die* (1954). **LIT**

1929   British novelist and playwright J. B. (John Boynton) Priestley publishes the novel *The Good Companions*. Among his later works will be the play *An Inspector Calls*, a domestic comedy, and the novel *The Image Men* (1968). **LIT**

1929   Experimental French writer and filmmaker Jean Cocteau publishes the novel *Les Enfants terribles*. Later works will include the plays *La voix humaine* (*The Human Voice*, 1930) and *La machine infernale* (*The Infernal Machine*, 1934). **LIT**

1929–1930   Austrian painter Oskar Kokoschka paints *Jerusalem*, one of his many landscapes of towns as seen from high above. **PAINT**

1929   The Museum of Modern Art opens in New York, with an exhibition of works of Paul Cézanne, Paul Gauguin, Georges Seurat, and Vincent van Gogh. In 1939 the museum will move to its current site on 53rd Street. **PAINT**

1929   Spanish painter Salvador Dalí joins the surrealist movement. Through his works, which embody a hallucinogenic sense of reality, he becomes one of surrealism's most famous artists. **PAINT**

··

"I don't think I ever tried to paint the American scene; I'm trying to paint myself."—Painter Edward Hopper, known as a major exponent of American scene painting, c. 1930

··

1929   American painter Edward Hopper paints *The Lighthouse at Two Lights*. **PAINT**

1929   German photographer August Sander publishes his collection of portraits of Germans, *Face of Our Time*. The work is both a model of the new objectivity movement and a commentary on the rise of Nazism. **PHOTO**

1930s   Faced with competition from film and radio, vaudeville declines and soon vanishes. **DRAMA**

1930s   Silkscreen, originally developed earlier this century for commercial textile printing, becomes a medium for fine artists. **GRAPH**

1930s   Popular songs of the day include "Body and Soul," "I Got Rhythm," "Georgia on My Mind," "Minnie the Moocher," "Goodnight, Sweetheart," "Brother, Can You Spare a Dime," "Night and Day," "Boulevard of Broken Dreams," "Stormy Weather," "Easter Parade," "Blue Moon," "The Continental," "Begin the Beguine," "Just One of Those Things," "I Can't Get Started," "Pennies From Heaven," "Bei Mir Bist Du Schön," "The Lady is a Tramp," "A Foggy Day in London Town," "Jeepers Creepers," "Falling in Love With Love," "Over the Rainbow," "Beer Barrel Polka," and "I'll Never Smile Again."   **MUSIC**

1930s   Much American popular music is generated by Broadway shows, particularly those of Richard Rodgers and Lorenz Hart, Cole Porter, and Irving Berlin.   **MUSIC**

1930s   Beginning with her first recordings in 1935, American jazz singer Billie Holiday establishes herself as a defining presence in jazz music. Despite drug and legal problems her career will continue until her death in 1959. Among her best known works are "Strange Fruit" and "Gloomy Sunday."   **MUSIC**

1930s   Using the newly developed hand-held cameras, photojournalists record world events large and small for popular magazines like *Life* and *Time*. Among the first successful photojournalists are Erich Salomon, Felix Man, Brassaï, and Henri Cartier-Bresson. Dorothy Lang, who chronicles the Great Depression for the Farm Security Administration, generates widespread compassion for the suffering, notably through her photos of migrant workers in California. **PHOTO**

1930s   Spanish sculptor Julio González establishes wrought iron as an important medium for sculpture while working in Paris. His pieces will influence artists in the 1960s and 1970s in creating violently expressive sculpture in wrought iron and welded steel.   **SCULP**

1930s   During this decade and next, radio comedies enjoy great success on the airwaves. Among the most popular are "The Jack Benny Show," "Fibber McGee and Molly," and "The Edgar Bergen–Charlie McCarthy Show."   **TV&R**

1930   Designed by Raymond Hood and John Mead Howells, the thirty-six-story Daily News Building is constructed in New York City. It houses the staff of the tabloid with the highest circulation in the United States.   **ARCH**

1930   Notable films include Lewis Milestone's *All Quiet on the Western Front*, Josef von Sternberg's *The Blue Angel*, and Clarence Brown's *Anna Christie*, starring international film star Greta Garbo.   **FILM**

1930   Approximately 250 million people around the world attend movies once a week, with 115 million of them Americans.   **FILM**

1930   In an attempt to counteract negative views of the American film in-dustry, the Motion Picture Production Code is developed by the Motion Picture Producers and Distributors of America (MPPDA). The rules regulating onscreen morality will become known as the Hays Code, after Will Hays, head of MPPDA.   **FILM**

1930   British poet W. H. (Wystan Hugh) Auden publishes *Poems*, including "This Lunar Beauty" and "Petition."   **LIT**

1930–1932   American classics scholar Edith Hamilton becomes known as a popularizer of ancient history with the publication of *The Greek Way* (1930) and *The Roman Way* (1932).   **LIT**

1930   British poet T. S. Eliot publishes the poem *Ash-Wednesday*, an ex-ploration of faith and religion in current times.   **LIT**

1930   In accepting the Nobel Prize in Literature, American novelist Sinclair Lewis makes a speech titled "The American Fear of Literature," critical of conservative antagonism toward contempo-rary writing.   **LIT**

1930   American poet Hart Crane publishes the multipart poem *The Bridge*. Both a celebration of the Brooklyn Bridge and an exploration of what Crane calls "the Myth of America," it will become his best-known work.   **LIT**

1930–1935   American writer Katherine Anne Porter publishes two collections of stories under the title *Flowering Judas*. Later short-story and short novel collections will include *The Leaning Tower and Other Stories* (1944) and *Pale Horse, Pale Rider* (1939).   **LIT**

1930–1936   American novelist John Dos Passos publishes the *U.S.A.* trilogy: *The 42nd Parallel* (1930), *1919* (1932), and *The Big Money* (1936). The books will become known for their blend of journalism, prose poet-ry, and sketches of important personages of the day and everyday people.   **LIT**

1930   Sir Adrian Boult becomes musical director of the newly formed BBC Symphony Orchestra.   **MUSIC**

1930   Russian composer Igor Stravinsky composes *Symphony of Psalms*.   **MUSIC**

1930   Dutch painter Piet Mondrian paints *Composition in Red, Yellow and Blue*.   **PAINT**

1930   Dutch painter Christian Küpper, known as Theo van Doesburg, pub-lishes *Art Concret*, a treatise outlining the nonfigurative abstract art that will be known as concrete art. The work is written in opposi-tion to the constructivist exhibition group known as the Cercle et Carré (Circle and Square).   **PAINT**

1930   American painter Grant Wood completes *American Gothic*. At an exhi-bition at the Art Institute of Chicago, it will win a bronze medal.   **PAINT**

1930–1931   American painter Thomas Hart Benton completes a number of murals of American life for the New School of Social Research in New York City. His stylized depiction of Americans will become prototypical.   **PAINT**

1930–1980   By capturing the "decisive moment" of an experience, French photographer Henri Cartier-Bresson becomes one of the most important photojournalists of the twentieth century. His work combines influences of several of the major artistic movements of the century, including surrealism and abstract art. Collections of his works will be found in *The Europeans* (1955) and *Man and Machine* (1969), among others.   **PHOTO**

1930–1950   American photographer Edward Weston establishes himself as a creator of sensuous but unadorned photographic images, such as his studies of female nudes.   **PHOTO**

1930–1950   American combat photographer Robert Capa illustrates the immediacy of war in his photos of the Spanish Civil War, notably the 1936 photo *Death of a Loyalist Soldier*, and of the D-Day invasion of World War II. He will be killed by a mine in Vietnam in 1954.   **PHOTO**

1931–1947   The Rockefeller Center complex is constructed in New York City.   **ARCH**

1931   The New Negro Art Theatre Dance Group, the first professional black dance group, is founded in New York by American dancer Helmsley Winfield.   **DANCE**

1931   Irish-born English choreographer Dame Ninette De Valois founds the Sadler's Wells Ballet School. She will direct the Sadler's Wells Ballet, which will eventually become the Royal Ballet.   **DANCE**

1931   The Group Theatre, a production company dedicated to presenting serious contemporary drama, is formed in New York City by Harold Clurman, Cheryl Crawford, and Lee Strasberg. It will present premieres of several works by American playwright Clifford Odets, including *Awake and Sing!* (1935), *Waiting for Lefty* (1935) and *Golden Boy* (1937) before closing in 1941.   **DRAMA**

1931   *Mourning Becomes Electra*, a thirteen-act trilogy by American playwright Eugene O'Neill, is produced. *Ah, Wilderness!*, an O'Neill comedy, will be produced in 1933.   **DRAMA**

1931   Notable films include Charlie Chaplin's *City Lights*, James Whale's *Frankenstein*, and Lewis Milestone's *The Front Page*.   **FILM**

1931   British novelist Virginia Woolf publishes the novel *The Waves*.   **LIT**

1931   Russian-born American anarchist Emma Goldman publishes her autobiography *Living My Life*.   **LIT**

1931   American novelist and critic Edmund Wilson publishes a book of literary essays, *Axel's Castle*. Among his subjects are James Joyce, Gertrude Stein, and William Butler Yeats.   **LIT**

1931   American historian and journalist Frederick Lewis Allen publishes an informal chronicle of the 1920s, *Only Yesterday*. The book will become a best-seller and will be followed by a sequel of the years after, *Since Yesterday*.   **LIT**

1931   American humorist James Thurber publishes his first collection of humorous essays, *The Owl and the Attic*. Later volumes will include *My Life and Hard Times* (1933) and *The Beast in Me and Other Animals* (1948). From the 1920s much of his work appeared in *The New Yorker*.   **LIT**

1931   Spanish painter Salvador Dalí paints *Persistence of Memory*.   **PAINT**

1931   French painter Henri Matisse completes *The Dance*, a series of murals at the Barnes Foundation in Merion, Pennsylvania.   **PAINT**

....

"[P]aper, tobacco, food, and a little whiskey." —American novelist William Faulkner's writing requirements, c. 1930s

....

1931–1932   American painter Ben Shahn gains prominence through his gouaches of the Sacco and Vanzetti trials. He had earlier created similar gouaches to illustrate the Dreyfus case.   **PAINT**

1932   Notable films include Mervyn LeRoy's *I Am a Fugitive from a Chain Gang*, Edmund Goulding's *Grand Hotel*, Fritz Lang's *M*, and René Clair's *À Nous la Liberté*.   **FILM**

1932   *Tarzan, the Ape Man* is the first Tarzan film to star American actor and Olympic swimming champion Johnny Weissmuller. Several Weissmuller-Tarzan sequels will follow.   **FILM**

1932   British poet W. H. Auden publishes the poetry collection *The Orators*.   **LIT**

1932–1962   American novelist William Faulkner publishes some of his best-known works, including *Light in August* (1932), *Absalom, Absalom!* (1936), *Intruder in the Dust* (1948), and *A Fable* (1954), which will win the Pulitzer Prize. His final work is *The Reivers* (1962).   **LIT**

1932   American novelist Pearl S. Buck publishes *The Good Earth*, about Chinese life, which will win the Pulitzer Prize.   **LIT**

1932   Italian poet Salvatore Quasimodo publishes the collection *Oboe sommerso*. His later works will include *Poesie nuove* (1942) and *La terra impareggiable* (1958).   **LIT**

1932   Irish novelist and short-story writer Sean O'Faolain publishes his first story collection, *Midsummer Night Madness*. Later works will include *A Nest of Simple Folk* (1933) and the story collections *The Man Who Invented Sin* (1947) and *The Talking Trees* (1979).   **LIT**

1932   British novelist Aldous Huxley publishes the futuristic satire *Brave New World*. His earlier works include *Crome Yellow* (1921) and *Point Counter Point* (1928).   **LIT**

1932   The London Philharmonic Orchestra is founded by Sir Thomas Beecham.   **MUSIC**

1932–1933 Mexican painter Diego Rivera paints the fresco series *Detroit Industry* in the Detroit Institute of Arts. With other Mexican painters such as José Clemente Orozco and David Alfaro Siqueiros, Rivera has led a revival of the fresco as a medium of public art.   **PAINT**

1932   Polaroid film, the first synthetic light-polarizing film, is developed by American inventor Edwin Herbert Land.   **PHOTO**

1932   American artist Alexander Calder creates a new form of sculpture of carefully balanced metal plates, rods, and wires which can be moved either by air currents or mechanical means. Marcel Duchamp will visit Calder's studio in Paris and name the constructions "mobile."   **SCULP**

1932–1945 Throughout his four terms in office, United States president Franklin Roosevelt employs radio to transmit regular broadcasts known as "fireside chats." They are early examples of the political power of a mass medium.   **TV&R**

1933   The highly influential Bauhaus school of architecture, which moved to Berlin from Dessau in 1932, is closed by the Third Reich.   **ARCH**

1933   Revolutionary Russian choreographer George Balanchine comes to the United States and, with Lincoln Kirstein, founds the School of American Ballet. In 1948 its dance company will become the New York City Ballet, with Kirstein its director.   **DANCE**

1933   American stage-trained dancer Fred Astaire (born Frederick Austerlitz) appears in his first film with American actress Ginger Rogers, *Flying Down to Rio*. The two will be paired in several films, including *Top Hat* (1935) and *Swing Time* (1936), through which they revolutionize the use of dance in films, making it a medium to further plot development and embody romance.   **DANCE**

1933   Adolf Hitler comes to power, and German playwright Bertolt Brecht and his family go into exile, moving to Switzerland, then to Denmark, then Finland, and finally to the United States in 1941. Brecht will write much of his major work abroad, including *The Caucasian Chalk Circle* in 1945, a drama set in war-torn Russian Georgia.   **DRAMA**

1933   Helen Hayes, among the preeminent actresses of twentieth-century
              American theater, takes on one of her most admired roles, as Mary
              Queen of Scots in Maxwell Anderson's *Mary of Scotland*. Her other
              notable roles include the title character in Laurence Housman's
              Victoria Reigns (1935), and Viola in Shakespeare's *Twelfth Night*
              (1940).   **DRAMA**

1933   Thingspiel, a type of pageant play staged outdoors, begins to flour-
              ish in Germany. The form promotes German nationalism—particu-
              larly its Nazi manifestation.   **DRAMA**

1933   *Bodas de sangre* (*Blood Wedding*), the first play in a tragic trilogy by
              the Spanish poet Federico García Lorca, is produced. *Yerma*, the
              second play, will be produced in 1934. *La casa de Bernarda Alba*
              (*The House of Bernarda Alba*) will be produced in 1945. This group
              of plays will be seen as Lorca's greatest work. *Blood Wedding* and
              Bernarda Alba continue to be revived frequently.   **DRAMA**

1933   Notable films include George Cukor's *Dinner at Eight*, Frank Lloyd's
              Calvacade, Fritz Lang's *The Testament of Dr. Mabuse*, and Merian C.
              Cooper and Ernest B. Schoedsack's *King Kong*.   **FILM**

1933   Irish poet and dramatist William Butler Yeats publishes the collec-
              tion *The Winding Stair and Other Poems*, which includes "For Anne
              Gregory," "Byzantium," and "A Woman Young and Old." Many of
              the poems in a collection published the previous year, *Words for
              Music Perhaps and Other Poems*, are incorporated into later editions
              of this collection.   **LIT**

1933   British poet Stephen Spender publishes his first important
              collection, *Poems*.   **LIT**

1933   American novelist Nathaniel West publishes the tragic novel about
              an advice-to-the-lovelorn columnist, *Miss Lonely-Hearts*. He also will
              be known for his dark 1939 novel *The Day of the Locust*.   **LIT**

1933   French novelist André Malraux publishes the novel *La Condition hu-
              maine* (*Man's Fate*). Among his later works will be the novel *L'Espoir*
              (*Man's Hope*, 1938) and *Le Temps du mépris* (*Days of Wrath*, 1935).   **LIT**

1933–1939   About 60,000 writers, artists, and musicians emigrate from
              Germany during the rise of Nazi power. Countless others will be
              murdered in the Nazi Holocaust in the following years.   **MISC**

1933   French-American composer Edgard Varèse, pioneer of electronic
              music, composes *Ionization* for thirteen percussionists. Other im-
              portant works of his will include *Density 21.5* for solo flute (1936),
              Equatorial (1934, revised 1961), and *Déserts* (1950–1954).   **MUSIC**

Diego Rivera and Frida Kahlo in New York. Photo by Carl van Vechten. *(Beinecke Rare Book and Manuscript Library, Yale University)*

1933–1950   German expressionist painter Max Beckmann begins the nearly
            two-decade-long project of painting the nine triptychs known as
            Departure. Begun in the year he was removed by the Nazis from his
            teaching position in Frankfurt, *Departure* reflects his views on life,
            society, and the human tendency toward evil.   **PAINT**

1933   Mexican painter Diego Rivera paints the fresco *Man at the
            Crossroads* for Rockefeller Center in New York City. Because the
            mural includes a portrait of founder of the Soviet Union Vladimir
            Lenin, it will eventually be replaced by a mural created by British
            painter Sir Frank Brangwyn.   **PAINT**

1933   Transylvanian-born French photographer Brassaï (born Gyula
            Halász) publishes the collection of scenes of Parisian street life, *Paris
            de nuit (The Secret Paris of the 30s)*. His eye for capturing the dark
            haunts of the city will make him known as "The Eye of Paris." **PHOTO**

1933   American Edwin H. Armstrong develops frequency modulation
            (FM), which reduces static and increases sound fidelity in radio
            transmission. The same year the all-metal radio tube is developed
            by the Marconiphone Company.   **TV&R**

1934   African-American painter Aaron Douglas produces murals celebrat-
            ing his community's African heritage for the Harlem branch of the
            New York Public Library.   **ARCH**

1934   *The Children's Hour*, the first play by American playwright Lillian
            Hellman, is produced. The story of two teachers whose lives are de-
            stroyed by a student's false accusations of lesbianism, this drama
            will be a success on Broadway.   **DRAMA**

1934   The American musical *Anything Goes*—with book by Guy Bolton,
            P. G. Wodehouse, Howard Lindsay, and Russel Crouse, and lyrics
            and music by Cole Porter—premieres on Nov. 21.   **DRAMA**

1934   Notable films include W. S. Van Dyke's *The Thin Man*, Alexander
            Korda's *The Private Life of Henry VIII*, and John Ford's *The Lost
            Patrol*.   **FILM**

1934   Frank Capra's *It Happened One Night* becomes the first film to cap-
            ture all four major Academy Awards—for best picture, actor, actress,
            and director. The comic love story about a runaway heiress and a
            newspaper reporter spurs the development of the new genre of
            screwball comedy. The scene in which star Clark Gable takes off his
            shirt to reveal his bare chest causes sales of men's undershirts to go
            on the decline.   **FILM**

1934   American novelist James M. Cain publishes the popular mystery
            novel *The Postman Always Rings Twice*. It will be the basis for films
            in 1946 and 1988.   **LIT**

1934   British novelist, poet, and critic Robert Graves publishes his most popular works, *I, Claudius* and *Claudius the God*, two historical novels narrated by the Roman emperor Claudius.   LIT

1934   Welsh poet Dylan Thomas publishes his first collection, *Eighteen Poems*, noted for their violent imagery and suggestive language.   LIT

1934   American critic Malcolm Cowley publishes *Exile's Return*, a memoir of the American writers of the "lost generation" who went to Europe in the post–World War I years, including Ernest Hemingway, F. Scott Fitzgerald, John Dos Passos, and Hart Crane.   LIT

1934   American novelist F. Scott Fitzgerald publishes the novel *Tender is the Night*.   LIT

1934   Danish short-story writer Isak Dinesen (pen name of Baroness Karen Blixen) publishes the collection *Seven Gothic Tales*. Her later work, *Out of Africa*, will be the basis of an Academy Award–winning film.   LIT

· ·

"For me a work must first have a vitality of its own. I do not mean a reflection of the vitality of life, of movement, physical action, frisking, dancing figures, and so on, but that a work can have in it a pent-up energy, an intense life of its own, independent of the object it may represent. When a work has this powerful vitality we do not connect the word Beauty with it. Beauty, in the later Greek or Renaissance sense, is not the aim in my sculpture."
—British sculptor Henry Moore, 1934

· ·

1934   German composer Paul Hindemith composes the opera and symphony *Mathis der Maler* (*Mathis the Painter*).   MUSIC

1935   Dance impresario Lincoln Kirstein's book *Dance* is the first important history of the art form by an American.   DANCE

1935   The Latin American rumba becomes a popular social dance in the United States and Europe.   DANCE

1935   *Night Must Fall*, a drama which Welsh actor and playwright Emlyn Williams both wrote and acted in, premieres.   DRAMA

1935   *Murder in the Cathedral*, a drama by British poet T. S. Eliot about the murder of Thomas à Becket, premieres in England.   DRAMA

1935   The American musical *Porgy and Bess*—with book and lyrics by Dubose Heyward and Ira Gershwin and music by George Gershwin—premieres on Oct. 10. It is considered a revolutionary blend of folk music and Broadway force.   DRAMA

THE MAKE-BELIEVE BALLROOM

*I*n New York City during the Great Depression, people who wanted to dance to the latest swing music didn't have to visit pricey ballrooms or settle for dime-a-dance joints. Instead an announcer named Martin Block on radio station WNEW-AM guided dancers onto the floor of "The Make-Believe Ballroom." Starting in the depths of the Depression in 1934, the program played only the hottest dance music of its day. As music changed over the decades, the show came to include swing, big band, and jazz sounds. Like its latter-day compatriot, "American Bandstand," personal appearances on "The Make-Believe Ballroom" signaled an artist's success.

Despite the birth of rock n' roll in the 1950s, "The Make-Believe Ballroom" remained true to its origins in twentieth-century American ballroom dance music. The "Ballroom" remained open until WNEW-AM went off the air in December 1992. For nearly sixty years it remained an archetypal example of radio's capacity for kindling imagination through sound.

1935   Notable films include Alfred Hitchcock's *The 39 Steps*, John Ford's *The Informer*, Frank Lloyd's *Mutiny on the Bounty*, and Rouben Mamoulian's *Becky Sharp*, the first three-color Technicolor feature film.   **FILM**

1935   Irish poet and dramatist William Butler Yeats publishes the collection *A Full Moon in March*. Many of its poems will later be gathered under the title *Parnell's Funeral and Other Poems* in his collected *Poems*. These include twelve "Supernatural Songs," such as "Ribh in Ecstasy," "What Magic Drum?," "The Four Ages of Man," and "Meru."   **LIT**

1935   British officer T. E. (Thomas Edward) Lawrence's *The Seven Pillars of Wisdom* is published. The account of his role in the Arab revolt against the Ottoman Empire was previously published in abbreviated form as *The Revolt in the Desert*, 1927. His account will be the basis for David Lean's film *Lawrence of Arabia* (1962).   **LIT**

1935   American novelist John O'Hara publishes *Butterfield 8*, introducing woman-about-town Gloria Wandrous.   **LIT**

1935   American memoirist Clarence Shepard Day Jr. publishes the hugely successful nostalgic reminiscence *Life With Father*. A sequel, *Life With Mother*, is published in 1937, after Day's death.   **LIT**

1935–1967   American philosopher and scholar Will Durant and his wife Ariel Durant publish the ten volumes of *The Story of Civilization* series, which presents philosophy to a wide audience. They include *Our Oriental Heritage* (1935), *The Life of Greece* (1939), *Caesar and Christ* (1944), *The Age of Faith* (1950), *The Renaissance* (1953), *The Reformation* (1957), *The Age of Reason Begins* (1961), *The Age of Louis XIV* (1963), *The Age of Voltaire* (1965), and *Rousseau and Revolution* (1967).   **LIT**

1935   American novelist Thomas Wolfe publishes *Of Time and the River.*   **LIT**

1935   American poet Wallace Stevens publishes the poem "The Idea of Order at Key West."   **LIT**

1935   Highly secretive novelist B. Traven, of undisclosed origin, publishes the dark novel *The Treasure of Sierra Madre.* It will be the basis for an Academy Award–winning motion picture.   **LIT**

1935   Swing music, an offshoot of jazz, becomes popular in the United States and Europe. Its defining practitioners include Benny Goodman, the Dorsey Brothers, and Glenn Miller.   **MUSIC**

1935   Belgian surrealist painter René Magritte paints *Les Promenades d'Euclid.*   **PAINT**

1935–1943   The Federal Arts Project is instituted under the auspices of the Works Progress Administration of the U.S. government, creating public art for the nation and providing jobs for thousands of unemployed artists and craftspeople during the Great Depression. Departments of the project include the Federal Art Project, the Federal Music Project, Federal Theatre Project, and the Federal Writers Project.   **PAINT**

1935–1939   British art historian Kenneth Clark completes a catalogue of Italian artist Leonardo da Vinci's drawings at Windsor Castle, Britain, and follows four years later with a monograph on the artist. These, along with other critical works, will establish him as a champion of art understanding.   **PAINT**

1935   British painter Ben Nicholson creates a series of cubist- and Mondrian-influenced reliefs that will put him at the forefront of British abstract artists. Between 1932 and 1951 he is married to British artist Barbara Hepworth.   **PAINT**

1935   Having already established himself as a leading abstract artist and contributor to art magazines, English painter and graphic artist John Piper becomes art editor of the avant-garde quarterly *Axis.*   **PAINT**

1936–1937   American architect Frank Lloyd Wright designs the Kaufmann house, "Falling Water," in Bear Run, Pennsylvania. The house is cantilevered over a waterfall.   **ARCH**

1936   The Moiseyev Dance Company is founded in Moscow by Russian
            dance impressario Igor Moiseyev. It will become known for its inter-
            pretations of Russian folk dances.   **DANCE**

1936   *An Actor Prepares*, the first of several books on acting by Russian
            actor and director Konstantin Stanislavsky, is published in English.
            In this work, which will be particularly influential in America (*see*
            1949, DRAMA), Stanislavsky sets out the approach to acting that he
            and his students have taken over the years at the Moscow Art
            Theater (*see* 1898, DRAMA). He encourages actors to draw on inner
            feelings and personal experiences to create realistic, full-bodied
            characters.   **DRAMA**

1936   *You Can't Take It With You*, a comedy by American playwrights Moss
            Hart and George S. Kaufman, premieres. It will receive the Pulitzer
            Prize. Hart and Kaufman will later write *The Man Who Came to
            Dinner* (1939).   **DRAMA**

1936   Notable films include Frank Capra's *Mr. Deeds Goes to Town*, Charlie
            Chaplin's *Modern Times*, Robert Z. Leonard's *The Great Ziegfeld*, and
            Fritz Lang's *Fury*.   **FILM**

1936   American novelist William Faulkner publishes the novel *Absalom,
            Absalom!*, which continues the story of the Compson family begun
            in *The Sound and the Fury* (1929).   **LIT**

1936   American novelist Margaret Mitchell publishes *Gone With the Wind*.
            The saga of Scarlett O'Hara, Rhett Butler, and the ravages experi-
            enced by the South during the Civil War will be a perennial best-
            seller. *See also* 1939, FILM.   **LIT**

1936   American broadcaster and lecturer Dale Carnegie publishes *How to
            Win Friends and Influence People*, one of the world's most successful
            how-to manifestos for building confidence.   **LIT**

1936   American writer James Agee and photographer Walker Evans pub-
            lish *Let Us Now Praise Famous Men*, an account of the poverty and
            quiet dignity of three sharecropping families in the South. The work
            had originally been commissioned by *Fortune* magazine.   **LIT**

1936   On Nov. 23 *Life* magazine begins publication in the United States
            under American businessman Henry Luce. It will become one of the
            most widely read weekly general-interest magazines in history.   **LIT**

1936   American composer Samuel Barber composes his best-known
            work, *Adagio for Strings*.   **MUSIC**

1936   American photographer Margaret Bourke-White takes the cover
            photo for the first issue of *Life*, of Fort Peck Dam in Montana. Her
            eye for drama and the sculptural qualities in photography will make
            her one of the most popular photojournalists of the twentieth
            century.   **PHOTO**

1936   The British Broadcasting Company (BBC) sets up the world's first electronic television system.   **TV&R**

1937   The Mordkin Ballet, the company that will become the American Ballet Theater, is founded. It will operate under the name of Mordkin Ballet until 1940, when it will be known as Ballet Theater. From 1956 it will be the American Ballet Theater.   **DANCE**

1937   Hungarian-born designer and architect Marcel Breuer establishes himself in the United States after more than a decade of designing furniture at the Bauhaus in Germany (1914–1928). His furniture designs using wood and steel tubing will have a lasting effect in modern design.   **DECO**

1937   *Le Voyageur sans bagages* (*Traveler without Luggage*), the first pièce noire—melancholy play—by French playwright Jean Anouilh, is produced. *La Sauvage* (*The Restless Heart*), another pièce noire, is produced in 1938.   **DRAMA**

1937   British actor Laurence Olivier joins the Old Vic theater company, where, over the next two seasons and under the direction of Tyrone Guthrie (*see* 1963, DRAMA), he will play Hamlet, Macbeth, Henry V, Iago, Coriolanus, and Sir Toby Belch (in *Twelfth Night*), establishing himself as an actor of great distinction. Over the following decades, he will pursue a very successful career as a stage and film actor and director.   **DRAMA**

1937   Notable films include Jean Renoir's *La Grande Illusion*, George Cukor's *Camille*, and Walt Disney's *Snow White and the Seven Dwarfs*, the first feature-length color animated Disney cartoon. **FILM**

1937   British novelist C. S. Forester begins his popular series of novels about naval hero Horatio Hornblower with *The Happy Return*. **LIT**

1937   British novelist J. R. R. Tolkien publishes the fantasy novel *The Hobbit*, introducing the intrepid hobbit Bilbo Baggins and the wizard Gandalf.   **LIT**

1937   British poet W. H. Auden publishes the poetry collection *On This Island* and the poem "Spain," concerning the Spanish Civil War, in which he served as an ambulance driver for the Republicans. **LIT**

1937   American novelist and journalist John Phillips Marquand publishes the popular saga *The Late George Apley*, which will win the Pulitzer Prize.   **LIT**

1937   American novelist Zora Neale Hurston publishes the African-American feminist novel, *Their Eyes Were Watching God*.   **LIT**

1937   American novelist John Steinbeck publishes *Of Mice and Men*. **LIT**

1937   British novelist Evelyn Waugh publishes *A Handful of Dust*. Later novels will include the comic novel *The Loved One* (1948) and *Brideshead Revisited*, which becomes the basis for a BBC-TV mini-series.   **LIT**

1937–1954   Arturo Toscanini is director of the National Broadcasting Company Symphony Orchestra, formed especially for him by NBC.   **MUSIC**

1937   German composer Carl Orff composes his scenic oratorio *Carmina Burana* based on twenty-five Latin poems from the thirteenth century.   **MUSIC**

1937   Russian composer Dmitry Shostakovich's masterpiece Symphony no. 5, Op. 47 is performed during the Russian Revolution twentieth-anniversary celebration.   **MUSIC**

1937   As part of its repression of modern art, the Third Reich presents an exhibition of *Entartete Kunst*, or degenerate art, in Munich. Among the artists condemned because their work does not adhere to Reich ideology are Vincent van Gogh, Henri Matisse, and Pablo Picasso. Thousands of works of modern artists are removed from galleries across Germany by the Nazis, many of them to be destroyed.   **PAINT**

1937   Spanish painter Pablo Picasso completes the painting *Guernica*, which captures the horror brought to the town of Guernica during the Spanish Civil War.   **PAINT**

1937   Romanian sculptor Constantin Brancusi creates his monumental ensemble for his hometown of Targu-Jiu, including the *Gate of the Kiss*, the *Table of Silence*, and *Endless Column*, which is nearly a hundred feet high.   **SCULP**

1938   The Lambeth walk becomes a popular social dance in the United States and Europe.   **DANCE**

1938   *Le Bal des Voleurs* (*Thieves' Carnival*), the first pièce rose—romantic play—by French playwright Jean Anouilh, is produced. *Léocadia* (*Time Remembered*), another pièce rose, will be produced in 1940.   **DRAMA**

1938   *The Corn is Green*, an autobiographical play by Welsh playwright and actor Emlyn Williams, is produced. The author also acts in the play, which is generally regarded as his best.   **DRAMA**

1938   *Our Town*, a play depicting small-town life by American playwright Thornton Wilder, premieres. Following a successful professional run, it will become a perennial high school drama club favorite.   **DRAMA**

1938   Notable films include Sergey Eisenstein's *Alexander Nevsky*, Frank Capra's *You Can't Take It with You*, and Alfred Hitchcock's *The Lady Vanishes*.   **FILM**

1938   In June *Action Comics* No. 1 introduces Superman, the caped hero
            with amazing superpowers, created by Jerry Siegel and Joe Shuster.
            Batman, created by Bob Kane, is introduced in the May 1939
            Detective Comics. In the coming decades, a horde of superheroes,
            most with special powers and secret identities, will flourish in
            American comic books.   **GRAPH**

1938   Irish poet and dramatist William Butler Yeats publishes the collec-
            tion *New Poems*, which includes "Lapis Lazuli," "Beautiful Lofty
            Things," "The Curse of Cromwell," "Parnell," and "The Municipal
            Gallery Re-visited."   **LIT**

1938   British novelist Daphne Du Maurier publishes *Rebecca*, which will
            be filmed by Alfred Hitchcock in 1940.   **LIT**

1938   British novelist, poet, and critic Robert Graves publishes the first
            edition of his *Collected Poems*.   **LIT**

1938   Poems published this year by Irish poet Louis MacNeice include
            "The Sunlight on the Garden," "Bagpipe Music," and "Good
            Dream."   **LIT**

1938   British novelist Graham Greene publishes *Brighton Rock*, his first
            novel explicitly exploring Catholic themes. Other Greene novels of
            this type will include *The Power and the Glory* (1940), *The Heart of
            the Matter* (1948), *The End of the Affair* (1951), and *The Quiet
            American* (1955).   **LIT**

1938   American novelist and journalist Marjorie Kinnan Rawlings publish-
            es the novel *The Yearling*, about a boy's attachment to a deer.   **LIT**

1938   German composer Werner Egk's opera *Peer Gynt* is produced in
            Berlin.   **MUSIC**

1938   American jazz musician Benny Goodman and his orchestra hold
            the first swing concert in Carnegie Hall, New York City. Members of
            his band include Harry James, Ziggy Elman, Gene Krupa, Lionel
            Hampton, and Count Basie.   **MUSIC**

1938   The Cloisters, a museum of medieval art, is built in upper
            Manhattan as a separate extension of the Metropolitan Museum of
            Art.   **PAINT**

1938   American naive painter Anna Mary "Grandma" Moses has the first ex-
            hibition of her work in a drugstore in Hoosick Falls, New York.   **PAINT**

1938   American photographer Walker Evans has his first showing at the
            Museum of Modern Art, providing the basis for his book *American
            Photographs*. Among his other works will be *Photographs* (1938) and
            First and Last (1978).   **PHOTO**

PORTRAITS IN THE SUBWAY

*O*ne of the earliest and most long-lived purposes for photography was the personal portrait. Although by the mid-1800s the photographic process had become inexpensive enough for even the average working person to afford a portrait, cumbersome equipment prohibited anything but a stationary, often self-conscious pose.

By the 1930s the hand-held single-lens camera allowed for more spontaneous views of events and people. Along with revolutionizing the recording of history through photojournalism in magazines like Time and Life, it made possible what American photographer Walker Evans called the "unposed portrait." He explored the possibilities of this type of portraiture on the trains of the New York subway.

Using a concealed camera, Evans photographed portraits of dozens upon dozens of what he called "unselfconscious captive sitters" during the late 1930s and early 1940s. Although he considered the subway a "dream 'location' for any portrait photographer weary of the studio and the parade of vanity," he also felt the artistic conflict of capturing the image of an unwitting subject. In a draft of a text to accompany his book of subway photos, he called his clandestine approach a "rude and imprudent invasion" and himself a "penitent spy and an apologetic voyeur."

The photographs were collected in the 1966 book Many Are Chosen, published two decades after Evans's original "invasion."

1938   American radio and theater impresario Orson Welles and his Mercury Players stage a radio drama based on the H. G. Wells novel *The War of the Worlds* on Oct. 30. So realistic is the broadcast that many listeners fear the country is being invaded by aliens.   **TV&R**

1939   American composer Aaron Copland's ballet *Billy the Kid* is produced in New York, and has a consciously created "American sound."   **DANCE**

1939   *My Heart's in the Highlands* and *The Time of Your Life*, plays by American playwright William Saroyan, premieres. *Time* will win the Pulitzer Prize, but Saroyan will decline it.   **DRAMA**

1939   *Ondine*, generally regarded as the best play by French novelist and playwright Jean Giraudoux, is produced.   **DRAMA**

1939   *The Little Foxes*, a drama by American playwright Lillian Hellman, is produced. A tale of greed and social climbing in a turn-of-the-century Southern family, this play will become Hellman's most famous work.   **DRAMA**

1939   In what will be considered the peak year of the Hollywood studio sys-
          tem, 400 movies are released, of which the biggest box-office suc-
          cess is David O. Selznick's MGM production of *Gone With the Wind*,
          directed by Victor Fleming. The adaptation of Margaret Mitchell's
          1936 novel of the Civil War and Reconstruction stars Vivien Leigh as
          Scarlett O'Hara and Clark Gable as Rhett Butler. Made for $3.9 mil-
          lion, it will, by the 1990s, have earned more than $79 million.   **FILM**

1939   Other Hollywood films of this year include Victor Fleming's *The
          Wizard of Oz*, Frank Capra's *Mr. Smith Goes to Washington*, John
          Ford's *Stagecoach* and *Drums Along the Mohawk*, George Stevens's
          Gunga Din, Howard Hawks's *Only Angels Have Wings*, William
          Dieterle's *The Hunchback of Notre Dame* and *Juarez*, George
          Marshall's *Destry Rides Again*, Sidney Lanfield's *The Hound of the
          Baskervilles*, George Cukor's *The Women*, Lewis Milestone's *Of Mice
          and Men*, William Wyler's *Wuthering Heights*, Sam Wood's *Goodbye,
          Mr. Chips*, and Edmund Goulding's *Dark Victory*.   **FILM**

1939   Significant films made outside the United States include, from France,
          Jean Renoir's *La Règle du jeu* (*The Rules of the Game*) and Marcel
          Carné's *Le Jour se lève* (*Daybreak*), and, from Britain, Zoltan Korda's
          The Four Feathers and Carol Reed's *The Stars Look Down*.   **FILM**

1939   After years of languishing in low-budget westerns, American actor
          John Wayne (born Marion Morrison) establishes himself as a proto-
          typical Hollywood star through his performance as the Ringo Kid in
          John Ford's *Stagecoach*.   **FILM**

1939   Irish poet and dramatist William Butler Yeats dies (*b.* 1865). His last
          collection, *Last Poems and Two Plays*, is published posthumously
          this year. It includes "The Black Tower," "Cuchulain Comforted,"
          "Long-legged Fly," "The Circus Animals' Desertion," and "Politics."
          Also included is "Under Ben Bulben," which gives the epitaph on
          Yeats's tombstone in Drumcliff churchyard under the mountain Ben
          Bulben in County Sligo, Ireland: "Cast a cold eye/On life, on
          death./Horseman, pass by!"   **LIT**

1939   American mystery novelist Raymond Chandler publishes his first
          novel, *The Big Sleep*, introducing hard-boiled private detective Philip
          Marlowe, who returns in a series of novels that also include
          Farewell, My Lovely (1940) and *The Lady in the Lake* (1943). The
          books will spawn a number of films.   **LIT**

1939   Irish writer James Joyce's novel *Finnegans Wake* is published in
          complete form. Previously published in parts as *Work in Progress*
          from 1928 to 1937, the experimental work is rich in verbal play and
          mythological, historical, and literary allusion. It centers on the
          dreams of Dublin tavern-keeper Humphrey Chimpden Earwicker
          and his family as they sleep through a single night.   **LIT**

1939   The *Collected Poems* of British poet A. E. Housman is published posthumously.   **LIT**

1939   British writer Christopher Isherwood publishes *Goodbye to Berlin*, a semiautobiographical fiction collection that includes the sketch "Sally Bowles," which will serve as the basis for John Van Druten's play *I Am a Camera* (1951), which in turn will provide the basis for the Broadway musical *Cabaret* (1968) and its Academy Award–winning film adaptation (1972).   **LIT**

1939   Welsh writer Richard Llewellyn publishes his novel of memory and Welsh mining life, *How Green Was My Valley*. The book becomes a best-seller in the United States and is made into an Academy Award–winning film by John Ford in 1941.   **LIT**

1939–1945   Well-known World War II correspondents include William Shirer, Ernie Pyle, A. J. Liebling, and radio commentator Edward R. Murrow, whose war reports begun with the words, "This is London," become famous.   **LIT**

1939   American novelist John Steinbeck publishes *The Grapes of Wrath*, an indictment of the treatment of those attempting to escape the ravages of the Dust Bowl and the Great Depression. The book will win the Pulitzer Prize and inspire an Oscar-winning film.   **LIT**

1939   American novelist and short-story writer Eudora Welty publishes the short story "Petrified Man."   **LIT**

1939–1940   Shortly after his death, two works by American novelist Thomas Wolfe are published: *The Web and the Rock* (1939) and *You Can't Go Home Again*. Both works concern the character George "Monk" Webber.   **LIT**

1939   Australian novelist Patrick White publishes his first novel *Happy Valley*. Later works will include *The Tree of Man* (1955) and *Voss* (1957).   **LIT**

1939   Following the Spanish Civil War, cellist Pablo Casals leaves Spain in protest against dictator Francisco Franco.   **MUSIC**

1939–1945   Popular World War II songs include "Roll Out the Barrel," "The White Cliffs of Dover," "I'll Be Seeing You," "Praise the Lord and Pass the Ammunition," "Hang Out the Washing on the Siegfried Line," and "Lili Marlene," sung memorably by German-born film star Marlene Dietrich.   **MUSIC**

1939   American composer Irving Berlin's "God Bless America" is popularized by singer Kate Smith, among others and becomes an informal anthem of the country. It also becomes one of Smith's signature songs. American folk composer Woody Guthrie will later respond to the song with his own socially inclusive brand of patriotism in "This Land Is Your Land."   **MUSIC**

1939–1941   Spanish painter Joan Miró paints the series *The Constellations*, twenty-three paintings in gouache and oil on paper, now considered among his finest works.   **PAINT**

1939–1958   American photographer Berenice Abbott, a former student of Man Ray, compiles a series of highly stylized photos that illustrate the laws of physics.   **PHOTO**

1939   American artist Joseph Cornell shows a series of surrealist "collage sculptures" and "constructions" in a solo exhibition at the Julien Levy Gallery in New York, consisting of hand-made boxes containing several manufactured items. Cornell's boxes will foreshadow Robert Rauschenberg's "combines" of the 1950s.   **SCULP**

1939   FM radios are first sold commercially.   **TV&R**

1940s   The jitterbug, a fast dance developed for the 4/4 syncopation of swing music, dominates the dance floor in the United States and Europe.   **DANCE**

1940s   Canada encourages the development of contemporary art by Eskimo craft workers practicing traditional styles. The works produced include carved figures in whalebone, ivory, and soapstone and lithographs printed with stone. The art of the Eskimo (or Inuit) peoples of the Bering Sea and Canada dates back at least 2,000 years.   **DECO**

THE CONSTELLATIONS OF WORLD WAR II

*J*ust as Pablo Picasso had been prompted by the Spanish Civil War to create one of his most intense works, Guernica, Spanish surrealist painter Joan Miró responded to the horrors of World War II by creating the twenty-three paintings that some would consider his finest works, the Constellation *series. In 1940, when he started the series of mainly gouache and oil studies, he had settled near Normandy, hoping to escape the path of World War II. However, when Hitler's troops bombed the region in May 1940 and France went under Vichy rule, Miró was forced to abandon his home. Back in Spain Miró saw the war escalate, yet was able to complete the paintings by the fall of 1941. Including such influential works as "The Passage of the Divine Bird" and "The Beautiful Bird Revealing the Unknown to a Pair of Lovers," the* Constellation *paintings radiate a delicacy, precision, and simultaneous wildness and serenity. They stand as a deliberate artistic response to the chaos of war.*

1940s	Popular songs of the decade include "South of the Border," "How High the Moon," "Oh, Johnny (How You Can Love)," "Blueberry Hill," "I Got It Bad and That Ain't Good," "Bewitched, Bothered, and Bewildered," "Chattanooga Choo-Choo," "That Old Black Magic," "Paper Doll," "Mairzy Doats," "People Will Say We're in Love," "Sentimental Journey," "Rum and Coca-Cola," "Come Rain or Come Shine," "Almost Like Being in Love," "Buttons and Bows," "Some Enchanted Evening," and "Bali Ha'i." **MUSIC**
1940s	African-American painter Jacob Lawrence begins to produce primitivistic, highly decorative works on ghetto life and other social themes. **PAINT**
1940s	French painter Georges Rouault, who developed his own form of expressionism, turns to creating religious art. **PAINT**
1940	The Katherine Dunham Dance Company debuts off-Broadway. Named for the African-American dancer and anthropologist, it will be followed in 1944 by the New York–based Katharine Dunham School of Dance, which will teach both dance and cultural studies. **DANCE**
1940	Walt Disney Productions releases the animated features *Pinocchio* and *Fantasia*. Other notable films of the year include Alfred Hitchcock's *Rebecca*, John Ford's *The Grapes of Wrath*, Charlie Chaplin's *The Great Dictator*, Sam Wood's *Our Town*, and the first of the Bing Crosby–Bob Hope–Dorothy Lamour "Road" movies from Paramount, Victor Schertzinger's *Road to Singapore*. **FILM**
1940	British poet W. H. Auden publishes the poetry collection *Another Time*, which includes "Lay Your Sleeping Head, My Love" and "In Memory of W. B. Yeats." **LIT**
1940	Welsh poet Dylan Thomas publishes the story collection *Portrait of the Artist as a Young Dog*. **LIT**
1940	American writer Ernest Hemingway publishes *For Whom the Bell Tolls*, about Robert Jordan, an American volunteer for the Loyalists during the Spanish Civil War, and his love for a young Spanish woman, Maria. **LIT**
1940	African-American novelist Richard Wright publishes *Native Son*. **LIT**
1940	American poet e. e. cummings publishes the poem about the span of human existence, *Anyone Lived in a Pretty How Town*. It will become one of his best-known works. **LIT**
1940	American novelist John O'Hara publishes the story collection *Pal Joey*. The title story, about a small-time heel, will be adapted by Richard Rodgers and Lorenz Hart into a Broadway musical. **LIT**
1940	American painter Anna Mary "Grandma" Moses has her first major one-person show in New York City, after being championed by collector Louis Calder. **PAINT**

Movie still from *Citizen Kane* by Orson Welles. *(Photosearch, Inc.)*

1940   French painter Pierre Bonnard, known for his luxurious use of color and great popularity with audiences and collectors, is elected a member of the Royal Academy.   **PAINT**

1940   In the United States, 30 million homes have radios.   **TV&R**

1941   German playwright Bertolt Brecht's play *Mutter Courage und ihre Kinder* (*Mother Courage and Her Children*) is produced. Brecht's *Leben des Galilei* (*The Life of Galileo*) and *Der gute Mensch von Sezuan* (*The Good Person of Szechuan*) will be produced in 1943.   **DRAMA**

1941   *Blithe Spirit*, a comedy by British actor and playwright Noel Coward, is produced in New York and London. Very popular, it will run in London for 1,997 performances.   **DRAMA**

1941   *Watch on the Rhine*, a political drama by American playwright Lillian Hellman, premieres. It will be followed by *The Searching Wind* (1944), a play also on political themes, and *Another Part of the Forest* (1946).   **DRAMA**

1941   RKO releases the film *Citizen Kane*, produced, directed, and co-
          scripted (with Herman J. Mankiewicz) by twenty-five-year-old Orson
          Welles. Welles's debut feature, a fictionalized biography of publish-
          ing tycoon William Randolph Hearst, is hailed by critics as a rich,
          innovative masterpiece of filmmaking, despite the efforts of Hearst
          supporters to block its release. Not a commercial success in its own
          day, it will be rereleased many times and win a place among the
          best films in history.   **FILM**

THE ENDING THAT ALMOST WASN'T: MEET JOHN DOE

*I*n his 1971 autobiography, The Name Above the Title, *director Frank
Capra writes that* Meet John Doe, *his first independent feature made
by Frank Capra Productions and not by Columbia, had five different
endings. His chapter on the movie is called, "Five Endings in Search of An
Audience."*

*In this 1941 movie, Capra planned to probe "the agony of disillusion-
ment and the wild, dark passions of mobs." In so doing, he hoped to con-
vince critics that the Academy Award–winning director of* It Happened
One Night *and* Mr. Smith Goes to Washington *could produce more than
"Capra-corn."*

*In the film, a drifter (Gary Cooper) is tempted by money and glory to be-
come John Doe, a radio celebrity and leader of a populist social movement.
When Doe defies the politician who is manipulating him (Edward Arnold),
he engineers Doe's downfall, and the American public turns against him.
"But now," says Capra, "what happens to John Doe?"*

*The film opened for two weeks in six major cities, with four different
endings. The endings varied on whether Doe jumped from a skyscraper (as
he announced he would do), and on who or what lead him to his decision.
Although the press received the movie well, Capra was displeased with all
of the endings. Not until he received a letter from a man who called himself
"John Doe" did he realize what the ending should be. The letter said in part,
"The only thing that can keep John Doe from jumping to death is the John
Does themselves . . . if they ask him."*

*Capra called his cast together and filmed Doe being saved at midnight by
the reporter (Barbara Stanwyck) who is in love with him, her editor (James
Gleason), and a group of ordinary people who have been helped by John
Doe. Still, Capra felt that this ending was "the best of a sorry lot." He felt he
had created a movie with no answers for an audience that needed them.*

1941   Other notable American films of the year include Howard Hawks's *Sergeant York*, Michael Curtiz's *Dive Bomber*, George Cukor's *The Philadelphia Story*, Victor Fleming's *Dr. Jekyll and Mr. Hyde*, John Ford's *How Green Was My Valley*, John Huston's *The Maltese Falcon*, Preston Sturges's *The Lady Eve*, George Waggner's *The Wolf Man*, and Walt Disney Productions' *Dumbo*.   **FILM**

1941   British novelist Virginia Woolf's last novel, *Between the Acts*, is published posthumously.   **LIT**

1941   The final, unfinished novel of American novelist F. Scott Fitzgerald, *The Last Tycoon*, is published posthumously.   **LIT**

1941   Hungarian-born British novelist Arthur Koestler publishes *Darkness at Noon*, about the terrors of totalitarianism. His later works will include the novel *The Ghost in the Machine* (1967) and *Janus: A Summing Up*. He will die by his own hand in 1983.   **LIT**

1941   Endowed by American businessman Paul Mellon in 1937, the National Gallery of Art opens in Washington, D.C.   **PAINT**

1941   American realist painter Edward Hopper completes *Nighthawks*, which epitomizes his ability to convey the alienation of urban life.   **PAINT**

1941   Several artists focus their works on the activity and effects of World War II, including Henry Moore (drawings of refugees in London), Paul Nash (*Bombers Over Berlin*), and Feliks Topolski (drawings of British armies).   **PAINT**

1941   American photographer Ansel Adams composes *Moonrise, Hernandez, New Mexico*, one of the dozens of his photographs that use composition and tonal variety to establish him as a foremost twentieth-century landscape photographer.   **PHOTO**

1942   *Rodeo*, choreographed by American dancer Agnes De Mille, premieres. In 1943 De Mille will bring ballet to the Broadway musical through her choreography of Rodgers's and Hammerstein's *Oklahoma!*   **DANCE**

1942   *The Skin of Our Teeth*, a play by American playwright Thornton Wilder, premieres.   **DRAMA**

1942   American actors Hume Cronyn and Jessica Tandy marry. In the years to come, they will appear together on stage many times. Notable joint performances will include Anton Chekhov's *Three Sisters* and Arthur Miller's *Death of a Salesman* during the first season of the Guthrie Theatre in Minneapolis (1963–1964), and in New York, Edward Albee's *A Delicate Balance* (1966) and Samuel Beckett's *Happy Days* (1972).   **DRAMA**

1942   Warner Bros. releases Michael Curtiz's *Casablanca*, starring
              Humphrey Bogart and Ingrid Bergman. The World War II romantic
              drama will become one of the most popular films of all time.
              Though released in a limited run this year, it will not be nominated
              for an Oscar until the 1943 awards, when it will win Oscars for best
              picture, director, and screenplay.   **FILM**

1942   Other notable American films of this year include Walt Disney
              Productions' *Bambi*, William Wyler's *Mrs. Miniver*, Michael Curtiz's
              Yankee Doodle Dandy, Mervyn LeRoy's *Random Harvest*, Irving
              Rapper's *Now, Voyager*, David Butler's *Road to Morocco*, and Sam
              Wood's *The Pride of the Yankees*.   **FILM**

1942   American political cartoonist Herblock (Herbert Block) wins his first
              Pulitzer Prize for his work. He will win a second Pulitzer Prize in
              1954.   **GRAPH**

1942   American novelist Cornelia Otis Skinner and American periodical
              editor Emily Kimbrough publish the sprightly novel *Our Hearts Were
              Young and Gay*. It will generate a film adaptation in 1944.   **LIT**

1942   Algerian-born French writer Albert Camus publishes the existential
              novel *The Stranger*. He also publishes the philosophical essay *The
              Myth of Sisyphus* (1942). Among his later works will be the novel
              The Plague (1947).   **LIT**

1942   British scholar and writer C. S. (Clive Staples) Lewis publishes his
              epistolary work on evil, *The Screwtape Letters*. Among his later
              works is the series of children's books, *The Chronicles of Narnia*.   **LIT**

1942   Magnetic recording tape, which will revolutionize the recording in-
              dustry, is invented.   **MUSIC**

1942   In the movie *Holiday Inn* singer Bing Crosby introduces Irving
              Berlin's "White Christmas," which almost immediately becomes a
              holiday song standard and one of the most widely recorded songs
              in history.   **MUSIC**

1942   German-born American painter Hans Hofmann paints *The Wind*, in
              which he experiments with drip techniques later applied on a larger
              scale by Jackson Pollock. *See* 1947, PAINT.   **PAINT**

1942   German sculptor Arno Breker opens an exhibition of monumental
              figurative sculpture illustrating the ideologies of Germany's Third
              Reich at the Musée de l'Orangerie.   **SCULP**

1943   Construction ends on the Pentagon, the largest office building in
              the world at 6.5 million square feet in size.   **ARCH**

1943   *Les Mouches* (*The Flies*), the first play by French philosopher and
              writer Jean-Paul Sartre, is produced.   **DRAMA**

1943   Mexican playwright Rodolfo Usigli's historical drama *Corona del sombra* (*Crown of Shadow*) is produced. He will also write the play *El Gesticulador* (*The Imposter*). Both will be seen as classics of Latin American theater.   **DRAMA**

1943   The American musical *Oklahoma!*—with book and lyrics by Oscar Hammerstein II, music by Richard Rodgers, and choreography by Agnes De Mille—premieres on March 31. This landmark work is revolutionary in having songs and dances that advance the story.   **DRAMA**

1943   Notable films include Sam Wood's *For Whom the Bell Tolls*, Howard Hughes's *The Outlaw*, Frank Borzage's *Stage Door Canteen*, Vincente Minnelli's *Cabin in the Sky*, Fred M. Wilcox's *Lassie Come Home*, Victor Fleming's *A Guy Named Joe*, and Arthur Lubin's *Phantom of the Opera*.   **FILM**

1943–1946   Notable foreign films include Roberto Rossellini's *Open City* (1946), David Lean's *Brief Encounter* (1946) and *Great Expectations* (1946), Laurence Olivier's *Henry V* (1944), and Sergey Eisenstein's *Ivan the Terrible* (1943).   **FILM**

1943   Russian-born American novelist Ayn Rand publishes *The Fountainhead*, the story of the rise of a talented though self-involved architect. The book, which becomes a best-seller, typifies the way Rand interweaves her objectivist philosophy into her works.   **LIT**

1943   British poet T. S. Eliot publishes the poem *Four Quartets*.   **LIT**

1943   French philosopher and writer Jean-Paul Sartre publishes the treatise *Being and Nothingness*, which provides the basis for existentialism. His later works include the play *No Exit*.   **LIT**

1943   French novelist, essayist, and aviator Antoine de Saint-Exupéry publishes the fable *Le Petit Prince* (*The Little Prince*), about the search for what is important in life. An earlier collection of stories and meditations is *Wind, Sand, and Stars* (1939).   **LIT**

1943   Now living in New York, Dutch painter Piet Mondrian completes *Broadway Boogie Woogie*, which will become one of his best-known works.   **PAINT**

1943   American abstract expressionist painter Jackson Pollock gains his first solo exhibition.   **PAINT**

1943   American painter Thomas Hart Benton paints *July Hay*.   **PAINT**

1943   British sculptor Barbara Hepworth initiates an individual sculptural style in a series of hollow wood pieces that combine painting and sculpture, surrealist biomorphisim, and organic abstraction.   **SCULP**

1944   American composer Aaron Copland's evocative ballet *Appalachian Spring*, is danced by Martha Graham in Washington, D.C..   **DANCE**

| 1944 | French playwright Jean Anouilh's drama *Antigone*, based on Sophocles' classic (*see* 442 B.C., DRAMA), is produced in Paris during the German Occupation. It will become Anouilh's best-known play outside of France.   **DRAMA** |

1944   *Huisclos* (*No Exit*), a drama by French philosopher and writer Jean-Paul Sartre, is produced. It will generally be viewed as Sartre's greatest theatrical work.   **DRAMA**

1944   Notable films include Leo McCarey's *Going My Way*, Vincente Minnelli's *Meet Me in St. Louis*, Mervyn LeRoy's *30 Seconds Over Tokyo*, George Cukor's *Gaslight*, Frank Capra's *Arsenic and Old Lace*, Howard Hawks's *To Have and Have Not*, and Clarence Brown's *National Velvet*.   **FILM**

c. 1944   Dutch artist M. C. Escher designs surrealist prints fraught with optical illusion, memorably of staircases leading in several directions at once.   **GRAPH**

1944   Canadian-born American writer Saul Bellow publishes his first novel, *Dangling Man*.   **LIT**

1944   Stationed in the South Pacific with the Army during World War II, American poet Karl Shapiro publishes the collection *V-Letter and Other Poems*, about the experience and effects of war. It will win the Pulitzer Prize.   **LIT**

1944   British writer Eric Arthur Blair, known as George Orwell, publishes the political fable *Animal Farm*. His later novels include the antitotalitarian work *1984*. Much of his nonfiction work will be published in *Collected Essays, Journalism and Letters* (1968).   **LIT**

1944   Argentinian short-story writer and poet Jorge Luis Borges publishes the collection *Ficciones*. His poetry will be collected in *Selected Poems: 1923–1967* (1972).   **LIT**

1944   American composer William Schuman's *Secular Cantata No. 2*, "A Free Song," wins the first Pulitzer Prize for music.   **MUSIC**

1944   English composer Ralph Vaughan Williams composes his masterpiece Symphony no. 5 in D.   **MUSIC**

1944   Thirty thousand fans riot at New York's Paramount Theater where Frank "The Voice" Sinatra is to appear. Sinatra also appeared at the Paramount in 1942, when his popularity was beginning to crest; by 1944 he is at peak popularity. *See also* 1967, MUSIC.   **MUSIC**

1944   American painter Arshile Gorky paints *The Liver Is the Cock's Comb*.   **PAINT**

1945–1958   American architect Frank Lloyd Wright designs the Guggenheim Museum, New York City.   **ARCH**

1945   After temporarily emigrating to the United States from occupied France in 1941, Russian-born designer and painter Marc Chagall designs costumes and sets for composer Igor Stravinsky's ballet *Firebird*.   **DANCE**

1945   *La Folle de Chaillot* (*The Madwoman of Chaillot*), a play by French novelist and playwright Jean Giraudoux, premieres in Paris. It will be revived many times, enjoying popularity both in France and abroad.   **DRAMA**

1945   *The Glass Menagerie*, the first critically and commerically successful play by American playwright Tennessee Williams, premieres. It tells the story of Laura, a young disabled woman living in a fantasy world, her disaffected brother Tom, and their domineering mother Amanda.   **DRAMA**

· ·

*"Painting is not done to decorate apartments. . . . It is
an instrument of war against brutality and darkness."
—Spanish painter Pablo Picasso, known for such
powerful denunciations of war as Guernica (1937)
and The Charnel House (1945); c. 1940s*

· ·

1945   Notable American films include Leo McCarey's *The Bells of St. Mary's*, Alfred Hitchcock's *Spellbound*, George Sidney's *Anchors Aweigh*, Billy Wilder's *The Lost Weekend*, Michael Curtiz's *Mildred Pierce*, Elia Kazan's *A Tree Grows in Brooklyn*.   **FILM**

1945   Political cartoonist Bill Mauldin wins the Pulitzer Prize for his works. He gained fame for his World War II cartoons and will win a second Pulitzer Prize in 1959.   **GRAPH**

1945   American novelist Kathleen Winsor publishes *Forever Amber*.   **LIT**

1945   Chinese writer Lao She's *Rickshaw Boy* is translated into English. His work is known for its satirical humor.   **LIT**

1945   African-American novelist Richard Wright publishes the autobiographical *Black Boy*.   **LIT**

1945   British composer Benjamin Britten's opera *Peter Grimes* opens in London. It is hailed as marking a new era in English opera and establishes his reputation worldwide.   **MUSIC**

1945   Swing music begins to be transformed into the more idiosyncratic and improvisational bebop, or bop, music. A prime force in bop music is American jazz saxophonist Charlie "Bird" Parker.   **MUSIC**

1945   Spanish painter Pablo Picasso paints *The Charnel House*.   **PAINT**

Duke Ellington and band. (*UPI/Bettmann*)

1945   Following the end of World War II this year, the center of the art world shifts from Paris to New York, where abstract expressionism will be the dominant movement in painting into the 1960s. Abstract expressionist works are typically large, bold, nonrepresentational works in revolt against traditional styles. Painters associated with the movement include Jackson Pollock, Arshile Gorky, Hans Hofmann, Franz Kline, Willem de Kooning, Lee Krasner, Barnett Newman, Mark Rothko, and Adolph Gottlieb. Avant-garde New York painters of the 1940s and 1950s are also referred to as the New York school.   **PAINT**

1945   Five thousand U.S. homes now have television sets. Three years from now (1948), the number will be 1 million homes. By 1968 Americans will own 78 million television sets.   **TV&R**

1946   American architect R. (Richard) Buckminster Fuller designs Dymaxion House.   **ARCH**

1946   The new Bodleian Library opens at Oxford University, England. **ARCH**

1946   What will become the New York City Ballet is founded as the Ballet Society by Russian-born choreographer George Balanchine and American dance impresario Lincoln Kirstein.   **DANCE**

1946   French actor and mime Marcel Marceau introduces his character
              Bip, a white-faced clown at the Théâtre de Poche in Paris. He will
              portray this character throughout the world for years to come. **DRAMA**

1946   *The Iceman Cometh*, a drama by American playwright Eugene
              O'Neill, premieres. O'Neill's *A Moon for the Misbegotten* will be pro-
              duced in 1947.   **DRAMA**

1946   Notable films include William Wyler's *The Best Years of Our Lives*,
              Frank Capra's *It's a Wonderful Life*, Walt Disney Productions' *Song
              of the South*, Howard Hawks's *The Big Sleep*, Charles Vidor's *Gilda*,
              King Vidor's *Duel in the Sun*, Alfred Hitchcock's *Notorious*, Tay
              Garnett's *The Postman Always Rings Twice*, Clarence Brown's *The
              Yearling*, Alfred E. Green's *The Jolson Story*, and Robert Siodmak's
              The Killers.   **FILM**

1946   American journalist John Hersey publishes *Hiroshima*, an account of
              the effects of the U.S. dropping the atomic bomb on that Japanese
              city. Written while Hersey was a war correspondent for *The New
              Yorker*, the work appeared in the magazine before being published
              as a book.   **LIT**

1946   American novelist Carson McCullers publishes *The Member of the
              Wedding*, the story of a young girl, Frankie, and how she views her
              brother's upcoming wedding.   **LIT**

1946   American poet Robert Lowell publishes the collection *Lord Weary's
              Castle*, which will win the Pulitzer Prize. Other collections will in-
              clude *Life Studies* (1959) and *For the Union Dead* (1964).   **LIT**

1946–1963   American poet William Carlos Williams publishes the first four
              books of his poem *Paterson* (for Paterson, N.J.) in 1946. Book V will
              be published in 1958; he will be working on Book VI at the time of
              his death in 1963.   **LIT**

1946   Greek novelist Nikos Kazantzakis publishes the novel *Zorba the
              Greek*. Both it and his later novel, *The Last Temptation of Christ*, will
              be made into films.   **LIT**

1946   French artist Jean Dubuffet gains his first exhibition. Employing
              common materials and an unrefined spontaneity, his work embod-
              ies the movement known as art brut.   **PAINT**

1946   Australian painter Sir Sidney Nolan begins a series of paintings cen-
              tered on national folk hero Ned Kelly. These works will be crucial to
              establishing his career; decades of continued work will lead him to
              become one of Australia's foremost artists.   **PAINT**

1947   *L'Invitation au château* (*Ring Round the Moon*), a play by French playwright Jean Anouilh, is produced. Anouilh's *La Répétition, ou l'Amour puni* (*The Rehearsal*) will be produced in 1950, *La Valse des toréadors* (*The Waltz of the Toreadors*) in 1952 and *Pauvre Bitos, ou le Dîner des têtes* (*Poor Bitos*) in 1956.   **DRAMA**

1947   *Les Bonnes* (*The Maids*), the first drama by French writer Jean Genet, is staged in Paris by French director Louis Jouvet. It is based on the true story of two sisters, maids in a provincial French home, who kill their abusive employers.   **DRAMA**

1947   *A Streetcar Named Desire*, a drama by American playwright Tennessee Williams, premieres. Character Blanche DuBois speaks a line—"I have always depended on the kindness of strangers"— which will become a famous camp phrase. In 1951 *Streetcar* will be filmed by Elia Kazan, the director of the original play.   **DRAMA**

1947   *All My Sons*, which will become the first successful play by American playwright Arthur Miller, premieres.   **DRAMA**

1947   Notable American films include Elia Kazan's *Gentleman's Agreement*, George Seaton's *Miracle on 34th Street*, Irving Reis's *The Bachelor and the Bobby-Soxer*, H. C. Potter's *The Farmer's Daughter*, Norman Z. McLeod's *Road to Rio*, Joseph L. Mankiewicz's *The Ghost and Mrs. Muir*, Chester Erskine's *The Egg and I*, Cecil B. De Mille's *Unconquered*, Otto Preminger's *Forever Amber*, and Michael Curtiz's *Life With Father*.   **FILM**

1947   Notable foreign films include Charlie Chaplin's *Monsieur Verdoux* and Michael Powell and Emeric Pressburger's *Black Narcissus*.   **FILM**

1947   American novelist James Michener publishes his first book, the short story collection *Tales of the South Pacific*, which wins the Pulitzer Prize and becomes the basis for the musical *South Pacific* (1949). He will later become the author of a series of long, popular, semidocumentary novels, including *Hawaii* (1959), *The Source* (1965), and *Centennial* (1974).   **LIT**

1947   American novelist John Steinbeck publishes the parablelike short novel *The Pearl*, about the disastrous consequences of finding a precious gem.   **LIT**

1947   British novelist Malcolm Lowry publishes *Under the Volcano*.   **LIT**

1947   German-born poet and playwright Nelly Sachs publishes the poetry collection *Dwellings of Death*, about the Holocaust. Later collections include *And No One Knows Where to Go* (1957).   **LIT**

1947   American composer Charles Ives wins the Pulitzer Prize for his Symphony no. 3, written in 1911.   **MUSIC**

1947   American painter Jackson Pollock begins painting in a "drip and splash" style, abandoning the traditional brush and easel for more chaotic methods of applying paint. The style, known as action painting, is one form of abstract expressionism. Pollock's *Composition No. 1* is a characteristic work. *See also* c. 1950, PAINT.   **PAINT**

1947   The one-step Polaroid camera is developed by American inventor Edwin Herbert Land.   **PHOTO**

1947   Swiss sculptor Max Bill erects *Continuity* in Zurich, a monument that is based on the principle of the Möbius strip or band, which possesses only a single surface and a single edge.   **SCULP**

1948   The Ballets de Paris de Roland Petit is founded by French dancer Roland Petit.   **DANCE**

1948   Russian-born choreographer George Balanchine becomes artistic director and choreographer of the New York City Ballet.   **DANCE**

1948   *Les Mains sales (Dirty Hands)*, a drama by French philosopher and writer Jean-Paul Sartre, is produced. Sartre's *Le Diable et le bon dieu (The Devil and the Good Lord)* will be staged in 1951. These plays and Sartre's earlier dramas reflect his existential philosophy.   **DRAMA**

1948   *Summer and Smoke*, a drama by American playwright Tennessee Williams, premieres. It will be followed by *The Rose Tattoo* (1951) and *Camino Real* (1953).   **DRAMA**

1948   Notable films include Howard Hawks's *Red River*, Norman Z. McLeod's *The Paleface*, George Sidney's *The Three Musketeers*, Jean Negulesco's *Johnny Belinda*, John Huston's *The Treasure of the Sierra Madre* and *Key Largo*, and Anatole Litvak's *The Snake Pit*.   **FILM**

1948   Notable foreign films include Michael Powell and Emeric Pressburger's *The Red Shoes*, Jules Dassin's *The Naked City*, Laurence Olivier's *Hamlet*, Carol Reed's *The Fallen Idol*, and Vittorio De Sica's *The Bicycle Thief*.   **FILM**

1948   British poet, novelist, and critic Robert Graves publishes *The White Goddess*, a study of mythology in relation to poetic inspiration.   **LIT**

1948   American novelist and short-story writer Truman Capote breaks onto the literary scene with the publication of *Other Voices, Other Rooms*. Later celebrated works will include the short novel about New York–original Holly Golightly, *Breakfast at Tiffany's* (1958), and the nonfiction-based novel *In Cold Blood* (1965).   **LIT**

1948   American novelist Norman Mailer publishes the World War II novel *The Naked and the Dead*.   **LIT**

1948   South African novelist Alan Paton publishes the novel *Cry, the Beloved Country*.   **LIT**

Movie still from *Royal Wedding* with Fred Astaire. *(Photosearch, Inc.)*

1948   German composer Richard Strauss composes his *Vier letzte Lieder* (*Four Last Lieder*) for soprano and orchestra.   **MUSIC**

1948   French musician Pierre Schaeffer inaugurates "musique concrète" at a Paris radio studio. It works by replacing the traditional material of music (instrumental and vocal sounds) with recorded sounds such as noises and percussion.   **MUSIC**

1948   The long-playing vinyl phonograph record is developed by CBS engineer Peter Goldmark. The record runs at a speed of 33⅓ r.p.m. and plays for about forty-five minutes. It will change the creation and marketing of popular music.   **MUSIC**

1948   American painter Robert Motherwell begins the series of works *Elegy to the Spanish Republic*, which will eventually encompass more than a hundred paintings.   **PAINT**

1948   American painter Andrew Wyeth comes to international prominence with his painting *Christina's World*.   **PAINT**

1948   American painter and member of the New York school Barnett Newman establishes himself as an abstract expressionist by the end of the 1940s, particularly with his monochromatic 1948 painting *Onement I*.   **PAINT**

1948   Swiss sculptor Alberto Giacometti displays very thin, frail, almost sticklike bronze figures at an exhibition in New York.   **SCULP**

1948   The transistor, which will greatly reduce the size of radios and televisions, is developed for Bell Laboratories by American physicists William Shockley, John Bardeen, and Walter Brattain.   **TV&R**

1948   "The Toast of the Town," later known as "The Ed Sullivan Show," debuts on TV. The variety show featuring acts ranging from top Broadway talent to vaudevillian exotica will run until 1971. It will be noted for memorable appearances by Elvis Presley and the Beatles.   **TV&R**

1949   The samba, a Latin American dance, becomes popular in the United States and Europe.   **DANCE**

1949   *The Cocktail Party*, a drawing-room comedy by the British poet T. S. Eliot, is performed at the Edinburgh Festival. *The Confidential Clerk* and *The Elder Statesman*, both comedies by Eliot, will be performed at the festival in 1953 and 1958, respectively.   **DRAMA**

1949   *Haute surveillance (Deathwatch)*, a drama by French writer Jean Genet, opens in a production that Genet helps direct.   **DRAMA**

1949   American director and teacher of acting Lee Strasberg becomes artistic director of the Actors Studio, a New York City workshop devoted to the Method, an inner-directed approach to acting derived from the ideas of Konstantin Stanislavsky (*see* 1936, DRAMA). Workshop members will include the American actors Marlon Brando, James Dean, Montgomery Clift, Geraldine Page, Shelley Winters, Dustin Hoffman, Robert De Niro, Al Pacino, and Ellen Burstyn.   **DRAMA**

1949   *Death of a Salesman*, a drama written by American playwright Arthur Miller and directed by Elia Kazan, premieres. This tale of traveling salesman Willy Loman and his family will win the Pulitzer Prize and will be considered by some to be Miller's best play and an example of modern tragedy.   **DRAMA**

1949   The American musical *South Pacific*—with book by Oscar Hammerstein II and Joshua Logan, lyrics by Hammerstein, and music by Richard Rogers—premieres on April 7. It stars Mary Martin and Ezio Pinza.   **DRAMA**

1949   Notable American films include George Cukor's *Adam's Rib*, Robert Rossen's *All the King's Men*, Cecil B. De Mille's *Samson and Delilah*, William A. Wellman's *Battleground*, Allan Dwan's *The Sands of Iwo Jima*, Howard Hawks's *I Was a Male War Bride*, Mervyn LeRoy's *Little Women*, and Henry King's *Twelve O'Clock High*.   **FILM**

1949   Notable foreign films include Carol Reed's *The Third Man*, Roberto Rossellini's *Stromboli*, and Jean-Pierre Melville's *Les Enfants terribles*.   **FILM**

1949   African-American poet Gwendolyn Brooks publishes the collection *Annie Allen*. The Chicago-based poems will win the Pulitzer Prize.   **LIT**

1949   British author Nancy Mitford publishes the novel of English society, *Love in a Cold Climate*. Later works will include *The Blessing* (1951).   **LIT**

1949–1950   French novelist Simone de Beauvoir publishes the philosophical treatise *The Second Sex*, about women. Among her later works is the novel *The Mandarins*.   **LIT**

1949   American short-story writer Shirley Jackson publishes the tale of small-town cruelty, "The Lottery."   **LIT**

1949   *Mode de valeurs et d'intensités* for piano, by French composer Olivier Messiaen, will greatly influence experimentalist composers Pierre Boulez and Karlheinz Stockhausen.   **MUSIC**

1949–1951   In thanks to the nuns who nursed him following operations for cancer, French painter Henri Matisse designs and creates artwork for the Chapel of the Rosary of Vence. The artwork includes murals on tile and stained-glass windows.   **PAINT**

1949   Austrian expressionist painter Oskar Kokoschka is given an exhibition at the Museum of Modern Art, New York City. During a decades-long career he has become known for his telling portraits of people and towns, as well as his work with the Wiener Werkstätte.   **PAINT**

1950s   The international style of architecture, originating in the work of such architects as Walter Gropius, Ludwig Mies van der Rohe, and Le Corbusier in the 1920s, becomes the preferred mode for building skyscrapers. *See* 1926, ARCH.   **ARCH**

1950s   The Royal Ballet is founded in London. Among the choreographers for this classically oriented ballet are Anthony Tudor and Sir Frederick Ashton. **DANCE**

1950s   Off-Broadway theater flourishes in New York City, gaining the attention of critics and increasingly presenting artistically and commercially successful shows. **DRAMA**

1950s   Spanish painter Joan Miró experiments with etchings, lithographs, and illustration of books, including *Ubu Roi*. **GRAPH**

1950s   Popular songs of the decade include "Mona Lisa," "Goodnight Irene," "In the Cool, Cool, Cool of the Evening," "Hello, Young Lovers," "Jambalaya," "I Love Paris," "(How Much is That) Doggie in the Window," "Stranger in Paradise," "Mister Sandman," "Young at Heart," "Three Coins in the Fountain," "Love is a Many-Splendored Thing," "Rock Around the Clock," "Hound Dog," "Blue Suede Shoes," "Que Sera Sera," "Young Love," "Maria," "Volare," "Mack the Knife," "Personality," "Tom Dooley," "High Hopes." **MUSIC**

1950s   American painter Willem de Kooning paints the highly abstracted, energetically painted *Woman* series. **PAINT**

· ·

"Art is art. Everything else is everything else."
—American abstract painter
Ad Reinhardt, c. 1950s

· ·

1950s   American abstract painter and art critic Ad Reinhardt, who works within many artistic styles, including abstract expressionism, turns to monochromatic painting during the decade. **PAINT**

1950s   American photographers Irving Penn and Richard Avedon become known for their expressive work in advertising and fashion photography for mass-market periodicals like *Life* and *Vogue*. In 1957 Avedon will serve as inspiration for the main character in the film *Funny Face* and will also act as its visual consultant. **PHOTO**

1950s   Russian-born American sculptor Louise Nevelson begins to construct images of found pieces of wood. Her objects will take on the form of large wall units in the 1960s, decorated with motifs inspired by sculpture on Mayan ruins. **SCULP**

1950s   Late this decade, American sculptor John Chamberlain produces works known as "junk sculpture" made of fragments of old machinery and parts of wrecked automobiles. **SCULP**

1950   The United Nations Building is completed in New York City. **ARCH**

1950   The one-act *La Cantatrice chauve* (*The Bald Soprano*), the first play by French absurdist playwright Eugène Ionesco, is produced. It will be followed by *La Leçon* (*The Lesson*, 1951), *Les Chaises* (*The Chairs*, 1952), *Victimes du devoir* (*Victims of Duty*, 1953), *Jacques, ou la Soumission* (*Jacques, or the Submission*, 1955), and several other short works.   **DRAMA**

1950   *Come Back Little Sheba*, the first and perhaps best drama by American playwright William Inge, is produced. The show stars actress Shirley Booth, who will also perform in the 1952 film version.   **DRAMA**

1950   The American musical *Guys and Dolls*—with book by Jo Swerling and Abe Burrows and music and lyrics by Frank Loesser—premieres on Nov. 24. It is based on stories by American yarn spinner Damon Runyon. The play will be revived successfully on Broadway in the 1990s.   **DRAMA**

1950   Notable films include Joseph L. Mankiewicz's *All About Eve*, John Huston's *The Asphalt Jungle*, Billy Wilder's *Sunset Boulevard*, George Cukor's *Born Yesterday*, Henry Koster's *Harvey*, Walt Disney Productions' *Cinderella*, Compton Bennett and Andrew Marton's *King Solomon's Mines*, George Sidney's *Annie Get Your Gun*, Walter Lang's *Cheaper by the Dozen*, and Vincente Minnelli's *Father of the Bride*.   **FILM**

1950   Notable foreign films include Akira Kurosawa's *Rashomon*, Max Ophuls's *La Ronde*, and Jean Cocteau's *Orphée*.   **FILM**

1950   American science-fiction writer and founder of the Church of Scientology Layfette Ronald (L. Ron) Hubbard publishes *Dianetics: The Modern Science of Mental Health*. The book becomes a best-seller and establishes the Scientology movement.   **LIT**

c. 1950   Color field painting is developed in the late 1940s and early 1950s by such artists as Barnett Newman, Mark Rothko, and Helen Frankenthaler. The paintings make use of large areas of single colors. The movement is sometimes considered a variety of abstract expressionism, sometimes a separate entity. It is related to post-painterly abstraction. *See* 1960s, PAINT.   **PAINT**

1950   Austrian painter Oskar Kokoschka paints the *Prometheus* ceiling for Count Seilern's house, Princes Gate, London.   **PAINT**

1950   American painter Jackson Pollock paints *Autumn Rhythm* and *One*.   **PAINT**

1950   American painter Mark Rothko paints *No. 10*.   **PAINT**

1950–1958   Spanish painter Joan Miró designs *Mur du Soleil* and *Mur de la Lune*, ceramic murals for the UNESCO building, New York City. The works are examples of his experimentation in forms that continued for the rest of his life.   **PAINT**

1950   American painter Franz Kline, known for his idiosyncratic expressive form of abstract expressionism, has his first one-man show in New York City.   **PAINT**

1950–1970   American photojournalist W. Eugene Smith is active, creating works of "reasoned passion" such as *Tokomo in Her Bath* (1971), which conveys the sorrow of a mother whose son has died of mercury poisoning.   **PHOTO**

1950–1980   French photographer Robert Doisneau uses wit to capture incidences of human pleasure and shortcoming, in such photos as *The Kiss* and *Side Glance* (1953).   **PHOTO**

1950   American photographer Paul Strand, who combines in his work humanism and principles of modern art, publishes the collection *Time in New England*. His later collections will include *Un Paese* (1955) and *Living Egypt* (1969).   **PHOTO**

1950–1951   The highest-rated TV program of the season is "Texaco Star Theater" (NBC). Other top-rated programs are "Your Show of Shows" (NBC) and "The Lone Ranger" (ABC).   **TV&R**

1951   The National Ballet of Canada is founded in Toronto by Celia Franca.   **DANCE**

1951   *The Autumn Garden*, a drama by American playwright Lillian Hellman, premieres. It will be followed by her stage adaptation of Voltaire's *Candide* (1956) and her play *Toys in the Attic* (1960).   **DRAMA**

1951   *Requiem for a Nun*, the only play by American novelist William Faulkner, is published. It is a sequel to his novel *Sanctuary*.   **DRAMA**

1951   Notable films include John Huston's *The African Queen*, Vincente Minnelli's *An American in Paris*, Robert Wise's *The Day the Earth Stood Still*, George Stevens's *A Place in the Sun*, Elia Kazan's *A Streetcar Named Desire*, Mervyn LeRoy's *Quo Vadis?*, Walt Disney Productions' *Alice in Wonderland*, George Sidney's *Show Boat*, and Richard Thorpe's *The Great Caruso*.   **FILM**

1951   British poet W. H. Auden publishes the poetry collection *Nones*, which includes the poem "Their Lonely Betters."   **LIT**

1951   Two years before his death, Welsh poet Dylan Thomas publishes the poem "Do Not Go Gentle Into That Good Night" (revised 1952). His *Collected Poems* will be published in 1953.   **LIT**

1951   Irish playwright and novelist Samuel Beckett, writing in French, publishes *Molloy* and *Malone meurt* (*Malone Dies*), the first two novels of a trilogy that concludes with *L'Innommable* (*The Unnamable*, 1953).   **LIT**

1951   American novelist James Jones publishes *From Here to Eternity*, a best-seller about U.S. Army life in Hawaii before the 1941 attack on Pearl Harbor.   **LIT**

1951   American author J. D. Salinger publishes the novel *The Catcher in the Rye*. Main character Holden Caulfield, who spends much of his energy striving to avoid phonies, will become a prototypical postwar young hero. Salinger's later works will include *Nine Stories* (1953), *Franny and Zooey* (1961), *Raise High the Roof Beam, Carpenters*, and *Seymour: An Introduction* (1963).   **LIT**

1951   American poet Langston Hughes publishes the poem "Harlem," which begins, "What happens to a dream deferred?" In its day it becomes a representative work for African-Americans, and will become one of Hughes's signature works.   **LIT**

1951–1953   Russian-born American writer Isaac Asimov publishes the science-fiction novels known as *The Foundation* trilogy (*Foundation*, *Foundation and Empire*, *Second Foundation*), which originally appeared as individual stories in pulp magazines.   **LIT**

1951   British composer Benjamin Britten's somber opera *Billy Budd* opens in London.   **MUSIC**

1951   Ralph Vaughan Williams's opera *The Pilgrim's Progress* opens in London.   **MUSIC**

1951   American composer John Cage writes *Imaginary Landscape No. 4* for twelve radios, twenty-four musicians, and a conductor. Each performance is unique because as the piece progresses, each radio is tuned to a different station and the volume is changed.   **MUSIC**

1951   American photographer Aaron Siskind creates the photo *New York 2*, an example of the trend toward abstraction in post–World War II photography.   **PHOTO**

1951–1952   The highest-rated TV program of the season is "Arthur Godfrey's Talent Scouts" (CBS). Other top-rated programs are "I Love Lucy" (CBS) and "Your Show of Shows" (NBC).   **TV&R**

1952   Finnish-American architect Eero Saarinen designs the General Motors Technical Center in Warren, Michigan. It is to be one of his many influential designs in the United States; another will be Dulles International Airport in Virginia.   **ARCH**

1952   The ballet Folklórico de México is founded in Mexico City by Amalia Hernández of the National Institute of Fine Arts. Originally conceived to create works for television, it will evolve into Mexico's national company.   **DANCE**

1952   American dancer and actor Gene Kelly establishes himself as a foremost dancer and choreographer with his starring role in the Stanley Donen film *Singin' in the Rain*. His supple, athletic approach contrasts with the cool, light style of Fred Astaire. Kelly's dance with umbrella in hand on a rain-drenched street will become a landmark film sequence.   **DANCE**

1952   *The Mousetrap* by Agatha Christie begins its run on the British stage. The longest-running play in theater history, performances continue without interruption to the present day.   **DRAMA**

1952   Circle-in-the-Square, a theater which will present acclaimed productions of work by Tennessee Williams, Eugene O'Neill, Dylan Thomas, and many others, opens in New York City on Feb. 2.   **DRAMA**

1952   The Cinerama widescreen process, developed by Fred Waller, is unveiled in the feature-length travelogue *This Is Cinerama*, narrated by Lowell Thomas and memorable for its realistic roller-coaster sequence.   **FILM**

1952   Notable films include Gene Kelly and Stanley Donen's *Singin' in the Rain*, Fred Zinnemann's *High Noon*, John Ford's *The Quiet Man*, Cecil B. De Mille's *The Greatest Show on Earth*, John Huston's *Moulin Rouge*, Charles Vidor's *Hans Christian Andersen*, and Charlie Chaplin's *Limelight*.   **FILM**

1952   Notable foreign films include Vittorio De Sica's *Umberto D.*   **FILM**

1952   American novelist John Steinbeck publishes the family saga and study of brotherly conflict, *East of Eden*.   **LIT**

1952   American novelist Ralph Ellison publishes *Invisible Man*, an archetypal view of the African-American experience. It will win the National Book Award.   **LIT**

1952   American novelist Bernard Malamud publishes the baseball novel *The Natural*, about the gifted but doomed player Roy Hobbes.   **LIT**

1952   American writer Ernest Hemingway publishes his short novel, *The Old Man and the Sea*, about the struggle of a Cuban fisherman to snare a marlin.   **LIT**

1952   American essayist E. B. White publishes *Charlotte's Web*, the story of a talented spider named Charlotte and a pig named Wilbur. It will become a classic children's novel.   **LIT**

1952   American poet Frank O'Hara publishes his first collection, *A City Winter*. Among his later collections will be *Oranges* (1953), *Meditations in an Emergency* (1957), and *Lunch Poems* (1964).   **LIT**

1952   German composer Hans Werner Henze's first opera *Boulevard Solitude* opens in Hanover.   **MUSIC**

1952   Welsh poet Dylan Thomas writes the radio play *Under Milk Wood*.   **TV&R**

1952   Hand-held transistor radios are first marketed in the United States by the Japanese company Sony.   **TV&R**

1952–1953   The highest-rated TV program of the season is "I Love Lucy" (CBS). Other top-rated programs include "Arthur Godfrey's Talent Scouts" (CBS) and "Dragnet" (NBC).   **TV&R**

1953   French playwright Jean Anouilh's *L'Alouette* (*The Lark*), a historical play about Joan of Arc, is produced. Anouilh's *Becket, ou l'Honneur de Dieu*, an historical play about Thomas à Becket, is produced. **DRAMA**

1953   Irish playwright and novelist Samuel Beckett's play *En Attendant Godot* (*Waiting for Godot*) is produced. It will be very popular in France and abroad, and it will be regarded by many as Beckett's greatest work. **DRAMA**

1953   *The Crucible*, a drama by American playwright Arthur Miller, premieres. The story of the witchcraft trials in seventeenth century Salem, Massachusetts, it is Miller's response to the witch-hunts of Senator Joseph McCarthy and the House Un-American Activities Committee. **DRAMA**

1953   Films of the year include Fred Zinnemann's *From Here to Eternity*, George Stevens's *Shane*, William Wyler's *Roman Holiday*, Billy Wilder's *Stalag 17*, Walt Disney Productions' *Peter Pan*, Byron Haskin's *War of the Worlds*, and John Ford's *Mogambo*. **FILM**

1953   Henry Koster's biblical epic *The Robe*, released by 20th Century-Fox and starring Richard Burton and Jean Simmons, is the first movie filmed in the widescreen process CinemaScope. **FILM**

1953   Arch Oboler's *Bwana Devil* is the first 3-D, or three-dimensional, film to be shown commercially. The 3-D effect requires the audience to wear special glasses. **FILM**

1953   Notable foreign films include Federico Fellini's *I Vitelloni*, considered by some his masterpiece. **FILM**

1953   African-American novelist and essayist James Baldwin publishes the novel *Go Tell It on the Mountain*, based in part on his life experiences in Harlem. **LIT**

1953   American poet Theodore Roethke publishes *The Waking: Poems 1933–1953*, which will win the Pulitzer Prize. Other collections include *Words for the Wind* (1959) and *The Far Field* (1964). **LIT**

1953   English science-fiction writer Arthur C. Clarke publishes the novel *Childhood's End*. **LIT**

1953   American abstract expressionist painter Larry Rivers completes *Washington Crossing the Delaware*, inspired by the nineteenth-century Emanuel Leutze painting of the same name. *See* 1851, PAINT. **PAINT**

1953   German sculptor Mathias Golritz establishes an experimental museum in Mexico City called The Echo to display massive geometric steel structures. His compositions will influence artists of the 1960s, who will emphasize the duplicability of their works by leaving the execution to others. **SCULP**

Akira Kurosawa's *Seven Samurai. (The Everett Collection)*

1953–1954   The highest-rated TV program of the season is "I Love Lucy." Other top-rated programs are "You Bet Your Life" (NBC) and "The Milton Berle Show" (NBC).   **TV&R**

1954   American dancer Robert Joffrey founds the Joffrey Ballet in New York. It will feature works by American choreographers Twyla Tharp and Alvin Ailey, among others.   **DANCE**

1954   French ballet impresario Maurice Béjart becomes director of the Ballets de l'Étoile.   **DANCE**

1954   American playwright Thornton Wilder's *The Matchmaker*, a rewrite of his earlier work *The Merchant of Yonkers*, premieres. It will be the basis for the highly successful musical *Hello, Dolly!* See 1964, DRAMA.   **DRAMA**

1954   Notable films include Elia Kazan's *On the Waterfront*, Alfred Hitchcock's *Rear Window*, Edward Dmytryk's *The Caine Mutiny*, Michael Curtiz's *White Christmas*, Richard Fleischer's *20,000 Leagues Under the Sea*, Anthony Mann's *The Glenn Miller Story*, George Cukor's *A Star Is Born*, George Seaton's *The Country Girl*, William A. Wellman's *The High and the Mighty*, and Jean Negulesco's *Three Coins in the Fountain*.   **FILM**

1954	Notable foreign films include Akira Kurosawa's *The Seven Samurai*, Federico Fellini's *La Strada*, and Henri-Georges Clouzot's *Diabolique*. **FILM**
1954–1955	British novelist J. R. R. Tolkien publishes the fantasy trilogy *The Lord of the Rings*, consisting of the novels *The Fellowship of the Rings, The Two Towers*, and *The Return of the King*. **LIT**
1954	British poet Cecil Day-Lewis publishes his *Collected Poems*. He began publishing poetry in the 1920s, when he was a member of the left-wing group of poets centering on W. H. Auden. **LIT**
1954	American novelist and short-story writer Eudora Welty publishes *The Ponder Heart*, a short novel. Other works include *The Robber Bridegroom* (1942) and several story collections, including *Delta Wedding* (1946). **LIT**
1954	Already a published poet, British novelist Kingsley Amis publishes the comic work *Lucky Jim*, his first novel. Later works will include *That Uncertain Feeling* (1955) and *Jake's Thing* (1978). He will win the Booker Prize for the novel *The Old Devils* (1986). His son Martin Amis will also write. *See* 1986, LIT. **LIT**
1954	British composer Benjamin Britten's eerie opera *The Turn of the Screw* opens in Venice. **MUSIC**
1954	Italian-born composer Gian Carlo Menotti's opera *The Saint of Bleecker Street* opens in New York. It wins the Pulitzer Prize in 1955. **MUSIC**
1954	Austrian-born composer Arnold Schoenberg's unfinished opera *Moses and Aron* opens posthumously in Hamburg. **MUSIC**
1954	The Newport Jazz Festival in Newport, Rhode Island, is held for the first time. The annual event will feature some of the most important jazz musicians in the business. **MUSIC**
1954	Tennessee-born singer Elvis Aaron Presley records his first commercially successful record, "That's All Right, Mama" and "Blue Moon of Kentucky." A subsequent contract with RCA, several gold records ("Hound Dog," "Don't Be Cruel," among others), a history-making appearance on "The Ed Sullivan Show," and a film career beginning with *Love Me Tender* will make him the most influential rock musician of the decade. **MUSIC**
1954	British painter Francis Bacon reworks Velázquez's portrait of Pope Leo X in *Head Surrounded by Sides of Beef*. **PAINT**
1954	British painter Graham Sutherland completes his *Portrait of Churchill*, which was disliked by the former British prime minister and eventually destroyed by his family. **PAINT**
1954	RCA markets the first color television set. **TV&R**

1954–1955　　The highest-rated TV program of the season is "I Love Lucy" (CBS). Other top-rated programs include "The Jackie Gleason Show" (CBS) and "The Toast of the Town" (CBS). **TV&R**

1954　　Televisions are found in 29 million American homes. **TV&R**

1954　　In an early example of the power of TV to affect national events, American journalist Edward R. Murrow mounts an influential attack on Communist-hunting Wisconsin Senator Joseph McCarthy on the program "See It Now." **TV&R**

1955　　Architect Frederick Gibberd designs the London Airport. **ARCH**

1955　　*Bus Stop*, a drama by the American playwright Willian Inge, is produced. His other works include *Picnic* in 1953 and *The Dark at the Top of the Stairs*, produced in 1957. **DRAMA**

1955　　*A View from the Bridge* and *A Memory of Two Mondays*, one-act plays by American playwright Arthur Miller, premiere. (*A View from the Bridge* will be expanded to three acts in 1956). This year Miller also marries actress Marilyn Monroe. *After the Fall*, a Miller drama which will open in 1964, will be seen by many as a depiction of the playwright's relationship with Monroe. **DRAMA**

1955　　*Cat on a Hot Tin Roof*, a drama by American playwright Tennessee Williams, premieres. Set on a Mississippi Delta plantation, it tells of the conflicts within a family following the father's diagnosis with cancer. A highly bowdlerized version of *Cat* will be made into a popular 1958 film starring Elizabeth Taylor, Paul Newman, and Burl Ives. **DRAMA**

1955　　Notable films include Delbert Mann's *Marty*, Alfred Hitchcock's *To Catch a Thief*, Joshua Logan's *Picnic*, John Ford and Mervyn LeRoy's *Mister Roberts*, Walt Disney Productions' *Lady and the Tramp*, Fred Zinnemann's *Oklahoma!*, and Henry King's *Love Is a Many Splendored Thing*. **FILM**

1955　　Notable foreign films include Ingmar Bergman's *Smiles of a Summer Night*, Jules Dassin's *Rififi*, and Laurence Olivier's *Richard III*. **FILM**

1955　　On Sept. 30 twenty-four-year-old American actor James Dean (*b.* Feb. 8, 1931) dies in a car crash after rocketing to stardom earlier this year with his intense performances in Nicholas Ray's *Rebel Without a Cause* and Elia Kazan's *East of Eden*. His third and last starring film, George Stevens's *Giant*, will be released next year. His status as a pop icon of troubled youth will only grow after his death. **FILM**

1955　　British poet Philip Larkin publishes the collection *The Less Deceived*. **LIT**

1955   American essayist and novelist Anne Morrow Lindbergh, wife of
                aviator Charles Lindbergh, publishes the memoiristic *Gift From the
                Sea*. For decades the philosophical book will remain a favorite
                among female readers.   **LIT**

1955–1963   African-American novelist and essayist James Baldwin publishes
                three collections of essays on race and society: *Notes of a Native Son*
                (1955); *Nobody Knows My Name* (1961); and *The Fire Next Time*
                (1963).   **LIT**

1955   Russian-born novelist Vladimir Nabokov publishes *Lolita*, a novel
                about a nymphet named Lolita Haze and a pedophile named
                Humbert Humbert, who falls in love with her. Originally published
                in France, it stirs controversy in the United States, where it will not
                be published until 1958.   **LIT**

1955   American poet Elizabeth Bishop publishes *Poems*, a collection of
                two books of poetry, *North & South* and *A Cold Spring*. She will be
                awarded the Pulitzer Prize in the same year for her work.   **LIT**

1955   British novelist William Golding publishes his novel of sin and
                chaos, *Lord of the Flies*.   **LIT**

1955   British composer Michael Tippett's visionary first opera *The
                Midsummer Marriage* opens in London.   **MUSIC**

c. 1955   In California American artist Richard Diebenkorn and other figura-
                tive expressionists break away from abstract expressionism, apply-
                ing brushwork inspired by the latter movement to studies of
                figures.   **PAINT**

1955   American painter Robert Rauschenberg creates the combine paint-
                ing *Bed*. Like such other works of his as *Canyon* (1959), it incorpo-
                rates collage, assorted objects, and energetic brushwork.   **PAINT**

1955   Spanish painter Salvador Dalí completes *The Lord's Supper*, a late
                example of the religiously oriented works he had been working on
                since the 1940s. Other such works include *The Crucifixion of St.
                John of the Cross* (1951).   **PAINT**

1955   Spanish painter Pablo Picasso's works are exhibited widely in
                Europe, notably in Munich, Hamburg, and Paris.   **PAINT**

1955   The humanistic international photography exhibit The Family of
                Man begins its run at the Museum of Modern Art, New York.
                Organized by photography department director Edward Steichen, it
                will become one of the most popular exhibitions of its day.   **PHOTO**

1955   Japanese-American sculptor Isamu Noguchi erects his Fountain of Peace for the UNESCO House in Paris. He will explore the Japanese tradition of garden-making and lay the foundation for the land art movement in the United States during the 1970s. The Isamu Noguchi Garden Museum will open in 1985 in Long Island City, New York.   **SCULP**

1955–1956   The highest-rated TV program of the season is "The $64,000 Question" (CBS). Other top-rated programs are "I Love Lucy" (CBS) and "The Ed Sullivan Show" (CBS).   **TV&R**

1955–1956   The thirty-nine half-hour episodes of the TV comedy "The Honeymooners" air on CBS. Starring comedians Jackie Gleason, Art Carney, Audrey Meadows, and Joyce Randolph as the protoptypical Brooklyn couples the Kramdens and Nortons, the series will gain a reputation as one of the most inspired comedies in TV history. It will gain cult status as new generations come to know it through reruns.   **TV&R**

1956–1958   German-born architect Ludwig Mies van der Rohe and American architect Philip Johnson design the Seagram Building in New York City, a classic work of the international style.   **ARCH**

1956   British playwright John Osborne's *Look Back in Anger* premieres in London. A forceful look at British working-class life, the play will be seen as a landmark work, the first of many "kitchen sink" dramas. Osborne's play *The Entertainer* will be produced in 1957, and his *Inadmissible Evidence* will premiere in 1964.   **DRAMA**

1956   *My Fair Lady*, an American musical based on George Bernard Shaw's *Pygmalion*, opens on Broadway. With a score by Alan Jay Lerner and Frederick Loewe, this show, directed by Moss Hart and starring Rex Harrison and Julie Andrews, will be enormously popular. *See also* 1914, DRAMA.   **DRAMA**

1956   *Long Day's Journey into Night*, a realistic, autobiographical drama written by American playwright Eugene O'Neill in 1941, is produced for the first time in New York. Winning O'Neill a Pulitzer posthumously, *Long Day's Journey* will be the playwright's most popular and, in the minds of many, best work.   **DRAMA**

1956   Notable American films include Cecil B. De Mille's *The Ten Commandments*, Michael Anderson's *Around the World in 80 Days*, Walter Lang's *The King and I*, George Stevens's *Giant*, Joshua Logan's *Bus Stop*, Henry King's *Carousel*, William Wyler's *Friendly Persuasion*, Robert Wise's *Somebody Up There Likes Me*, and Charles Walters's *High Society*.   **FILM**

1956   Notable foreign films include Jean Renoir's *Paris Does Strange Things*, Alain Resnais's *Night and Fog*, and Ingmar Bergman's *The Seventh Seal*.   **FILM**

1956   American novelist Grace Metalious publishes *Peyton Place*, a critical melodrama of small-town life.   **LIT**

1956   American Beat poet Allen Ginsberg publishes the epic, personal poem "Howl." In the late 1950s in the United States, the poem was deemed obscene, but charges were eventually dropped.   **LIT**

1956   American novelist Saul Bellow publishes *Seize the Day*, a collection of three short stories, a play, and a short novel.   **LIT**

1956   American poet Richard Wilbur publishes his third collection of poems, *Things of This World*, which will win the Pulitzer Prize and National Book Award. Other collections include *Ceremony* (1950) and *The Beautiful Changes* (1947).   **LIT**

1956   British painter Richard Hamilton paints the collage *Just What Is It That Makes Today's Home So Different, So Appealing?*, which anticipates the popular culture concerns of pop art. *See* 1960s, PAINT.   **PAINT**

1956   American painter Ellsworth Kelly creates *Atlantic*, an example of hard edge painting, which emphasizes sharp edges around color areas.   **PAINT**

1956–1957   The highest-rated TV program of the season is "I Love Lucy" (CBS). Other top-rated programs are "The Ed Sullivan Show" (CBS) and "The Jack Benny Show" (CBS).   **TV&R**

1957   Russian composer Igor Stravinsky's ballet *Agon*, a prominent example of his final period of twelve-tone serial music, opens in Paris.**DANCE**

•••

"I have learned that nothing matters but the final picture."
—American film producer David O. Selznick, 1957

•••

1957   Irish playwright Samuel Beckett's play *Fin de partie* (*Endgame*) is produced in London. Beckett's monologue *Krapp's Last Tape* will be produced in 1958.   **DRAMA**

1957   *Le Balcon* (*The Balcony*), a drama by French writer Jean Genet, is produced in London. Set in an elite brothel during a revolution, it is both ritualistic and realistic.   **DRAMA**

1957   The dramatic musical *West Side Story* opens on Broadway. Inspired by Shakespeare's *Romeo and Juliet*, it is choreographed by Jerome Robbins, with music by Leonard Bernstein and lyrics by Stephen Sondheim. The musical, which explores cultural hatreds through the conflicts between young Puerto Ricans and more established immigrants in New York City, heralds a turn toward musicals with darker themes.   **DRAMA**

THE WEST SIDE OF WEST SIDE STORY

*I*n 1949 producer Jerome Robbins conceived the idea for a Broadway musical based on Romeo and Juliet. *According to composer Leonard Bernstein, the musical would tell "a tragic story in musical-comedy terms, using only musical-comedy techniques," and would be set amid the current conflicts of the day. In the 1949 plans for the play, that meant the differences between Catholics and Jews.*

But by 1955 one of the major conflicts of the day had become the gang wars between newly immigrated Puerto Ricans and established ethnic groups on New York's near West Side. "[W]e . . . have come up with what I think is going to be it," wrote Bernstein, "two teen-age gangs, one the war-ring Puerto Ricans, the other self-styled 'Americans.' Suddenly it all springs to life. I hear rhythms and pulses, and—most of all—I can sort of feel the form." Romeo and Juliet *was becoming* West Side Story.

West Side Story *made its Broadway debut on September 26, 1957. It won two Tony awards and was hailed for its groundbreaking integration of music, dance, and social commentary.*

More than thirty-five years after its debut, West Side Story *remains fresh in part because the conflicts that spurred its plot still fuel urban life. However, the West Side that gave title to the play has disappeared. In 1962 the depressed New York neighborhood was cleared to make room for the glittering theater complex known as Lincoln Center. The razing of the buildings that made way for Lincoln Center erased the West Side of* West Side Story.

1957	Notable American films include Frank Borzage's *A Farewell to Arms*, Stanley Donen's *Funny Face*, Sidney Lumet's *12 Angry Men*, Billy Wilder's *Witness for the Prosecution*, Joshua Logan's *Sayonara*, Robert Stevenson's *Old Yeller*, Rouben Mamoulian's *Silk Stockings*, Nunnally Johnson's *The Three Faces of Eve*, and Mark Robson's *Peyton Place*. **FILM**
1957	Notable foreign films include David Lean's *Bridge on the River Kwai* and Charlie Chaplin's *A King in New York*. **FILM**
1957	American Beat writer Jack Kerouac publishes *On the Road*, a novel with commentary about a trip across the United States. The book becomes known as a signature work of the Beat Generation. **LIT**
1957	American writer James Agee publishes the novel *A Death in the Family*, based on his father's death. It will win a Pulitzer Prize. **LIT**
1957	Russian-born novelist Vladimir Nabokov publishes the novel *Pnin*. **LIT**

1957	American writer Mary McCarthy publishes a memoir of her difficult childhood, *Memories of a Catholic Girlhood*. **LIT**
1957	American novelist and short-story writer John Cheever publishes the novel *The Wapshot Chronicle*. **LIT**
1957	British poet Ted (Edward James) Hughes publishes his first collection, *The Hawk in the Rain*, to great success. Later volumes will include *Crow* (1970) and *Selected Poems: 1957–1967* (1972). The husband of American poet Sylvia Plath, he will edit her *Selected Poems* (1985). **LIT**
1957	Russian novelist Boris Pasternak publishes the novel *Doctor Zhivago*. He will decline the Nobel Prize for it in 1958. **LIT**
1957–1958	French tapestry artist and sculptor Henri-Georges Adam completes the monument *Beacon of the Dead*, for display at the Nazi World War II death camp Auschwitz. **SCULP**
1957–1958	The highest-rated TV program of the season is "Gunsmoke" (CBS). Other top-rated programs are "Have Gun Will Travel" (CBS) and "General Electric Theater" (CBS). **TV&R**
1957	Stereo (or stereophonic) records, which allow for the projection of sound from two sources, become popular in the United States and Europe. **TV&R**
1957	American radio personality Dick Clark moves his pop music and dance program "American Bandstand" to television, where it will become an influential pop music forum. **TV&R**
1958	The cha-cha, a Latin-inspired dance, becomes popular in the United States and Europe. **DANCE**
1958	American dancer Alvin Ailey founds the Alvin Ailey American Dance Theatre. Among its best-known works will be the American spirituals-inspired "Revelations," which premieres in 1960. Among its most celebrated dancers will be Judith Jamison, who will become director of the troupe following Ailey's death in 1989. **DANCE**
1958	German playwright Bertolt Brecht's *Der Aufhaltsame Aufstieg des Arturo Ui* (*The Resistible Rise of Arturo Ui*) is produced. Brecht's *Die Heilige Johanna der Schlachthöfe* (*St. Joan of the Stockyards*), which transposes the legend of Joan of Arc to twentieth century Chicago, will be staged in 1959. **DRAMA**
1958	*The Birthday Party*, the first full-length play by British playwright Harold Pinter, premieres in London. **DRAMA**
1958	*Suddenly Last Summer*, a drama by American playwright Tennessee Williams, opens. It will be made into a popular 1959 movie starring Katharine Hepburn, Elizabeth Taylor, and Montgomery Clift. **DRAMA**

1958 Notable American films include Alfred Hitchcock's *Vertigo*, Stanley Kramer's *The Defiant Ones*, Joshua Logan's *South Pacific*, Morton Da Costa's *Auntie Mame*, Richard Brooks's *Cat on a Hot Tin Roof*, Vincente Minnelli's *Gigi*, George Abbott and Stanley Donen's *Damn Yankees*, John Sturges's *The Old Man and the Sea*, and Mervyn LeRoy's *No Time for Sergeants*. **FILM**

1958 Notable foreign films include Jacques Tati's *Mon Oncle*, and Andrej Wajda's *Ashes and Diamonds*. **FILM**

1958 British novelist T. H. White concludes the tetralogy *The Once and Future King*, consisting of four novels based on Arthurian legend, beginning with *The Sword in the Stone* (1939). **LIT**

1958–1972 American science-fiction novelist Ursula K. Le Guin publishes her *Earthsea* trilogy, about the Wizard Ged on the islands of Earthsea. **LIT**

1958 American poet Ezra Pound is released from a U.S. federal insane asylum after being placed there instead of facing trial for treason during World War II. **LIT**

1958 Nigerian writer Chinua Achebe publishes his novel of colonial rule, *Things Fall Apart*. Among his later works are the story collection *Girls at War* (1972) and the novel *Arrow of God* (1964). **LIT**

1958 The Tchaikovsky piano competition in Moscow is won by American Van Cliburn. **MUSIC**

1958 American composer Samuel Barber's opera *Vanessa*, with a libretto by Italian-born composer Gian Carlo Menotti, wins the Pulitzer Prize. **MUSIC**

1958–1969 American composer Leonard Bernstein serves as musical director of the New York Philharmonic Orchestra, helping it achieve increased prestige and boosting concert attendance. **MUSIC**

1958 In New York American artist Jasper Johns has his first one-man show. Among his best-known works will be the series *Targets*, *Flags*, and *Numbers*, heavily textured encaustic paintings of everyday two-dimensional objects. **PAINT**

1958–1959 American New York school painter Mark Rothko completes his *Black on Maroon* and *Red on Maroon* paintings, a group of nine creations considered among his masterworks. The works were originally created for a New York City restaurant. **PAINT**

1958 American photographer Minor White takes the photograph *Ritual Branch*, an example of the influence of abstract expressionism on his work. **PHOTO**

1958–1959 The highest-rated TV program of the season is "Gunsmoke" (CBS). Other top-rated programs are "Wagon Train" (NBC) and "I've Got a Secret" (CBS). **TV&R**

1959–1970   Russian ballerina Natalia Makarova dances with the Kirov Ballet, be-
             coming known as one of the most inspired interpreters of dance in
             the twentieth century. Among her roles are Giselle in *Giselle* and
             Odette/Odile in *Swan Lake*.   **DANCE**

1959   *Tueur sans gages* (*The Killer*), a full-length drama by French ab-
             surdist playwright Eugène Ionesco, is produced. Elie Berenger, the
             play's central character, will reappear in Ionesco's *Rhinocéros* (pro-
             duced in 1960) and *Le Roi se meurt* (*Exit the King*, 1962).   **DRAMA**

1959   *Les Nègres* (*The Blacks*), a play by French writer Jean Genet, opens.
             It will have a long off-Broadway run in 1961.   **DRAMA**

1959   *The Zoo Story*, a one-act drama that is the first play by American
             playwright Edward Albee, premieres in Berlin. Albee's *The Death of
             Bessie Smith* and *The American Dream*, both one-act plays, will pre-
             miere in 1960 and 1961, respectively.   **DRAMA**

1959   *A Raisin in the Sun*, a drama by African-American playwright
             Lorraine Hansberry, is produced. It is the first play written by a
             black woman to be staged on Broadway, and it will enjoy great criti-
             cal and commercial success.   **DRAMA**

1959   *Sweet Bird of Youth*, a drama by American playwright Tennessee
             Williams, premieres. *The Night of the Iguana* will open in 1961. **DRAMA**

1959   The American musical *Gypsy*—starring Ethel Merman, with book by
             Arthur Laurente, lyrics by Stephen Sondheim and music by Jule
             Styne—premieres on May 21. It will be revived on Broadway in the
             1990s, with Tyne Daly in the starring role.   **DRAMA**

1959   Notable American films include William Wyler's *Ben-Hur*, Otto
             Preminger's *Anatomy of a Murder* and *Porgy and Bess*, Alfred
             Hitchcock's *North by Northwest*, Billy Wilder's *Some Like It Hot*,
             George Stevens's *The Diary of Anne Frank*, Fred Zinnemann's *The
             Nun's Story*, Michael Gordon's *Pillow Talk*, and Howard Hawks's *Rio
             Bravo*.   **FILM**

1959   Notable foreign films include Federico Fellini's *La Dolce Vita*, Carol
             Reed's *Our Man in Havana*, and Alain Resnais's *Hiroshima, Mon
             Amour*.   **FILM**

1959   American science-fiction writer Walter M. Miller Jr. publishes *A
             Canticle for Liebowitz*, concerning the monastic preservation of civi-
             lization after a nuclear holocaust.   **LIT**

1959   American short-story writer Grace Paley publishes her first collec-
             tion *The Little Disturbances of Man*. Her later collections will include
             Enormous Changes at the Last Minute (1974) and *Later the Same Day*
             (1985).   **LIT**

1959   American novelist William Burroughs publishes the darkly outra-
             geous novel *Naked Lunch*.   **LIT**

A WRITER GROWS IN BROOKLYN

W hile many American writers have aspired to making their name in the bright lights of Manhattan, a large number have plied their craft just over the river in the unheralded borough of Brooklyn.

For some, like Neil Simon or Alfred Kazin, Brooklyn was a birthplace and a source of memory. For others, like Truman Capote, it was a destination. As he put it in his essay, "A House on the Heights" (1959), "I live in Brooklyn. By choice."

Among those who have passed through Brooklyn long enough to immortalize the borough in their works and be counted as native sons or daughters are:

Truman Capote—lived for part of his adulthood in Brooklyn Heights. Reimagined Brooklyn in the essays "Brooklyn" (1946) and "A House on the Heights" (1959).

Alfred Kazin—born and raised in Brownsville, Brooklyn. Recalled in memoir A Walker in the City (1951).

Marianne Moore—lived for part of her later adult life in Brooklyn. Immortalized Brooklyn Bridge in poem "Granite and Steel" (1966).

Neil Simon—born and raised in Brooklyn. Remembered Brooklyn in autobiographical play Brighton Beach Memoirs (1983).

Walt Whitman—attended grade school in Brooklyn, edited the Brooklyn Times and Brooklyn Daily Eagle, had his self-published Leaves of Grass printed there in 1855. Remembered Brooklyn in "Crossing Brooklyn Ferry" (1856).

Thomas Wolfe—lived there for three years writing the novel October Fair, parts of which were incorporated into Of Time and the River (1935). Recalled South Brooklyn in short story "Only the Dead Know Brooklyn."

1959	German novelist Günter Grass publishes *The Tin Drum*, about the rise of Nazism in the town of Danzig. It will become part of the Danzig Trilogy, the other novels of which are *Cat and Mouse* (1963) and *Dog Years* (1965). **LIT**
1959	American photographer and filmmaker Robert Frank publishes the controversial book of photographs *The Americans*, which provides pointed, ironic commentary on the emptiness of modern American existence. **PHOTO**
1959–1960	The highest-rated TV program of the season is "Gunsmoke" (CBS). Other top-rated programs are "Father Knows Best" (CBS) and "Perry Mason" (CBS). **TV&R**
1960s	The Stuttart Ballet, the first important German ballet troupe, is founded. **DANCE**

1960s   Popular songs of the decade include "The Twist," "Where the Boys Are," "Moon River," "(Theme from) Exodus," "Days of Wine and Roses," "Blowin' in the Wind," "Those Lazy, Hazy, Crazy Days of Summer," "I Want to Hold Your Hand," "Like a Rolling Stone," "Hello, Dolly!," "Satisfaction," "Baby Love," "My Girl," "King of the Road," "Downtown," "A Hard Day's Night," "Eleanor Rigby," "Born Free," "Ballad of the Green Berets," "Hey Jude," "Mrs. Robinson," "Aquarius/Let the Sun Shine," and "A Boy Named Sue."   **MUSIC**

1960s   Pop art, influenced by popular culture and commercial art, comes into fashion. The movement is linked most memorably with American artist Andy Warhol, whose works include repeated rows of images of such products and celebrities as Campbell's Soup, Coca-Cola bottles, Marilyn Monroe, and Elvis Presley, achieved through silkscreen printing.   **PAINT**

1960s   Post-painterly abstraction, a movement that rejects the textured surfaces of abstract expressionism for large areas of unmodulated color, is practiced by artists such as Helen Frankenthaler, Morris Louis, Kenneth Noland, Frank Stella, and Ellsworth Kelly.   **PAINT**

1960s   American pop artist Tom Wesselmann paints the series *The Great American Nude*.   **PAINT**

1960s   After having his works exhibited in the Family of Man exhibit at the Museum of Modern Art in 1955, American photographer Garry Winogrand becomes known for his lively "street" photography.   **PHOTO**

1960s   American artist George Segal creates life-sized white plaster figures cast from life to be placed among everyday elements of the real environment.   **SCULP**

1960s   American artist Dan Flavin appropriates the fluorescent light tube as his sculptural medium for pieces he calls "Icons."   **SCULP**

1960s   Swedish-born American artist Claes Oldenburg reflects the pop art agenda by looking to popular urban culture for sources and material for a series of soft sculptures of commonplace, vastly enlarged objects.   **SCULP**

1960s   Conceptual art, an artistic approach in which the idea behind the work, rather than its aesthetically pleasing execution, is of greatest value. Often everyday objects are presented in these artworks, as in American artist Joseph Kosuth's *One and Three Chairs*.   **SCULP**

1960   Swiss architect Le Corbusier designs the Monastery La Tourette at Eveux, near Lyons, France.   **ARCH**

1960   Philadelphia-born singer Chubby Checker spurs a dance craze with his recording of the Hank Ballard song "The Twist." The song reaches number 1 on pop music charts in 1960 and 1961, and spurs the development of dance halls known as discotheques.   **DANCE**

Dollar Signs, by Andy Warhol. (© *1992* by the *Andy Warhol Foundation*)

1960   British playwright Harold Pinter's drama *The Caretaker* is produced. Pinter's *The Homecoming* will be produced in 1965.   **DRAMA**

1960   *Oh Dad, Poor Dad, Mamma's Hung You in the Closet and I'm Feelin' So Sad*, a black comedy by American playwright Arthur Kopit, is produced.   **DRAMA**

1960   The musical *The Fantasticks* by Tom Jones and Harvey Schmidt premieres in New York in May. It will continue its uninterrupted run thirty-five years on.   **DRAMA**

1960   Notable American films include Billy Wilder's *The Apartment*, Stanley Kubrick's *Spartacus*, Alfred Hitchcock's *Psycho*, John Sturges's *The Magnificent Seven* (a western remake of Akira Kurosawa's *The Seven Samurai*, Japan, 1954), Otto Preminger's *Exodus*, John Wayne's *The Alamo*, Daniel Mann's *Butterfield 8*, and Richard Brooks's *Elmer Gantry*.   **FILM**

1960   Notable foreign films include Luchino Visconti's *Rocco and His Brothers*, Karel Reisz's *Saturday Night and Sunday Morning*, and Jules Dassin's *Never on Sunday*.   **FILM**

1960   American novelist John Barth publishes *The Sot-Weed Factor*, a novel based on the life of satirist Ebenezer Cook, author of the 1708 work *The Sot-Weed Factor; or A Voyage to Maryland*. The book will be revised in 1966.   **LIT**

1960   American writer John Updike publishes the novel *Rabbit, Run*, the first of several novels about suburbanite Harry Angstrom. Later *Rabbit* novels will include *Rabbit Redux* (1971), *Rabbit is Rich* (1981), and *Rabbit at Rest* (1990).   **LIT**

1960   American novelist Harper Lee publishes *To Kill a Mockingbird*, a haunting tale of childhood and racial injustice. Her first novel will win the Pulitzer Prize.   **LIT**

1960   American composer Elliott Carter's String Quartet no. 2 wins the Pulitzer Prize.   **MUSIC**

1960   Leading postwar Dutch abstract artist Karel Appel, known for the strong expressiveness of his work, wins the Guggenheim Award for abstract painting for his work, *Woman With Ostrich*.   **PAINT**

1960–1961   The highest-rated TV program of the season is "Gunsmoke" (CBS). Other top-rated programs are "The Andy Griffith Show" (CBS) and "The Untouchables" (ABC).   **TV&R**

1960   Approximately 100 million television sets are in homes in the United States and Europe, with 85 million of them in the United States.   **TV&R**

1960   Presidential candidates Vice President Richard Nixon and Senator John Kennedy appear in a televised presidential debate. The TV camera favors the youthful-looking Kennedy and harms the perspiring Nixon.   **TV&R**

1961   Irish playwright Samuel Beckett's monologue *Oh! Les Beaux Jours* (*Happy Days*) is produced. Beckett's plays *Comédie* (*Play*) and *Va et Vient* (*Come and Go*) will be produced in 1963 and 1966, respectively.   **DRAMA**

1961   The Shakepeare Memorial Theatre Company becomes the Royal Shakespeare Company. Under the guidance of British director Peter Hall, the company will present a variety of classical and modern plays at Aldwych Theatre in London, while performing mostly Shakespeare at Stratford-Upon-Avon.   **DRAMA**

1961   Cafe La Mama, which will be called La Mama Experimental Theater Club, is founded by Ellen Stewart in New York City. This avant-garde theater group will provide a venue for new and experimental plays.   **DRAMA**

1961   Notable films include Blake Edwards's *Breakfast at Tiffany's*, Robert Wise and Jerome Robbins's *West Side Story*, J. Lee Thompson's *The Guns of Navarone*, Anthony Mann's *El Cid*, Robert Stevenson's *The Absent-Minded Professor*, Stanley Kramer's *Judgment at Nuremburg*, John Ford's *Two Rode Together*, and Delbert Mann's *Lover Come Back*.   **FILM**

1961   John Huston's *The Misfits* is the last film of actors Clark Gable and Marilyn Monroe. Gable died in 1960; Monroe will die on Aug. 5, 1962.   **FILM**

1961   Notable foreign films include François Truffaut's *Jules and Jim*, Alain Resnais's *Last Year at Marienbad*, and Luis Buñuel's *Viridiana*.   **FILM**

1961   American journalist Theodore H. White publishes the Pulitzer Prize–winning *The Making of the President: 1960*, an influential account of the 1960 presidential campaign.   **LIT**

1961   American novelist Walker Percy publishes his first novel, *The Moviegoer*, the story of inveterate moviegoer Binx Bolling, who finds himself on a spiritual and philosophical quest.   **LIT**

1961   Under his birth name LeRoi (LeRoy) Jones, African-American poet and playwright Amiri Baraka publishes his first collection of poetry, *Preface to a Twenty Volume Suicide Note*. Jones will assume the name Amiri Baraka ("blessed prince") in 1967.   **LIT**

1961   American novelist Joseph Heller publishes his satire of World War II, *Catch-22*, the title phrase of which will become part of the American lexicon.   **LIT**

1961   West Indian novelist and essayist V. S. (Vidiadhar Surajprasad) Naipaul publishes the novel *A House for Mr. Biswas*. Among his later novels is *The Mimic Men* (1967). His nonfiction works will include *Among the Believers: An Islamic Journey* (1981) and *Finding the Center: Two Narratives* (1985).   **LIT**

1961   British novelist Iris Murdoch publishes the novel *A Severed Head*. Her later works will include *The Book and the Brotherhood* (1987).   **LIT**

1961   British novelist Muriel Spark publishes the novel *The Prime of Miss Jean Brodie*, about an idiosyncratic teacher and her pupils.   **LIT**

1961   American composer Walter Piston's Symphony no. 7 wins the Pulitzer Prize.   **MUSIC**

1961   American folk singer Bob Dylan (born Robert Zimmerman) makes his first concert appearance at Folk City in Greenwich Village. By the end of the decade, his songs of cultural commentary and disaffection will become anthems of his age.   **MUSIC**

1961   German-born painter Hans Hofmann paints *The Golden Wall*.   **PAINT**

1961   The Museum of the Chinese Revolution opens in Beijing, China.   **PAINT**

1961   British painter Allen Jones establishes himself as a pop artist in the "Young Contemporaries" pop art exhibition in London.   **PAINT**

1961–1962   The highest-rated TV program of the season is "Wagon Train" (NBC). Other top-rated programs are "Bonanza" (NBC) and "Hazel" (NBC).   **TV&R**

1962   British ballerina Margot Fonteyn and Russian dancer Rudolf Nureyev begin their lengthy partnership in London's Royal Ballet.   **DANCE**

1962   The New York Shakepeare Festival, which had been founded in 1954 by American director Joseph Papp, moves to the Delacorte Theater, an open-air facility built for it in New York City's Central Park. The company presents Shakespeare plays, and later it will stage other classical and contemporary works as well. Admission will always be free. The festival continues to operate to the present day.   **DRAMA**

1962   *The Milk Train Doesn't Stop Here Anymore*, a drama by Tennessee Williams, premieres. It will be followed by *In the Bar of a Tokyo Hotel* (1969), *Small Craft Warnings* (1972), *Vieux Carré* (1977), *Clothes for a Summer Hotel* (1980), and several other plays that generally will be seen as minor works.   **DRAMA**

1962   *Who's Afraid of Virginia Woolf?*, the first full-length play by American playwright Edward Albee, premieres in New York City. The tale of an evening of drinking and "games" in the home of a New England college professor, this powerful, popular drama will be seen by many as Albee's best work and a great modern play. It will be filmed in 1966 by director Mike Nichols, with Elizabeth Taylor and Richard Burton playing the leading roles.   **DRAMA**

1962   David Lean's *Lawrence of Arabia*, released by Columbia, introduces Peter O'Toole as British officer T. E. Lawrence and Egyptian actor Omar Sharif as Bedouin leader Sherif Ali. With a screenplay by playwright Robert Bolt, the epic film draws on Lawrence's classic account of his adventures in Arabia, *The Seven Pillars of Wisdom* (1935).   **FILM**

1962 — Notable American films include *How the West Was Won* by John Ford, George Marshall, and Henry Hathaway, and *The Longest Day* by Andrew Marton, Ken Annakin, and Bernhard Wicki. Also released this year are Morton Da Costa's *The Music Man*, Blake Edwards's *The Days of Wine and Roses*, Mervyn LeRoy's *Gypsy*, Robert Mulligan's *To Kill a Mockingbird*, and John Frankenheimer's *The Manchurian Candidate*. **FILM**

1962 — John Ford's *The Man Who Shot Liberty Valance* is the first film to team American stars James Stewart and John Wayne. **FILM**

1962 — Terence Young's *Dr. No* makes a star of Sean Connery as superspy James Bond. The film is the first in a long series of films that will successively star Connery, George Lazenby, Roger Moore, and Timothy Dalton as Bond. **FILM**

1962 — Notable foreign films include Jean-Luc Godard's *My Life to Live* and Vittorio De Sica's *The Condemned of Altona*. **FILM**

1962 — American short-story writer and novelist Katherine Anne Porter publishes the novel *Ship of Fools*. **LIT**

1962 — American novelist Ken Kesey publishes the novel *One Flew Over the Cuckoo's Nest*, about life inside a psychiatric ward. The book, which will become an Academy Award–winning film in 1975, is based on Kesey's earlier experiences and work in an asylum. **LIT**

1962 — Russian-born novelist Vladimir Nabokov publishes *Pale Fire*, a novel consisting of a poem written by professor John Shade and the lengthy commentary of editor Charles Kinbote. **LIT**

1962 — English novelist Doris Lessing publishes the feminist novel about a woman's search for self-definition *The Golden Notebook*. She has also written the short-story collection *The Habit of Loving*. **LIT**

1962 — Russian novelist Aleksandr Solzhenitsyn publishes his first novel, *One Day in the life of Ivan Denisovich*, about a twenty-four-hour span in a Stalinist prison camp. He will win the Nobel Prize for literature in 1970 for his works, which will include *Cancer Ward* (1968) and *The First Circle* (1968). **LIT**

1962 — English novelist and critic Anthony Burgess publishes his futuristic novel of a highly violent society, *A Clockwork Orange*. Among his other works will be the novel *The Long Day Wanes* (1964). **LIT**

1962 — Conductor Leopold Stokowski founds the American Symphony Orchestra in New York City. **MUSIC**

1962 — British composer Michael Tippett's opera *King Priam*, with its sparse and abrasive style, opens. **MUSIC**

1962 — To mark the opening of Britain's Coventry cathedral, British composer Benjamin Britten composes *War Requiem*, which interweaves music with verse by war poets. **MUSIC**

1962   American composer Robert Ward's opera *The Crucible*, produced in New York in 1961, wins the Pulitzer Prize.   **MUSIC**

1962   American folk-singing group Peter, Paul, and Mary (Peter Yarrow, Paul Stookey, and Mary Travers) spark a new generation's interest in folk music through protest songs like "If I Had a Hammer" and, in the next year, "Blowin' in the Wind."   **MUSIC**

1962   Soul music begins to enter into mainstream tastes with performers like Sam Cooke, whose 1962 dance tune "Twistin' the Night Away" and earlier love ballad "Wonderful World" (1960) place him on the charts.   **MUSIC**

1962–1963   The highest-rated TV program of the season is "The Beverly Hillbillies" (CBS). Other top-rated programs are "The Red Skelton Show" (CBS) and "Ben Casey" (ABC).   **TV&R**

1962   American First Lady Jacqueline Kennedy conducts a nationally televised tour of the White House, which receives critical acclaim and high ratings.   **TV&R**

....

"The true writer has nothing to say. What counts is the way he says it."—French novelist Alain Robbe-Grillet, For a New Novel, 1963

....

1963   The musical comedy *A Funny Thing Happened on the Way to the Forum*, with book by Burt Shevelove and Larry Gelbart and music and lyrics by Stephen Sondheim, premieres on Broadway. Starring Zero Mostel as Pseudolus, the musical is based on the work of Roman playwright Plautus (*see* 254 B.C., DRAMA). It will be filmed in 1966.   **DRAMA**

1963   American playwright Neil Simon's *Barefoot in the Park* is produced. It will be followed by *The Odd Couple* (1965), *Plaza Suite* (1968), *The Last of the Red Hot Lovers* (1969), *The Prisoner of Second Avenue* (1971), *Chapter Two* (1977), *Brighton Beach Memoirs* (1983), and *Biloxi Blues* (1984); as well as by Simon books for several musicals, including *Sweet Charity* (1966) and *Promises, Promises* (1968). Nearly all of Simon's plays will be enormous commerical successes.   **DRAMA**

1963   Notable American films include Alfred Hitchcock's *The Birds*, Stanley Kramer's *It's a Mad Mad Mad Mad World*, Billy Wilder's *Irma La Douce*, John Sturges's *The Great Escape*, Martin Ritt's *Hud*, Ralph Nelson's *Lilies of the Field*, Jerry Lewis's *The Nutty Professor*, and George Sidney's *Bye Bye Birdie*.   **FILM**

1963   The most notorious screen couple of the day is American actress Elizabeth Taylor and British actor Richard Burton, who met while filming Joseph L. Mankiewicz's expensive flop *Cleopatra*, released this year. Taylor and Burton divorce their spouses and go on to marry and divorce each other twice, while costarring together in a number of films, including Mike Nichols's *Who's Afraid of Virginia Woolf?* (1966). **FILM**

1963   Notable foreign films include Tony Richardson's *Tom Jones*, Terence Young's *From Russia With Love*, Robert Bresson's *Pickpocket*, Federico Fellini's *8 1/2*, Luchino Visconti's *The Leopard*, Ingmar Bergman's *The Silence*, and Orson Welles's *The Trial*. **FILM**

1963   American director William Asher's *Beach Party* is the first in a series of teen-oriented beach films starring Frankie Avalon and Annette Funicello, with Harvey Lembeck as slow-witted biker Eric Von Zipper. **FILM**

1963   British novelist John le Carré (pen name of David Cornwell) publishes the international best-seller *The Spy Who Came in from the Cold*, marked by his distinct blend of moral analysis and espionage adventure. Le Carré will become known particularly for the shrewd, aging secret agent George Smiley, hero of a series of novels including *Tinker, Tailor, Soldier, Spy* (1974). **LIT**

1963   American writer Mary McCarthy publishes the novel *The Group*, a biting, comic look at the lives of several graduates of a prominent women's college. **LIT**

1963   Japanese novelist Mishima Yukio (born Kimitake Hiraoka) publishes *The Sailor Who Fell from Grace With the Sea*. Among his other works is *Confessions of Mask* (1949). **LIT**

1963   The Beach Boys' pop paeans to the surfing way of life, "Surfin' Safari" and "Surfin' USA," mark the beginning of a rock subgenre called the California sound. Anthems to the automobile like "Little Deuce Coupe" will add to the mystique of the Beach Boys as the most important California troubadours. **MUSIC**

1963   The Liverpool-based rock group the Beatles sweeps England with the rhythm-and-blues-influenced hits "Love Me Do," "Please Please Me," "From Me to You," and "She Loves You." Over the decade the group, consisting of John Lennon, Paul McCartney, George Harrison, and Ringo Starr (Richard Starkey), will become an international cultural force and change the face of twentieth-century popular music. **MUSIC**

1963   American pop artist Roy Lichtenstein paints *Wham!*, one of his many works that blow up comic book images, faithfully reproducing the dots and primary colors. **PAINT**

1963   The Guggenheim Museum in New York City holds an exhibition of pop art, including works by Andy Warhol and Robert Rauschenberg. **PAINT**

1963–1964   The highest-rated TV program of the season is "The Beverly Hillbillies" (CBS). Other top-rated programs are "The Dick Van Dyke Show" (CBS) and "Petticoat Junction" (CBS).   **TV&R**

1963   The four-day television coverage of the assassination and burial of President John F. Kennedy will redefine the medium as a unifying public force.   **TV&R**

1964   A spate of frenetic go-go dances, including the monkey, the watusi, and the frug become popular in U.S. and European discotheques and go-go clubs.   **DANCE**

1964   *Entertaining Mr. Sloane*, the first play by British playwright Joe Orton, is produced. His other black comedies *Loot* and *What the Butler Saw* will be produced in 1966 and 1969, respectively.   **DRAMA**

1964   *Incident at Vichy*, a historical drama by American playwright Arthur Miller, premieres. In 1968 Miller's drama *The Price* will open.   **DRAMA**

1964   American playwright Edward Albee's *Tiny Alice* is produced in New York City. The difficult, dense work puzzles many critics and theatergoers.   **DRAMA**

1964   The American musical *Hello, Dolly!*, starring Carol Channing, with book by Michael Stewart and lyrics and music by Jerry Herman, premieres on Jan. 16. It is based on the Thornton Wilder play *The Matchmaker*.   **DRAMA**

1964   The American musical *Fiddler on the Roof* premieres on Sept. 22. Starring Zero Mostel and Bea Arthur, with book by Joseph Stein, lyrics by Sheldon Harnick and music by Jerry Bock, the play about tradition and change in a Russian Jewish family will be revived often after its initial run.   **DRAMA**

1964   Notable American films include Robert Stevenson's *Mary Poppins*, George Cukor's *My Fair Lady*, Anthony Mann's *The Fall of the Roman Empire*, Edward Dmytryk's *The Carpetbaggers*, Norman Jewison's *Send Me No Flowers*, George Pal's *The Seven Faces of Dr. Lao*, Richard Quine's *Sex and the Single Girl*, and Blake Edwards's *The Pink Panther*.   **FILM**

1964   Sidney Lumet's drama *Fail-Safe* and Stanley Kubrick's black comedy *Dr. Strangelove or How I Learned to Stop Worrying and Love the Bomb* both depict the accidental triggering of nuclear war.   **FILM**

1964   Sergio Leone's *A Fistful of Dollars*, the first of his "spaghetti westerns," makes a star of American actor Clint Eastwood as the laconic "Man With No Name."   **FILM**

1964   Other notable international films include Carl Dreyer's *Gertrud*, Vittorio De Sica's *Marriage Italian-Style* and *Yesterday, Today, and Tomorrow*, Masaki Kobayashi's *Kwaidan*, Guy Hamilton's *Goldfinger*, Richard Lester's *A Hard Day's Night*, and Peter Glenville's *Becket*. **FILM**

COMPETITION FOR THE SINGING NUN

On December 26, 1963, one month after the assassination of President John F. Kennedy, the number 1 pop hit in America was "Dominique" by Belgian religious singer Soeur Sourire, known as the Singing Nun. American musical tastes were about to be altered radically, for this was also the day that the Beatles released their single "I Want to Hold Your Hand."

Already a sensation in England and continental Europe, the Liverpool-based band, with their mop-top haircuts and lapelless jackets, now became extraordinarily popular in America as well. Aided by their appearance on "The Ed Sullivan Show" in February 1964, the Beatles—John Lennon, Paul McCartney, George Harrison, and Ringo Starr—occupied the top five places in the charts by March. By the end of 1964 they had released twenty-nine singles, including such original hits as "She Loves You," "Can't Buy Me Love," "Please Please Me," "I Saw Her Standing There," "From Me to You," "All My Loving," "Do You Want to Know a Secret," and "A Hard Day's Night," and covers of other artists' songs such as "Twist and Shout" and "Roll Over Beethoven." Driving across the country that spring, folk singer Bob Dylan found the Beatles ubiquitous on the radio, though, as he put it, "I kept it to myself that I really dug them."

As proof of the eclecticism of American popular culture, the Singing Nun was not completely overwhelmed. In 1966, the same year that John Lennon declared in an interview that the Beatles were more popular than Jesus, the MGM musical biography The Singing Nun, starring Debbie Reynolds and Ricardo Montalban, was a big box-office success. Its most memorable song was "Dominique."

1964   American mystery writer John D. MacDonald publishes the novels *The Deep Blue Good-By* and *Nightmare in Pink*, part of the long-running series featuring the detective Travis McGee and having a color in the title.   **LIT**

1964   *A Moveable Feast*, the autobiographical recounting of the post–World War I European life of American writer Ernest Hemingway is published posthumously, following his self-inflicted death.   **LIT**

1964   The Museum of African Art is founded in Washington, D.C. It will later be incorporated into the Smithsonian Institution (1979) and renamed the National Museum of African Art (1981).   **MISC**

GIMMICK SITCOMS

*F*aced with the turbulent social changes of the 1960s, producers of American TV comedy took the only sensible course: they ignored it. Though Mr. Ed once flirted with becoming a beatnik and a rock-and-roll group once passed through Gilligan's Island, for the most part TV situation comedies in the days before "All in the Family" (1971–1979) stayed away from social issues. Instead, outlandish fantasies, improbably blended with shades of quiet suburban life, were the order of the day. Here are some of the strangest TV gimmicks of the gimmick decade:

"The Addams Family" (1964–1966)—macabre but funny family
"The Beverly Hillbillies" (1962–1971)—hillbillies move to Beverly Hills
"Bewitched" (1964–1972)—ad executive marries a witch
"Mr. Ed" (1961–1966)—a talking horse
"The Flying Nun" (1967–1970)—a flying nun
"Gilligan's Island" (1964–1967)—castaways shipwrecked on funny island
"I Dream of Jeannie" (1965–1970)—astronaut finds beautiful genie in bottle
"It's About Time" (1966–1967)—astronauts are stranded in the past
"The Munsters" (1964–1966)—monstrous but funny family
"My Favorite Martian" (1963–1966)—bachelor lives with Martian
"My Living Doll" (1964–1965)—bachelor lives with beautiful robot
"My Mother the Car" (1965–1966)—mother is reincarnated as car

1964	American composer Roger Sessions composes the opera *Montezuma*. **MUSIC**
1964	Beatlemania sweeps the United States, as the British rock band the Beatles releases six number 1 hits during the year, more than any other new act in rock history. They win this year's Grammy Award for Best New Artist, star in Richard Lester's film *A Hard Day's Night*, and make a famous appearance on television's "The Ed Sullivan Show." The Beatles will continue to be the decade's most popular band until their breakup in 1970. *See* 1963, MUSIC. **MUSIC**
1964	The British rock band the Rolling Stones, with their lead singer Mick Jagger, release their first album, *The Rolling Stones: England's Newest Hitmakers*. Their angry, energetic sound will help define 1960s youth rebellion, through songs such as "Satisfaction," "Get Off My Cloud," and "Paint It Black." **MUSIC**
1964	American painter Helen Frankenthaler paints *Interior Landscape*. **PAINT**
1964	American painter Ellsworth Kelly paints *Red/Blue*. **PAINT**

1964   The nonrepresentational artistic style known as op art, which relies on optical illusions that often imply movement, comes into fashion in the fine and popular arts.   **PAINT**

1964   American sculptor David Smith erects his stainless steel *Cubi* series outside his farm at Bolton Landing, New York. The pieces will eventually be placed in major museums.   **SCULP**

1964–1965   The highest-rated TV program of the season is "Bonanza" (NBC). Other top-rated programs are "Bewitched" (ABC) and "The Fugitive" (ABC).   **TV&R**

1965   Robert Wise's *The Sound of Music*, based on the Rodgers and Hammerstein stage musical and starring Julie Andrews and Christopher Plummer, is released by 20th Century-Fox. It will unseat *Gone With the Wind* (1939) to become the top-grossing film of all time. *See also* 1972, FILM.   **FILM**

1965   Other notable American films include David Lean's *Doctor Zhivago*, Carol Reed's *The Agony and the Ecstasy*, Otto Preminger's *Bunny Lake Is Missing*, Elliot Silverstein's *Cat Ballou*, George Stevens's *The Greatest Story Ever Told*, Blake Edwards's *The Great Race*, and Fred Coe's *A Thousand Clowns*.   **FILM**

1965   Notable international films include Richard Lester's *Help!*, John Schlesinger's *Darling*, Jean-Luc Godard's *Alphaville*, Jean Cocteau's *The Testament of Orpheus*, Michelangelo Antonioni's *Red Desert*, Roman Polanski's *Repulsion*, and Federico Fellini's *Juliet of the Spirits*.   **FILM**

1965   American director James Ivory, working in India, gains international notice with the drama *Shakespeare Wallah*, coscripted with Polish-born Ruth Prawer Jhabvala and produced by Indian Ismail Merchant. The Merchant-Ivory-Jhabvala team will become known in the 1980s and 1990s for their British-made, beautifully mounted, emotionally nuanced literary adaptations, including *A Room With a View* (1985) and *Howards End* (1992).   **FILM**

1965   American novelist Frank Herbert publishes the science-fiction classic *Dune*, first in a series of novels about the desert planet Arrakis that will also include *Dune Messiah* (1969) and *Children of Dune* (1976).   **LIT**

1965   American poet Randall Jarrell publishes a collection of autobiographical poems, *The Lost World*.   **LIT**

1965   Based on a number of interviews with the African-American leader, American writer Alex Haley writes *The Autobiography of Malcolm X*. The book is published near the time of Malcolm X's assassination in 1965.   **LIT**

1965   American journalist Tom Wolfe ushers in the age of new journalism with the publication of *The Kandy-Kolored Tangerine-Flake Streamline Baby*. He will follow it in 1968 with *The Electric Kool-Aid Acid Test*, based on the experiences of American novelist Ken Kesey.   **LIT**

1965   British novelist John Fowles publishes *The Magus*. Among his later works is *The French Lieutenant's Woman* (1969).   **LIT**

1965   Italian novelist Italo Calvino publishes the short-story collection *Cosmicomics*. He will be known for his fantastic, ironic writing in this and other works, including *Mr. Palomar* (1985).   **LIT**

1965   Playing songs like Bob Dylan's "Tambourine Man," the Byrds become early experimenters with electronically amplified folk music, creating a subgenre of popular music called "folk rock."   **MUSIC**

1965   The all-girl group the Supremes becomes the female examplar of the Detroit-based Motown sound with the hits "Stop! In the Name of Love," "Back in My Arms Again," and "I Hear a Symphony." Led by Diana Ross, the Supremes will become the most popular female singing group of the decade.   **MUSIC**

1965   American artist Frank Stella paints *Empress of India*.   **PAINT**

1965   His work gaining newfound interest since the 1950s, an exhibition of Swiss sculptor Alberto Giacometti's work is held in London.   **SCULP**

1965–1966   The highest-rated TV program of the season is "Bonanza" (NBC). Other top-rated programs are "Gomer Pyle, U.S.M.C." (CBS) and "Batman" (ABC).   **TV&R**

1966   American architect Robert Venturi publishes *Complexities and Contradictions in Modern Architecture*. He becomes a leading figure in postmodernist architecture, which advocates an eclectic style that makes use of popular culture, historical associations, and humor.   **ARCH**

1966   American playwright Edward Albee's drama *A Delicate Balance* is produced in New York City. It will be awarded the Pulitzer Prize.   **DRAMA**

1966   *Les Paravents* (*The Screens*), a drama by French writer Jean Genet, opens in Paris.   **DRAMA**

1966   Notable American films include Mike Nichols's *Who's Afraid of Virginia Woolf?*, Jack Smight's *Harper*, John Ford's *7 Women*, Billy Wilder's *The Fortune Cookie*, Alfred Hitchcock's *Torn Curtain*, and Norman Jewison's *The Russians Are Coming, The Russians Are Coming*.   **FILM**

1966   Notable international films include Michelangelo Antonioni's *Blowup*, Roman Polanski's *Cul-de-Sac*, François Truffaut's *Fahrenheit 451*, Fred Zinnemann's *A Man for All Seasons*, Orson Welles's *Chimes at Midnight*, Ingmar Bergman's *Persona*, Claude Lelouch's *A Man and a Woman*, Pier Paolo Pasolini's *The Gospel According to St. Matthew*, and Sergio Leone's *The Good, the Bad, and the Ugly*.   **FILM**

1966   Chinese writer Lao She (*b.* 1899) dies during the Cultural Revolution, reportedly killed for writing works opposed by the state.   **LIT**

1966   American novelist Bernard Malamud publishes *The Fixer*. The story of anti-Semitism in Russia in the early twentieth century will win the Pulitzer Prize.   **LIT**

••

"We're more popular than Jesus now."—British musician John Lennon on the popularity of the Beatles, 1966

••

1966   American writer Susan Sontag publishes the essay collection, *Against Interpretation*, which establishes her as a critic of culture and the arts.   **LIT**

1966   American novelist John Barth publishes *Giles-Goat Boy*.   **LIT**

1966   Irish poet Seamus (Justin) Heaney publishes the collection *Death of a Naturalist*. Later collections include *Door into the Dark* (1969). He will also publish a prose collection, *Preoccupations: Selected Prose 1968–1978*.   **LIT**

1966–1983   French-born American diarist Anaïs Nin publishes the multivolume *Diary of Anaïs Nin*. Written up to her death in 1977, part of the work is published posthumously.   **LIT**

1966   American composer Samuel Barber's opera *Antony and Cleopatra* opens the Metropolitan Opera Company's first season at Lincoln Center in New York.   **MUSIC**

1966   After an absence of several years from the pop charts, Frank Sinatra returns with *Strangers in the Night*, which will win the Grammy Award for Record of the Year. Although he will continue to enjoy concert and some chart success over the decades, his next massive success will be the 1993 album of pairings with contemporary artists, *Duets*.   **MUSIC**

1966   The Jewish Museum of New York opens an exhibition of minimal sculpture called "Primary Structures," featuring such artists as Donald Judd, Sol LeWitt, and Carl André.   **SCULP**

1966–1967   The highest-rated TV program of the season is "Bonanza" (NBC). Other top-rated programs are "The Lucy Show" (CBS) and "Green Acres" (CBS).   **TV&R**

The Beatles. *(The Everett Collection)*

1967   The John Hancock Center opens in Chicago. More than 1,100 feet in
            height, it is, at its completion, the second tallest building in the
            world, but will fall to fifth place by 1973.   **ARCH**

1967   *Rosencrantz and Guildenstern Are Dead*, a drama by Czech-born
            British playwright Tom Stoppard, is produced. His later plays will in-
            clude *After Magritte* (produced in 1970), *Travesties* (1974), and *The
            Real Thing* (1982).   **DRAMA**

1967   *Relatively Speaking*, a comedy by British playwright Alan Ayckbourn,
            premieres. His comedies *Absurd Person Singular* and *Bedroom Farce*
            will be produced in 1973 and 1977, respectively.   **DRAMA**

1967   One of the first rock musicals, *Hair* opens in New York on Oct. 29,
            with book and lyrics by Gerome Ragni and James Rado and music
            by Galt MacDermott. Billed as an "American tribal love-rock musi-
            cal," it will become a cultural marker of its time.   **DRAMA**

1967   American on- and offscreen couple Spencer Tracy and Katharine
            Hepburn star in their last of nine films they made together, Stanley
            Kramer's *Guess Who's Coming to Dinner*. Tracy, who wins an
            Academy Award for his performance, dies this year. Their other
            films include *Adam's Rib* (1949) and *Pat and Mike* (1952).   **FILM**

1967   Notable American films include Arthur Penn's *Bonnie and Clyde*,
              Mike Nichols's *The Graduate*, Norman Jewison's *In the Heat of the
              Night*, Joshua Logan's *Camelot*, Don Chaffey's *Fantastic Voyage*, and
              Walt Disney Productions' *The Jungle Book*.   **FILM**

1967   Notable foreign films include Joseph Strick's *Ulysses*, Robert
              Aldrich's *The Dirty Dozen*, Luis Buñuel's *Belle de Jour*, Jacques Tati's
              Playtime, Philippe de Broca's *King of Hearts*, and Bo Widerberg's
              Elvira Madigan.   **FILM**

1967   American novelist Ira Levin publishes *Rosemary's Baby*, about a
              New York woman who carries the devil's child. The book becomes
              a best-seller and the basis for a successful film by Roman Polanski
              (1968).   **LIT**

1967   American essayist and journalist Norman Podhoretz publishes a
              memoir of his young adult life in New York, *Making It*.   **LIT**

1967   American novelist Richard Brautigan publishes *Trout Fishing in
              America*, which will become a cult favorite in the 1960s.   **LIT**

1967   Colombian novelist and short-story writer Gabriel García Márquez
              publishes the saga of magic realism, *One Hundred Years of Solitude*.
              It establishes him as an important modern talent. Later works will
              include *Chronicle of a Death Foretold* (1982) and *Love in the Time of
              Cholera* (1988).   **LIT**

1967   Aretha Franklin establishes herself as the "Queen of Soul" with her
              rendition of Otis Redding's "Respect."   **MUSIC**

1967   The Monterey Pop Festival in Monterey, California, makes stars of
              Janis Joplin, Jimi Hendrix, and Otis Redding. All three will be dead
              within three years. Redding dies this year, on December 10, in a plane
              crash. His posthumously released ballad "(Sittin' on) The Dock of the
              Bay" is a number 1 hit. Joplin and Hendrix die in 1970.   **MUSIC**

1967   Cream, the British "supergroup" famed for its lengthy, improvisa-
              tional live performances, is formed. Following its breakup two years
              later, guitarist Eric Clapton will eventually achieve success as a solo
              artist.   **MUSIC**

1967   Brooklyn-born singer Barbra Streisand presents a highly touted con-
              cert in Central Park, New York City. It is attended by approximately
              135,000 fans.   **MUSIC**

1967   American painter Richard Diebenkorn begins painting the *Ocean
              Park* series, which he will continue for decades.   **PAINT**

1967   American painter Romare Bearden creates the collage *Three Folk
              Musicians*. Over the decades of his work, Bearden's paintings and
              collages, influenced by cubism and African sculpture, build a pene-
              trating view of African-American experience.   **PAINT**

1967–1968   The highest-rated TV program of the season is "The Andy Griffith Show" (CBS). Other top-rated programs are "Family Affair" (CBS) and "The Dean Martin Show" (NBC).   **TV&R**

1968   The columns of the Parthenon in Athens, Greece, face serious problems of erosion and are in danger of crumbling.   **ARCH**

1968   Designed by architect Eero Saarinen, the Gateway Arch in St. Louis, Missouri, is completed and dedicated.   **ARCH**

1968   The foundations of the Temple of Herod are discovered by Benjamin Masar of Jerusalem University. The temple was destroyed in A.D. 70.   **ARCH**

1968   Polish director Jerzy Grotowski publishes *Towards a Poor Theatre*, a book in which he presents his concept of actor-based theater, theater which is derived from the mental and physical resources of its actors.   **DRAMA**

1968   *The Increased Difficulty of Concentration*, an abstract drama by Czech playwright Vaclav Havel, is produced. In 1989, Havel will become president of Czechoslovakia (since 1993, the Czech Republic).   **DRAMA**

1968   The Theatres Act is passed, abolishing government censorship of theater in England. Previously, the Lord Chamberlain's Office had had the power to prevent the public performance of plays it deemed morally offensive.   **DRAMA**

1968   American actor James Earl Jones, widely considered to be the greatest black actor of his generation, opens on Broadway in *The Great White Hope*, a play by Howard Slacker about boxer Jack Johnson. Jones will appear in many classical and contemporary stage, film, and television roles, including Othello and Macbeth for Joseph Papp's New York Shakespeare Festival.   **DRAMA**

1968   Notable American films include Peter Yates's *Bullitt*, William Wyler's *Funny Girl*, John Wayne's *The Green Berets*, Gene Saks's *The Odd Couple*, Franklin J. Schaffner's *Planet of the Apes*, Mel Brooks's *The Producers*, Roman Polanski's *Rosemary's Baby*, and George A. Romero's *Night of the Living Dead*.   **FILM**

1968   Notable foreign films include Stanley Kubrick's *2001: A Space Odyssey*, Carol Reed's *Oliver!*, George Dunning's animated Beatles film *Yellow Submarine*, Franco Zeffirelli's *Romeo and Juliet*, Andrej Wajda's *Gates to Paradise*, Alain Resnais's *Je t'aime, Je t'aime*, François Truffaut's *The Bride Wore Black*, Roger Vadim's *Barbarella*, Jean-Luc Godard's *Weekend*, Ingmar Bergman's *Shame*, and Sergei Bondarchuk's *War and Peace*.   **FILM**

1968   While in prison African-American political activist Eldridge Cleaver writes *Soul on Ice*, a personal treatise on anger and violence in young African-Americans.   **LIT**

1968 American novelist and essayist Joan Didion publishes the essay collection *Slouching Toward Bethlehem*. Like her 1979 collection *The White Album*, it examines the decay of modern culture, often seen through the California experience. **LIT**

1968 American avant-garde composer Philip Glass presents his *Pieces in the Shape of a Square* in New York. **MUSIC**

1968 German electronic music pioneer Karlheinz Stockhausen composes the experimental work *Spiral* for a soloist with short-wave radio receiver. **MUSIC**

1968 German composer Hans Werner Henze's oratorio *The Raft of Medusa*, a musical protest against inhumanity, is performed. **MUSIC**

1968 American photorealist Chuck Close paints *Self-Portrait*. Photorealists (also called superrealists or hyperrealists) paint with the precise, exhaustive detail found in photographs, and often work from photographs. Other photorealists include Don Eddy, Richard Estes, and Audrey Flack. **PAINT**

1968–1969 The highest-rated TV program of the season is "Rowan & Martin's Laugh-In" (NBC). Other top-rated programs are "Mayberry R.F.D." (CBS) and "Julia" (NBC). **TV&R**

1969 The Dance Theater of Harlem is founded by American dancer Arthur Mitchell. The first black principal dancer for the American Ballet Theater and member of the New York City Ballet, Mitchell is said to have been prompted to develop an American dance company upon hearing of the death of Martin Luther King Jr. **DANCE**

1969 The Body Politic, a nonprofit theater, is founded in Chicago. Its emergence marks the beginning of the city's Off-Loop theater movement. Victory Gardens Theater, Steppenwolf Theatre Company, Wisdom Bridge Theatre, and others will soon be established, providing Midwesterners with high quality, inexpensively priced plays. **DRAMA**

1969 Notable American films include Paul Mazursky's *Bob and Carol and Ted and Alice*, George Roy Hill's *Butch Cassidy and the Sundance Kid*, Arthur Penn's *Alice's Restaurant*, Robert Stevenson's *The Love Bug*, Dennis Hopper's *Easy Rider*, John Schlesinger's *Midnight Cowboy*, Bob Fosse's *Sweet Charity*, Henry Hathaway's *True Grit*, Sydney Pollack's *They Shoot Horses, Don't They?*, and Sam Peckinpah's *The Wild Bunch*. **FILM**

1969 Notable foreign films include Charles Jarrott's *Anne of the Thousand Days*, Karel Reisz's *Isadora*, Richard Attenborough's *Oh! What a Lovely War*, Ingmar Bergman's *The Passion of Anna*, Eric Rohmer's *My Night at Maud's*, François Truffaut's *The Wild Child*, Constantin Costa-Gavras's *Z*, and Federico Fellini's *Fellini Satyricon*. **FILM**

1969   American novelist Mario Puzo publishes *The Godfather.* The saga of
             the Corleone crime family will become a best-seller and will gener-
             ate three films.   **LIT**

1969   American poet John Berryman publishes the complete collection of
             his 385 poems in *The Dream Songs.* In process since 1955, it will
             win the National Book Award and Bollingen Prize.   **LIT**

1969   American novelist Kurt Vonnegut publishes his antiwar novel
             Slaughterhouse-Five, which ranges through time and into outer
             space as the author struggles to come to terms with the firebomb-
             ing of Dresden during World War II.   **LIT**

1969–1971   Avant-garde French composer Pierre Boulez becomes director of
             the New York Philharmonic.   **MUSIC**

1969   The Woodstock Music and Art Fair, near Bethel, New York, attracts
             more than 400,000 enthusiasts for three days of "peace, love and
             music." Dozens of musicians perform, including The Who, Jim
             Hendrix, Janis Joplin, The Grateful Dead, Sly & the Family Stone,
             Joe Cocker, Santana, and Joan Baez. A defining moment for the
             baby-boomer generation, it will be commemorated in 1994 by a
             cross-generational Woodstock concert near the original site. **MUSIC**

1969   *Tommy,* the world's first rock opera, by Peter Townshend of The
             Who, is performed in New York City. It will be made into a Ken
             Russell film in 1975 and adapted into a Tony-winning Broadway
             musical in 1993.   **MUSIC**

1969–1970   The highest-rated TV program of the season is "Rowan & Martin's
             Laugh-In" (NBC). Other top-rated programs are "Gunsmoke" (CBS)
             and "Family Affair" (CBS).   **TV&R**

1970s   Popular songs of the decade include "Bridge Over Troubled Water,"
             "Your Song," "Stairway to Heaven," "It's Too Late," "Imagine,"
             "(Theme from) Shaft," "American Pie," "Aqualung," "Killing Me
             Softly," "Superstition," "The Way We Were," "Born to Run," "Taxi,"
             "(You're) Havin' My Baby," "Feelings," "The Hustle," "(Don't Stop)
             Thinkin' About Tomorrow," "Stayin' Alive," "Hotel California,"
             "Piano Man," "Maggie May," "ABC," and "Bad Girls."   **MUSIC**

1970s   American feminist artist Miriam Shapiro becomes well known for
             her decorative mixed-media works on fabric, associated with the
             pattern and decoration movement.   **PAINT**

1970s   German-born British photographer Bill Brandt and American pho-
             tographer Jerry Uelsmann represent two photographers practicing
             the movement toward the fantastic in photography. The movement
             effects a troubled representation of reality through the use of photo-
             graphic manipulation.   **PHOTO**

1970s   American artist Duane Hanson creates strikingly realistic figures
             from models using painted polyester and fiberglass.   **SCULP**

1970   Notable American films include Bob Rafelson's *Five Easy Pieces*,
             George Seaton's *Airport*, Athur Hiller's *Love Story*, Robert Altman's
             *M*A*S*H* and *Brewster McCloud*, Mike Nichols's *Catch-22*, Arthur
             Penn's *Little Big Man*, Franklin J. Schaffner's *Patton*, Howard
             Hawks's *Rio Lobo*, Don Siegel's *Two Mules for Sister Sara*, and
             Michelangelo Antonioni's *Zabriskie Point*.   **FILM**

1970   Notable British films include Ken Russell's *The Music Lovers*, Billy
             Wilder's *The Private Life of Sherlock Holmes*, and David Lean's
             Ryan's Daughter. Other foreign films include *Tora! Tora! Tora!* by
             Richard Fleischer, Toshio Masuda, and Kinji Fukasuku, François
             Truffaut's *Bed and Board*, Elio Petri's *Investigation of a Citizen Above
             Suspicion*, Akira Kurosawa's *Dode's Kaden*, and Luis Buñuel's
             Tristana.   **FILM**

c. 1970   American artist Philip Pearlstein creates paintings of nude figures,
             often in domestic surroundings, that are minutely realistic and
             unidealized. His work is related to photorealism, though more emo-
             tional in tone and based on live models rather than photographs.
             See also 1968, PAINT.   **PAINT**

· ·

**"I learned right in the beginning from Jack [John] Ford,
and I learned what not to do by watching Cecil B.
DeMille."—American film director Howard Hawks
on his role models, c. 1970s**

· ·

1970   American photographer and physician Eliot Porter publishes the
             collection of wildlife photos, *Appalachian Wilderness*. Among his lat-
             er collections will be *Birds of North America—A Personal Selection*
             (1972) and *Eliot Porter's Southwest* (1985).   **PHOTO**

1970   American artist Robert Smithson completes his major earthwork
             piece, *Spiral Jetty*, a mud and rock coil in the Great Salt Lake. The
             work is not intended to endure as Smithson allows for the process
             of erosion to take place. The project will survive only in
             photographs.   **SCULP**

1970–1971   The highest-rated TV program of the season is "Marcus Welby,
             M.D." (ABC). Other top-rated programs are "Here's Lucy" (CBS) and
             "Ironside" (NBC).   **TV&R**

1971   The Standard Oil of Indiana Building opens in Chicago, outstripping
             the John Hancock Center in height. *See* 1967, ARCH.   **ARCH**

1971   The witty and idiosyncratic dance troupe, the Pilobolus Dance Theater, is founded by Americans Robb Pendleton and Jonathan Wolken.   **DANCE**

1971   *The Basic Training of Pavlo Hummel* and *Sticks and Bones*, two dramas by American playwright David Rabe, are produced in New York City. The first is about an American soldier in Vietnam. The second is about a Vietnam veteran who has just returned to America.   **DRAMA**

··

"[W]hat I'm doing is harmless to these people really, and there's no malevolence in it and there's no deception in it, and it is done in a great tradition, examples of which are Daumier and Goya."—American photographer Walker Evans on the ethics of documentary photography, 1971

··

1971   Notable American films include William Friedkin's *The French Connection*, Peter Bogdanovich's *The Last Picture Show*, Robert Mulligan's *Summer of '42*, Norman Jewison's *Fiddler on the Roof*, T. C. Frank's *Billy Jack*, Robert Wise's *The Andromeda Strain*, Mike Nichols's *Carnal Knowledge*, Don Siegel's *Dirty Harry*, Alan J. Pakula's *Klute*, Robert Altman's *McCabe and Mrs. Miller*, Clint Eastwood's *Play Misty for Me*, Gordon Parks's *Shaft*, and George Lucas's *THX 1138*.   **FILM**

1971   Notable British films include Ken Russell's *The Devils*, Joseph Losey's *The Go-Between*, Sam Peckinpah's *Straw Dogs*, John Schlesinger's *Sunday Bloody Sunday*, and Stanley Kubrick's *A Clockwork Orange*. Other foreign films include Louis Malle's *Murmur of the Heart*, Nicolas Roeg's *Walkabout*, François Truffaut's *Anne and Muriel*, Eric Rohmer's *Claire's Knee*, Ingmar Bergman's *The Touch*, and Bernardo Bertolucci's *The Conformist*.   **FILM**

1971   A year after his death, British novelist E. M. Forster's novel *Maurice*, concerning a homosexual relationship, is published for the first time since it was written around 1912.   **LIT**

1971   Filmmaker and writer Woody Allen publishes his first collection of essays, *Getting Even*. Other books will include *Without Feathers* (1975), *Side Effects* (1980), and *The Floating Light Bulb* (1982).   **LIT**

1971   American artist Chris Burden has himself shot in the left arm by a friend for the artwork called *Shoot*.   **MISC**

1971   American songwriter Carole King wins the Grammy Award for Best Contemporary Vocal Performer, Female, and her album *Tapestry* wins for Album of the Year. The album will sell more than 15 million copies and help to usher in an era of singer-songwriters, such as Carly Simon, Jackson Brown, and others. Previously, King had been part of a phenomenally successful 1960s songwriting team with Gerry Goffin; their work included "Up On the Roof" and "Locomotion." **MUSIC**

1971   Progressive rock, featuring such groups as Jethro Tull and Pink Floyd, becomes popular. The Philly sound develops in Philadelphia as a soul music rival to Detroit's Motown, with groups like the Stylistics and the Spinners. **MUSIC**

1971   American painter Willem de Kooning paints *Amityville*. **PAINT**

1971   The situation comedy "All in the Family" begins its eight-year run on CBS. Starring Carroll O'Connor as the bigoted Archie Bunker and Jean Stapleton as his devoted, cockeyed wife Edith, it will poke fun at contemporary attitudes with a groundbreaking openness. It will be the highest-rated TV program of the 1971–1972 season alongside other top-rated programs such as "The Flip Wilson Show" (NBC) and "Gunsmoke" (CBS). **TV&R**

···

"What's your name?"
"Cary Grant."
"You don't look like Cary Grant."
"I know—nobody does."
—British actor Cary Grant to a
hotel reservation clerk, 1971

···

1971   Television advertisements for cigarettes are banned in the United States. Print advertisements remain legal. **TV&R**

1971   American public television begins broadcasting "Masterpiece Theatre," the long-running anthology series showcasing British dramatic programs, usually broadcast in several parts and often based on literary works. In years to come, PBS will offer many programs first seen in Britain, including Alistair Cooke's "America" (BBC, 1972) and "Monty Python's Flying Circus" (BBC, 1969–1974). **TV&R**

1972   The World Trade Center, designed by American architect Minoru Yamasaki, opens in New York City. With its twin 110-story towers rising 1,377 feet, it is briefly the tallest building in the world before being displaced the next year by the Sears Tower. Both are taller than the previous record-holder, the Empire State Building. *See also* 1931, ARCH; 1973, ARCH. **ARCH**

1972   San Francisco's skyline is redefined by the pyramidal Transamerica Building, designed by William L. Pereira Associates and opening this year.   **ARCH**

1972   The campy musical *Grease*, set in the 1950s, opens on Broadway and a nostalgia craze sweeps the United States. The play will be revived on Broadway in 1994.   **DRAMA**

1972   *The Tooth of Crime*, a drama by American playwright Sam Shephard, premieres. Shepard's *The Curse of the Starving Class* will be produced in 1977.   **DRAMA**

1972   American performance artist Laurie Anderson—who will become known for multimedia performance pieces mixing photography, film, drawings, animation, the spoken word, and music—presents *Story Show*, one of her first works.   **DRAMA**

1972   Paramount releases Francis Ford Coppola's *The Godfather*, starring Marlon Brando, Al Pacino, Robert Duvall, and James Caan. The epic saga of the Corleone crime family is based on the novel by Mario Puzo, with a screenplay by Puzo and Coppola. The film sets a new record for all-time box office sales. It will win three Oscars, including a Best Actor Oscar refused by Marlon Brando, and will lead to two sequels. *See* 1974, FILM; 1990, FILM.   **FILM**

1972   Other notable American films include Bob Fosse's *Cabaret*, John Boorman's *Deliverance*, Alfred Hitchcock's *Frenzy*, Michael Ritchie's *The Candidate*, Ronald Neame's *The Poseidon Adventure*, Martin Ritt's *Sounder*, Peter Bogdanovich's *What's Up, Doc?*, and Gordon Parks Jr.'s *Superfly*.   **FILM**

1972   Notable foreign films include Ken Russell's *The Boy Friend*, Peter Medak's *The Ruling Class*, Joseph L. Mankiewicz's *Sleuth*, Luis Buñuel's *The Discreet Charm of the Bourgeoisie*, Eric Rohmer's *Chloe in the Afternoon*, Robert Bresson's *Four Nights of a Dreamer*, Werner Herzog's *Aguirre, the Wrath of God*, Jerzy Skolimowski's *King, Queen, Knave*, Federico Fellini's *Roma*, and Ingmar Bergman's *Cries and Whispers*.   **FILM**

1972   British novelist Margaret Drabble publishes *The Needle's Eye*. Other novels include *A Summer Bird-Cage* (1963) and *The Garrick Year* (1964).   **LIT**

1972   American composer Leonard Bernstein presents his Mass for the opening of the John F. Kennedy Center for the Performing Arts in Washington D.C..   **MUSIC**

1972   American singer Helen Reddy makes the feminist anthem "I Am Woman" the pop rallying cry of the women's liberation movement.   **MUSIC**

1972 | American artist Andy Warhol paints *Mao*, executed with silkscreen and paint on canvas.   **PAINT**

1972 | In Italy Michelangelo's sculpture *Pietà* is mutilated with a hammer by a vandal.   **SCULP**

1972–1973 | The highest-rated TV program of the season is "All in the Family" (CBS). Other top-rated programs are "Sanford and Son" (NBC) and "Maude" (CBS).   **TV&R**

1973 | The Sears Tower, the tallest building in the world at 110 stories and 1,454 feet, opens in Chicago, designed by Skidmore, Owings & Merrill. *See also* 1972, ARCH.   **ARCH**

1973 | American playwright Lanford Wilson's *The Hot l Baltimore* is produced. It will run off-Broadway for 1,166 performances. Wilson's *Balm in Gilead* had been produced in 1965. His *5th of July* and *Talley's Folly* will be produced in 1978 and 1979, respectively.   **DRAMA**

1973 | British playwright Peter Shaffer's drama *Equus* is produced. His historical play *Amadeus* will be produced in 1979. Both will be great successes; *Amadeus* will be made into an Academy Award–winning movie in 1984.   **DRAMA**

1973 | Notable American films include George Roy Hill's *The Sting*, George Lucas's *American Graffiti*, William Friedkin's *The Exorcist*, Sidney Lumet's *Serpico*, Sydney Pollack's *The Way We Were*, Clint Eastwood's *High Plains Drifter*, Robert Altman's *The Long Goodbye*, Martin Scorsese's *Mean Streets*, John Waters's *Pink Flamingos*, Woody Allen's *Sleeper*, and Mel Brooks's *Blazing Saddles*.   **FILM**

1973 | Notable foreign films include Lindsay Anderson's *O Lucky Man*, Fred Zinnemann's *The Day of the Jackal*, François Truffaut's *Day for Night*, Jean-Luc Godard's *Tout Va Bien*, Cheng Chang Ho's *Five Fingers of Death*, Bernardo Bertolucci's *Last Tango in Paris*, Djibril Diop Mambety's *Touki-Bouki*, and Ingmar Bergman's *Scenes from a Marriage*.   **FILM**

1973 | The erotic film *Deep Throat* is ruled "indisputably and irredeemably obscene" by a New York Criminal Court judge. The film, one of many sexploitation entries during the 1960s and 1970s, creates an uproar (and increases business) across the United States.   **FILM**

1973 | Bernardo Bertolucci's highly charged *Last Tango in Paris*, starring Marlon Brando and Maria Schneider, generates controversy for its sexual frankness. In its day it marks the limits to which an artistic film can take the presentation of sex on-screen.   **FILM**

1973 | American novelist Erica Jong publishes *Fear of Flying*, a best-selling novel about a woman, Isadora Wing, who practices sexual freedom. The book will generate controversy and many imitators.   **LIT**

1973   American novelist Thomas Pynchon publishes *Gravity's Rainbow*, his darkly comic, phantasmagoric novel of German missile development during World War II.   **LIT**

1973–1975   Russian novelist Aleksandr Solzhenitsyn writes the novel *The Gulag Archipeligo*. It will bring about his exile to the West in 1974. Twenty years later, in 1994, following the fall of the Soviet Union, he will return to Russia.   **LIT**

1973   American poet Adrienne Rich publishes the collection *Diving into the Wreck*, which, like her collections over the previous decade, takes a feminist approach to women's experiences. Her 1976 prose collection *Of Woman Born* will concentrate on the experience and public perception of motherhood.   **LIT**

1973   British science-fiction writer Arthur C. Clarke publishes the novel *Rendezvous with Rama*.   **LIT**

1973   British composer Benjamin Britten's *Death In Venice* premieres. **MUSIC**

1973   From Honolulu American rock musician Elvis Presley presents a globally televised concert to benefit the battleship *Arizona*.   **MUSIC**

1973   Rock influenced by country-western music reaches mainstream American audiences through groups such as the Allman Brothers Band, ZZ Top, and the Marshall Tucker Band.   **MUSIC**

1973–1974   The highest-rated TV program of the season is "All in the Family" (CBS). Other top-rated programs are "The Sonny and Cher Comedy Hour" (CBS) and "The Mary Tyler Moore Show" (CBS).   **TV&R**

1974   Citing personal and artistic reasons, Russian ballet dancer Mikhail Baryshnikov, of the Kirov Ballet, defects to the West while touring with the Bolshoi Ballet in Toronto.   **DANCE**

1974   Notable American dance works include George Balanchine's *Coppelia*, Jerome Robbins's *Four Bagatelles* and *Dybbuk Variations*, and Eliot Feld's *Sephardic Songs*.   **DANCE**

1974   Notable American films include Francis Ford Coppola's *The Godfather Part II* and *The Conversation*, Mel Brooks's *Young Frankenstein*, Roman Polanski's *Chinatown*, Martin Scorsese's *Alice Doesn't Live Here Anymore*, Terrence Malick's *Badlands*, Robert Aldrich's *The Longest Yard*, Tobe Hooper's *The Texas Chainsaw Massacre*, Jack Haley Jr.'s *That's Entertainment*, John Guillermin's *The Towering Inferno*, and Steven Spielberg's *The Sugarland Express*. **FILM**

1974   Notable foreign films include John Boorman's *Zardoz*, Richard Lester's *The Three Musketeers*, Ted Kotcheff's *The Apprenticeship of Duddy Kravitz*, Louis Malle's *Lacombe, Lucien*, Alain Resnais's *Stavisky*, Rainer Werner Fassbinder's *Effi Briest*, Federico Fellini's *Amarcord*, Vittorio De Sica's *The Voyage*, and Ingmar Bergman's *The Magic Flute*.   **FILM**

1974   British poet Philip Larkin publishes his final book of poems, *High Windows*, including the poems "The Old Fools" and "The Building." **LIT**

1974   American essayist Annie Dillard publishes the collection of nature essays, *Pilgrim at Tinker Creek*, which will win the Pulitzer Prize. **LIT**

1974   American publishing phenomenon Stephen King publishes his first novel, *Carrie*, the story of a lonely girl with telekinetic powers. King's brand of horror in works such as *The Shining* (1977), *Misery* (1987), and *Needful Things* (1991), will dominate the fiction bestseller list for decades. **LIT**

••

"I saw rock 'n' roll's future and its name is Bruce Springsteen."—American music critic Jon Landau, who became Springsteen's manager, 1974

••

1974   Notable musical works include German composer Hans Werner Henze's opera *Rachel, la cubana*, German composer Mauricio Kagel's String Quartet and *Mirum fur Tuba*, and British composer Elisabeth Luytens's *The Winter of the World* and *Plenum III*. **MUSIC**

1974   American artist Jasper Johns creates the oil, encaustic, and collage on canvas work *Corpse and Mirror*. **PAINT**

1974–1975   The highest-rated TV program of the season is "All in the Family" (CBS). Other top-rated programs are "M*A*S*H" (CBS) and "The Waltons" (CBS). **TV&R**

1975   Notable dance works include American choreographer Merce Cunningham's *Rebus* and *Changing Steps/Loops*, Russian-born choreographer George Balanchine's *Sheherezade*, and Soviet choreographer Yuri Grigorivich's *Ivan the Terrible*. **DANCE**

1975   British playwright Harold Pinter's *No Man's Land* is produced. His drama *Betrayal* will be produced in 1978. **DRAMA**

1975   American playwright Edward Albee's *Seascape* premieres in a production directed by the author. It will win the Pulitzer Prize. **DRAMA**

1975   The American musical *A Chorus Line*—with book by James Kirkwood and Nicholas Dante, lyrics by Edward Kleban, and music by Marvin Hamlisch—premieres on April 15. The high-concept, behind-the-scenes musical will become Broadway's all-time longest-running show. **DRAMA**

1975   Steven Spielberg's *Jaws* becomes the all-time box office champion,
             unseating *The Godfather* (1972). Starring Roy Scheider, Robert Shaw,
             and Richard Dreyfuss, the shark thriller is based on the best-selling
             novel by Peter Benchley. The film establishes Spielberg as a major
             director and helps to establish the summer blockbuster as a driving
             force in the way Hollywood studios plan their annual schedule of
             films.   **FILM**

1975   Other notable American films of the year include Robert Altman's
             Nashville, Milos Forman's *One Flew Over the Cuckoo's Nest*, Sidney
             Lumet's *Dog Day Afternoon*, Hal Ashby's *Shampoo*, John Milius's *The
             Wind and the Lion*, John Schlesinger's *The Day of the Locust*, and
             Woody Allen's *Love and Death*.   **FILM**

1975   Notable British films include Stanley Kubrick's *Barry Lyndon*, John
             Huston's *The Man Who Would Be King*, Terry Gilliam's *Monty Python
             and the Holy Grail*, and Ken Russell's *Tommy*. Other foreign films in-
             clude Akira Kurosawa's *Dersu Uzala*, Peter Weir's *Picnic at Hanging
             Rock*, François Truffaut's *The Story of Adele H.*, Werner Herzog's
             Every Man for Himself and God Against All, and Michelangelo
             Antonioni's *The Passenger*.   **FILM**

1975   British painter David Hockney creates stage sets for a production of
             Stravinsky's 1951 opera *The Rake's Progress*.   **MUSIC**

1975   American opera singer Beverly Sills makes her Metropolitan Opera
             debut in Rossini's *The Siege of Corinth*.   **MUSIC**

1975   Notable musical works include Finnish composer Aulis Sallinen's
             opera *Ratsumies*, American composer Charles Wuorinen's opera
             The W. of Babylon, American composer Carmen Moore's *Wildfires
             and Field Songs* and *Museum Piece*, American composer Virgil
             Thomson's *Family Portrait*, Swiss composer Heinz Holliger's
             Quartet for Strings, and British composer Benjamin Britten's *Sacred
             and Profane* for five unaccompanied voices.   **MUSIC**

1975   New Jersey-born rock musician Bruce Springsteen records the al-
             bum *Born to Run*, which plumbs traditional American longings for
             love, freedom, and the open road. The album immediately makes
             him a rock icon; the title song becomes a rock anthem.   **MUSIC**

1975   American producer-songwriter Van McCoy's instrumental hit "The
             Hustle" ushers in the most popular dance craze since the twist. As
             disco music becomes popular, the hustle remains its archetypal
             incarnation.   **MUSIC**

1975   American painter Jasper Johns creates several encaustic crosshatched
             works, including *Weeping Women* and *The Barber's Tree*.   **PAINT**

1975   American painter Willem de Kooning paints *Whose Name Was Writ
             in Water*.   **PAINT**

1975   American artist Roy Lichtenstein paints *Cubist Still Life with Lemons*.   **PAINT**

1975   The Japanese company Sony introduces the Betamax, the first home videocassette recorder (VCR). A competing format, VHS, made by JVC, will become the dominant system in American homes during the 1980s.   **TV&R**

1975–1976   The highest-rated TV program of the season is "All in the Family" (CBS). Other top-rated programs are "Laverne & Shirley" (ABC) and "Rhoda" (CBS).   **TV&R**

1976   *For Colored Girls Who Have Considered Suicide When the Rainbow is Enuf*, a drama by African-American playwright Ntozake Shange, is produced. It will be very successful critically and commercially.   **DRAMA**

1976   Mexican playwright Oscar Villegas's *Atlantida* (*Atlantis*) is produced.   **DRAMA**

1976   Notable American films include Sidney Lumet's *Network*, Martin Scorsese's *Taxi Driver*, Alan J. Pakula's *All the President's Men*, John Avildsen's *Rocky*, Richard Donner's *The Omen*, and Brian De Palma's *Carrie*.   **FILM**

1976   Notable foreign films include François Truffaut's *Small Change*, Wim Wenders's *Kings of the Road*, Alain Tanner's *Jonah Who Will Be 25 in the Year 2000*, Ingmar Bergman's *Face to Face*, Eric Rohmer's *The Marquise of O*, and Richard Lester's *Robin and Marian*.   **FILM**

1976   Chinese-American writer Maxine Hong Kingston publishes *The Woman Warrior: Memoirs of a Girlhood Among Ghosts*, about the women in her Chinese family.   **LIT**

1976   American short-story writer Raymond Carver publishes the collection, *Will You Please Be Quiet, Please*, which establishes him as an important modern talent. Later collections will include *What We Talk About When We Talk About Love* (1981), *Cathedral* (1983), and *Where I'm Calling From* (1988).   **LIT**

1976   American conductor and opera director Sarah Caldwell is the first woman to conduct New York's Metropolitan Opera, with a performance of *La Traviata*.   **MUSIC**

1976   The opera *Einstein on the Beach* by American composers Philip Glass and Robert Wilson premieres at the Avignon Festival in France to immediate acclaim.   **MUSIC**

1976   Musical works commissioned to celebrate the U.S. bicentennial include John Cage's *Renga* with *Apartment House 1776*, Morton Subotnick's *Before the Butterfly*, and Gian Carlo Menotti's Symphony no. 1.   **MUSIC**

1976   Punk rock bands such as Blondie and the Ramones perform at such
              New York clubs as Max's Kansas City and CBGB. In England, the
              Sex Pistols release their first single, "Anarchy in the U.K.," and in
              the following year, their banned anti-monarchy song "God Save the
              Queen" reaches number one on the British pop charts.   **MUSIC**

1976   Disco becomes the dominant pop music form, making stars of
              artists such as Donna Summer, Gloria Gaynor, the Andrea True
              Connection, and K.C. & the Sunshine Band.   **MUSIC**

1976   The British rock group Queen enjoys huge success with the album
              A Night at the Opera, which includes their best-known song,
              "Bohemian Rhapsody." In 1991 their lead singer Freddie Mercury
              will die of AIDS.   **MUSIC**

1976   American painter Andrew Wyeth depicts Andy Warhol in *Portrait of
              Andy*.   **PAINT**

1976   American painter Elizabeth Murray paints *Beginner*.   **PAINT**

1976   American painter Alfred Leslie paints *Our Family in 1976*.   **PAINT**

1976   American photographer Richard Avedon publishes the collection
              Portraits, which contains his seemingly unadorned yet compelling,
              sometimes disturbing views of people.   **PHOTO**

1976   In April Bulgarian-born artist Christo works with sixty-five workers
              to install his *Running Fence*, a nylon ribbon twenty-five miles long
              strung through the California countryside between the Pacific coast
              and the town of Petaluma. The project will begin to be dismantled
              in October.   **SCULP**

1976–1977   The highest-rated TV program of the season is "Happy Days" (ABC).
              Other top-rated programs are "M*A*S*H" (CBS) and "The Six
              Million Dollar Man" (ABC).   **TV&R**

1977   British architect Richard Rogers and Italian architect Renzo Piano
              design the Pompidou Center, an art museum and performing arts
              center in Paris.   **ARCH**

1977   The modern aluminum-faced Citicorp Center opens in New York
              City. Designed by Hugh Stubbins & Associates, it marks the city sky-
              line with its sharply diagonal roof. The firm also designs the Federal
              Reserve Bank Building, which opens in Boston this year.   **ARCH**

1977   Notable dance works include American choreographer Twyla
              Tharp's *Simon Medley* and *MUD*.   **DANCE**

1977   *American Buffalo*, a drama by American playwright David Mamet,
              premieres, providing Mamet with his Broadway debut.   **DRAMA**

1977   The American musical *Annie*, based on the comic strip *Little Orphan
              Annie*, premieres on April 21. Its book is by Thomas Meehan, lyrics
              by Martin Charnin, and music by Charles Strouse.   **DRAMA**

1977   Notable American films include Steven Spielberg's *Close Encounters of the Third Kind*, Fred Zinnemann's *Julia*, Herbert Ross's *The Turning Point*, and John Badham's *Saturday Night Fever*. Woody Allen and his film *Annie Hall* win Oscars for Best Picture, Director, and Original Screenplay, setting a new, more serious direction for the filmmaker, whose earlier films were purely comic.   **FILM**

1977   Notable foreign films include Luis Buñuel's *That Obscure Object of Desire*, Moshe Mizrahi's *Madame Rosa*, Bruce Beresford's *The Getting of Wisdom*, Claude Goretta's *The Lacemaker*, Paolo and Vittori Taviani's *Padre Padrone*, and Bernardo Bertolucci's *1900*.   **FILM**

1977   George Lucas's *Star Wars*, released by 20th Century-Fox, sets a new all-time box office record, establishes Lucas as an independent entertainment mogul, and opens the way for a flood of big-budget science-fiction blockbusters. Two sequels will follow, *The Empire Strikes Back* (1980) and *The Return of the Jedi* (1983).   **FILM**

1977   British novelist Barbara Pym publishes the novel *Quartet in Autumn*, her first major success since her novels of the 1950s, including *Excellent Women* (1952).   **LIT**

1977   Notable American musical works include Leon Kirchner's opera *Lily*, Ned Rorem's organ suite *A Quaker Reader*, Elliott Carter's *A Symphony of Three Orchestras*, George Crumb's large-scale orchestral work *Star-Child*, Roque Cordero's *Soliloquies No. 3* for solo clarinet, Leonard Bernstein's *Songfest*, and Roger Sessions's *Five Pieces for Piano*.   **MUSIC**

1977   British singer and songwriter Elvis Costello (born Declan MacManus) makes his name as an idiosyncratic musician and commentator on the human condition with his album *My Aim Is True*.   **MUSIC**

1977   Rock musician Elvis Presley dies at Graceland, his Memphis home on Aug. 16. Speculation arises that his dependence on prescribed drugs played a role in his death. So intense is the loyalty of his fans that decades after his death pilgrimages will be made to his home and grave, making Presley the foremost celebrity icon of American pop culture.   **MUSIC**

1977   British painter David Hockney paints *Looking at Pictures on a Screen* and *My Parents*.   **PAINT**

1977   American painter Robert Moskowitz paints *The Swimmer*.   **PAINT**

1977   French painter Balthus (Count Balthasaiklossowski) paints *Nude in Profile*.   **PAINT**

1977   American artist Cindy Sherman creates the photographic series *Untitled Film Stills*.   **PHOTO**

1977–1988   The highest-rated TV program of the season is "Laverne & Shirley" (ABC). Other top-rated programs are "60 Minutes" (CBS) and "Charlie's Angels" (ABC).   **TV&R**

1977   For eight consecutive nights the TV mini-series "Roots" (ABC), about a black family's history through slavery and freedom in the United States, is broadcast to record-breaking ratings.   **TV&R**

1978   Chinese-American architect I. M. Pei designs the east wing of the National Gallery of Art in Washington, D.C.   **ARCH**

1978   Notable dance works include Belgian choreographer Maurice Béjart's *Gaité Parisienne* and American choreographer Martha Graham's *The Owl and the Pussycat, Ecuatorial*, and *The Flute of Pan*.   **DANCE**

1978   *Buried Child*, a drama by American playwright Sam Shepard, premieres. It will win the Pulitzer Prize. Shepard's *True West* and *A Lie of the Mind* will be produced in 1980 and 1985, respectively.   **DRAMA**

1978   Notable American films include Michael Cimino's *The Deer Hunter*, Warren Beatty's *Heaven Can Wait*, John Carpenter's *Halloween*, Hal Ashby's *Coming Home*, John Landis's *National Lampoon's Animal House*, and Richard Donner's *Superman*.   **FILM**

1978   Notable foreign films include Bertrand Blier's *Get Out Your Handkerchiefs*, Billy Wilder's *Fedora*, Rainer Werner Fassbinder's *The Marriage of Maria Braun*, Claude Chabrol's *Violette*, and Ingmar Bergman's *Autumn Sonata*.   **FILM**

1978   British novelist Graham Greene publishes *The Human Factor*, a spy thriller with the moral concerns typical of his work. *See also* 1938, LIT.   **LIT**

1978   The Metropolitan Opera transmits its first live telecast from New York, *La Bohème* with Renata Scotto and Luciano Pavarotti.   **MUSIC**

1978   György Ligeti's opera *Le Grand Macabre* premieres in Sweden; Krzysztof Penderecki's opera *Paradise Lost* and Concerto for Violin premiere in the United States.   **MUSIC**

1978   Notable American musical works include Samuel Barber's *Third Essay for Orchestra*, Charles Wuorinen's *Percussion Symphony* and *Two-Part Symphony*, Morton Subotnick's *Dance! Cloudless Sulphur* for tape and dancers, and Elie Siegmeister's *A Set of Houses* and *City Songs*. French composer Pierre Boulez premieres an orchestral version of his *Notations*; German composer Isang Yun premieres *Muak (Fantasy for Orchestra*.   **MUSIC**

1978   American painter Elizabeth Murray paints *Children Meeting*.   **PAINT**

1978   In New York the "Bad Painters" and "New Imagists" exhibitions launch a new form of representational art called neo-expressionism, which uses expressive color and brushwork and intentionally primitive styles. Artists associated with the movement include American painter Joan Brown and German painter Anselm Kiefer.   **PAINT**

1978–1979   The highest-rated TV program of the season is "Laverne & Shirley" (ABC). Other top-rated programs are "Mork & Mindy" (ABC) and "All in the Family" (CBS).   **TV&R**

1979   Russian ballet dancers Alexander Godunov and Leonid and Valentina Kozlov defect to the United States during a tour of the Bolshoi Ballet, in which they were principal dancers.   **DANCE**

1979   The works of nineteenth-century Danish choreographer Auguste Bournonville are introduced to the United States in a national tour by the Royal Danish Ballet.   **DANCE**

1979   British composers Andrew Lloyd Webber and Tim Rice see the premiere of their rock opera musical *Evita* on Broadway. It will begin a near-dominance of Webber musicals in American theater over the coming two decades.   **DRAMA**

1979   British playwright Caryl Churchill's *Cloud Nine*, a comedy about sex roles and imperialism, is produced. She had previously written *Vinegar Tom* (produced in 1976). Churchill's *Top Girls* will be produced in 1982, *Serious Money* in 1987.   **DRAMA**

1979   American actor and playwright Spalding Gray begins to write and perform a series of autobiographical monologues, which will include *Sex and Death to the Age of 14, Booze, Cars and College Girls, India and After, Interviewing the Audience*, and *Swimming to Cambodia*. He will be at the forefront of the new field of performance art.   **DRAMA**

1979   Notable American films include Blake Edwards's *10*, Robert Benton's *Kramer vs. Kramer*, Woody Allen's *Manhattan*, James Bridges's *The China Syndrome*, Francis Ford Coppola's *Apocalype Now*, Peter Yates's *Breaking Away*, and Martin Ritt's *Norma Rae*. **FILM**

1979   Notable foreign films include Bruce Beresford's *Breaker Morant*, George Miller's *Mad Max*, Luis Buñuel's *L'Age d'Or*, Luchino Visconti's *The Innocent*, and Rainer Werner Fassbinder's *Despair*.   **FILM**

1979   American journalist Tom Wolfe publishes *The Right Stuff*, an iconoclastic study of the seven Mercury astronauts. It will be the basis of a 1983 film.   **LIT**

1979   British poet Thom Gunn publishes *Selected Poems: 1950–1975*. Later works include *The Passages of Joy* (1982) and *The Occasions of Poetry* (1982).   **LIT**

1979   South African novelist Nadine Gordimer publishes the political nov-
           el *Burger's Daughter*. Among her other works are the novel *The
           Conservationist* (1974) and the story collection *Something Out There*
           (1984).   **LIT**

1979   Other notable literary works include American Norman Mailer's *The
           Executioner's Song*, a novel about real-life killer Gary Gilmore; West
           Indian V. S. Naipaul's *A Bend in the River*; American William
           Styron's *Sophie's Choice*; American Geoffrey Wolff's study of his fa-
           ther, *The Duke of Deception*; American Joan Didion's *The White
           Album*; and American Robert Penn Warren's collection *Now and
           Then: Poems 1976–1978*.   **LIT**

1979   The world's oldest orchestra, founded in 1548, Dresden State
           Orchestra, gives its first New York performance at Lincoln Center,
           featuring the music of Beethoven, Mozart, and Brahms.   **MUSIC**

1979   American opera singer Beverly Sills retires as a singer and becomes
           the music director of the New York City Opera.   **MUSIC**

1979   American painter Philip Johnson executes *Paintsplats*; American
           artist Claes Oldenburg creates *Model* and *Crusoe Umbrella*.   **PAINT**

1979   Mexican artist Rufino Tamayo gains his first major United States ret-
           rospective at New York's Whitney Museum of American Art.   **PAINT**

1979   The growing popularity of minimalist art is suggested in U.S. exhibi-
           tions of artists such as Joseph Beuys and Richard Artschwager. **PAINT**

1979   American artist Judy Chicago organizes a team of women artists for
           the collaborative feminist project *The Dinner Party*. The place set-
           tings at the large triangular table represent thirty-nine women from
           history. The suggestion of vaginal shapes in the abstract designs of
           some of the plates causes controversy.   **SCULP**

1979   A retrospective of the works of sculptor George Segal is held at the
           Walker Art Center in Minneapolis.   **SCULP**

1979–1980   The highest-rated TV program of the season is "60 Minutes" (CBS).
           Other top-rated programs are "Three's Company" (ABC) and
           "That's Incredible" (ABC).   **TV&R**

1980s   Break dancing, based on urban street dancing, becomes popular in
           the United States.   **DANCE**

1980s   American artist Keith Haring becomes famous for his white chalk-
           line drawings on black backgrounds in empty advertising sign-
           boards in New York City subway stations.   **GRAPH**

1980s   Popular songs of the decade include "Sailing," "Bette Davis Eyes,"
               "Up Where We Belong," "Ebony and Ivory," "Every Breath You
               Take," "Born in the U.S.A.," "Material Girl," "Thriller," "Beat It,"
               "Karma Chameleon," "What's Love Got to Do With It," "Purple
               Rain," "We Are the World," "Graceland," "That's What Friends Are
               For," "Somewhere Out There," "Don't Worry, Be Happy," "Sweet
               Child O' Mine," "So Emotional," "Forever Your Girl," "Girl You
               Know It's True," and "Straight Up."   **MUSIC**

1980   American architects Philip Johnson and John Burgee design the
               Crystal Cathedral in Garden Grove, California.   **ARCH**

1980   The U.S. architectural firm Gruzen & Partners designs New York
               City's Grand Hyatt Hotel, with an atrium four stories high.   **ARCH**

1980   American avant-garde choreographer Laura Dean's first ballet,
               Night, premieres with the Joffrey Ballet.   **DANCE**

1980   Notable American films include Jim Abrahams's *Airplane!*, Irvin
               Kershner's *The Empire Strikes Back*, Martin Scorsese's *Raging Bull*,
               James Bridges's *Urban Cowboy*, Robert Redford's *Ordinary People*,
               and Stanley Kubrick's *The Shining*.   **FILM**

1980   Notable foreign films include Gillian Armstrong's *My Brilliant
               Career*, François Truffaut's *The Last Metro*, Akira Kurosawa's
               Kagemusha, Vladimir Menshov's *Moscow Does Not Believe in Tears*,
               and Jamie Uys's *The Gods Must Be Crazy*.   **FILM**

1980   South African novelist J. M. Coetzee, known for his fictional explo-
               rations of imperialism and apartheid, publishes *Waiting for the
               Barbarians*.   **LIT**

1980   Italian semiotician and essayist Umberto Eco publishes his first nov-
               el *The Name of the Rose*. The cerebral tale of murder in a Benedictine
               monastery becomes a surprise international best-seller.   **LIT**

1980   Other notable literary works include the posthumously published
               novel by American John Kennedy Toole, *A Confederacy of Dunces*;
               South African Andre Brink's *A Dry White Season*; Italian Italo
               Calvino's collection, *Italian Folktales*; American Walker Percy's *The
               Second Coming*; Briton P. D. James's *Innocent Blood*; American
               Donald R. Justice's collection, *Selected Poems*; and American Philip
               Levine's two collections, *Ashes* and *7 Years From Somewhere*.   **LIT**

1980   In celebration of the 200th birthday of Los Angeles, the opera *The
               Sinking of the Titanic* by West German William Dieter Siebert has its
               United States premiere at the University of California, Los Angeles.
               The opera requires the performance area to become a ship that
               must be deserted by its audience.   **MUSIC**

1980   The Pulitzer Prize–winning symphony *In Memory of a Summer Day*
               by David Del Tredici premieres in St. Louis.   **MUSIC**

1980   On Dec. 8 ex-Beatle John Lennon is shot and killed outside his apartment building in New York City by deranged fan Mark Chapman. His album with wife Yoko Ono *Double Fantasy*, released earlier in the year, will reach number 1 on the pop music charts.   **MUSIC**

1980   German painter Anselm Kiefer executes *To the Unknown Painter*.   **PAINT**

1980   A few months before his death this year, the Metropolitan Museum of Art presents an exhibit of American artist Clyfford Still's abstract paintings, the museum's largest-ever one-man exhibition by a living artist.   **PAINT**

1980   A major retrospective of Spanish painter Pablo Picasso draws record crowds at the Museum of Modern Art, New York City.   **PAINT**

1980   American photographer Irving Penn publishes the collection *Flowers*, which contains many of his arresting recent works.   **PHOTO**

1980   American artist Jeff Koons begins a sculptural program called "The New" consisting of a series of vacuum cleaners encased in Plexiglas with flourescent lights, displayed next to advertising posters.   **SCULP**

1980   American entrepreneur Ted Turner founds the Cable News Network (CNN). Over the next few years, cable television stations of many kinds will proliferate.   **TV&R**

1980–1981   The highest-rated TV program of the season is "Dallas" (CBS). Other top-rated programs are "The Love Boat" (ABC) and "Little House on the Prairie" (NBC).   **TV&R**

1981   Several experimental dance festivals are held across the United States, including the American Dance Festival in Durham, North Carolina, and a "Next Wave" program at the Brooklyn Academy of Music. Dancers include Americans Laura Dean and Trisha Brown.   **DANCE**

1981   Notable American films include Steven Spielberg's *Raiders of the Lost Ark*, Louis Malle's *Atlantic City*, Warren Beatty's *Reds*, and Mark Rydell's *On Golden Pond*.   **FILM**

1981   Notable foreign films include Hugh Hudson's *Chariots of Fire*, Peter Weir's *Gallipoli*, Rainer Werner Fassbinder's *Lili Marleen*, Bill Forsyth's *Gregory's Girl*, and Karel Reisz's *The French Lieutenant's Woman*.   **FILM**

1981   Notable literary works include American Toni Morrison's *Tar Baby*; Briton D. M. Thomas's *The White Hotel*; American John Updike's third "Rabbit" novel *Rabbit Is Rich*; American Donald Barthelme's *Sixty Stories*; Argentinian Jorge Luis Borges's *Borges: A Reader*; and American Lisel Mueller's *The Morning of the Poem*.   **LIT**

1981   The first exhibition of pre-Columbian art exhibited outside Central America, called "Between Continents; Between Seas: Pre-Columbian Art of Costa Rica," is shown at the National Gallery of Art, Washington, D.C.   **MISC**

1981   American composer Roger Sessions's Concerto for Orchestra is pre-
             miered in Boston; American composer Ned Rorem's Double
             Concerto for Cello and Piano is debuted in Cincinnati.   **MUSIC**

1981   American composer Philip Glass premieres two operas: *The Panther*
             at the Houston Opera and *Satyagraha* at the Brooklyn Academy of
             Music.   **MUSIC**

1981   A triple bill of works by Russian composer Igor Stravinsky, with designs
             by David Hockney, is staged at the Metropolitan Opera House.   **MUSIC**

1981   Symphony in F Major, a newly discovered work of Wolfgang
             Amadeus Mozart, is premiered near Munich, West Germany. The
             piece was written when Mozart was nine years old.   **MUSIC**

1981   After an eleven-year separation, American folk duo Paul Simon and
             Art Garfunkel reunite for a widely attended concert in New York's
             Central Park. They will reunite again for a sellout concert series in
             1993.   **MUSIC**

1981   On Aug. 1 MTV takes to the air with its first video, "Video Killed the
             Radio Star" by the Buggles. The use of videos will revolutionize the
             way rock music is presented to its audience, making it as much a
             visual as an aural medium.   **MUSIC**

1981   American artist Robert Ryman paints *Paramount*.   **PAINT**

1981   American artist Romare Bearden creates the collage *Artist with
             Painting and Model*.   **PAINT**

1981   American painter Alice Neel executes *Self-Portrait*.   **PAINT**

1981   American artist Robert Moskowitz creates the pastel on paper work
             Red Mill.   **PAINT**

1981   Pop sculptor Claes Oldenburg creates the thirty-eight-foot *Flashlight*
             for the University of Nevada at Reno.   **SCULP**

1981–1982   The highest-rated program of the season is "Dallas" (CBS). Other
             top-rated programs are "60 Minutes" (CBS) and "The Dukes of
             Hazzard" (CBS).   **TV&R**

1982   Chinese-American architect I. M. Pei designs the Fragrant Hills
             Hotel in Beijing, China, and the Texas Commerce Tower in
             Houston, Texas.   **ARCH**

1982   American architect Michael Graves designs the Humana Building
             in Louisville, Kentucky, an important work of postmodern
             architecture.   **ARCH**

1982   The Vietnam Veteran's Memorial, designed by American architect
             Maya Lin, is completed in Washington, D.C. The stark wall of
             names of those killed in the war stirs great controversy.   **ARCH**

1982   *Master Harold . . . and the Boys*, a drama about apartheid by South African playwright Athol Fugard, premieres. In 1984 his *The Road to Mecca* will be produced.   **DRAMA**

1982   American playwright Christopher Durang's comedy *Sister Mary Ignatius Explains It All for You* premieres. Durang's *Beyond Therapy* and *The Marriage of Bette and Boo* will be produced in 1982 and 1985, respectively.   **DRAMA**

1982   Notable films include Steven Spielberg's *E.T., The Extra Terrestrial*, Sydney Pollack's *Tootsie*, Taylor Hackford's *An Officer and a Gentleman*, Tobe Hooper's *Poltergeist*, Wayne Wang's *Chan is Missing*, and Blake Edward's *Victor/Victoria*.   **FILM**

1982   Notable foreign films include Jean-Jacques Beineix's *Diva*, Daniel Vigne's *The Return of Martin Guerre*, Richard Attenborough's *Gandhi*, and Rainer Werner Fassbinder's *Lola*.   **FILM**

1982   American novelist Anne Tyler publishes *Dinner at the Homesick Restaurant*, the story of a troubled family. The book is instrumental in establishing Tyler's themes and her popularity.   **LIT**

1982   American novelist and poet Alice Walker publishes the epistolary novel *The Color Purple*, about the struggles of African-American women in the South.   **LIT**

1982   Australian novelist Thomas Keneally publishes *Schindler's Ark*, a novelistic account of European businessman's Oskar Schindler's moves to save Jews from death during the Holocaust. In the United States the novel will be known as *Schindler's List*.   **LIT**

1982   Other notable literary works include American Saul Bellow's *The Dean's December*; American Paul Theroux's *The Mosquito Coast*; and Briton Graham Greene's *Monsignor Quixote*.   **LIT**

1982   American singer Michael Jackson, late of the Motown group the Jackson Five, becomes a recording superstar with his album *Thriller*. Six of the nine album cuts become major hits, most notably "Beat It" and "Billie Jean." Jackson's fashion preferences (a gloved hand) and his stylized expressive dance steps exert a powerful influence on early 1980s culture.   **MUSIC**

1982   American painter Joseph Beuys executes *Monuments to the Stag*. **PAINT**

1982   American painter Elizabeth Murray paints *Keyhole*.   **PAINT**

1982–1983   The highest-rated TV program of the season is "60 Minutes" (CBS). Other top-rated programs are "M*A*S*H" (CBS) and "Magnum, P.I." (CBS).   **TV&R**

1983   Two new buildings by leading architects are erected on Madison Avenue in New York City: Philip Johnson's AT&T building at 56th Street and Edward Larrabee Barnes's IBM building at 57th Street. **ARCH**

1983   American architect Frank Gehry designs the Norton house in Venice, California.   **ARCH**

1983   Rudolf Nureyev, a former Russian ballet dancer who defected to the West, becomes director of the Paris Opera Ballet.   **DANCE**

1983   American choreographer Paul Taylor's *Sunset* is premiered.   **DANCE**

1983   *Glengarry Glen Ross*, a drama by American playwright David Mamet, is produced. It will win the Pulitzer Prize.   **DRAMA**

1983   Notable American films include James L. Brooks's *Terms of Endearment*, Lawrence Kasdan's *The Big Chill*, Adrian Lyne's *Flashdance*, Paul Brickman's *Risky Business*, John Badham's *War Games*, Woody Allen's *Zelig*, and Peter Weir's *The Year of Living Dangerously*.   **FILM**

· ·

"Westerns are successful throughout the world because nobody says anything."
—American film star James Stewart, 1983

· ·

1983   Notable foreign films include Ingmar Bergman's *Fanny and Alexander*, Federico Fellini's *And the Ship Sails On*, Ettore Scola's *La Nuit de Varennes*, and Lewis Gilbert's *Educating Rita*.   **FILM**

1983   American novelist and short-story writer Mark Helprin publishes *Winter's Tale*, a complex and fanciful epic of New York City.   **LIT**

1983   American writer John Updike publishes the essay collection *Hugging the Shore*, which will win the Pulitzer Prize.   **LIT**

1983   British novelist Fay Weldon publishes *The Life and Loves of a She-Devil*. Among her earlier works are *The Fat Woman's Joke* (1967).   **LIT**

1983   Other notable literary works include Briton John le Carré's *The Little Drummer Girl*; Pulitzer Prize–winning American Galway Kinnell's *Selected Poems*; Colombian Gabriel García Márquez's *Chronicle of a Death Foretold*; American Lewis Thomas's essay collection, *Late Night Thoughts on Listening to Mahler's Ninth Symphony*; and American Raymond Carver's *Cathedral*.   **LIT**

1983   American composer William Mayer's opera *A Death in the Family*, based on the James Agee novel, is premiered at the Minnesota Opera.   **MUSIC**

1983   The Nashville Network premieres on cable television, highlighting the growing mainstream interest in country-and-western music.   **MUSIC**

1983   The British rock group the Police gain wide success with their album *Synchronicity*. The group's bleak, intellectual outlook is highlighted in hit songs such as the paean to possessive love, "Every Breath You Take."   **MUSIC**

| 1983 | American artist Jasper Johns paints *Racing Thoughts*. | PAINT |

1983   American painter Brice Marden paints *Elements IV*.   **PAINT**

1983   In photos like *Gregory Watching the Snow Fall*, British painter David Hockney creates collages influenced by the painting movements of the twentieth century.   **PHOTO**

1983   American sculptor Richard Serra erects *Clara-Clara* in the Jardin des Tuileries. The huge steel creation will be a part of his "Prop" series on exhibition at the Georges Pompidou Center in France.   **SCULP**

· ·

"What is directing? It's trying to use a lot of people and some very, very heavy apparatus and give it the lightness of a pen while you are writing."—British film director David Lean, c. 1983

· ·

1983–1984   The highest-rated TV program of the season is "Dallas" (CBS). Other top-rated programs are "Dynasty" (ABC) and "Falcon Crest" (CBS). **TV&R**

1984   The Martha Graham dance troupe presents its first interpretation of the Stravinsky ballet *The Rite of Spring*.   **DANCE**

1984   African-American playwright August Wilson's play *Ma Rainey's Black Bottom* premieres. It will be followed by *Joe Turner's Come and Gone* (produced in 1986), *Fences* (1987), and *The Piano Lesson* (1988).   **DRAMA**

1984   Notable American films include Milos Forman's *Amadeus*, Steven Spielberg's *Indiana Jones and the Temple of Doom*, Sergio Leone's *Once Upon a Time in America*, Ron Howard's *Splash*, Martin Brest's *Beverly Hills Cop*, and Jim Jarmusch's *Stranger Than Paradise*.   **FILM**

1984   Notable foreign films include Roland Joffe's *The Killing Fields*, David Lean's *A Passage to India*, Andrei Tarkovsky's *Nostalghia*, and Neil Jordan's *The Company of Wolves*.   **FILM**

1984   American novelist and short-story writer Louise Erdrich publishes her novel *Love Medicine*, an exploration of three generations of Turtle Mountain Chippewas in the Great Plains.   **LIT**

1984   A collection of the works of American poet Richard Hugo, *Making Certain It Goes On: The Collected Poems*, is published posthumously. **LIT**

1984   British novelist Julian Barnes publishes *Flaubert's Parrot*, a fictional blend of biography and fantasy.   **LIT**

1984   Czech novelist and short-story writer Milan Kundera, known for writing on political and erotic themes, publishes his best-known novel, *The Unbearable Lightness of Being*.   **LIT**

1984   American novelist Jay McInerney publishes *Bright Lights, Big City*, the story of a rootless young professional in New York City.   **LIT**

1984   Other notable literary works include American Eudora Welty's writing memoir *One Writer's Beginnings*; Briton Angela Carter's *Nights at the Circus*; American Philip Levine's *Selected Poems*; Briton J. G. Ballard's *Empire of the Sun*; and American Joan Didion's novel *Democracy*.   **LIT**

1984   Two exhibitions from the People's Republic of China tour the United States: Contemporary Chinese Painting and an exhibition on loan from the Shanghai Museum of artifacts from the Neolithic era.   **MISC**

1984   Irish rock musician Bob Geldof of the Boomtown Rats organizes Band Aid to record the song, "Do They Know It's Christmas?" to aid Ethiopian famine relief. Members from fifteen rock bands participate in the internationally successful venture, including David Bowie, Phil Collins, Sting, George Michael, and Duran Duran.   **MUSIC**

1984   The success of American singer-songwriter Bruce Springsteen's *Born in the USA* album and tour establishes him as a rock superstar.   **MUSIC**

1984   American painters Andy Warhol, Jean-Michel Basquiat, and Francesco Clemente paint *Polestar*.   **PAINT**

1985   New works by American choreographer Paul Taylor include *Last Look* and *Roses*; new works by Russian-born choreographer George Balanchine include *Native Green*.   **DANCE**

1985   Notable films include Robert Zemeckis's *Back to the Future*, Sydney Pollack's *Out of Africa*, Peter Weir's *Witness*, Ron Howard's *Cocoon*, and Lewis Teague's *The Jewel of the Nile*.   **FILM**

1985   Notable foreign films include Agnès Varda's *Vagabond*, Jean-Luc Godard's *Hail Mary*, Dorris Dorrie's *Men*, Akira Kurosawa's *Ran*, Terry Gilliam's *Brazil*, and Stephen Frears's *My Beautiful Laundrette*.   **FILM**

1985   American novelist Anne Tyler publishes the novel *The Accidental Tourist*, a family drama about a disaffected travel writer and a dog trainer who find love.   **LIT**

1985   Other notable literary works include American Larry McMurtry's *Lonesome Dove*; Italian Italo Calvino's *Mr. Palomar*; Mexican Carlos Fuentes's *The Old Gringo*; and Chilean Isabel Allende's *The House of the Spirits*.   **LIT**

1985   American composer Stephen Albert's Pulitzer Prize–winning work *Symphony, RiverRun*, premieres in Washington, D.C.   **MUSIC**

1985   To provide aid to Africa, American composer Quincy Jones arranges the recording of the Michael Jackson–Lionel Richie anthem of global solidarity, "We Are the World." It is recorded in January by more than thirty top vocal artists, including Michael Jackson, Bruce Springsteen, Billy Joel, Cyndi Lauper, Lionel Richie, Kenny Rogers, and Stevie Wonder.   **MUSIC**

1985   In July Irish rock musician Bob Geldof organizes Live Aid, benefit concerts held in London and Philadelphia that feature more than fifty pop stars, including Bob Dylan, Tina Turner, David Bowie, and Neil Young.   **MUSIC**

1985   American singer Madonna (Madonna Louise Vernon Ciccone) cements her place as an eighties pop icon with the album *Like a Virgin*. Her outrageous attitude and chameleonlike changes of image will contribute as much as her music to her success.   **MUSIC**

1985   Canadian-American painter Dorothea Rockburne paints *Interior Perspective* (*Discordant Harmony*).   **PAINT**

1985   Red Grooms: Retrospective, 1956–1984, a collection of the works of the modern American artist, is held at the Pennsylvania Academy of Fine Arts.   **PAINT**

1985   American artist Cindy Sherman completes the photographic series *Grotesques*.   **PHOTO**

1985   Bulgarian-born artist Christo wraps the Pont Neuf Bridge in Paris with 47,680 square yards of tan nylon.   **SCULP**

1985   A collection of works by American sculptor Mark di Suvero is exhibited at the Storm King Art Center in Mountainville, New York, in celebration of the center's twenty-fifth anniversary.   **SCULP**

1985   American sculptor Louise Bourgeois has her first large-scale exhibition at the Museum of Modern Art.   **SCULP**

1985–1986   The highest-rated TV program of the season is "Dynasty" (ABC). Other top-rated programs are "The Cosby Show" (NBC), "Dallas" (CBS), and "Family Ties" (NBC).   **TV&R**

1986   Notable films include Woody Allen's *Hannah and Her Sisters*, Oliver Stone's *Platoon*, Francis Ford Coppola's *Peggy Sue Got Married*, James Cameron's *Aliens*, Rob Reiner's *Stand By Me*, and Tony Scott's *Top Gun*.   **FILM**

1986   Notable foreign films include James Ivory's *A Room With a View*, Jovan Acin's *Hey Babu Riba*, Chen Kaige's *Yellow Earth*, Claude Berri's *Manon of the Spring*, Alain Cavalier's *Therese*, Alex Cox's *Sid and Nancy*, Neil Jordan's *Mona Lisa*, and Bertrand Tavernier's *Round Midnight*.   **FILM**

1986–1991 American writer and artist Art Spiegelman redefines the graphic novel with *Maus: A Survivor's Tale*, about his father's experiences in a concentration camp during World War II and his life afterward. The book, published in two parts, will win the Pulitzer Prize. **GRAPH**

1986 Canadian novelist and poet Margaret Atwood publishes the speculative gender work *The Handmaid's Tale*. Earlier novels include *Surfacing* (1972) and *Bodily Harm* (1983). Her collections of poetry include *The Animals in That Country* (1968) and *Selected Poems* (1976). **LIT**

1986 British writer Martin Amis, son of novelist Kingsley Amis (*see* 1954, LIT), publishes the short-story collection *Einstein's Monsters*, centered on the theme of nuclear war. **LIT**

1986 Other notable literary works include Italian Primo Levi's *The Monkey's Wrench*; Briton Iris Murdoch's *The Good Apprentice*; American Oliver Sacks's study of his patients, *The Man Who Mistook His Wife for a Hat*; American Louise Erdrich's *The Beet Queen*; West Indian-born Derek Walcott's *Collected Poems 1948-1984*; American Robert Coles's examination, *The Moral Life of Children*; and American Robert Stone's *Children of Light*. **LIT**

1986 Russian-born pianist Vladimir Horowitz holds his first concert in Moscow since his departure in 1925. The widely attended concert was not acknowledged by the Soviet government. **MUSIC**

1986 American composer Anthony Davis's opera *X* (*The Life and Times of Malcolm X*), has its formal premiere at the New York City Opera. **MUSIC**

1986 Rap music, which began in the mid-seventies among black and Hispanic youth in New York City's outer boroughs, becomes increasingly popular. The Queens-based Run-DMC's album *Raisin' Hell* is the first of the genre to go platinum. **MUSIC**

1986 American artist Roy Lichtenstein paints *Mural with Blue Brushstroke* for the lobby of New York's Equitable Life Assurance Center. **PAIN**

1986 "Diego Rivera: A Retrospective," the first retrospective exhibition of the Mexican painter of murals, opens at the Detroit Institute of Arts and travels internationally during the next year. **PAINT**

1986 A newly developing artistic movement, neo-geo, which combines abstract painting and representational sculpture, is featured in several shows in American galleries and museums. **PAINT**

1986–1987 The highest-rated TV program of the season is "The Cosby Show" (NBC). Other top-rated programs are "Murder, She Wrote" (CBS), "Cheers" (NBC), and "Miami Vice" (NBC). **TV&R**

1987 Japanese architect Kenzo Tange wins the Pritzker Architecture Prize. In England community architect Ralph Erskine wins the Royal Gold Medal for Architecture. **ARCH**

1987   Belgian choreographer Maurice Béjart permanently moves his
             Ballet of the Twentieth Century from Brussels, Belgium, to
             Lausanne, Switzerland.   **DANCE**

1987   Notable American films include James L. Brooks's *Broadcast News*,
             Adrian Lyne's *Fatal Attraction*, Norman Jewison's *Moonstruck*,
             Leonard Nimoy's *Three Men and a Baby*, and Brian De Palma's *The
             Untouchables*.   **FILM**

•••

"What civilians do not understand—and to a writer
anyone not a writer is a civilian—is that writing is
manual labor of the mind: a job, like laying pipe."
—American novelist and screenwriter
John Gregory Dunne, 1987

•••

1987   Notable foreign films include Louis Malle's *Au Revoir Les Enfants*,
             Gabriel Axel's *Babette's Feast*, Richard Attenborough's *Cry Freedom*,
             John Boorman's *Hope and Glory*, Juzo Itami's *A Taxing Woman*,
             Stephen Frears's *Sammy and Rosie Get Laid*, and Bernardo
             Bertolucci's *The Last Emperor*.   **FILM**

1987   American journalist Tom Wolfe publishes the novel *The Bonfire of
             the Vanities*, a satire of eighties greed, race relations, and criminal
             justice.   **LIT**

1987   Other notable American literary works include Toni Morrison's
             Beloved, T. Coraghessan Boyle's *World's End*, Joyce Carol Oates's
             You Must Remember This, and Annie Dillard's memoir, *An American
             Childhood*. In England Irish-born Brian Moore publishes *The Colour
             of Blood* and Nigerian-born Amos Tutuola publishes *Pauper, Brawler,
             and Slanderer*. In Germany Friedrich Dürrenmatt publishes the nov-
             el *Der Auftrag*.   **LIT**

1987   New musical works include American composer Steven Paulus's
             Construction Symphony, French composer Olivier Messiaen's *Bird
             Sketches* for piano, and British composer Robert Saxton's choral
             work *I Will Awake the Dawn*.   **MUSIC**

1987   American painter Brice Marden executes *Diptych*; American painter
             Robert Ryman paints *Constant*.   **PAINT**

1987   The first retrospective of German neoexpressionist artist Anselm
             Kiefer begins at the Art Institute of Chicago and travels to
             Philadelphia, Los Angeles, and New York in 1988.   **PAINT**

1987–1988   The highest-rated TV program of the season is "The Cosby Show"
             (NBC). Other top-rated programs are "Cheers" (NBC), "Night Court"
             (NBC), and "Moonlighting" (ABC).   **TV&R**

Entrance to the Louvre designed by I. M. Pei. *(French Government Tourist Office)*

1988   As part of a national architecture project called Grands Projets, France's Louvre Museum is remodeled by Chinese-American architect I. M. Pei. One element is a modern sixty-five-foot glass pyramid. **ARCH**

1988   Several activities between United States and Soviet ballets and dance troupes mark improving relations between the countries, including the exchange of guest artists between the New York City and Bolshoi Ballets. **DANCE**

1988   American playwright Wendy Wasserstein's drama about womanhood and feminism, *The Heidi Chronicles*, is produced. It will win the Pulitzer Prize and a Tony award. Her play *The Sisters Rosensweig* will be produced in 1993. **DRAMA**

1988   Notable American films include Steven Frears's *Dangerous Liaisons*, Lawrence Kasdan's *The Accidental Tourist*, Penny Marshall's *Big*, Jonathan Demme's *Married to the Mob*, Barry Levinson's *Rain Man*, and Robert Zemeckis's *Who Framed Roger Rabbit*. **FILM**

1988   Notable foreign films include David Cronenberg's *Dead Ringers*, Zhang Yimou's *Red Sorghum*, Giuseppe Tornatore's *Cinema Paradiso*, Bertrand Tavernier's *Beatrice*, and Wim Wenders's *Wings of Desire*. **FILM**

1988   American novelist Don De Lillo publishes the novel *Libra*, which uses the Lee Harvey Oswald assassination of President John Kennedy to explore larger meanings in modern America. **LIT**

1988   Other notable literary works include Briton Fay Weldon's *The Hearts and Lives of Men*; Colombian Gabriel García Márquez's *Love in the Time of Cholera*; American Raymond Carver's collection, *Where I'm Calling From*; and Nigerian Chinua Achebe's *Anthills of the Savannah*.   LIT

1988   Poetic works include U.S. poet laureate Richard Wilbur's *New and Collected Poems*; Polish poet Czeslaw Milosz's *The Collected Poems: 1931–1987*; Nigerian poet Wole Soyinka's *Mandela's Earth and Other Poems*; Russian-American poet Joseph Brodsky's *To Urania*; and American poet John Hollander's *Harp Lake*.   LIT

1988   The Shaping of Daimyo Culture 1185–1868, the most wide-ranging exhibition of works from the Japanese feudal age, begins at the National Gallery of Art, Washington, D.C.   MISC

1988   On the occasion of American composer Elliott Carter's eightieth birthday, his Oboe Concerto receives its American debut with the San Francisco Symphony Orchestra.   MUSIC

1988   The first operas by American composer John Cage, *Europeras 1 & 2*, are premiered in Purchase, New York.   MUSIC

1988   Heavy metal groups like Guns n' Roses, Def Leppard, Van Halen, Metallica, and the Scorpions gain popularity, countering a resurgence of classic rock from the sixties and seventies.   MUSIC

1988–1989   The highest-rated TV program of the season is "The Cosby Show" (NBC). Other top-rated programs are "Roseanne" (ABC), "A Different World" (NBC), and "Cheers" (NBC).   TV&R

1989   Chinese-American architect I. M. Pei designs the Bank of China building in Hong Kong.   ARCH

1989   Architect Pierre Fakhoury designs the Basilica of Our Lady of Peace in Yamoussoukro, Ivory Coast, the tallest church in Christendom, with a dome 525 feet high.   ARCH

1989   Conflicts with the board of trustees lead Russian dancer Mikhail Baryshnikov to resign as artistic director of the American Ballet Theater, a post he held since 1980.   DANCE

1989   Notable films of the year include Tim Burton's *Batman*, Bruce Beresford's *Driving Miss Daisy*, Gus Van Sant's *Drugstore Cowboy*, Kenneth Branagh's *Henry V*, Jim Sheridan's *My Left Foot*, Steven Soderbergh's *sex, lies and videotape*, and Oliver Stone's *Born on the Fourth of July*.   FILM

1989   Notable foreign films include Jane Campion's *Sweetie*, Peter Greenaway's *The Cook, The Thief, His Wife and Her Lover*, Wayne Wang's *Life is Cheap . . . But Toilet Paper is Expensive*, Percy Adlon's *Rosalie Goes Shopping*, and Patrice Leconte's *Monsieur Hire*.   FILM

Mikhail Baryshnikov in Eliot Feld's *Santa Fe Saga*. (*UPI/Bettmann*)

1989   The first films designated for inclusion in the National Film Registry,
        part of the 1988 National Film Preservation Act that honors works
        that are "culturally, historically, or esthetically significant," are *The
        Best Years of Our Lives* (1946); *Casablanca* (1942); *Citizen Kane*
        (1941); *The Crowd* (1928); *Dr. Strangelove, or, How I Learned to Stop
        Worrying and Love the Bomb* (1964); *The General* (1927); *Gone With
        the Wind* (1939); *The Grapes of Wrath* (1940); *High Noon* (1952);
        Intolerance (1916); *The Learning Tree* (1969); *The Maltese Falcon*

(1941); *Mr. Smith Goes to Washington* (1939); *Modern Times* (1936); *Nanook of the North* (1922); *On the Waterfront* (1954); *The Searchers* (1956); *Singin' in the Rain* (1952); *Snow White and the Seven Dwarfs* (1937); *Some Like It Hot* (1959); *Star Wars* (1977); *Sunrise* (1927); *Sunset Boulevard* (1950); *Vertigo* (1958); and *The Wizard of Oz* (1939).   **FILM**

1989   Indian-born British writer Salman Rushdie publishes the novel *The Satanic Verses*, resulting in a death sentence from the government of Iran, which accuses him of blasphemy against Islam. Rushdie is forced to go into hiding, which will continue for years. His other works include *Midnight's Children* (1981).   **LIT**

1989   Other notable literary works include American E. L. Doctorow's *Billy Bathgate*; American Allan Gurganus's *Oldest Living Confederate Widow Tells All*; American Amy Tan's first work, *The Joy Luck Club*; and American John Berryman's *Collected Poems, 1937–1971*, published posthumously.   **LIT**

1989   In Oct. a bill is passed in the U.S. Congress that prohibits the National Endowment for the Arts (NEA) from funding artworks deemed obscene as defined in a 1973 ruling by the U.S. Supreme Court. It will prompt NEA chairman John Frohnmayer to ask artists to sign antiobscenity loyalty oaths, which will in turn result in the refusal of some artists and organizations to accept NEA grants.   **MISC**

c. 1989   Vinyl records are phased out of music stores, replaced by the cleaner-sounding, smaller, and more expensive compact discs.   **MUSIC**

1989   A retrospective of the works of modern American painter Helen Frankenthaler opens at the Museum of Modern Art in New York and travels across the United States.   **PAINT**

1989–1990   The highest-rated TV program of the season is "Roseanne" (ABC). Other top-rated programs are "LA Law" (NBC), "The Wonder Years" (ABC), and "60 Minutes" (CBS).   **TV&R**

1990   Japanese architect Kenzo Tange designs the twin tower City Hall in Tokyo.   **ARCH**

1990   The renovated main building at Ellis Island in New York harbor is opened to the public in Sept. Once the initial processing center for millions of immigrants to the United States, it is now a museum of immigration. Architects include Beyer Blinder Belle of New York City and Notter Finegold + Alexander of Boston.   **ARCH**

1990   American dancer and choreographer Martha Graham premieres her first work accompanied by popular music: *Maple Leaf Rag*, set to the music of American ragtime composer Scott Joplin.   **DANCE**

1990   The largest gathering of U.S. dance companies ever held takes place at the 1990 Dance Biennial in France.   **DANCE**

1990   Notable films include Kevin Costner's *Dances With Wolves*, Penny Marshall's *Awakenings*, Andrew Bergman's *The Freshman*, Martin Scorsese's *Goodfellas*, Chris Columbus's *Home Alone*, Paul Verhoven's *Total Recall*, Francis Ford Coppola's *The Godfather Part III*, and Peter Weir's *Green Card*. **FILM**

1990   Notable foreign films include Pedro Almodóvar's *Tie Me Up! Tie Me Down!*, Jim Sheridan's *The Field*, and Akira Kurosawa's *Akira Kurosawa's Dreams*. **FILM**

1990   American artist Jenny Holzer, known for her electronic signs of pointed social and political statement, is awarded the grand prize at the Venice Biennale in Italy. **GRAPH**

1990   Notable literary works include American John Updike's final novel about Rabbit Angstrom, *Rabbit at Rest*; South African J. M. Coetzee's *Age of Iron*; Irish Edna O'Brien's collection, *Lantern Slides*; Briton A. S. Byatt's *Possession*; and American Thomas Pynchon's *Vineland*, his first work in seventeen years. **LIT**

1990   American poetic works include Anthony E. Hecht's *The Transparent Man* and U.S. poet laureate Mark Strand's *The Continuous Life*. **LIT**

1990   The National Endowment for the Arts revokes grants to four American performance artists whose work is deemed sexually controversial: Karen Finley, John Fleck, Holly Hughes, and Tim Miller. In a similar move, the NEA revokes grants to the University of Pennsylvania's Institute of Contemporary Art, the sponsor of a photographic exhibition of erotic works by American photographer Robert Mapplethorpe. *See also* 1990, PHOTO. **MISC**

1990   American composer Mel Powell's concerto *Duplicates*, winner of the Pulitzer Prize for Music, premieres at the Los Angeles Philharmonic. **MUSIC**

1990   In October American composer Leonard Bernstein announces his retirement as musical director of the New York Philharmonic, five days before his death from a heart attack. Among his compositions are the ballet *Fancy Free* (1944) and the musical *West Side Story* (1957). **MUSIC**

1990   In March a decade-long project to clean and restore paintings by Michelangelo in Rome's Sistine Chapel is completed. **PAINT**

1990   An exhibition of sexually suggestive photographs by American photographer Robert Mapplethorpe at the Contemporary Arts Center in Cincinnati, Ohio, prompts public protests and a lawsuit against the Center's director Dennis Barrie. He will be acquitted of obscenity charges by the Ohio municipal court. *See also* 1990, MISC. **PHOTO**

1990–1991   Top-rated TV shows include "Roseanne" (ABC), "Cheers" (NBC), "60 Minutes" (CBS), and "Murphy Brown" (CBS). **TV&R**

HIGH-PRICED ART

*T*hough great art is priceless, art dealers and collectors depend on being able to judge its price. A new record for the cost of a painting was set on May 15, 1990, when Japanese paper tycoon Ryoei Saito paid $82.5 million for Portrait of Dr. Gachet *(1890) by Dutch painter Vincent van Gogh. The work of living artists is valued at considerably lower levels, but most people would still find it hard to raise the $20.68 million paid for the abstract painting* Interchange *(1955) created by American painter Willem de Kooning. Purchased by the Japanese dealer-collector "Mountain Tortoise" on November 8, 1989, the work fetched the highest price ever for a painting by a living artist.*

Van Gogh's pen-and-ink drawing Jardin de Fleurs *(1888) became the most expensive drawing ever sold, for $8.36 million on November 14, 1990. The most expensive sculpture bought at action was the bronze garden ornament* The Dancing Faun *created by Dutch sculptor Adriaan de Vries (c. 1545–1626); it sold for £6.82 million ($12 million) on December 7, 1989.*

However, prices paid at auction may not be the best criterion for judging which artistic works are the most valuable. After all, the world's most valuable pieces are not for sale, though there is one industry intimately concerned with judging their worth in dollars and cents. On that basis, the most valuable painting in the world is Leonardo da Vinci's Mona Lisa *(c. 1503), which was assessed for insurance purposes at $100 million at the time of its move in 1962 from the Louvre in Paris for temporary exhibition in the United States.*

1991	American choreographer Merce Cunningham creates the performance *Trackers*. **DANCE**
1991	Notable American films include Jonathan Demme's *Silence of the Lambs*, Barry Levinson's *Bugsy*, John Singleton's *Boyz N the Hood*, Ridley Scott's *Thelma & Louise*, Oliver Stone's *JFK*, and Terry Gilliam's *The Fisher King*. **FILM**
1991	*Beauty and the Beast*, a Disney studios animated film featuring the voice of Angela Lansbury and the music of Howard Ashman and Alan Menken, becomes the first animated movie to be nominated for an Oscar for Best Picture. **FILM**
1991	Notable international films include Claude Chabrol's *Madame Bovary*, Carlos Saura's *Ay, Carmela!*, Zhang Yimou's *Raise the Red Lantern*, Gabriele Salvatores's *Mediterraneo*, and Sven Nykvist's *The Ox*. **FILM**

1991   Notable literary works include American Diane Wood Middlebrook's biography, *Anne Sexton*, which will raise questions about its gathering of sources; South African Nadine Gordimer's collection *Jump and Other Stories*; American Amy Tan's *The Kitchen God's Wife*; and Canadian Douglas Coupland's *Generation X: Tales for an Accelerated Culture*.   **LIT**

1991   American poetic works include John Ashbery's *Flow Chart*, Philip Levine's *What Work Is*, and William Bronk's collections, *Death Is the Place*, *Life Supports*, and *Living Instead*.   **LIT**

1991   An exhibition, "Degenerate Art: The Fate of the Avant-Garde in Nazi Germany," which features works repressed by Hitler during his rule, begins its tour in Los Angeles. By the end of next year it will have traveled internationally and will have completed its tour in Berlin. **MISC**

1991   The controversial opera *The Death of Klinghoffer*, by composer John Adams and librettist Alice Goodman, premieres at the Brooklyn Academy of Music. It is based on the experiences of American tourist Leon Klinghoffer, who died at the hands of pro-Palestinian terrorists on the cruise ship the *Achille Lauro*.   **MUSIC**

1991   Natalie Cole's Grammy-winning album *Unforgettable* is a personal tribute to her father, singer Nat King Cole, with twenty-two of his classic hits rerecorded on the LP. She is able to sing "duets" with him through advanced electronic techniques.   **MUSIC**

1991   The American cross-country musical tour Lollapalooza begins its run at Irvine Meadows Amphitheater, near Los Angeles. The tour, arranged by musician Perry Farrell of the group Jane's Addiction, features such alternative rock groups as Siouxsie and the Banshees, Living Colour, Nine Inch Nails, Butthole Surfers, and Jane's Addiction. After traveling to more than twenty cities this year, it will become an annual event.   **MUSIC**

1991   Bulgarian-born artist Christo sets up his umbrella project, in which 1,340 blue umbrellas are positioned in Japan and 1,760 yellow umbrellas are put up in California. Accidents in both places causing injury to two people lead to an early dismantling of the project. **SCULP**

1991–1992   Top-rated TV shows include "Cheers" (NBC), "Murphy Brown" (CBS), and "Roseanne" (ABC).   **TV&R**

1992   The one-hundredth anniversary of Tchaikovsky's Christmas ballet *The Nutcracker* is celebrated with myriad presentations worldwide, including an idiosyncratic adaptation called *The Hard Nut* at the Brooklyn Academy of Music.   **DANCE**

1992   Notable American films include Clint Eastwood's *Unforgiven*, Spike Lee's *Malcolm X*, Robert Altman's *The Player*, Martin Brest's *Scent of a Woman*, and Francis Ford Coppola's *Bram Stoker's "Dracula."* **FILM**

1992   Notable foreign films include Régis Wargnier's *Indochine*, Neil Jordan's *The Crying Game*, James Ivory's *Howards End*, Alfonso Arau's *Like Water for Chocolate*, and Richard Attenborough's *Chaplin*.   **FILM**

1992   Notable literary works include Briton Peter Ackroyd's *English Music*; Nigerian Ben Okri's *The Famished Road*; American Terry McMillan's *Waiting to Exhale*; and American Cormac McCarthy's *All the Pretty Horses*.   **LIT**

1992   American poetic works include Tess Gallagher's collection *Moon Crossing Bridge*, William Bronk's *Some Words*, John Ashbery's *Hotel Lautréamont*, and David Ferry's *Gilgamesh*.   **LIT**

1992   The opera *The Voyage* by American composer Philip Glass, which celebrates the 500th anniversary of explorer Christopher Columbus's first voyage to the New World, premieres at New York's Metropolitan Opera.   **MUSIC**

1992   Country music continues to rise in popularity, with performers like Garth Brooks, Reba McEntire, Vince Gill, Clint Black, and Wynonna and Naomi Judd.   **MUSIC**

1992–1993   Pop music is challenged by "alternative" rock, specifically "grunge" groups like Nirvana, Stone Temple Pilots, and Pearl Jam, with their heavy guitar sound, and "gangster rappers" like Snoop Doggy Dogg and Ice-T, whose lyrics are filled with images of street violence. **MUSIC**

1992–1993   Top-rated TV shows include "Roseanne" (ABC), "Northern Exposure" (CBS), "Seinfeld" (NBC), and "60 Minutes" (CBS).   **TV&R**

1992   In May, after nearly three decades of dominating the late-night TV talk show forum, Nebraska-born comedian Johnny Carson retires as host of "The Tonight Show" (NBC). He is replaced by comedian Jay Leno.   **TV&R**

1993   American inventor and engineer Chuck Hoberman completes *Iris Dome* and *Expanding Geodesic Sphere*, examples of his large-scale work combining architecture, robotics, and sculpture.   **ARCH**

1993   Honoring the memories of the six million Jews and five million others systematically killed during the Nazi Holocaust (1933–1945), the United States Holocaust Memorial Museum opens in Washington, D.C. It is designed by architect James I. Freed of the firm Pei Cobb Freed & Partners.   **ARCH**

1993   To spark interest from younger audiences, the Joffrey Ballet premieres a new ballet, *Billboards*, which features the music of American rock musician Prince.   **DANCE**

1993   American dancer and choreographer Twyla Tharp teams with Russian dancer Mikhail Baryshnikov in a national tour called *Cutting Up*.   **DANCE**

1993   American playwright Terence McNally's *A Perfect Ganesh* is produced. Previous works had included *Frankie and Johnny in the Clair de Lune* (produced in 1988), *The Lisbon Traviata* (1989), and *Lips Together, Teeth Apart* (1991).   **DRAMA**

1993   American playwright Tony Kushner's *Angels in America: A Gay Fantasia on National Themes, Part I: Millennium Approaches* opens on Broadway at the Walter Kerr Theater. It will win the Pulitzer Prize and several Tony awards. *Part II: Perestroika* will be produced later in the year.   **DRAMA**

1993   Notable American films include Steven Spielberg's *Jurassic Park*, Jonathan Demme's *Philadelphia*, Martin Scorsese's *The Age of Innocence*, Andrew Davis's *The Fugitive*, and Wolfgang Petersen's *In the Line of Fire*.   **FILM**

1993   Notable foreign films include Chen Kaige's *Farewell My Concubine*, Fernando Trueba's *Belle Epoque*, Ang Lee's *The Wedding Banquet*, Mike Leigh's *Naked*, James Ivory's *The Remains of the Day*, and Jane Campion's *The Piano*.   **FILM**

1993   The comic book hero Superman dies at the hands of the villain Doomsday in *Superman* No. 75 (on sale since November 1992). Later this year, his editors find a way to bring him back to life. *See also* 1938, GRAPH.   **GRAPH**

1993   Notable literary works include Irish Roddy Doyle's *Paddy Clarke Ha Ha Ha*, which will win the Booker Prize; Indian Vikram Seth's *A Suitable Boy*; American E. Annie Proulx's *The Shipping News*, which will win the National Book Award; and Japanese Banana Yoshimoto's *Kitchen*.   **LIT**

1993   American novelist Alan Lightman's *Einstein's Dreams* interweaves narrative with a discussion of the properties of physics.   **LIT**

1993   American poet Maya Angelou composes the poem "On the Pulse of Morning" for the inauguration of President Bill Clinton. Other original works of poetry this year include A. R. Ammons's *Garbage* and Donald Hall's *The Museum of Clear Ideas*.   **LIT**

1993   American poet Rita Dove is named U.S. poet laureate. In 1986 she was awarded the Pulitzer Prize for *Thomas and Beulah*.   **LIT**

1993   The Biennial Exhibition at the Whitney Museum of American Art in New York sparks criticism for its choice of politically driven works and objects that were not artistic in origin.   **MISC**

1993   The 45th annual Venice Biennale begins in Venice, Italy, on June 13. The American representative for this international exhibition is sculptor Louise Bourgeois, who will be the subject of a retrospective show the following year at the Brooklyn Museum.   **MISC**

Maya Angelou *(Women's Wear Daily)*

1993   The Vienna Festival premieres two new operas: *Homage to Zhivago* by Russian composer Alfred Schnittke and *The Cave* by American composer Steve Reich.   **MUSIC**

1993   American abstract painter Robert Ryman receives his first compre- hensive retrospective at the Museum of Modern Art. He is known for his studies of the sensual, tactile elements of the medium, no- tably in his "white paintings."   **PAINT**

1993   Japanese sculptor Osami Tamaka creates constructions drawn from Asian and minimalist sources consisting of weathered wood beams and blocks of white paraffin wax.   **SCULP**

1993–1994   Top-rated TV shows include "Home Improvement" (ABC), "Seinfeld" (NBC), and "Frasier" (NBC).   **TV&R**

1993   After more than a decade as host of NBC's "Late Night," Indiana- born comedian David Letterman becomes host of the new "Late Show" on CBS. His move to a rival network sparks a late night talk show rivalry with NBC's Jay Leno and "The Tonight Show." *See* 1992, TV&R.   **TV&R**

1994   French architect Christian de Portzamparc wins the Pritzker Prize. He is best known for the City of Music center in Paris.   **ARCH**

1994   A $150 grant from the Minneapolis, Minnesota, Walker Art Center to a performance artist who performs ritual skin carving to heighten AIDS awareness prompts stern Congressional debate and a 5 percent cut in the National Endowment for the Arts budget for 1994–1995.   **DRAMA**

1994   *Three Tall Women*, by American playwright Edward Albee, premieres. It will win the Pulitzer Prize for drama.   **DRAMA**

1994   Dominating the Broadway stage this year are musical revivals, including *Damn Yankees*, *Grease*, and *Carousel*. They are spurred by the recent successful revivals of *Gypsy* and *Guys and Dolls*.   **DRAMA**

··

"In general, my music seeks the awareness of motion we have in flying or of driving a car and not the plodding of horses or the marching of soldiers that pervades the motion patterns of older music."—American composer Elliott Carter, 1994

··

1994   After nearly two decades of directing some of the top money-making movie successes in history (*Jaws*, *E.T., The Extra-Terrestrial*, *Raiders of the Lost Ark*), American director Steven Spielberg wins artistic accolades and the Best Picture and Best Director Academy Award for the Holocaust-inspired drama *Schindler's List*.   **FILM**

1994   Notable films include Jan de Bont's *Speed*, Mike Newell's *Four Weddings and a Funeral*, the Walt Disney Company's *The Lion King*, Robert Redford's *Quiz Show*, Bob Zemeckis's *Forrest Gump*, and Quentin Tarantino's *Pulp Fiction*.   **FILM**

1994   West Indian writer V. S. Naipaul publishes the autobiographically influenced series of linked stories, *A Way in the World*.   **LIT**

1994   American novelist E. L. Doctorow publishes *The Waterworks*, which, like other Doctorow novels such as *Ragtime* (1976) and *Billy Bathgate* (1989), is set in New York City of the historical past.   **LIT**

1994   A concert to celebrate the World Cup soccer finals features tenors José Carreras, Placido Domingo, and Luciano Pavarotti. Featuring classical and popular works, it is broadcast worldwide, reaching an audience of over a billion people.   **MUSIC**

1994   New York City's Metropolitan Opera dismisses soprano Kathleen Battle for "unprofessional actions" during rehearsals.   **MUSIC**

1994   After a decades-long absence from the concert stage, American singer Barbra Streisand mounts an international concert tour. Despite costly tickets, the tour plays to sellout audiences.   **MUSIC**

IN MEMORIAM

*E*ver since the lethal syndrome known as AIDS was first diagnosed in the 1980s, the world of the arts has been devastated by the disease. Here are a few of the figures from many fields of artistic endeavor who have been lost to AIDS:

Peter Allen, entertainer and songwriter, 1992
Howard Ashman, composer for theater and film, 1991
Michael Bennett, director and choreographer, 1987
Alan Buchsbaum, architect, 1987
Scott Burton, sculptor, 1989
Ian Charleson, actor, 1990
Bruce Chatwin, travel writer, 1989
James Crabe, cinematographer, 1989
Nicholas Dante, playwright, 1991
Brad Davis, actor, 1991
Denholm Elliott, actor, 1992
Perry Ellis, fashion designer, 1986
Vincent Fourcade, interior designer, 1992
Choo-San Goh, choreographer, 1987
Halston, fashion designer, 1990
Keith Haring, graffiti artist, 1990
Rock Hudson, actor, 1985
Paul Jacobs, pianist and harpsichordist, 1983
Derek Jarman, filmmaker, 1994
Philipp Jung, set designer, 1992
Larry Kert, singer and actor, 1991
Wilford Leach, theater director, 1988
Liberace, entertainer and pianist, 1987
Charles Ludlam, actor, playwright, and director, 1987
Robert Mapplethorpe, photographer, 1989
Freddie Mercury, singer and lyricist, 1991
Rudolf Nureyev, dancer, 1993
Anthony Perkins, actor, 1992
Leonard Raver, organist, 1992
Robert Reed, actor, 1992
Paul Russell, dancer, 1991
Bill Sherwood, filmmaker, 1990
Jack Smith, performance artist and filmmaker, 1989
Burton Taylor, dancer, 1991
Paul Thek, installation artist, 1988
Tim Wengerd, dancer and choreographer, 1989
John Wilson, dancer and choreographer, 1992
Ricky Wilson, guitar player, 1985
David Wojnarowicz, mixed-media artist, 1992

1994   American singer and songwriter Kurt Cobain, leader of the alternative rock group Nirvana and reputed musical spokesperson for "Generation X," commits suicide. Recordings commemorating Cobain from such musicians as Neil Young, Sinéad O'Connor, and R.E.M. will follow later in the year.   **MUSIC**

1994   Contemporary artists exhibited in New York's galleries this year include painter Pat Adams, nouveau surréaliste sculptor Robert Gober, Jenny Holzer, Ann Agee, Donald Lipski, Julian Schnabel, John Baldessari, and Richard Serra.   **PAINT**

1994   Two multimedia installations by the late composer John Cage are exhibited in New York: "Rolywholyover A Circus" and "The First Meeting of the Satie Society."   **PAINT**

1994   The Andy Warhol Museum opens in a converted warehouse in the artist's hometown of Pittsburgh, Pennsylvania.   **PAINT**

1994   The work of American photographer Lee Friedlander is exhibited at the Museum of Modern Art. Beginning in 1979, his extended series of photographic studies has explored the nature of human communication.   **PHOTO**

1994   The German parliament votes to approve Bulgarian-born artist Christo's plan to wrap the Reichstag Building in a million square feet of silver fabric for two weeks in 1995.   **SCULP**

APPENDIX:
BIRTH AND DEATH DATES

The field of artistic endeavor in which these artists gained their greatest prominence is indicated by the following codes:

A	Architecture
DA	Dance
DE	Decorative Arts
DR	Drama
F	Film
L	Literature
M	Music
PA	Painting and Graphic Arts
PH	Photography
S	Sculpture
T	Television & Radio

Adam, Robert (A)	1728–1792	Anderson, Sherwood (L)	1876–1941
Adams, Ansel (PH)	1902–1984	André, Carl (S)	1935–
Adams, Henry Brooks (L)	1838–1918	Andrea del Sarto (PA)	1486–1530
Addison, Joseph (L)	1672–1719	Andrews, Julie (M)	1935–
Aeschylus (DR)	c. 525–c. 456 B.C.	Angelico, Fra	
Ailey, Alvin (DA)	1931–1989	(Guido di Pietro) (PA)	c. 1400–1455
Albee, Edward (DR)	1928–	Angelou, Maya (L)	1928–
Albéniz, Isaac (M)	1860–1909	Anouilh, Jean (DR)	1910–1987
Albers, Josef (PA)	1888–1976	Antelami, Benedetto (S)	fl. 12th cent.
Alberti, Leon Battista (A)	1404–1472	Antonioni, Michelangelo (F)	1912–
Alcott, Louisa May (L)	1832–1888	Aristophanes (DR)	c. 448–c.380 B.C.
Alda, Alan (T)	1936–	Aristotle (L)	384–322 B.C.
Alger, Horatio (L)	1832–1899	Armstrong, Louis (M)	1900–1971
Allen, Fred (T)	1894–1956	Arnaz, Desi (T)	1917–1986
Allen, Gracie (T)	1902–1964	Arness, James (T)	1923–
Allen, Woody (F)	1935–	Arnold, Matthew (L)	1822–1888
Alonso, Alicia (DA)	1921–	Arp, Jean (Hans) (PA)	1887–1966
Altman, Robert (F)	1925–	Ashbery, John (L)	1927–
Andersen, Hans Christian (L)	1805–1875	Ashton, Frederick (DA)	1906–1988
Anderson, Laurie (DR)	1947–	Asimov, Isaac (L)	1920–1992

APPENDIX

Astaire, Fred (DA)	1899–1986	Bellow, Saul (L)	1915–
Atget, Eugène (PH)	1857–1927	Benét, Stephen Vincent (L)	1898–1943
Attenborough, Richard (F)	1923–	Bennett, Tony (M)	1926–
Atwood, Margaret (L)	1939–	Benny, Jack (T)	1894–1974
Auden, W. H. (L)	1907–1973	Berg, Alban (M)	1885–1935
Austen, Jane (L)	1775–1817	Bergé, Jacques (S)	1696–1756
Bacall, Lauren (F)	1924–	Bergen, Edgar (T)	1903–1978
Bach, Johann Sebastian (M)	1685–1750	Bergman, Ingmar (F)	1918–
Bacon, Francis (L)	1561–1626	Bergman, Ingrid (F)	1915–1982
Bacon, Francis (PA)	1910–1992	Berlage, Hendrik P. (A)	1856–1934
Baez, Joan (M)	1941–	Berle, Milton (T)	1908–
Baker, Josephine (M)	1906–1975	Berlin, Irving (M)	1888–1989
Balanchine, George (DA)	1904–1983	Berlioz, Louis-Hector (M)	1803–1869
Baldwin, James (L)	1924–1987	Bernhardt, Sarah (DR)	1844–1923
Ball, Lucille (T)	1911–1989	Bernini, Gian Lorenzo (S)	1598–1680
Balzac, Honoré de (L)	1799–1850	Bernstein, Leonard (M)	1918–1990
Bancroft, Anne (F)	1931–	Berruguette, Alonso (S)	c. 1489–1561
Bara, Theda (F)	1885–1955	Berry, Chuck (M)	1926–
Baraka, Imamu Amiri		Berryman, John (L)	1914–1972
(LeRoi Jones) (L)	1934–	Bertolucci, Bernardo (F)	1940–
Barber, Samuel (M)	1910–1981	Bierce, Ambrose (L)	1842–1914?
Barlach, Ernst (S)	1870–1938	Bill, Max (S)	1908–
Barrie, James (DR)	1860–1937	Bizet, Georges (M)	1838–1875
Barrymore, Ethel (DR)	1879–1959	Blake, William (L)	1757–1827
Barrymore, John (DR)	1882–1942	Blitzstein, Marc (M)	1905–1964
Barrymore, Lionel (DR)	1878–1954	Bloch, Ernest (M)	1880–1959
Barth, John (L)	1930–	Boccioni, Umberto (PA)	1882–1916
Barthelme, Donald (L)	1931–1989	Bogart, Humphrey (F)	1899–1957
Bartholdi, Frédéric Auguste (S)	1834–1904	Bogdanovich, Peter (F)	1939–
Bartók, Béla (M)	1881–1945	Böll, Heinrich (L)	1917–
Baryshnikov, Mikhail (DA)	1948–	Bonnard, Pierre (PA)	1867–1947
Bashō (L)	1644–1694	Booth, Edwin Thomas (DR)	1833–1893
Battle, Kathleen (M)	1948–	Booth, John Wilkes (DR)	1839–1865
Baudelaire, Charles Pierre (L)	1821–1867	Booth, Junius Brutus, Jr. (DR)	1821–1883
Baum, L. Frank (L)	1856–1919	Booth, Junius Brutus, Sr. (DR)	1796–1852
Beardsley, Aubrey (PA)	1872–1898	Borges, Jorge Luis (L)	1899–1987
Beatty, Warren (F)	1937–	Borglum, Gutzon (S)	1867–1941
Beaumont, Francis (DR)	1584–1616	Borodin, Aleksandr (M)	1833–1887
Beckett, Samuel (DR)	1906–1990	Borzage, Frank (F)	1893–1962
Beethoven, Ludwig van (M)	1770–1827	Bosch, Hieronymus (PA)	c. 1450–1516
Behn, Aphra (DR)	1640–1689	Boswell, James (L)	1740–1795
Behrens, Peter (A)	1868–1940	Botticelli, Sandro (PA)	c. 1444–1510
Béjart, Maurice (DA)	1928–	Bouchardon, Edme (S)	1698–1762
Bellini, Gentile (PA)	1429–1507	Boulez, Pierre (M)	1925–
Bellini, Giovanni (PA)	c. 1430–1516	Bourke-White, Margaret (PH)	1904–1971

Bournonville, Auguste (DA)	1805–1879	Bustelli, Franz Anton (S)	1723–1763
Bowen, Daniel (S)	1760–1856	Butler, Samuel (L)	1835–1902
Bracci, Pietro (S)	1700–1773	Buxtehude, Dietrich (M)	1637–1707
Bradstreet, Anne (L)	c. 1612–1672	Byrd, William (M)	1543–1623
Brady, Mathew (PH)	1823–1896	Byron, Lord	
Brahms, Johannes (M)	1833–1897	(George Gordon) (L)	1788–1824
Bramante		Caccini, Giulio (M)	c. 1545–1618
(Donato d'Agnolo) (A)	1444–1514	Caesar, Sid (T)	1922–
Branagh, Kenneth (F)	1960–	Caffiéri, Jean Jacques (S)	1725–1792
Brancusi, Constantin (S)	1876–1957	Cage, John (M)	1912–1992
Brando, Marlon (F)	1924–	Cagney, James (F)	1899–1986
Braque, Georges (PA)	1882–1963	Caine, Michael (F)	1933–
Brecht, Bertolt (DR)	1898–1956	Calder, Alexander (S)	1898–1976
Brennan, Walter (F)	1894–1974	Calderón de la Barca,	
Britten, Benjamin (M)	1913–1976	Pedro (DR)	1600–1681
Brontë, Charlotte (L)	1816–1855	Callas, Maria (M)	1923–1977
Brontë, Emily (L)	1818–1848	Calvino, Italo (L)	1923–1985
Brown, James (M)	1933–	Cameron, Julia Margaret (PH)	1815–1879
Browne, Thomas (L)	1605–1682	Campbell, Mrs. Patrick	
Browning, Elizabeth Barrett (L)	1806–1861	(Beatrice Stella Tanner) (DR)	1865–1940
Browning, Robert (L)	1812–1889	Campion, Jane (F)	1955–
Bruch, Max (M)	1838–1920	Camus, Albert (L)	1913–1960
Bruckner, Anton (M)	1824–1896	Canova, Antonio (S)	1757–1822
Bruegel,		Cantor, Eddie (M)	1892–1964
Pieter, the Elder (PA)	c. 1525–1569	Capa, Robert (PH)	1913–1954
Bruhn, Erik (DA)	1929–	Capek, Karel (L)	1890–1938
Brunelleschi, Filippo (A)	1377–1446	Capote, Truman (L)	1924–1984
Bryant, William Cullen (L)	1794–1878	Capra, Frank (F)	1897–1991
Brynner, Yul (F)	1915–1985	Caravaggio, Michelangelo (PA)	c. 1565–1609
Buck, Pearl S. (L)	1892–1973	Carlyle, Thomas (L)	1795–1881
Bulfinch, Charles (A)	1763–1844	Carmichael, Hoagy (M)	1899–1981
Bulwer-Lytton, Edward (L)	1803–1873	Carmona, Luis Salvador (S)	1709–1767
Buñuel, Luis (F)	1900–1983	Carney, Art (T)	1918–
Bunyan, John (L)	1628–1688	Carpeaux, Jean-Baptiste (S)	1827–1875
Burbage, Richard (DR)	c. 1567–1619	Carreras, José (M)	1946–
Burke, Edmund (L)	1729–1797	Carroll, Lewis	
Burne-Jones, Edward (PA)	1833–1898	(Charles Dodgson) (L)	1832–1898
Burnett, Carol (T)	1933–	Carson, Johnny (T)	1925–
Burney, Fanny (L)	1752–1840	Carter, Elliott (M)	1908–
Burns, George (T)	1896–	Cartier-Bresson, Henri (PH)	1906–
Burns, Robert (L)	1759–1796	Caruso, Enrico (M)	1873–1921
Burr, Raymond (T)	1917–1993	Cash, Johnny (M)	1932–
Burroughs, Edgar Rice (L)	1875–1950	Castle, Vernon (DA)	1887–1918
Burroughs, William S. (L)	1914–	Castro, Felipe de (S)	1711–1775
Burton, Richard (F)	1925–1984	Cather, Willa (L)	1873–1947

Catullus (L)	c. 84–54 B.C.
Cellini, Benvenuto (S)	1500–1571
Cervantes, Miguel de (L)	1547–1616
Cézanne, Paul (PA)	1839–1906
Chagall, Marc (PA)	1889–1985
Chamberlain, John (S)	1927–
Chandler, Raymond (L)	1888–1959
Chaney, Lon (F)	1883–1930
Chaplin, Charlie (F)	1889–1979
Chardin, Jean-Baptiste-Siméon (PA)	1699–1779
Charisse, Cyd (DA)	1921–
Charles, Ray (M)	1930–
Chaucer, Geoffrey (L)	c. 1340–1400
Chávez, Carlos (M)	1899–1978
Cheever, John (L)	1912–1982
Chekhov, Anton (DR)	1860–1904
Chen Kaige (F)	1952–
Cher (M)	1946–
Chevalier, Maurice (M)	1888–1972
Chirico, Giorgio de (PA)	1888–1978
Chopin, Frédéric-François (M)	1810–1849
Chopin, Kate (L)	1851–1904
Chrétien de Troyes (L)	fl. 1165–1190
Christie, Agatha (L)	1891–1976
Christo (Christo Javacheff) (S)	1935–
Churchill, Caryl (DR)	1938–
Cicero, Marcus Tullius (L)	106–43 B.C
Cimabue (Bencivieni di Pepo) (PA)	c. 1240–1302
Clapton, Eric (M)	1945–
Clark, Dick (T)	1929–
Cline, Patsy (M)	1932–1963
Clodion (Claude Michel) (S)	1738–1814
Close, Glenn (F)	1947–
Coetzee, J. M. (L)	1940–
Cohan, George M.	1878–1942
Colbert, Claudette (F)	1905–
Cole, Nat King (M)	1919–1965
Coleridge, Samuel Taylor (L)	1772–1834
Colette, Sidonie-Gabrielle (L)	1873–1954
Collot, Marie Anne (S)	1748–1821
Colman, Ronald (F)	1891–1958
Confucius (L)	c. 551–479 B.C.
Congreve, William (DR)	1670–1729
Connery, Sean (F)	1930–
Conrad, Joseph (L)	1857–1924
Constable, John (PA)	1776–1837
Cooke, Sam (M)	1931–1964
Cooper, Gary (F)	1901–1961
Cooper, James Fenimore (L)	1789–1851
Copland, Aaron (M)	1900–1990
Coppola, Francis Ford (F)	1939–
Corneille, Pierre (DR)	1606–1684
Cornell, Katharine (DR)	1893–1974
Corot, Jean-Baptiste-Camille (PA)	1796–1875
Corradini, Antonio (S)	1668–1752
Correggio (Antonio Allegri) (PA)	c. 1494–1534
Cosby, Bill (T)	1937–
Costner, Kevin (F)	1955–
Couperin, François	1668–1733
Courbet, Gustave (PA)	1819–1877
Coward, Noel (DR)	1899–1973
Cowell, Henry Dixon (M)	1897–1965
Coysevox, Antoine (S)	1640–1720
Cozens, Alexander (PA)	1717–1786
Cranach, Lucas, the Elder (PA)	1472–1553
Crane, Hart (L)	1899–1932
Crane, Stephen (L)	1871–1900
Crawford, Joan (F)	1904–1977
Cronkite, Walter (T)	1916–
Cronyn, Hume (DR)	1911–
Crosby, Bing (M)	1903–1977
Cruise, Tom (F)	1962–
Cruz, Juana Inés de la (DR)	1651–1695
Cukor, George (F)	1899–1983
cummings, e.e. (Edward Estlin) (L)	1894–1962
Cunningham, Merce (DA)	1922–
Curtis, Tony (F)	1925–
Curtiz, Michael (F)	1888–1962
Czerny, Karl (M)	1791–1857
Daguerre, Louis-Jacques (PH)	1789–1851
Dalí, Salvador (PA)	1904–1989
Daltrey, Roger (M)	1945–
d'Amboise, Jacques (DA)	1934–
Danilova, Alexandra (DA)	1904–
Dante Alighieri (L)	1265–1321

Darin, Bobby (M)	1936–1973
Daumier, Honoré (PA)	1808–1879
David, Jacques-Louis (PA)	1748–1825
Davies, Arthur Bowen (PA)	1862–1928
Davis, Bette (F)	1908–1989
Davis, Geena (F)	1957–
Davis, Miles (M)	1926–1992
Davis, Sammy, Jr. (M)	1925–1990
Davis, Stuart (PA)	1894–1964
Day, Doris (M)	1924–
Day-Lewis, Daniel (F)	1957–
Dean, James (F)	1931–1955
Debussy, Claude (M)	1862–1918
Defoe, Daniel (L)	c. 1600–1731
Degas, Edgar (PA)	1834–1917
de Havilland, Olivia (F)	1916–
De Hooch (Hoogh), Pieter (PA)	c. 1629–1677
de Kooning, Willem (PA)	1904–
Delacroix, Eugène (PA)	1798–1863
Delibes, Léo (M)	1838–1891
Delius, Frederick (M)	1862–1934
Della Robbia, Andrea (PA)	1435–c. 1525
Della Robbia, Luca (PA)	c. 1400–1482
De Mille, Agnes (DA)	1905–1993
De Mille, Cecil B. (F)	1881–1959
Demme, Jonathan (F)	1944–
Demuth, Charles (PA)	1883–1935
De Niro, Robert (F)	1943–
De Palma, Brian (F)	1940–
De Sica, Vittorio (F)	1902–1974
Desprez, Josquin (M)	c. 1440–1521
Diaghilev, Sergei (DA)	1872–1929
Dickens, Charles (L)	1812–1870
Dickinson, Emily (L)	1830–1886
Dickson, W. K. L. (F)	1860–1935
Diderot, Denis (L)	1713–1784
Didion, Joan (L)	1934–
Diebenkorn, Richard (PA)	1922–
Dietrich, Marlene (F)	1901–1992
Dillard, Annie (L)	1945–
Dinesen, Isak (Karen Blixen) (L)	1885–1962
Disney, Walt (F)	1901–1966
Doctorow, E. L. (L)	1931–
Domenico Veneziano (PA)	?–1461
Domingo, Placido (M)	1941–
Domino, Fats (M)	1929–
Donahue, Phil (T)	1935–
Donatello (S)	1386–1466
Donen, Stanley (F)	1924–
Donizetti, Gaetano (M)	1797–1848
Donne, John (L)	1572–1631
Doré, Gustave (PA)	1832–1883
Dorsey, Jimmy (M)	1904–1957
Dorsey, Tommy (M)	1905–1956
Dos Passos, John (L)	1896–1970
Dostoyevsky, Fyodor (L)	1821–1881
Douglas, Kirk (F)	1916–
Dove, Arthur (PA)	1880–1946
Dowland, John (M)	c. 1563–1626
Doyle, Arthur Conan (L)	1858–1930
Dreiser, Theodore (L)	1871–1945
Dressler, Marie (F)	1869–1934
Dreyfuss, Richard (F)	1947–
Dryden, John (L)	1631–1700
Dubuffet, Jean (PA)	1901–1985
Duchamp, Marcel (S)	1887–1968
Dufay, Guillaume (M)	c. 1400–1474
Dufy, Raoul (PA)	1887–1953
Dukas, Paul (M)	1865–1935
Dumas, Alexandre, père (L)	1802–1870
Duncan, Isadora (DA)	1878–1927
Dunstable, John (M)	c. 1380–1453
Durang, Christopher (DR)	1949–
Dürer, Albrecht (PA)	1471–1528
Dvořák, Antonín (M)	1841–1904
Dylan, Bob (M)	1941–
Eakins, Thomas (PA)	1844–1916
Eastwood, Clint (F)	1930–
Edison, Thomas Alva (F)	1847–1931
Edwards, Blake (F)	1922–
Eglevsky, André (DA)	1917–1977
Eisenstein, Sergey (F)	1898–1948
Elgar, Edward (M)	1857–1934
Eliot, George (Mary Ann Evans) (L)	1819–1880
Eliot, T. S. (L)	1888–1965
Ellington, Duke (M)	1899–1974
Ellison, Ralph (L)	1914–1994

Elsheimer, Adam (PA)	1578–1610	Frank, Robert (PH)	1924–
Elssler, Fanny (DA)	1810–1884	Frankenheimer, John (F)	1930–
Emerson, Ralph Waldo (L)	1803–1882	Frankenthaler, Helen (PA)	1928–
Ensor, James (PA)	1860–1949	Franklin, Aretha (M)	1942–
Ernst, Max (PA)	1891–1976	Franklin, Benjamin (L)	1706–1790
Etting, Ruth (M)	1896–1978	Frescobaldi, Girolano (M)	1583–1643
Euripides (DR)	c. 480–406 B.C.	Friedkin, William (F)	1939–
Evans, Edith (DR)	1888–1965	Frost, Robert (L)	1874–1963
Evans, Walker (PH)	1903–1975	Fuentes, Carlos (L)	1929–
Eyck, Jan van (PA)	c. 1370–c. 1440	Fugard, Athol (DR)	1932–
Fairbanks, Douglas (F)	1883–1939	Fuller, R. Buckminster (A)	1895–1983
Falconet, Étienne (S)	1716–1791	Gable, Clark (F)	1901–1960
Falla, Manuel de (M)	1876–1946	Gabo, Naum (S)	1890–1977
Farquhar, George (DR)	1678–1707	Gainsborough, Thomas (PA)	1727–1788
Farrow, Mia (F)	1945–	Galsworthy, John (DR)	1867–1933
Faulkner, William (L)	1897–1962	Gance, Abel (F)	1889–1981
Fauré, Gabriel (M)	1845–1924	Garbo, Greta (F)	1905–1990
Fawcett, Farrah (T)	1946–	García Lorca, Federico (L)	1898–1936
Feininger, Lyonel (PA)	1871–1956	García Márquez, Gabriel (L)	1928–
Fellini, Federico (F)	1920–1993	Gardner, Alexander (PH)	1821–1882
Feydeau, Georges (DR)	1862–1921	Garfunkel, Art (M)	1942–
Field, Sally (F)	1946–	Garland, Judy (M)	1922–1969
Fielding, Henry (L)	1707–1754	Garner, James (T)	1928–
Fitzgerald, F. Scott (L)	1896–1940	Garrick, David (DR)	1717–1779
Fitzgerald, Ella (M)	1918–	Gaskell, Elizabeth (L)	1810–1865
Flaubert, Gustave (L)	1821–1880	Gay, John (DR)	1685–1732
Flavin, Dan (S)	1933–	Genet, Jean (DR)	1910–1986
Flaxman, John (S)	1755–1826	Gershwin, Ira (M)	1896–1983
Fleming, Victor (F)	1883–1949	Gershwin, George (M)	1898–1937
Fletcher, John (DR)	1579–1625	Ghiberti, Lorenzo (S)	c. 1381–1455
Fokine, Michel (DA)	1880–1942	Giacometti, Alberto (S)	1901–1966
Fonda, Henry (F)	1905–1982	Giambologna (S)	1529–1608
Fonda, Jane (F)	1937–	Gibbons, Orlando (M)	1585–1625
Fontanne, Lynn		Gide, André (L)	1869–1951
(Lillie Louise) (DR)	1887–1983	Gielgud, John (DR)	1904–
Fonteyn, Margot (DA)	1919–1991	Gillespie, Dizzy (M)	1917–1993
Ford, Ford Madox (L)	1873–1939	Ginsberg, Allen (L)	1926–
Ford, Harrison (F)	1942–	Giorgione (PA)	c. 1476–1510
Ford, John (F)	1895–1973	Giotto di Bondone (PA)	c. 1267–1337
Forman, Milos (F)	1932–	Girardon, François (S)	1628–1565
Forster, E. M. (L)	1879–1970	Giraudoux, Jean (DR)	1882–1944
Fosse, Bob (M)	1927–1987	Gish, Dorothy (F)	1898–1968
Foster, Jodie (F)	1962–	Gish, Lillian (F)	1896–1993
Foster, Stephen (M)	1826–1864	Glass, Philip (M)	1937–
Franck, César (M)	1822–1890	Gleason, Jackie (T)	1916–1987

Glinka, Mikhail (M)	1804–1857	Haley, Bill (M)	1925–1981
Gluck,		Hammerstein II, Oscar (M)	1895–1960
Christoph Willibald von (M)	1714–1787	Hammett, Dashiell (L)	1894–1961
Godard, Jean–Luc (F)	1930–	Hamsun, Knut (L)	1859–1952
Godfrey, Arthur (T)	1903–1983	Handel, George Frideric (M)	1685–1759
Goeritz, Mathias (S)	1915–	Handy, W. C. (M)	1873–1958
Goethe,		Hanks, Tom (F)	1956–
Johann Wolfgang von (L)	1749–1832	Hansberry, Lorraine (DR)	1930–1965
Gogol, Nikolai (L)	1809–1852	Hanson, Duane (S)	1925–
Goldberg, Whoopi (F)	1949–	Hanson, Howard (M)	1896–1981
Golding, William (L)	1911–1993	Hardy, Oliver (F)	1892–1957
Goldoni, Carlo (DR)	1707–1793	Hardy, Thomas (L)	1840–1928
Goldsmith, Oliver (L)	1728–1774	Harlow, Jean (F)	1911–1937
González, Julio (S)	1872–1942	Harrison, George (M)	1943–
Gorky, Arshile (PA)	1904–1948	Harrison, Rex (F)	1908–1990
Gorky, Maksim (DR)	1868–1936	Hart, William S. (F)	1865–1946
Goujon, Jean (S)	c. 1510–1565	Hart, Moss (DR)	1904–1961
Gounod, Charles (M)	1818–1893	Hart, Lorenz (M)	1895–1943
Goya, Francisco de (PA)	1746–1828	Harte, Bret (L)	1836–1902
Grable, Betty (F)	1916–1973	Hartley, Marsden (PA)	1877–1943
Graham, Martha (DA)	1895–1991	Hauptmann, Gerhart (DR)	1862–1946
Granados, Enrique (M)	1867–1916	Havel, Vaclav (DR)	1936–
Grant, Cary (F)	1904–1986	Hawkes, John (L)	1925–
Grass, Günter (L)	1927–	Hawks, Howard (F)	1896–1977
Gray, Spalding (DR)	1941–	Hawthorne, Nathaniel (L)	1804–1864
Greco, El (Doménikos		Haydn, Franz Joseph (M)	1732–1809
Theotokópoulos) (PA)	c.1541–1614	Haydn, Johann Michael (M)	1737–1806
Greenough, Horatio (S)	1805–1852	Hayes, Helen (DR)	1900–1993
Greuze, Jean-Baptiste (PA)	1725–1805	Hayworth, Rita (F)	1918–1987
Grieg, Edvard (M)	1843–1907	Hazlitt, William (L)	1778–1830
Griffith, Andy (T)	1926–	Hecht, Ben (DR)	1894–1964
Griffith, D. W. (F)	1875–1948	Heine, Heinrich (L)	1797–1856
Grimm, Jakob (L)	1785–1863	Heller, Joseph (L)	1923–
Grimm, Wilhelm (L)	1786–1859	Hellman, Lillian (DR)	1905–1984
Gris, Juan (PA)	1887–1972	Hemingway, Ernest (L)	1899–1961
Gropius, Walter (A)	1883–1969	Hendrix, Jimi (M)	1942–1970
Grosz, George (PA)	1893–1959	Henri, Robert (PA)	1865–1929
Grotowski, Jerzy (DR)	1933–	Henry, O.	
Grünewald, Matthias (PA)	c. 1475–1528	(William S. Porter) (L)	1862–1910
Guinness, Alec (F)	1914–	Henson, Jim (T)	1936–1990
Guthrie, Tyrone (DR)	1900–1971	Hepburn, Katharine (F)	1907–
Guthrie, Woody (M)	1912–1967	Hepburn, Audrey (F)	1929–1993
Hackman, Gene (F)	1931–	Hepworth, Barbara (S)	1903–1975
Hagen, Uta Thyra (DR)	1919–	Herbert, George (L)	1593–1633
Hagman, Larry (T)	1931–	Heredia, José Maria (L)	1803–1839

APPENDIX

Herrick, Robert (L)	1591–1674	Ingres,	
Hesse, Hermann (L)	1877–1962	Jean-Auguste-Dominique (PA)	1780–1867
Heston, Charlton (F)	1923–	Ionesco, Eugène (DR)	1912–1994
Hildebrandt,		Irving, Henry (DR)	1838–1905
Johann Lukas von (S)	1668–1745	Irving, Washington (L)	1783–1859
Hindemith, Paul (M)	1895–1963	Isherwood, Christopher (L)	1904–1986
Hitchcock, Alfred (F)	1899–1980	Ivanov, Lev (DA)	1834–1905
Hockney, David (PA)	1937–	Ives, Charles Edward (M)	1874–1954
Hoffman, Dustin (F)	1937–	Jackson, Michael (M)	1958–
Hofmann, Hans (PA)	1880–1966	Jackson, Shirley (L)	1919–1965
Hogarth, William (PA)	1697–1764	Jagger, Mick (M)	1943–
Holbein, Hans,		James, Harry (M)	1916–1983
the Younger (PA)	c. 1497–1543	James, Henry (L)	1843–1916
Holden, William (F)	1918–1981	Janáček, Leoš (M)	1854–1928
Holiday, Billie (M)	1915–1959	Jenny, William Le Baron (A)	1832–1907
Holliday, Judy (F)	1922–1965	Joffrey, Robert (DA)	1930–1988
Holly, Buddy (M)	1936–1959	Johns, Jasper (PA)	1930–
Holst, Gustav (M)	1874–1934	Johnson, Philip (A)	1906–
Homer (L)	c. 9th cent. B.C.	Johnson, Samuel (L)	1709–1784
Homer, Winslow (PA)	1836–1910	Jolson, Al (M)	1886–1953
Honegger, Arthur (M)	1892–1955	Jones, Inigo (A)	1573–1652
Hope, Bob (F)	1903–	Jones, James Earl (DR)	1931–
Hopkins, Anthony (F)	1937–	Jonson, Ben (DR)	1572–1637
Hopper, Edward (PA)	1882–1967	Jooss, Kurt (DA)	1901–1979
Horace (L)	65–8 B.C.	Joplin, Scott (M)	1868–1917
Horne, Marilyn (M)	1934–	Joplin, Janis (M)	1943–1970
Horton, Lester (DA)	1906–1958	Joyce, James (L)	1882–1941
Houdon, Jean-Antoine (S)	1741–1828	Judd, Donald (S)	1928–1994
Housman, A. E. (L)	1859–1936	Juvenal (L)	60–140
Houston, Whitney (M)	1963–	Kafka, Franz (L)	1883–1924
Howells, William Dean (L)	1837–1920	Kahlo, Frida (PA)	1907–1954
Hughes, Langston (L)	1902–1967	Kahn, Louis Isador (A)	1901–1974
Hugo, Victor (L)	1802–1885	Kandinsky, Wassily (PA)	1866–1944
Humperdinck, Engelbert (M)	1854–1921	Karloff, Boris (F)	1887–1969
Humphrey, Doris (DA)	1895–1958	Karsavina, Tamara (DA)	1885–1978
Hunt, Richard Morris (A)	1828–1895	Kaufman, George S. (DR)	1889–1961
Hunter, Holly (F)	1958–	Kazan, Elia (DR)	1909–
Hurston, Zora Neale (L)	1901–1960	Kazantzakis, Nikos (L)	1883–1957
Hurt, William (F)	1950–	Kean, Edmund (DR)	1789–1833
Huston, John (F)	1906–1987	Keaton, Buster (F)	1895–1966
Ibsen, Henrik (DR)	1828–1906	Keaton, Diane (F)	1946–
Indiana, Robert (PA)	1928–	Keats, John (L)	1795–1821
Inge, William (DR)	1913–1973	Kelly, Gene (DA)	1912–
Ingemann, Bernard Severin (L)	1789–1862	Kelly, Grace (F)	1928–1982
Ingram, Rex (F)	1895–1969	Kemble, Fanny (DR)	1809–1893

Kemble, John Philip (DR)	1757–1823
Kemble, Charles (DR)	1775–1854
Kent, Rockwell (PA)	1882–1971
Kern, Jerome (M)	1885–1945
Kerouac, Jack (L)	1922–1969
Kertész, André (PH)	1894–1985
Kesey, Ken (L)	1935–
Khachaturian, Aram (M)	1903–1978
King, Carole (M)	1942–
Kipling, Rudyard (L)	1865–1936
Kirstein, Lincoln (DA)	1907–
Klee, Paul (PA)	1879–1940
Klimt, Gustav (PA)	1862–1918
Kline, Franz (PA)	1910–1962
Kodály, Zoltán (M)	1882–1967
Kokoschka, Oskar (PA)	1886–1980
Kollwitz, Käthe (PA)	1867–1945
Koons, Jeff (S)	1955–
Korda, Alexander (F)	1893–1956
Kovacs, Ernie (T)	1919–1962
Kubrick, Stanley (F)	1928–
Kurosawa, Akira (F)	1910–
Kyd, Thomas (DR)	1558–1594
Lagerlöf, Selma (L)	1858–1940
Lamb, Charles (L)	1775–1834
Lancaster, Burt (F)	1913–
Landon, Michael (T)	1936–1991
Lange, Dorothea (PH)	1895–1965
Lanza, Mario (M)	1921–1959
Lao–tzu (L)	c. 6th cent. BC
Lardner, Ring (L)	1885–1933
Lasso, Orlando di (M)	1532–1594
Latrobe, Benjamin Henry (A)	1766–1820
Laughton, Charles (F)	1899–1962
Laurel, Stanley (F)	1890–1965
Lawler, Ray (DR)	1921–
Lawrence, D. H. (L)	1885–1930
Lean, David (F)	1908–1991
Lear, Edward (L)	1812–1888
Lear, Norman (T)	1922–
Le Brun, Charles (PA)	1619–1690
Le Corbusier (Charles Jeanneret) (A)	1887–1965
Lee, Spike (F)	1957–
Le Gallienne, Eva (DR)	1899–1991

Le Gros, Pierre (S)	1666–1719
Lehmbruck, Wilhelm (S)	1881–1919
Leigh, Vivien (F)	1913–1967
Le Lorrain, Robert (S)	1666–1743
Lemmon, Jack (F)	1925–
Lemoyne, Jean–Baptiste (S)	1704–1778
Lennon, John (M)	1940–1980
Leonardo da Vinci (PA)	1452–1519
Leoncavallo, Ruggiero (M)	1857–1919
Lermontov, Mikhail (L)	1814–1841
Lerner, Alan Jay (M)	1918–1986
Lessing, Doris (L)	1919–
Letterman, David (T)	1947–
Levinson, Barry (F)	1942–
Lewes, George Henry (DR)	1817–1878
Lewis, Jerry Lee (M)	1935–
Lewis, Sinclair (L)	1885–1951
LeWitt, Sol (S)	1928–
Li Po (L)	701–762
Lichtenstein, Roy (PA)	1932–
Ligeti, György (M)	1923–
Lind, Jenny (M)	1820–1887
Lippi, Fra Filippo (PA)	c. 1406–1469
Liszt, Franz (M)	1811–1886
Little Richard (M)	1932–
Lloyd, Harold (F)	1893–1971
Lloyd Webber, Andrew (M)	1948–
Loesser, Frank (M)	1910–1969
Loewe, Frederick (M)	1904–1988
Lombard, Carole (F)	1908–1942
Lombardo, Tullio (S)	c. 1455–1532
London, Jack (L)	1876–1916
Longfellow, Henry Wadsworth (L)	1807–1882
Loren, Sophia (F)	1934–
Lorenzi, Battista (S)	1527–1594
Lorrain, Claude (PA)	1600–1682
Louis, Morris (PA)	1912–1962
Lowell, Amy (L)	1874–1925
Lowell, James Russell (L)	1819–1891
Lowell, Robert (L)	1917–1977
Lowry, Malcolm (L)	1909–1957
Loy, Myrna (F)	1905–1993
Lubitsch, Ernst (F)	1892–1947
Lucas, George (F)	1944–

Lugosi, Bela (F)	1882–1956	Maugham,	
Lully, Jean-Baptiste (M)	1632–1687	William Somserset (L)	1874–1965
Lumet, Sidney (F)	1924–	Maupassant, Guy de (L)	1850–1893
Lumière, Auguste (F)	1862–1954	Mauriac, François (L)	1885–1970
Lumière, Louis (F)	1864–1948	McCarey, Leo (F)	1898–1969
Lunt, Alfred (DR)	1892–1977	McCarthy, Mary (L)	1912–1989
Macaulay,		McCartney, Paul (M)	1942–
Thomas Babington (L)	1800–1859	McIntire, Samuel (S)	1757–1811
MacDowell, Edward (M)	1860–1908	McNally, Terence (DR)	1939–
Machado de Assis, Joaquim (L)	1839–1908	Meadows, Audrey (T)	1924–
Machiavelli, Niccolò (L)	1469–1527	Méliès, Georges (F)	1861–1938
MacLaine, Shirley (F)	1934–	Melville, Herman (L)	1819–1891
Maeterlinck, Maurice (DR)	1862–1949	Menander (DR)	c. 324–293 B.C.
Magritte, René (PA)	1898–1967	Mencken, H. L. (L)	1880–1956
Mahler, Gustav (M)	1860–1911	Mendelssohn, Felix (M)	1809–1847
Mailer, Norman (L)	1923–	Menotti, Gian Carlo (M)	1911–
Makarova, Natalia (DA)	1940–	Meredith, George (L)	1828–1909
Mallarmé, Stephane (L)	1842–1898	Mérimée, Prosper (L)	1803–1870
Malory, Thomas (L)	?–1471	Messiaen, Olivier (M)	1908–1993
Malraux, André (L)	1901–1976	Meyerbeer, Giacomo (M)	1791–1864
Mamet, David (DR)	1947–	Michelangelo Buonarroti (S)	1475–1564
Man Ray (PA)	1890–1977	Middleton, Thomas (DR)	1570–1627
Mancini, Henry (M)	1924–1994	Midler, Bette (M)	1945–
Mandelstam, Osip (L)	1891–1938	Mies van der Rohe, Ludwig (A)	1886–1969
Manet, Édouard (PA)	1832–1883	Milland, Ray (F)	1907–1986
Mankiewicz, Joseph L. (F)	1909–1993	Millay, Edna St. Vincent (L)	1892–1950
Mann, Anthony (F)	1906–1967	Miller, Arthur (DR)	1915–
Mann, Thomas (L)	1875–1955	Miller, Glenn (M)	1904–1994
Mantegna, Andrea (PA)	1431–1506	Miller, Henry (L)	1891–1980
Marceau, Marcel (DR)	1923–	Millet, Jean-François (PA)	1814–1875
March, Fredric (F)	1897–1975	Mills, Robert (A)	1781–1855
Marivaux, Pierre Carlet de (DR)	1688–1763	Milton, John (L)	1608–1674
Marlowe, Christopher (DR)	1564–1593	Minnelli, Liza (M)	1946–
Marsh, Reginald (PA)	1898–1954	Minnelli, Vincente (F)	1903–1986
Martí, José (L)	1853–1895	Miró, Joan (PA)	1893–1983
Marvell, Andrew (L)	1621–1678	Mistral, Frédéric (L)	1830–1914
Marx, Chico (Leonard) (F)	1886–1961	Mitchell, Arthur (DA)	1934–
Marx, Groucho (Julius) (F)	1890–1977	Mitchell, Margaret (L)	1900–1949
Marx, Harpo (Arthur) (F)	1888–1964	Modigliani, Amedeo (PA)	1884–1920
Masaccio (Tommaso		Moiseyev, Igor (DA)	1906–
di Simone Guidi) (PA)	1401–1428	Molière	
Mascagni, Pietro (M)	1863–1945	(Jean-Baptiste Poquelin) (DR)	1622–1673
Massenet, Jules (M)	1842–1912	Molnár, Ferenc (DR)	1878–1952
Massine, Léonide (DA)	1896–1979	Mondrian, Piet (PA)	1872–1944
Matisse, Henri (PA)	1869–1954	Monet, Claude (PA)	1840–1926

Monk, Thelonious (M)	1917–1982
Monroe, Marilyn (F)	1926–1962
Montaigne, Michel de (L)	1533–1592
Montañes, Juan (S)	1568–1649
Monteverdi, Claudio (M)	1567–1643
Montgomery, Elizabeth (T)	1933–
Moon, Keith (M)	1947–1978
Moore, Douglas (M)	1893–1969
Moore, Henry (PA)	1898–1986
Moore, Marianne (L)	1887–1972
Moore, Mary Tyler (T)	1937–
Morisot, Berthe (PA)	1841–1895
Morley, Thomas (M)	1557–1602
Morris, William (DE)	1834–1896
Morrison, Toni (Chloe Wofford) (L)	1931–
Moses, "Grandma" Anna (PA)	1860–1961
Motherwell, Robert (PA)	1915–
Mozart, Wolfgang Amadeus (M)	1756–1791
Munch, Edvard (PA)	1863–1944
Murasaki, Shikibu (L)	c. 978–1026
Murillo, Bartolomé Esteban (PA)	1617–1682
Murrow, Edward R. (T)	1908–1965
Musset, Alfred de (DR)	1810–1857
Mussorgsky, Modest (M)	1839–1881
Muybridge, Eadweard (PH)	1830–1904
Myron (S)	c. 480–440 B.C.
Nabokov, Vladimir (L)	1899–1977
Naipaul, V. S. (L)	1932–
Nanni di Banco (S)	c. 1384–1421
Nelson, Harriet Hilliard (T)	1914–
Nelson, Ozzie (T)	1907–1975
Neruda, Pablo (L)	1904–1973
Neumann, Johann Balthasar (S)	1687–1753
Nevelson, Louise (S)	1900–1988
Newhart, Bob (T)	1929–
Newman, Barnett (PA)	1905–1971
Newman, Paul (F)	1925–
Nichols, Mike (F)	1931–
Nicholson, Jack (F)	1937–
Niepce, Joseph N. (PH)	1765–1833
Nijinsky, Vaslav (DA)	1890–1950
Nikolais, Alwin (DA)	1912–1993
Niven, David (F)	1909–1983
Noguchi, Isamu (S)	1904–1988
Norris, Frank (L)	1870–1902
Nureyev, Rudolf (DA)	1938–1993
Oates, Joyce Carol (L)	1938–
O'Casey, Sean (John Casey) (DR)	1880–1964
O'Connor, Carroll (T)	1924–
O'Connor, Flannery (L)	1925–1964
Offenbach, Jacques (M)	1819–1980
O'Keeffe, Georgia (PA)	1887–1987
Oldenburg, Claes (S)	1929–
Olivier, Laurence (DR)	1907–1989
Omar Khayyam (L)	1048–1131
O'Neill, Eugene (DR)	1888–1953
Orff, Carl (M)	1895–1982
Orozco, José Clemente (PA)	1883–1949
Orton, Joe (DR)	1933–1967
Orwell, George (Eric Blair) (L)	1903–1950
Osborne, John (DR)	1929–
Oshima, Nagisa (F)	1932–
O'Toole, Peter (F)	1932–
Ouedraogo, Idrissa (F)	1952–
Ovid (L)	43 B.C.–A.D. 17
Pachelbel, Johann (M)	1653–1706
Pacher, Michael (S)	1435–1498
Pacino, Al (F)	1940–
Paderewski, Ignace (M)	1860–1941
Paine, Thomas (L)	1737–1809
Palladio, Andrea (A)	1508–1580
Palmer, Erastus Dow (S)	1817–1904
Papp, Joseph (DR)	1921–1991
Parker, Charlie (M)	1920–1955
Parks, Gordon (F)	1912–
Parrish, Maxfield (PA)	1870–1966
Pasternak, Boris (L)	1890–1960
Pavarotti, Luciano (M)	1935–
Pavlova, Anna (DA)	1881–1931
Paxton, Joseph (A)	1801–1865
Paz, Octavio (L)	1914–
Peck, Gregory (F)	1916–
Pei, I. M. (A)	1917–
Pepys, Samuel (L)	1633–1703
Percy, Walker (L)	1916–1990

Peri, Jacopo (M)	1561–1633	Prokofiev, Sergey (M)	1891–1953
Permoser, Balthasar (S)	1651–1732	Proust, Marcel (L)	1871–1922
Perrot, Jules (DA)	1810–1910	Puccini, Giacomo (M)	1858–1924
Petipa, Marius (DA)	1822–1910	Puget, Pierre (S)	1620–1694
Petit, Roland (DA)	1924–	Pugin, Augustus (A)	1812–1852
Petrarch (L)	1304–1374	Purcell, Henry (M)	1659–1695
Petronius (L)	?–66	Pushkin, Aleksandr (L)	1799–1837
Pfeiffer, Michelle (F)	1957–	Pyle, Howard (PA)	1853–1911
Phidias (S)	c. 500–c. 432 B.C.	Pynchon, Thomas (L)	1937–
Piaf, Edith (M)	1915–1963	Queirolo, Francesco (S)	1704–1762
Picasso, Pablo (PA)	1881–1973	Quercia, Jacopo della (S)	c. 1374–1438
Pickford, Mary (F)	1893–1979	Rabe, David (DR)	1940–
Piero della Francesca (PA)	c. 1420–1492	Rabelais, François (L)	c. 1494–1553
Pigalle, Jean-Baptiste (S)	1714–1785	Rachel (Élisa Félix) (DR)	1820–1858
Pilon, Germain (S)	c. 1535–1590	Rachmaninoff, Sergey (M)	1873–1943
Pindar (L)	c. 522–439 B.C.	Racine, Jean (DR)	1639–1699
Pinero, Arthur Wing (DR)	1855–1934	Rameau, Jean-Philippe (M)	1683–1764
Pinter, Harold (DR)	1930–	Raphael (Raffaello Sanzio) (PA)	1483–1520
Pirandello, Luigi (DR)	1867–1936	Rauschenberg, Robert (PA)	1925–
Pisano, Giovanni (S)	c. 1245–1314	Ravel, Maurice (M)	1875–1937
Pisano, Nicola (S)	c. 1220–c. 1284	Redding, Otis (M)	1941–1967
Pissarro, Camille (PA)	1830–1903	Redford, Robert (F)	1937–
Piston, Walter (M)	1894–1976	Redgrave, Michael (DR)	1908–1985
Plath, Sylvia (L)	1932–1963	Redgrave, Vanessa (F)	1937–
Plato (L)	c. 428–347 B.C.	Reed, Carol (F)	1906–1976
Plautus (DR)	c. 254–184 B.C.	Rembrandt van Rijn (PA)	1606–1669
Plutarch (L)	c. 48–122	Renoir, Jean (F)	1894–1979
Poe, Edgar Allan (L)	1809–1849	Renoir, Pierre-Auguste (PA)	1841–1919
Poitier, Sidney (F)	1924–	Resnais, Alan (F)	1922–
Polanski, Roman (F)	1933–	Reynolds, Joshua (PA)	1723–1792
Pollaiuolo, Antonio del (S)	1431–1498	Ribera, José de (PA)	1591–1652
Pollock, Jackson (PA)	1912–1956	Ribera, Pedro de (S)	1681–1742
Pope, Alexander (L)	1688–1744	Richard, Keith (M)	1943–
Porter, Cole (M)	1891–1964	Richardson, Henry Hobson (A)	1838–1886
Porter, Edwin S. (F)	1869–1941	Richardson, Ralph (DR)	1902–1983
Porter, Katherine Anne (L)	1890–1980	Riis, Jacob (PH)	1849–1914
Pound, Ezra (L)	1885–1972	Rilke, Rainer Maria (L)	1875–1926
Poussin, Nicolas (PA)	1594–1665	Rimbaud, Arthur (L)	1854–1891
Power, Tyrone (F)	1913–1958	Rimsky-Korsakov, Nicolay (M)	1844–1908
Praxiteles (S)	c. 370–333 B.C.	Rivera, Diego (PA)	1886–1957
Préault, Auguste (S)	1809–1879	Rivers, Larry (PA)	1923–
Preminger, Otto (F)	1905–1986	Robards, Jason, Jr. (DR)	1922–
Prendergast, Maurice (PA)	1859–1924	Robbe-Grillet, Alain (L)	1922–
Presley, Elvis (M)	1935–1977	Robbins, Jerome (DA)	1918–
Primaticcio, Francesco (S)	1504–1570	Robeson, Paul (DR)	1898–1976

Robinson, Edward G. (F)	1893–1973
Robinson, Henry Peach (PH)	1830–1901
Rockwell, Norman (PA)	1894–1978
Rodgers, Richard (M)	1902–1979
Rogers, Ginger (F)	1911–
Roseanne (T)	1952–
Ross, Diana (M)	1944–
Rossellini, Roberto (F)	1906–1977
Rossellino, Antonio (S)	1427–1479
Rossellino, Bernardo (S)	1409–1464
Rossetti, Christina (L)	1830–1894
Rossetti, Dante Gabriel (PA)	1828–1882
Rossini, Gioacchino (M)	1792–1868
Rostand, Edmond (DR)	1868–1918
Roth, Philip (L)	1933–
Rothko, Mark (PA)	1903–1970
Rouault, Georges (PA)	1871–1958
Roubillac, Louis-François (S)	c. 1700–1762
Rousseau, Henri (PA)	1844–1910
Rubens, Peter Paul (PA)	1577–1640
Rubinstein, Anton (M)	1829–1894
Rude, François (S)	1784–1855
Rush, William (S)	1756–1833
Rushdie, Salman (L)	1947–
Saarinen, Eero (A)	1910–1961
Saarinen, Eliel (A)	1873–1950
St. Denis, Ruth (DA)	1877–1968
Saint–Saëns, Camille (M)	1835–1921
Salinger, J. D. (L)	1919–
Salvi, Nicola (S)	1697–1751
Sánchez, Florencio (DR)	1875–1910
Sand, George (Amandine Dudevant) (L)	1804–1876
Sandburg, Carl (L)	1878–1967
Sander, August (PH)	1876–1964
Sappho (L)	7th cent. B.C.
Sarandon, Susan (F)	1946–
Sargent, John Singer (PA)	1856–1925
Saroyan, William (L)	1908–1981
Sartre, Jean-Paul (DR)	1905–1980
Satie, Erik	1866–1925
Scarlatti, Domenico (M)	1685–1757
Schlesinger, John (F)	1926–
Schlüter, Andreas (S)	1664–1714
Schoenberg, Arnold (M)	1874–1951
Schubert, Franz (M)	1797–1828
Schultz, Hart Merriam (Lone Wolf) (S)	1882–1970
Schumann, Clara Wieck (M)	1819–1896
Schumann, Robert (M)	1810–1856
Schütz, Heinrich (M)	1585–1672
Schwarzenegger, Arnold (F)	1947–
Scopas (S)	fl. 4th–cent. B.C.
Scorsese, Martin (F)	1942–
Scott, George C. (F)	1926–
Scott, Walter (L)	1771–1832
Scriabin, Aleksandr (M)	1872–1915
Seeger, Pete (M)	1919–
Segal, George (S)	1924–
Selznick, David O. (F)	1902–1965
Sembene, Ousmane (F)	1923–
Seneca, Lucius Annaeus (DR)	c. 4 B.C.–A.D. 65
Serling, Rod (T)	1924–1975
Serra, Richard (S)	1939–
Sessions, Roger (M)	1896–1985
Seurat, Georges (PA)	1859–1891
Sexton, Anne (L)	1928–1974
Shaffer, Peter (DR)	1926–
Shahn, Ben (PA)	1898–1969
Shakespeare, William (DR)	1564–1616
Shange, Ntozake (DR)	1948–
Shaw, Artie (M)	1910–
Shaw, George Bernard (DR)	1856–1950
Shearer, Norma (F)	1900–1983
Sheeler, Charles (PA)	1883–1965
Shelley, Mary Wollstonecraft (L)	1797–1851
Shelley, Percy Bysshe (L)	1792–1822
Shepard, Sam (DR)	1943–
Sheridan, Richard Brinsley (DR)	1751–1816
Shostakovich, Dmitry (M)	1906–1975
Sibelius, Jean (M)	1865–1957
Siddons, Sarah (DR)	1755–1831
Sidney, Philip (L)	1554–1586
Sills, Beverly (M)	1929–
Siloé, Diego de (S)	c. 1495–1563
Simon, Neil (DR)	1927–
Simon, Paul (M)	1942–
Sinatra, Frank (M)	1915–

Sinclair, Upton (L)	1878–1968	Stravinsky, Igor (M)	1882–1971
Singer, Isaac Bashevis (L)	1904–1991	Streep, Meryl (F)	1951–
Sisley, Alfred (PA)	1839–1899	Streisand, Barbra (M)	1942–
Skelton, Red (T)	1910–	Strindberg, August (DR)	1849–1912
Skillin, Simeon, Jr. (S)	1757–1806	Stroheim, Erich von (F)	1885–1957
Skillin, Simeon, Sr. (S)	1716–1778	Styron, William (L)	1925–
Skillin, John (S)	1746–1800	Sullivan, Arthur (M)	1842–1900
Sluter, Claus (S)	?–1405	Sullivan, Ed (T)	1901–1974
Smith, Bessie (M)	1894–1937	Sullivan, Louis Henry (A)	1856–1924
Smith, David (S)	1906–1965	Sully, Thomas (PA)	1783–1872
Smith, Maggie (DR)	1934–	Swift, Jonathan (L)	1667–1745
Smith, W. Eugene (PH)	1918–1978	Swinburne, Algernon Charles (L)	1837–1909
Smithson, Robert (S)	1938–1973	Synge, John Millington (DR)	1871–1909
Solzhenitsyn, Aleksandr (L)	1918–	Taglioni, Maria (DA)	1804–1884
Sondheim, Stephen (M)	1930–	Tagore, Rabindranath (DR)	1861–1941
Sophocles (DR)	c. 496–c.406 B.C.	Talbot,	
Sousa, John Philip	1854–1932	William Henry Fox (PH)	1800–1877
Southey, Robert (L)	1774–1843	Tallchief, Maria (DA)	1925–
Soyinka, Wole (L)	1934–	Tallis, Thomas (M)	c. 1505–1583
Spacek, Sissy (F)	1949–	Tamaka, Osami (S)	1952–
Spenser, Edmund (L)	c. 1552–1599	Tamayo, Rufino (PA)	1899–1991
Spielberg, Steven (F)	1947–	Tandy, Jessica (DR)	1909–1994
Springsteen, Bruce (M)	1949–	Tanizaki, Junichiro (L)	1886–1965
Stallone, Sylvester (F)	1946–	Tanner, Henry O. (PA)	1859–1937
Stanwyck, Barbara (F)	1907–1990	Tatlin, Vladimir (S)	1885–1953
Stapleton, Jean (T)	1923–	Taylor, Elizabeth (F)	1932–
Starr, Ringo (M)	1940–	Taylor, Paul (DA)	1930–
Steele, Richard (L)	1672–1729	Tchaikovsky, Pyotr Ilich (M)	1840–1893
Steichen, Edward (PH)	1879–1973	Telemann, Georg Philipp (M)	1681–1767
Stein, Gertrude (L)	1874–1946	Tennyson, Alfred (Lord) (L)	1809–1892
Steinbeck, John (L)	1902–1968	Terry, Ellen (DR)	1847–1928
Stella, Frank (PA)	1936–	Thackeray,	
Sterne, Laurence (L)	1713–1768	William Makepeace (L)	1811–1863
Stevens, George (F)	1904–1975	Tharp, Twyla (DA)	1941–
Stevens, Wallace (L)	1879–1955	Thomas, Danny (T)	1912–1991
Stevenson, Robert Louis (L)	1850–1894	Thomas, Dylan (L)	1914–1953
Stewart, James (F)	1908–	Thompson, Emma (F)	1959–
Stieglitz, Alfred (PH)	1864–1946	Thomson, Virgil (M)	1896–1989
Still, Clyfford (PA)	1904–1980	Thoreau, Henry David (L)	1817–1862
Stoker, Bram (L)	1847–1912	Tiffany, Louis Comfort (DE)	1848–1933
Stone, Oliver (F)	1946–	Tinguely, Jean (S)	1925–
Stoppard, Tom (DR)	1937–	Tintoretto	
Stowe, Harriet Beecher (L)	1811–1896	(Jacopo Robusti) (PA)	1518–1594
Strauss, Johann (M)	1825–1899	Tippett, Michael (M)	1905–
Strauss, Richard (M)	1864–1949	Titian (Tiziano Vecelli) (PA)	c. 1490–1576

Tocqueville, Alexis de (L)	1805–1859
Tolstoy, Leo (L)	1828–1910
Tomé, Narciso (S)	1690–1742
Tomlin, Lily (F)	1939–
Toulouse-Lautrec,	
Henri de (PA)	1864–1901
Townshend, Peter (M)	1945–
Tracy, Spencer (F)	1900–1967
Trollope, Anthony (L)	1815–1882
Truffaut, François (F)	1932–1984
Tucker, Sophie (M)	1884–1966
Tudor, Anthony (DA)	1909–
Turgenev, Ivan (L)	1818–1883
Turner, Joseph M. W. (PA)	1775–1851
Turner,	
Robert Edward (Ted) (T)	1938–
Turner, Tina (M)	1938–
Twain, Mark	
(Samuel L. Clemens) (L)	1835–1910
Tyler, Anne (L)	1941–
Uccello, Paolo	c. 1396–1475
Uelsmann, Jerry (PH)	1934–
Updike, John (L)	1932–
Usigli, Rodolfo (DR)	1905–1979
Valentino, Rudolph (F)	1895–1926
Vallee, Rudy (M)	1901–1986
Van Der Zee, James (PH)	1886–1983
Van Dyck, Anthony (PA)	1599–1641
Van Dyke, Dick (T)	1925–
van Gogh, Vincent (PA)	1853–1890
Varda, Agnès (F)	1928–
Varèse, Edgar (M)	1883–1965
Vargas Llosa, Mario (L)	1936–
Vasari, Giorgio (PA)	1511–1574
Vaughan, Sarah (M)	1924–1990
Vaughan Williams, Ralph (M)	1872–1958
Velásquez, Diego (PA)	1599–1660
Verdi, Giuseppi (M)	1813–1901
Vergara, Ignacio de (S)	1715–1776
Vergil (L)	70–19 BC
Verlaine, Paul (L)	1844–1896
Vermeer, Jan (PA)	1632–1675
Verne, Jules (L)	1828–1905
Veronese, Paolo (PA)	1528–1588
Verrocchio, Andrea del (S)	1435–1488

Vestris, Gaetan (DA)	1729–1808
Vidor, King (F)	1894–1982
Villa–Lobos, Heitor (M)	1887–1959
Villela, Edward (DA)	1936–
Vivaldi, Antonio (M)	1678–1741
Voltaire	
(François-Marie Arouet) (DR)	1694–1778
Vonnegut, Kurt, Jr. (L)	1922–
Vuillard, Édouard (PA)	1868–1940
Wagner, Otto (A)	1841–1918
Wagner, Richard (M)	1813–1883
Walker, Alice (L)	1944–
Walters, Barbara (T)	1931–
Walton, William (M)	1902–1983
Ward, John Quincy Adams (S)	1830–1910
Warhol, Andy (PA)	1930–1987
Warren, Robert Penn (L)	1905–1989
Washington, Denzel (F)	1954–
Wasserstein, Wendy (DR)	1950–
Waters, John (F)	1946–
Wayne, John (F)	1907–1979
Webb, Jack (T)	1920–1982
Weber, Carl Maria von (M)	1786–1826
Webern, Anton von (M)	1883–1945
Webster, John (DR)	c. 1580–1634
Wedekind, Frank (DR)	1864–1918
Weidman, Charles (DA)	1901–1975
Weill, Kurt (M)	1900–1950
Welch, John (S)	1711–1789
Welles, Orson (F)	1915–1985
Wells, H. G. (L)	1866–1946
Welty, Eudora (L)	1909–
Wertmuller, Lina (F)	1928–
West, Benjamin (PA)	1738–1820
Weston, Edward (PH)	1886–1958
Weyden, Rogier van der (PA)	c. 1400–1464
Wharton, Edith (L)	1862–1937
Whistler, James A. M. (PA)	1834–1903
White, E. B. (L)	1899–1985
White, Stanford (A)	1853–1906
Whitman, Walt (L)	1819–1892
Whittier, John Greenleaf (L)	1807–1892
Wilde, Oscar (DR)	1854–1900
Wilder, Billy (F)	1906–
Wilder, Thornton (DR)	1897–1975

Willaert, Adriaan (M)	1490–1562
Williams, Emlyn (DR)	1905–1987
Williams, Hank (M)	1923–1953
Williams, Tennessee (DR)	1911–1983
Williams, William Carlos (L)	1883–1963
Wilson, August (DR)	1945–
Wilson, Edmund (L)	1895–1972
Wilson, Lanford (DR)	1937–
Wilton, Joseph (S)	1722–1803
Winfrey, Oprah (T)	1954–
Wise, Robert (F)	1914–
Wodehouse, P. G. (L)	1881–1975
Wolfe, Thomas (L)	1900–1938
Wolfe, Tom (L)	1931–
Wonder, Stevie (M)	1950–
Wood, Grant (PA)	1891–1942
Woodward, Joanne (F)	1930–
Woolf, Virginia (L)	1882–1941
Wordsworth, William (L)	1770–1850
Wouk, Herman (L)	1915–
Wren, Christopher (A)	1632–1723
Wright, Frank Lloyd (A)	1869–1959
Wright, Joseph (S)	1756–1793
Wright, Patience Lovell (S)	1725–1786
Wright, Richard (L)	1908–1960
Wycherley, William (DR)	1640–1716
Wyeth, Andrew (PA)	1917–
Wyler, William (F)	1902–1981
Wynette, Tammy (M)	1942–
Yeats, William Butler (L)	1865–1939
Zimmerman, Johann Baptist (S)	1680–1758
Zinnemann, Fred (F)	1907–
Zola, Émile (L)	1840–1902
Zurburán, Francisco de (PA)	1598–1664

BIBLIOGRAPHY

Abrams, M. H., ed. *The Norton Anthology of English Literature*, rev. ed. New York: W. W. Norton & Co., 1968.

Adepegba, C. O. *Yoruba Metal Sculpture*. Ibaadan: Ibaadan University Press, 1991.

Amiet, Pierre. *Art of the Ancient Near East*. New York: Harry N. Abrams, 1980.

Ammer, Christine. *Harper's Dictionary of Music*. New York: Harper & Row, 1972.

Ancient Treasures in Terracotta of Mali and Ghana. New York: African-American Institute, 1981.

Apel, Willi. *Harvard Dictionary of Music*, 2d ed. Cambridge, MA: The Belknap Press, Harvard University Press, 1972.

Art of the Congo. Minneapolis, MN: Walker Art Center, 1967.

Austin, William A. *Music In the 20th Century: from Debussy through Stravinsky*. New York: W. W. Norton & Company, 1966.

Balanchine, George, and Francis Mason. *101 Stories of the Great Ballets*. New York: Anchor/Doubleday, 1989.

Banham, Martin, ed. *The Cambridge Guide to World Theatre*. Cambridge, UK: Cambridge University Press, 1988.

Barnett, R. D. *Assyrian Sculpture in the British Museum*. London: McClelland and Stewart, 1975.

Bauer, Marion, Ethel Peyser, and Elizabeth E. Rogers. *Music Through the Ages*, 3d ed. New York: G. P. Putnam's Sons, 1967.

Benét's Reader's Encyclopedia, 3d ed. New York: Harper & Row, 1987.

Bishop, Robert. *American Folk Sculpture*. New York: E. P. Dutton and Co., 1974.

Blom, Eric. *Grove's Dictionary of Music and Musicians*, 5th ed. New York: St. Martin's Press, 1962.

Bordman, Gerald. *The Oxford Companion to American Theatre*. Oxford, UK: Oxford University Press, 1984.

Brooks, Tim. *The Complete Directory to Prime Time TV Stars: 1946-Present*. New York: Ballantine, 1987.

Brooks, Tim, and Earle Marsh. *The Complete Directory to Prime Time Network TV Shows: 1946-Present*. New York: Ballantine, 1985.

Brose, David S.. *Ancient Art of the American Woodland Indians*. New York: Harry N. Abrams, 1985.

BIBLIOGRAPHY

Burbank, Richard. *Twentieth Century Music: Orchestral, Chamber, Operatic, & Dance Music 1900–1980*. New York: Facts On File, 1984.

Cheney, Sheldon. *Sculpture of the World*. New York: Viking Press, 1968.

Chilvers, Ian, Harold Osborne, and Dennis Farr. *The Oxford Dictionary of Art*. Oxford, UK: Oxford University Press, 1988.

Corey, Melinda, and George Ochoa. *A Cast of Thousands: A Compendium of Who Played What in Film*. New York: Facts On File, 1992.

Craven, Wayne. *Sculpture in America*. New York: Thomas Y. Crowell Co., 1968.

Easby, Elizabeth Kennedy, and John F. Scott. *Before Cortés: Sculpture of Middle America*. New York: Metropolitan Museum of Art, 1970.

Editions d'Art Albert Skira. *Sculpture: Fifteenth to Eighteenth Century*. New York: Rizzoli International Publications, 1987.

Ewen, David. *American Composers: A Biographical Dictionary*. New York: G. P. Putnam's Sons, 1982.

Eyo, Ekpo. *Two Thousand Years of Nigerian Art*. Lagos, Nigeria: Federal Dept. of Antiquities, 1977.

Ferrier, Jean-Louis. *Art of Our Century*. New York: Prentice Hall, 1988.

Gammond, Peter. *Classical Music: An Illustrated Guide to Composers*. New York: Acorn Publishing, 1980.

Godine, David R. *200 Years of American Sculpture*. New York: Whitney Museum of American Art, 1976.

Goulding, Phil G. *Classical Music: The 50 Greatest Composers and Their 1000 Greatest Works*. New York: Fawcett Columbine, 1992.

Gray, Anne. *The Popular Guide to Classical Music*. New York: Carol Publishing Group, 1993.

Grout, Donald Jay, and Claude V. Palisca. *A History of Western Music*, 4th ed. New York: W. W. Norton & Company, 1980.

Grun, Bernard. *The Timetables of History*, 3d ed. New York: Simon & Schuster, 1975.

Hafner, German. *Art of Crete, Mycenae, and Greece*. New York: Harry N. Abrams, 1968.

Hardy, Phil, and Dave Laing. *The Faber Companion to 20th-Century Popular Music*. London: Faber and Faber, 1990.

Hartnoll, Phyllis, ed. *The Oxford Companion to the Theatre*, 4th ed. Oxford, UK: Oxford University Press, 1983.

Haskins, James. *Black Dance in America*. New York: HarperCollins, 1990.

Higgins, Reynold. *Minoan and Mycenaen Art*. London: Thames and Hudson, 1967.

Highwater, Jamake. *Arts of the Indian Americas*. New York: Harper & Row, 1983.

Hochman, Stanley. *McGraw-Hill Encyclopedia of World Drama*. New York: McGraw-Hill, 1984.

Janson, H. W, and Anthony F. Janson. *History of Art*, 4th ed. New York: Harry N. Abrams, 1991.

BIBLIOGRAPHY

Jasen, David A. *Tin Pan Alley*. New York: Donald I. Fine, 1988.

Jones, Arthur F. *HarperCollins College Outline: Introduction to Art*. New York: HarperPerennial, 1992.

Katz, Ephraim. *The Film Encyclopedia*, 2d ed. New York: HarperPerennial, 1994.

Kirkpatrick, John, et al. *The New Grove Twentieth-Century American Masters*. New York: W. W. Norton & Co., 1987.

Lapiner, Alan. *Pre-Columbian Art of South America*. New York: Harry N. Abrams, 1976.

Leroi-Gourhan, André. *Treasures of Prehistoric Art*. New York,: Harry N. Abrams, 1968.

Levy, Judith S., and Agnes Greenhall. *The Concise Columbia Encyclopedia*. New York: Avon, 1983.

Lucie-Smith, Edward. *The Thames and Hudson Dictionary of Art Terms*. London: Thames and Hudson Ltd., 1988.

The Metropolitan Museum of Art Guide. New York: The Metropolitan Museum of Art, 1983.

Michalowski, Kazimierz. *Great Sculpture of Ancient Egypt*. New York: William Morrow and Co., 1978.

Minott, Charles. *HarperCollins College Outline: History of Art*. New York: HarperPerennial, 1992.

Murray, Margaret Alice. *Egyptian Sculpture*. London: Duckworth, 1930.

Nite, Norm N. *Rock On Almanac, The First Four Decades of Rock 'n' Roll: A Chronology*. New York: Harper & Row, 1989.

O'Neil, Thomas. *The Grammy's: For the Record*. New York: Penguin Books, 1993.

Osborne, Harold, ed. *An Illustrated Companion to the Decorative Arts*. London: Wordsworth Editions, 1989.

Ousby, Ian, ed. *The Cambridge Guide to Literature in English*. Cambridge, UK: Cambridge University Press, 1988.

Pericot-Garcia, Luis. *Prehistoric and Primitive Art*. New York: Harry N. Abrams, 1967.

Perkins, George, Barbara Perkins, and Phillip Leininger. *Benét's Reader's Encyclopedia of American Literature*. New York: HarperCollins, 1991.

Pollitt, J. J. *Art and Experience in Classical Greece*. New York: Cambridge University Press, 1988.

Post, Chandler. *A History of European and American Sculpture*, Cambridge, MA: Harvard University Press, 1921.

Read, Herbert, ed. *The Thames and Hudson Dictionary of Art*. London: Thames and Hudson, 1985.

Rosenblum, Robert, and H. W. Janson. *19th-Century Art*. Englewood Cliffs, NJ: Prentice-Hall, and New York: Harry N. Abrams, 1984.

Rothschild, Lincoln. *Sculpture Through the Ages*. New York: McGraw-Hill, 1942.

BIBLIOGRAPHY

Sackett, Susan. *The Hollywood Reporter Book of Box Office Hits*. New York: Billboard Books, 1990.

Sandars, N. K. *Prehistoric Art in Europe*. Baltimore, MD: Penguin Books, 1968.

Scarre, Chris. *Smithsonian Timelines of the Ancient World*. London: Dorling Kindersley, 1993.

Sculpture Since the Sixties. New York: Whitney Museum of American Art, 1988.

Shaw, Arnold. *Dictionary of American Pop/Rock*. New York: Schirmer Books, 1982.

Slonimsky, Nicolas. *The Concise Baker's Biographical Dictionary of Musicians*. New York: Schirmer Books, 1988.

Stern, Jane, and Michael Stern. *Jane & Michael Stern's Encyclopedia of Pop Culture*. New York: HarperPerennial, 1992.

Strong, Donald. *Roman Art and Architecture*. Middlesex, England: Penguin Books, 1988.

Trager, James. *The People's Chronology*. New York: Henry Holt & Co., 1992.

Westrup, Sir Jack, F. L. L. Harrison, and Conrad Wilson. *Collins Dictionary of Music*, 3d ed. London: Collins, 1988.

Wetterau, Bruce. *The New York Public Library Book of Chronologies*. New York: Prentice-Hall, 1990.

Wheeler, Mortimer. *Roman Art and Architecture*. London: Thames and Hudson, 1979.

Who's Who in America. New Providence, NJ: Marquis Who's Who, 1993.

INDEX

INDEX

INDEX

INDEX

INDEX

Dos Passos, John, 253
Dostoyevsky, Fyodor, 39, 179, 181, 183, 190
Dou, Gerrit, 101
Doughty, Thomas, 153
Douglas, Aaron, 259
Dove, Rita, 354
Dowland, John, 94–95
Dowson, Ernest, 191
Doyle, Arthur Conan, 195
Doyle, Roddy, 354
Drabble, Margaret, 325
Drama: commedia dell'arte, 81, 127; Greece, 18; Kabuki theater, 93; liturgical dramas, 44; masques, 59, 101–2, 106; morality plays, 52, 61, 68; mystery plays, 52, 54, 58; Nō, 55; passion plays, 55; restoration drama, 112, 116
Drayton, Michael, 91, 96, 98
Dreiser, Theodore, 218, 224, 244
Dreyer, Carl, 248, 311
Dryden, John, 108, 110–16
Du Bois, W. E. B., 214
Dubuffet, Jean, 280
Du Camp, Maxime, 165
Duccio (Duccio di Buoninsegna), 54–55
Duchamp, Marcel, 227, 230, 232, 234, 256
Dudevant, Amandine. See Sand, George
Dufay, Guillaume, 61
Dufy, Raoul, 217, 236
Dumas, Alexandre, fils, 169, 172
Dumas, Alexandre, père, 163
Du Maurier, Daphne, 266
Du Maurier, George, 202
Dunbar, Paul Laurence, 203
Duncan, Isadora, 213
Dunham, Katherine, 271
Dunne, Finley Peter, 206
Dunning, George, 319
Dunstable, John, 62
Durand, Asher B., 153
Durang, Christopher, 339
Durant, Ariel, 262
Durant, Will, 262
Dürer, Albrecht, 66, 68, 72, 74–76, 78–79
Durey, Louis, 232
Dürrenmatt, Friedrich, 345
Duse, Eleonora, 210
Duvall, Robert, 325
Dvořák, Antonín, 194, 201, 211
Dwan, Allan, 241, 285
Dyer, Sir Edward, 88
Dyes, 5; indigo, 52; mauve, 174; tie-dyeing, 40; Tyrian purple, 11
Dylan, Bob, 307, 312

E

Eakins, Thomas, 187, 195, 201
Earl, Ralph, 140
Eastman, George, 197
Eastwood, Clint, 311, 323, 326, 352
Eco, Umberto, 336
Edison, Thomas Alva, 189, 195, 199, 202
"Ed Sullivan Show, The," 284, 313
Edwards, Blake, 306, 308, 311, 314, 334, 339
Edwards, Jonathan, 125
Egk, Werner, 266
Eiffel, Gustave, 187, 197
Eisenstein, Sergey, 244, 248, 265, 276
Elgar, Edward, 213
Elgin Marbles, 144
El Greco, 87, 89–90, 92, 96
Eliot, George, 166
Eliot, T. S. (Thomas Stearns), 215, 231, 240, 253, 260, 276, 284
Ellington, Duke, 234, 279
Ellison, Ralph, 290
El Mudo, 86
Elssler, Fanny, 156, 158, 166–67
Emerson, Peter Henry, 199
Emerson, Ralph Waldo, 157–58, 160–61, 166
Érard, Sébastien, 137
Erasmus, Desiderius, 74
Erdrich, Louise, 341, 344
Ernst, Max, 239, 243
Escher, M. C., 277
Etowah culture (Mississippi), 52
Euphuism, 87
Euripides, 22–24
Evans, Frederick Henry, 198, 213
Evans, Walker, 263, 266–67
Eyck, Hubert van, 61
Eyck, Jan van, 61–62

F

Fabian Arts Group, 219
Fabian Society, 193
Fabritius, Carel, 101, 106
Fairbanks, Douglas, 229, 241, 243
Fakhoury, Pierre, 347
Falconet, Étienne, 119, 137
Falla, Manuel de, 231
Fan K'uan, 46
Farquhar, George, 117, 119
Fassbinder, Rainer Werner, 327, 333–34, 337, 339
Faulkner, William, 251, 255, 263, 288
Feld, Eliot, 327, *348*
Félix, Élisa. See Rachel

INDEX

INDEX

INDEX

INDEX

Le Gray, Gustave, 166
Le Gros, Pierre, 116
Le Guin, Ursula K., 300
Lehár, Franz, 219
Lehmbruck, Wilhelm, 221
Leichner, Ludwig, 179
Leigh, Mike, 354
Leigh, Vivien, 268
Le Lorrain, Robert, 125
Lelouch, Claude, 316
Lely, Sir Peter, 108
Lemon, William, 140
Lemoyne, Jean-Baptiste, 129
Lennon, John, 310, 312, 337
Lenôtre, André, 111
Leonardo da Vinci, 65–68, 70, 72, 76, 351
Leone, Sergio, 311, 316, 341
Léonin (Leoninus), 50
Leopardi, Count Giacomo, 152
Lermontov, Mikhail, 160
Lerner, Alan Jay, 296
LeRoy, Mervyn, 255, 275, 277, 285, 288, 294, 300, 308
Lescot, Pierre, 82
Leslie, Alfred, 331
Leslie, Frank, 172
Lessing, Doris, 308
Lester, Richard, 311, 313–14, 327, 330
Leutze, Emanuel, 168
Le Vau, Louis, 111
Levi, Primo, 344
Levin, Ira, 318
Levine, Philip, 336, 342, 352
Levinson, Barry, 346, 351
Lewes, George Henry, 166
Lewis, C. S. (Clive Staples), 275
Lewis, Matthew, 140
Lewis, Sinclair, 237, 240, 244, 250, 253
Lewis, Wyndham, 220, 230
Leyster, Judith, 101
Lichtenstein, Roy, 310, 330, 344
Liebermann, Max, 201
Liebling, A. J., 269
Ligeti, György, 333
Lightman, Alan, 354
Limburg, Herman, 60
Limburg, Jean, 60
Limburg, Paul, 60
Lin, Maya, 338
Lincoln, Abraham, 178
Lind, Johanna Maria (Jenny), 158, 166
Lindbergh, Anne Morrow, 295
Lindsay, Vachel, 227
Li Po (Li T'ai-po), 42

Lippi, Filippino, 67–68
Lippi, Fra Filippo, 62–63, 67
Lipski, Donald, 358
Lismer, Arthur, 237
Liszt, Franz, 152, 161, 164, 171
Livy, 29
Llewellyn, Richard, 269
Lloyd, Frank, 257, 261
Lloyd, Harold, 241, 244
Locke, Matthew, 106–8, 112
Loesser, Frank, 287
Loewe, Frederick, 296
Logan, Joshua, 285, 294, 296, 298, 300, 318
Lo Kuan-chung, 55
Lombardo, Tullio, 68
Lone Wolf, 236
Longfellow, Henry Wadsworth, 161, 172, 175
Lorenzi, Battista, 86
Lorenzo the Magnificent (Medici), 59
Loris, Heinrich (Henricus Glareanus), 82
Lorrain, Claude, 102, 114
Losey, Joseph, 323
Loti, Pierre, 180
Lotto, Lorenzo, 74, 79
Lovelace, Richard, 102, 105
Lowell, Robert, 280
Lowry, Malcolm, 281
Lubitsch, Ernst, 233, 250
Lucan, 33
Lucas, George, 323, 326, 332
Luce, Henry, 242, 263
Luciani, Sebastiano. See del Piombo, Sebastiano
Lucian of Samosata, 34
Lucius Accius, 28
Lucius Africanus, 26
Lucretius, 29
Lu Hsün, 192
Luks, George, 220, 245
Lully, Jean-Baptiste, 93, 104, 106, 112
Lumet, Sidney, 298, 311, 326, 329–30
Lumière, Auguste, 202
Lumière, Louis, 202
Luther, Martin, 69
Luytens, Elisabeth, 328
Lyceum Theater School of Acting, 193
Lyly, John, 87
Lyne, Adrian, 340, 345
Lysippus, 25

M

Mac-, Mc-,: Names beginning with Mc- are alphabetized as Mac-.
Macaulay, Thomas Babington, 161

INDEX

McCarey, Leo, 277–78
McCarthy, Cormac, 353
McCarthy, Mary, 299, 310, 312
McCartney, Paul, 310, 312
McCay, Winsor, 216, 233
McCoy, Van, 329
McCullers, Carson, 280
MacDermott, Galt, 317
Macdonald, J. E. H., 237
MacDonald, John D., 312
Machado de Assis, Joachim Maria, 210
Machaut, Guillaume de, 57–58
Machiavelli, Niccolò, 75, 77
McInerney, Jay, 342
McIntire, Samuel, 140
McIntyre, James, 208
MacLeish, Archibald, 249
McLeod, Norman Z., 281–82
MacManus, Declan. See Costello, Elvis
McMillan, Terry, 353
McMurtry, Larry, 342
McNally, Terence, 354
MacNeice, Louis, 266
Maderna, Carlo, 73, 96
Madonna, 343
Maeterlinck, Maurice, 233
Magritte, René, 243, 246, 262
Mahler, Gustav, 204, 219, 224
Mailer, Norman, 282, 335
Makarova, Natalia, 301
Malamud, Bernard, 290, 316
Malevich, Kasimir, 233
Mallarmé, Stéphane, 187
Malle, Louis, 323, 327, 337, 345
Malory, Sir Thomas, 67
Malraux, André, 257
Mambety, Djibril Diop, 326
Mamet, David, 331, 340
Mamoulian, Rouben, 261, 298
Man, Felix, 252
Manet, Édouard, 178, 193
Mankiewicz, Herman J., 273
Mankiewicz, Joseph L., 281, 287, 310, 325
Mann, Anthony, 292, 306, 311
Mann, Delbert, 294, 306
Mann, Thomas, 211
Mansart, François, 102
Mansfield, Katherine, 219
Mantegna, Andrea, 65–66
Manzoni, Alessandro, 153
Maori art, 142
Mapplethorpe, Robert, 350, 357
Marazzoli, Marco, 103
Marbeck, John, 82
Marc, Franz, 190, 224

Marceau, Marcel, 280
Marcus Aurelius, 34
Marden, Brice, 341, 345
Marey, Étienne-Jules, 189, 192
Marinetti, Filippo Thommaso, 221
Marini, Biagio, 99
Marionettes. See Puppets
Marivaux, Pierre Carlet de, 120
Marlowe, Christopher, 87–90, 92, 98
Marot, Clément, 80
Marquand, John Phillips, 264
Marquis, Don, 247
Marshall, George, 268, 308
Marshall, Penny, 346, 350
Martí, José, 193
Martin, John, 148
Martini, Simone, 57
Marton, Andrew, 287, 308
Marvell, Andrew, 113–14
Marville, Charles, 166
Masaccio (Tommaso di Giovanni di
  Simone Guidi), 59, 61
Masar, Benjamin, 319
Masks, African, 190
Masolino (Tommaso di Cristoforo Fini), 62
Massenet, Jules, 222
Massys, Quentin, 76
Masters, Edgar Lee, 230
Masuda, Toshio, 322
Mather, Cotton, 116
Matisse, Henri, 208, 216–17, 222, 224,
  255, 265, 285
Maugham, William Somerset, 230, 238
Mauldin, Bill, 278
Maupassant, Guy de, 193
Mauriac, François, 247
Mayan culture, 29–30, 42
Mayer, William, 340
Mazzocchi, Virgilio, 103
Mazzola, Girolamo Francesco. See
  Parmigianino
Meadows, Audrey, 296
Medak, Peter, 325
Meehan, Thomas, 331
Méliès, Georges, 211
Melville, Herman, 164–65, 168, 170, 243
Melville, Jean-Pierre, 285
Memmi, Lippo, 57
Menander, 26
Mencken, H. L., 220, 234–35, 243
Mendelssohn, Felix, 153–54, 156, 159, 164
Mengozzi-Colonna, Gerolamo, 126
Mengs, Anton, 130
Meng-tzu (Mencius), 25
Menotti, Gian Carlo, 293, 300, 330

INDEX

koto, 37; lure, 12; lute, 7, 9, 42, 94; lyre, 7, 18; oboe, 9; organ, 42, 46, 52, 96, 134; piano, 118, 124, 137, 170; reed pipe, 42; sistrum, 9; string, 14; theremin, 243; trumpet, 9, 11, 14, 42; vina, 17; viol, 94; viola, 110; violin, 84, 99, 110; xylophone, 42

Musical notation: musical staff, 47; neumes, 42, 47, 52; time signature, 53

Musset, Alfred de, 156

Mussorgsky, Modest, 185

Muybridge, Eadweard, 189

Myron, 20

N

Nabokov, Vladimir, 295, 298, 308

Nadar, 151

Naipaul, V. S. (Vidiadhar Surajprasad), 306, 335, 356

Nanni di Banco, 60

Nash, Paul, 274

Nash, Thomas, 91, 93

Nashville Group, 235

Nathan, George Jean, 243

Navajo, 159

Navarrete, Juan Fernández de. See El Mudo

Nazca culture (Peru), 35

Neel, Alice, 338

Negre, Charles, 166

Negulesco, Jean, 282, 292

Nelson, Ralph, 309

Nemirovich-Danchenko, Vladimir, 206

Neruda, Jan, 189

Neruda, Pablo, 243

Neumann, Johann Balthasar, 125

Neuys, Joseph, 339

Nevelson, Louise, 286

Newell, Mike, 356

Newman, Barnett, 279, 284, 287

Newman, John Henry, 179

Nichols, Anne, 239

Nichols, Mike, 310, 315, 318, 322–23

Nicholson, Ben, 262

Niepce, Joseph-Nicéphore, 152

Nijinsky, Vaslav, 223

Nin, Anaïs, 316

Noguchi, Isamu, 296

Nolan, Sir Sidney, 280

Nolde, Emil, 218

Norem, Ned, 338

Norris, Frank, 211

Novels: Newgate novels, 154; penny dreadfuls, 165; dime novels, 165

Nureyev, Rudolf, 307, 340, 357

Nykvist, Sven, 351

O

Oates, Joyce Carol, 345

Oboler, Arch, 291

O'Brien, Edna, 350

O'Casey, Sean, 241–42, 246, 250

O'Connor, Carroll, 324

Odets, Clifford, 254

O'Faolain, Sean, 255

O'Flaherty, Liam, 245

O'Hara, Frank, 290

O'Hara, John, 261, 271

O'Keeffe, Georgia, 220, 247

Okri, Ben, 353

Oldenburg, Claes, 303, 335, 338

Olivier, Laurence, 264, 276, 282, 294

Olmec culture (Mexico), 11–12, 13, 16

Olmsted, Frederick Law, 174

O'Neill, Eugene, 193, 236, 238–39, 243, 246, 248, 254, 280, 290, 296

O'Neill, James, 193

Ophuls, Max, 287

Orff, Carl, 265

Ormandy, Eugene, 225

Orozco, José Clemente, 256

Orton, Joe, 311

Orwell, George, 277

Osborne, John, 296

Ostrovsky, Aleksandr Nikolayevich, 171

O'Sullivan, Timothy, 185

O'Toole, Peter, 307

Ovid, 30–32, 39

Owen, Wilfrid, 237

Ozenfant, Amédée, 233

P

Pacino, Al, 284, 325

Paganini, Niccolò, 140, 145

Pagodas, 38

Paine, Thomas, 136, 139

Painting: fresco, 60; oil paint, 71; palette, 60; scroll, 34; tempera, 60

Pakula, Alan J., 323, 330

Paley, Grace, 301

Palladio, Andrea, 81–82, 85–86

Palma, Jacopo. See Vecchio, Palma

Palmer, Erastus Dow, 176

Papp, Joseph, 307

Paracas culture (Peru), 14

Parks, Gordon, 323, 325

Parmigianino, 78–80

Parthenon, 21, 23, 319

Pasolini, Pier Paolo, 316

Pasternak, Boris, 299

Pater, Walter, 182–83, 191

Paton, Alan, 282

INDEX

INDEX

Pugin, Augustus, 156, 160, 196
Puppets, 40, 93, 115, 196; Karagoz, 52; Punch and Judy shows, 93
Purcell, Henry, 114–15
Pushkin, Aleksandr, 151, 153
Puzo, Mario, 321
Pyle, Ernie, 269
Pym, Barbara, 332
Pynchon, Thomas, 327, 350
Pythagoras, 17

Q

Quasimodo, Salvatore, 255
Queen, Ellery, 250
Queirolo, Francesco, 129
Quercia, Jacopo della, 62
Quintilian, 33
Quintus Ennius, 27

R

Rabe, David, 323
Rabelais, François, 80
Rachel (Élisa Félix), 156, 158
Rachmaninoff, Sergey, 211
Racine, Jean, 109–12
Radcliffe, Ann, 140
Rado, James, 317
Ragni, Gerome, 317
Raleigh, Sir Walter, 90, 98
Rameau, Jean-Philippe, 120
Rand, Ayn, 276
Randolph, Joyce, 296
Raphael, 72–75, 77
Rauschenberg, Robert, 295, 310
Ravel, Maurice, 236, 247
Rawlings, Marjorie Kinnan, 266
Ray, Man, 206–7, 236, 270
Ray, Nicholas, 294
Raymond, Henry, 167
Read, Charles, 168
Recuay culture (Peru), 31
Redding, Otis, 318
Reddy, Helen, 325
Redford, Robert, 336, 356
Reed, Carol, 268, 282, 285, 301, 314, 319
Reger, Max, 230
Reich, Steve, 355
Reinhardt, Ad, 286
Reis, Irving, 281
Reisz, Karel, 305, 320, 337
Rejlander, Oscar, 175
Remarque, Erich Maria, 251
Rembrandt, 101–2, 104, 106–8, 110–11
Renoir, Jean, 243, 264, 268, 296
Renoir, Pierre-Auguste, 185, 189, 192

Resnais, Alain, 296, 301, 306, 319, 327
Reyes Basualto, Neftalí Ricardo. *See* Neruda, Pablo
Reymont, Wladyslaw, 207
Reynolds, Debbie, 312
Reynolds, Sir Joshua, 119, 128, 132–34
Ribera, José de, 101, 104, 106
Ribera, Pedro de, 122
Rice, Elmer, 241
Rice, Thomas, 150
Rice, Tim, 334
Rich, Adrienne, 327
Richardson, Henry Hobson, 194
Richardson, Jonathan, 119
Richardson, Samuel, 125–26
Richardson, Tony, 310
Riemenschneider, Tilman, 74–75
Rietveld, Gerrit Thomas, 231, 242
Rigaud, Hyacinthe, 116
Riis, Jacob, 199
Riley, John, 114
Rilke, Rainer Maria, 217
Rimbaud, Arthur, 182
Rimsky-Korsakov, Nikolay, 184–85, 196, 220
Ripa, Cesare, 90
Ritt, Martin, 309, 325, 334
Rivera, Diego, 256, *258*, 259, 344
Rivers, Larry, 291
Robbins, Jerome, 297–98, 306, 327
Robinson, Edwin Arlington, 204, 240
Robinson, Henry Peach, 175
Robusti, Jacopo. *See* Tintoretto
Rock art, 2–3, *3*
Rockburne, Dorothea, 343
Rodgers, Richard, 252, 271, 276, 285
Rodin, Auguste, 190, 192, 194, 198, 205–6
Roethke, Theodore, 291
Rogers, Ginger, 256
Rogers, Richard, 331
Roget, Peter Mark, 169
Rohmer, Eric, 320, 323, 325, 330
Rolling Stones, 313
Romano, Giulio, 69
Rorem, Ned, 332, 338
Ross, Diana, 315
Rosselli, Cosimo, 67
Rossellini, Roberto, 276, 285
Rossellino, Bernardo, 63
Rossetti, Christina, 177
Rossetti, Dante Gabriel, 164–66, 171, 175, 192
Rossini, Gioacchino, 154
Rossiter, Philip, 94

INDEX

INDEX

INDEX

INDEX